THE JAPANESE IDEOLOGY

The Japanese Ideology

A MARXIST CRITIQUE OF LIBERALISM AND FASCISM

Tosaka Jun

Translated by Robert Stolz

Columbia University Press
New York

Columbia University Press
Publishers Since 1893
New York   Chichester, West Sussex
cup.columbia.edu
Translation copyright © 2024 Columbia University Press
All rights reserved

Library of Congress Cataloging-in-Publication Data
Names: Tosaka, Jun, 1900–1945, author.
Title: The Japanese Ideology : a Marxist critique of liberalism and fascism / Tosaka Jun ; translated by Robert Stolz.
Other titles: Nihon ideorogi ron. English.
Description: New York : Columbia University Press, 2024. | Includes bibliographical references and index.
Identifiers: LCCN 2024008302 (print) | LCCN 2024008303 (ebook) | ISBN 9780231216524 (hardback) | ISBN 9780231216531 (trade paperback) | ISBN 9780231561297 (ebook)
Subjects: LCSH: Ideology—Japan—History—20th century. | Fascism—Japan. | Liberalism—Japan. | Marxist criticism. | Philosophy, Japanese—20th century.
Classification: LCC B823.3 .T6813 2024 (print) | LCC B823.3 (ebook) | DDC 320.53/3095209043—dc23/eng/20240318
LC record available at https://lccn.loc.gov/2024008302
LC ebook record available at https://lccn.loc.gov/2024008303

Cover design: Chang Jae Lee
Cover image: © Shutterstock

CONTENTS

INTRODUCTION BY ROBERT STOLZ   ix

ACKNOWLEDGMENTS   xxxiii

Preface   1
Preface to the Revised Edition   3
Supplemental Preface to the Revised Edition   4

Part I. Foundation for a Critique of Japanism

Chapter One
Problems in Contemporary Japanese Thought: Japanism, Liberalism, Materialism   7

Chapter Two
Foundation for a Critique of Japanism: A Critique of Philological Philosophy   19

Chapter Three
An Analysis of "Common Sense": Toward a Resolution of Two Contradictions in Social Common Sense   39

Chapter Four
On Enlightenment: The Meaning and Necessity
of Enlightenment Today   61

Chapter Five
A Scientific Critique of Culture: An Outline for a Critique
of National Purification   77

Chapter Six
Japanist Ideology: Japanese Spiritualism, Japanese Agrarian
Fundamentalism, Japanese Pan-Asianism   88

Chapter Seven
Japanese Ethics and Anthropology: An Analysis of the
Social Meaning of Watsuji Tetsurō's Ethics   104

Chapter Eight
An Analysis of the Restorationist Phenomenon:
On the Famialism Analogy   117

Chapter Nine
The Essence of Cultural Control: An Analysis of Various Aspects
of Cultural Control in Contemporary Japan   128

Chapter Ten
The Fate of Japanism: From Fascism to the Ideology of
the Imperial Way   136

Part II: Foundation for a Critique of Liberalism

Chapter Eleven
Modern Idealism in Disguise: Foundation for a Critique of
"Hermeneutic Philosophy"   147

Chapter Twelve
"The Logic of Nothingness," Is It a Logic?: On Nishida's
Philosophical Method   163

CONTENTS

Chapter Thirteen
The Sorcery of "Totality": Takahashi Satomi's
Philosophical Method   174

Chapter Fourteen
Literature and Philosophy in an Age of Reaction: On the
Delusions of "Literaturism"   186

Chapter Fifteen
The Essence of "Literary Liberalism": The Progressive and
Reactionary Nature of "Liberals"   196

Chapter Sixteen
The Consciousness and Class Theory of the Intelligentsia:
Against the So-Called "Class Theory of Intelligence"   203

Chapter Seventeen
Doubts on the Theory of the Intelligentsia: Is the Current
Problematization of the Intelligentsia Mistaken?   210

Chapter Eighteen
The Theory of the Intelligentsia and the Theory of Technology:
A Reexamination of the Theory of Technology   220

Chapter Nineteen
Liberal Philosophy and Materialism: Against Two Types
of Liberal Philosophy   230

Chapter Twenty
Contemporary Japanese Thought: The Superiority of
Materialism for the Question of Thought   242

Part III: The Masses and Socialism in an "Age of Reaction"

Chapter Twenty-one
The Current Meaning of "Progressive"
and "Reactionary"   259

Chapter Twenty-two
A Reconsideration of the Masses   273

Chapter Twenty-three
Liberalism, Fascism, Socialism   282

Afterword: A *Japanese Ideology* for Our Time   293

NOTES   303

BIBLIOGRAPHY   325

INDEX   329

INTRODUCTION

Tosaka Jun (1900–1945) was one of the most trenchant and committed philosophers and cultural critics in 1930s Japan, and perhaps the most creative and important theorist of dialectical materialism in the world. He not only cofounded and edited the important journal *Materialism Studies* (*Yuibutsuron kenkyū*) from 1932 to 1938, but he also published major works on a broad range of topics from the scientific method, theories of ideology, popular customs, and the global nature of modern capitalism and fascism.[1] The text translated here, *The Japanese Ideology* (*Nihon ideorogi ron*, 1935, revised 1936), Tosaka's magisterial critique of Japanese liberalism and fascism, places him with Antonio Gramsci, Walter Benjamin, and Ernst Bloch as contemporary theorists of capitalism, ideology, and fascism. Yet in this this text he goes beyond even those thinkers' analyses in providing a philosophical critique of the Japanese ideology from the perspective of a robust historical and dialectical materialism; he ruthlessly critiques liberalism's deep yet unacknowledged complicity with Japanese fascism by demonstrating how both liberal and fascist thought accompanied and ideologically concealed the historical and material actuality of Japan's colonization of East Asia. *The Japanese Ideology* also makes a rare, but crucial intervention in Marxist thought with its critique of the "Asiatic Mode of Production" and its hidden reliance on the metaphysical notion of "the East," a framing device that has exceeded its moment and persists as the basis of postwar Area Studies.

As a student specializing in the philosophy of math and science working from 1921 to 1926 under the leading members of the Kyoto School of Philosophy, Nishida Kitarō and Tanabe Hajime, Tosaka occupies a key intersection of the neo-Kantian and Hegelian methods of his teachers and the theoretical commitments of 1920s Japanese Marxism following the founding of the Japanese Communist Party in 1922 and the translation of Soviet thought.[2] Forced out of his position at Hōsei University in Tokyo in 1934 and arrested multiple times in the state's crackdown on "dangerous thought" in the 1930s, he was last arrested in 1940 and died in prison of malnutrition and mistreatment in Nagano on August 9, 1945, the day of the Nagasaki bombing and the Soviet invasion of Manchuria.

Tosaka represents the highest example of the new theoretical and critical Japanese Marxism of the 1920s. In 1932, Tosaka, Miki Kiyoshi, Fukumoto Kazuo, and Hani Gorō founded the Institute for Materialism Studies (Yuibutsuron kenkyūkai, or *yuiken*)—whose key members included Oka Kunio, Nagata Hiroshi, and Hattori Shisō—less than a year after the Manchurian Incident and the same year as the establishment of the Japanese puppet state of Manchukuo. The *yuiken* brought a theoretical coherence and a deep connection with history to Japanese Marxism,[3] independent of the debates within Western and Orthodox Marxism, a position that was arguably unsurpassed anywhere. Early members included philosophers, journalists, a mathematician, two physicists, three biologists, and one historian. Founding member Kōzai Yoshishige recalls that initially the group was extremely diverse, "a group of scientists (*gakujutsusha*) with an interest in materialism (*yuibutsuron*)."[4] But under increasing state repression in the 1930s the more moderate members left, so that when shut down by the state in 1938 it was an association of extremely dedicated materialists.

Tosaka headed the *yuiken* beginning in 1933 and, after his dismissal from Hōsei, served as the group's secretary and the editor of its journal *Materialism Studies*. Following the attempted fascist coup of February 26, 1936, he was forced into hiding for several months. The *yuiken* continued until 1938 when, under tremendous pressure from government censors and police, Tosaka recommended it "voluntarily" disband. Its members' energies were briefly channeled into a new journal, *Art & Science* (*Gakugei*). The name itself reflected the hegemony of the culturalist discourse in Japanese society, one of the main objects of criticism and critique in *The Japanese Ideology*. The new journal lasted barely six months before many of its members, including Tosaka, were arrested in the "*yuiken* incident" of 1938.

Miki and Hani had studied in Germany, Miki under Heidegger at Marburg in 1923, and both were both steeped in materialist philosophy by Miki's return to Japan in 1925. In October they began the journal *Under the Banner of New Science* in conscious imitation of the German original *Unter der Banner des Marxismus*. That same year Miki translated the main points of *The German Ideology* and "Theses on Feuerbach," both of which were expanded and republished in 1930. Other translation projects included the introduction of Soviet thought when *yuiken* members Nagata Hiroshi and Kawauchi Tadahiko, students of the Russian literature department at Tokyo *gaigo gakkō*, translated Plekhanov's *The Development of the Monistic View of History*, Deborin's *Philosophy of Dialectical Materialism*, and most importantly for Tosaka and the *yuiken*, Ōmori Gitarō's Japanese translation of Lenin's *Materialism and Empirio-criticism* (1909; Jpn, 1927). Kōzai described the importance of Lenin's text for the group: "Lenin had forcefully—but merely—explained the need for this type of progressive natural science, together with philosophical materialists, to fight reactionary ideology,"[5] adding that it fell to the *yuiken* to answer Lenin's challenge and develop materialism into a workable antifascist theory.

The heart of Tosaka's dialectical materialism is grounded in the primacy and the agency of historical time, locating philosophical thought within its own historical moment, something he called "the principle of everydayness" (*nichijōsei*). The principle of everydayness is worked out in two fundamental texts from which Tosaka developed not only his materialist method, but also his theory of ideology: "On Space" (*Kūkanron*, 1931) and "The Principle of Everydayness and Historical Time" (*Nichijōsei no genri to rekishiteki jikan*, 1934).[6] His theory insisted on the material "actuality" of historically lived experience that constitutes the mutual dependency of history and philosophy, and insisting on philosophy's constant "answerability" to history.[7] Prefiguring by more than two decades Lukács's postwar critique of *Lebens* philosophy and vitalism in *The Destruction of Reason* (1952), Tosaka's project was at once part of the Kyoto School's prewar Hegelian and phenomenological philosophical project that sought to "overcome the modern"—manifested in the twin crises of contemporary philosophy and capitalist collapse—and a relentless materialist rejection of it. His teachers and fellow students at Kyoto University largely rejected a Marxist understanding of thought and history, centering their thought on the utopian and epiphanic analyses of the everyday in its process of becoming centered on the communal life of the folk culminating in the state, and later empire.[8] But Tosaka refused at all turns to see all ahistorical entities, the folk, or the nation or state, as the appropriate unit of analysis for history or philosophy. Instead he insisted on locating Japan and Japanese modernity within the "global"—expressed in the decidedly nonutopian and nonteleological global capitalism (imperialism) as the discontinuous and contradictory force structuring the necessary relationship of history and philosophy.

Everydayness as a theory of the everyday embedded in historical time—so different from the flat, ahistorical, apolitical, and vulgar "everyday" of positivisms and empiricisms of his moment, as well as from today's Latourian and Object Oriented Ontology—describes the space of material practice grounded in the historically embedded present that may be captured by culture or the state or other forces but is never reducible to them. Like Althusser's later concept of overdetermination, an inescapable everydayness thus remains "open" and available as the site of historical intervention. In Tosaka's thought, everydayness operates like Heisenberg's uncertainty principle in physics.[9] It describes the foundational, material substratum of our lives, what Harry D. Harootunian has called "the minimal unity of the everyday," and what Tosaka glossed as "the truth of the streets"[10]: "Our *consciousness* may indeed live in the phenomenological concept of time—but it is equally obvious that our *bodies* cannot."[11] "There is no escaping the fact that people live [*seikatsu suru*] within historical time. It is the *time of our lives*; we must now re-mind ourselves of this fact."[12]

In both "On Space" and "The Principle of Everydayness and Historical Time," Tosaka, like Lenin, links time and space in a dialectical relationship mediated by matter in motion.[13] Further, the historical moment exists in a constantly renegotiable relationship to the totality of historical time. While the present moment always exists within historical time, Tosaka makes an important inversion of the relationship between the "now" and the totality that resembles, but owes nothing to, Walter Benjamin's notion of *Jeztzeit*, which brings historical time under the aegis of the everyday. For Tosaka, any given historical period, ultimately defined by its political form (*seikaku*, "character"), is not the foundation for the establishment of an additive historical continuum: "Quite the contrary, [the historical period itself] is first defined by reference to the totality of the periodizations of historical time.... Against the whole of historical time, the period is given a configured orientation."[14] "Configured" in this sentence is a translation of Tosaka's original German terms: *konfigural*, *Konfiguralität*, and *konfigurieren* written in the Roman alphabet (very close but owing nothing to Benjamin's "constellations"). Tosaka takes these terms from discrete mathematics, the study of finite systems and objects that have distinct values—such as integers and logical statements, and unlike ideological forms such as the folk or the nation that do not flow into one another forming a smooth continuity as they appear to do in mere thought. In discrete mathematics, what is excluded is continuity itself.

Thus, as for Jorge Luis Borges's Pierre Menard, simple repetition cannot have the same meaning, and its meaning must be placed in a configured relation to the whole of historicial time.[15] An example from *The Japanese Ideology* shows this method in action: the reemergence of calls for Romanticism in Japan in the 1930s requires asking what this new Romanticism is reacting against, as it cannot be the same as its original incarnation which arose in reaction to the historical Enlightenment. As Tosaka puts it, the requirements of the principle of everydayness and historical time force us to render the ideological nature of 1930s Romanticism as at once "more general and also more particular."[16] This means that every now embedded within the totality of historical time is a specific, grounded temporality that itself has its own meaning and values given by this "now's" position within the whole of historical time; or, put into contemporary language, repetition creates a difference.

Using this historical method as a basis for his critique of ideology, in *An Outline of Ideology* (*Ideorogi gairon*, 1932), Tosaka sets up a series of increasingly refined articulations of philosophical traditions from a general worldview, a corresponding particular theory of being (*sonzairon*), and finally, a logic. While a logic is the last to develop, it is the most immediately accessible and thus should be the starting point for any critique. Like Benjamin's focus on the details of everyday life, Tosaka's critical historical method centered on the principle of everydayness is used to reveal the lived expressions of these philosophical categories, from thought (thought for Tosaka is something that must have a social existence, something that is *put to use*; see chapter 1), common sense, and finally popular custom (*fūzoku*). When an intellectual system of thought becomes "unconscious" and located in a "common sense," it becomes difficult to locate in the social field, but nonetheless operates like a "field of force" influencing nearby objects in what could appear to a superficial sociology as spooky action at a distance. Even more, "it is a kind of *idealist line of force that disciplines and develops the average and the majority.*" This slippery social space may be uncovered through embedding present thought into the totality of historical time (see *The Japanese Ideology* chapters 3–4). Finally, an intellectual system can be even further "unthought" by becoming popular custom—"popular custom is the skin that 'thought' wears"—seen in things like gestures, expressions, and clothing.[17] This analysis of common sense and customs will authorize Tosaka to declare that even in the age of fascist ascendancy of the 1930s, the "unconscious common sense" of Japanese thought remained the idealist worldview of liberalism inherited from the Meiji period (1868–1912; see chapter 1).

Consistent with the Marxist view of capitalist societies as inherently class-ridden, there were two discrete worldviews, bourgeois and proletarian, which in turn mapped to the philosophical traditions of idealism and materialism, each with their respective theories of being, logics, and common sense in the 1930s. Importantly, proletarian common sense and customs are those that come not from a narrow, economistic definition of those who sell their labor-power for a wage—throughout his work Tosaka insists on including the unemployed and their families in any analysis of "worker."[18] Rather, the "worker" here is all those who cannot live in the empty, homogeneous time of philosophical idealism, all who are forced by the social relations of production to inhabit a material everydayness structured by the working day and the "phantom-like objectivity" of value as socially necessary labor time.[19] Crucially, this material everydayness thus imposes an immediate and historical perspective with its own hierarchy of values specific to it. To those who inhabit the contemplative utopias of the realm of pure thought and mere possibility—"postulated individuals, people impossibly rich in leisure time" on whom "the now" does not impinge—there is never the urgency of the everyday and it can appear that the "merely possible" worlds of culture and art are the heart of life and practice, but at the cost that practice has been reduced to mere interpretation and musing.[20] By the standards of such an ahistorical utopia, all jobs have equal value, the hazard of dealing with infinite sums. Yet for those who will not live forever, in other words, those compelled to live within the confines of an "open" everydayness—that is, a finite life of practice bounded by Heidegger's "famous death,"[21] but one now governed by the demands of the working day—require a historical method and a valorizing process based in the materialist now of "today." Forced to answer to this "now" embedded in history, the bifurcation of idealist utopias that stand outside and above a vulgar everyday life of the laboring masses produced by advanced capitalism collapses: "All practical work, all historical narratives, all human action must take this [configured] present as the point of origin."[22] Even the deadline for the manuscript Tosaka is writing is governed by these historical circumstances and pressures of "the now." Here is the political payoff of the difference between Tosaka's present governed by an everydayness circumscribed by historical time and practice, and Heidegger's "being-toward-death" as a merely contemplative Dasein satisfied with, at best, "the mute interiority of phenomenology.[23]" In its place we find Tosaka's active, actual, "worker" stretching from the factory floor to writing desks of Marxist theorists.

Tosaka categorizes worldview, being, and logic as the *subjects and objects* of a sort of evolutionary "descent," later glossed as "historical necessity," through historical time. Those categories that cease to explain historical reality stop developing and become archaisms, which in turn means that their continued deployment in a very different historical present renders them a pure ideology of continuity despite the discontinuous and actual "truth of the streets."[24] Far from the discovery of a historical (cultural) continuity, using these archaisms as a guide to present practice is a regression. In one of Tosaka's key neologisms, these archaisms signal a "primitivization-ism" (*genshikashugi*[25]), whereby history is "made to flow backward" (see below and chapter 2). Idealism, fascist and liberal (including bourgeois sociology and economics), must therefore content itself with analyzing artificially static moments of equilibrium and identity, from the perfection of commodity prices to the ahistorical universality of Pareto power distributions. While varied, more than anything, these static, metaphysical archaisms went by the name of (national) culture. The key for Tosaka's historical theory is that, unlike idealism, materialism's dialectical logic grounded in an everydayness of the working day is able to grasp a world in motion, that is, it alone is able to grasp history in its "actuality."[26] Materialist common sense is therefore adequate to the actual crisis of capitalist society in a way that liberalism and fascism's formal logic cannot be. It was from this space of everydayness during the global crisis of the 1930s that he was able to see the true face of fascism.

THE JAPANESE IDEOLOGY AND THE QUESTION OF FASCISM

In the final chapter of the June 1936, second edition of *The Japanese Ideology*, Tosaka writes as an aside, "It should no longer be an issue as to whether or not Japan is fascist." The immediate reference is surely to the attempted coup d'état of February 26, 1936, in central Tokyo, which took place after the first edition of *The Japanese Ideology*—when junior military officers, inspired by Kita Ikki's emperor-centered national socialism, seized control of downtown Tokyo for three days, only surrendering when the emperor intervened and naval warships were brought into Tokyo Bay, their guns trained on the putschists' positions. The Febraury 26 Incident ended in a defeat of the romantic, self-sacrificing, *bushidō*-inspired version of the Imperial Way faction (*kōdō-ha*) of Japanese fascism—and people like Ishihara Kanji, the architect of the Manchurian Incident—at the hands of the more technocratic Control faction (*tōsei-ha*) of "new bureaucrats" represented by people like Kishi Nobusuke[27] and Tōjō Hideki, who argued for Japan to be remade as a total war state of massive economic combinations (*tōseikai*) coordinated by the military.[28] Yet despite these real and violent differences within the Japanese right, *The Japanese Ideology* is a ruthless analysis arguing against such an accidental and contingent understanding of emperor worshippers versus technocrats in favor of a much deeper and ominous understanding, not only of Japanese fascism but also fascism itself. Intensely historical and global, Tosaka's criticism does not posit Japan, or any other nation-state, including "socialism in one country," as a stable unit of analysis that experiences the contortions of the historical world as a discrete, identitarian subject. Fascism is a global *form* found in some way throughout the advanced capitalist world. Put another way, it is not the case that the economic, political, social, and cultural crises of 1930s global capitalism *found expression in* Japan, but that the economic, political, social, and cultural crises of global capitalism *are* "Japan."

Of course, Tosaka's simple, declarative statement on Japan's fascist nature quoted above is full of exasperation. Had he lived, that exasperation would have survived into the postwar historiographical debate on Japan and fascism by both Western and Japanese scholars. As is well known, the definition of fascism has been a huge subject of debate in both Western and Japanese literature. Defining fascism has been so fraught that Kevin Passmore, in the introduction to his updated, second edition of *Fascism: A Very Short Introduction*, notes that although in the first edition he defined fascism not theoretically, but phenomenologically, as a list of necessary traits—most problematic from Tosaka's perspective being the cult of a single leader (*fürherprinzip*) or a mass party "from below"[29]—in the introduction to the second edition he rejects this phenomenological approach as inadequate, but then leaves the rest of the book intact, making the book disavow itself.[30] Other theorists of fascism have completely abandoned the search for definitions and insist fascism is merely a postwar, academic, and historiographical construction.[31] Further, in the overwhelming majority of more general works on fascism, Japan is not considered, is dismissed as being not fascist without much justification, or is shunted off to an appendix where it is cheacked against a list of sort-of, maybe, but not-quite fascist characteristics.[32]

It is impossible not to notice that nearly the entirety of this scholarship on Japan and fascism recapitulates the old modernization theory–inspired Western debate on Japan as sort-of, maybe, but not-quite modern—which was never more than a thinly veiled statement that Japan was not quite Western.[33] In the end, these doubts on Japan's modernity and fascism are the same debate, and the conclusion can only be that Japan was never modern enough to be fascist. Thus, even the absence of true fascism in Japan serves as another dark marker of incomplete Westernization and discusses Japan once again as characterized first and foremost by what it lacks. This repetition of Japan as not quite modern and thus not quite fascist actually hints at a truth of fascism—something that Tosaka will argue in *The Japanese Ideology*: for all its insistence on the importance of the archaic past, fascism is inherently modern and global in form; as he will demonstrate, fascism's archaic categories do not indicate a failed or incomplete transition to full modernity; they are not *remnants* of a past that has simply lingered,[34] but are, in contrast, *revenants* actively resurrected and deployed in the capitalist and democratic present.

Of course, in Japan Studies, too, there is also a long debate over whether or not Japan was fascist. In the postwar period, both modernization theory and the often orientalist cultural and literary studies of Area Studies vehemently insist that the fascist label is inappropriate to Japan. Most recent scholarship on Japan and fascism mirrors the Cold War belief that Japan was an example of an incomplete modernity, and in favor or surface-level sensitivity to culture (especially literature), rejects the fascist label for Japan, from a sometimes unacknowledged, sometimes explicit, orientalist view of Japan as sui generis and so not subject to foreign modes of analysis and categorical organization[35]—thereby repeating a major claim of Japanist ideologues like Watsuji Tetsurō and many others (see chapters 6–8, 12–13). Since modernization theory's (partial) demise in the wake of the US-Vietnam War, Area Studies has redeployed the old orientalist framework dependent on a hard line between East and West in superficially less racist language without engaging with the critique of Area Studies or the unproblematic adoption of the nation-state and its culture as the relevant unit of analysis. In the frantic effort to spare Japan from the fascist label, both Western and Japan Studies texts have offered many alternatives. The long list includes: incomplete, or Maruyama Masao's still-born,[36] modernity; the "emperor system"; militarism;[37] radical shintoism;[38] totalitarianism (often in the sentimental, Dostoeyevskian sense of Judeo-Christian right and wrong that Hannah Arendt used it[39]); and many others. Thus, like modernity before it, the question of Japanese fascism cuts right to the heart of Area Studies' refusal to problematize the metaphysical binary of East and West.

In Japan Studies, perhaps the most common alternative to fascism is simply ultranationalism. Despite its popularity we can dismiss this untheorized "ultranationalism" quickly. The very name suggests a nationalist continuum at which some (quantitative?) threshold good nationalism becomes bad nationalism. This would make "ultranationalism" reducible to the ridiculous question: Nationalism, how much is too much? (But, whereas ultranationalism is easily dismissed at the level of theory, its popularity requires a deeper investigation.) Ultranationalism is also often used by Western scholars of fascism as well. Roger Griffin's definition makes ultranationalism the linchpin: "Fascism is a genus of political ideology whose mythic core and its various permutations is a palingenetic form of populist ultranationalism."[40] Likewise, the modifier "radical" of a term like "radical shintoism" to describe a modern capitalist society points to the same problem and ends with the same result—while also doing the extra ideological work of applying a religious method and categories to history and society. Theorists such as Zeev Sternhell[41] and Robert Paxton acknowledge that fascism is difficult to locate on the standard right-left ideological axis, and occasionally note the affinities between liberalism and fascism, but then flee from the implications of this insight. Paxton's *Anatomy of Fascism* still relies on the theory of bad "excess" beyond good liberal moderation in his nine-point definition. Indeed, rather than a mere list of fascist traits, Paxton's famous nine-points are, in fact, much more like nine steps or stages that, like the "ultra-" of ultranationalism, are merely another attempt to locate the never-located point at which the general categories and logic of good liberal nationalism tips over into the bad "ultranationalism" of fascism, at which point any further investigation is dropped, making the tipping point never anything more than some personal ideology of the author. Here these authors unwittingly re-present the central thesis of *The Japanese Ideology*: that there is too much of a shared philosophical base—"a real relationship between liberalism and fascism"[42]—for liberalism to be effectively marshaled against fascism.

Unlike Paxton and so many others, Tosaka proceeds to face this problem head on and develop a social scientific, and much more chilling, definition of fascism. As he states in chapter 20, "in place of a sociological map of the intellectual field using left, right, and center, or Marxism, fascism, and liberalism, I must construct a map built on more rational contents—which is to say, we need a more philosophical map."[43] *The Japanese Ideology* is that philosophical map.

The first edition of *The Japanese Ideology* (1935) is split into two sections of ten chapters each. Part I, a critique of "Japanism," which in chapter 1 Tosaka calls "the Japanese form of fascism," considers fascism to be indicative of a global moment of the crisis of capitalism in the 1930s. Part II offers a similar critique of liberalism. Three chapters were added to the second edition of 1936 and are presented here as part III: "The Masses and Socialism in an 'Age of Reaction.'" As the title suggests, *The Japanese Ideology* consciously updates Marx and Engels's *The German Ideology* (1845) for the global fascist moment of the 1930s and replaces Feuerbach and Stirner with Heidegger and his Japanese disciples as the main interlocutors. The primary issue of the book is to overcome and negate the phenomenon of fascist thought in Japan after the Japanese state responded to the global crisis of the 1930s with imperialism and police powers in the service of finance capital. It does so by philosophically critiquing the metaphysical, hermeneutic, and philological method of "the Japanese Ideology," which was a combination of the "emperor system," the capitalist mode of production, and, crucially, the idealist thought and method of Japanese liberalism that pioneered and shared much of the later fascist idealisms and metaphysics. The conclusion is that socialism (historical and dialectical materialism) is the only system of thought capable of combatting the idealism that sustains Japanese fascism.

In chapter 1 Tosaka makes his most significant claim that "there is a real relationship between liberalism and fascism" which shares "a family resemblance," in that both rejected the historical world, becoming idealist philosophies of (mere) interpretation, existing not in the world of historical "actuality" but merely in the "world of meaning":

> Now notwithstanding liberalism's origins within, as it were, an economic liberalism—meaning liberalism and liberal consciousness—there is a direct connection between that origin and political democracy. But liberal thought is absolutely not reducible to the concept of democracy—liberalism encompasses a much wider field. Liberal thought is able to gather unto itself all sorts of other contents.
>
> Indeed, we should have fundamental doubts whether liberalism even exists as an independent and singular form of thought at all.... For the sake of argument, let's assume such a liberal philosophy has in fact been developed. Even so, any resulting of "liberalism" would not be confined to absolute fidelity to the totality of liberal thought. That is because all sorts of idealist contents have entered into it, and if such idealist contents were in fact to be organized into a philosophical system, there is no assurance that such a system would be compatible with the original "liberalism."

As he will brilliantly and provocatively show in his key category of "constitutional fascism," because of this shared metaphysical and hermeneutic (and philological) basis, liberalism may become fascism (Japanism) *sono mama* (as is); that is, liberalism may become Japanism without breaking with its philosophical, categorical, logical, or methodological commitments. *The Japanese Ideology* is perhaps best read through this term *sono mama*, which blurs and threatens to erase the break between parts I and II of the book.

As promised, throughout *The Japanese Ideology* Tosaka rejects the superficial, bourgeois *sociologies* of left, right, and center in favor of a much deeper, *social scientific* antagonism between materialism and idealism. In the twenty-three chapters of meticulous critical analysis of the forms of appearance of various political, economic, and (especially cultural) movements and thought in contemporary Japan, the central insight of *The Japanese Ideology* is that liberalism and fascism exist on the same side of the dividing line between a critical, materialist social science and the idealist, and ultimately incoherent, "philosophies" and superficial "sociologies" of both fascism and liberalism. In short, though liberalism and fascism may not be precisely reducible to each other—they are closer to a Janus-faced ideology—their shared base and "family resemblance" nonetheless leaves liberalism defenseless in a fight against fascism.[44] At best this results in the ultimate liberal conceit, and the politically dangerous delusion, that liberalism is a middle ground from which one may oppose the "excesses" of both left and right. (It is also, of course, the source of much of the *tenkō* phenomenon[45] in which many "leftists" so easily recanted their positions and accommodated themselves to the wartime state and its nationalist sloganeering.)

Though Tosaka insists that historical liberalism was never a completely coherent philosophy because of its origins in a negative theory of "freedom from" political, economic, and social constraints, he does grant that it once had some symbiotic relationship to liberal economics and liberal politics in the earlier periods of capitalism. But it is also true that with the historical development of capitalism's own forces and relations of production, a liberal capitalism of individual commodity owners selling their commodities on the market had long since been replaced by monopoly capitalism and imperialism. This history of capitalism's own life processes means that the only form of liberalism that remains in 1930 is a "cultural liberalism" dangerously divorced from economic and political freedom, and always in danger of becoming a free-floating, purely personal ideology of the individual personality grounded in nothing but the mind of the liberal author. Further, it is only these superficial differences that allow liberals to imagine that they oppose fascism, which may be true, but they are only able to do so from personal feelings at the level of *content* (while as we shall see, fascism is first and foremost a *form*). They are thus what Tosaka will call "sentimental liberals" (*kibuntekina jiyūshugisha*) with no social, economic, or political grounding. "We can therefore see that liberalism is theoretically defenseless against a philosophy that uses liberalism's own logic and methods to break with classic factional fidelities and slides toward Japanism. That liberalism or liberal philosophy does not become Japanism has no basis in theory. It is merely a *personal attitude* or stance of any given author" (chapter 1; emphasis added here). Thus, when liberals oppose fascism they do so from a purely emotional standpoint and, as Tosaka states again and again, emotions "should not be respected as political principles."[46] Such an imagined, liberal "middle ground" is politically dangerous; for in the end there is no such thing as a purely negative form of "freedom from" with no relation to its actual, material, historical moment because for something to be considered "thought" it must be used—it must be deployed in the attempt to solve "actual" social problems, meaning it must become active and positive—but in doing so, this means it must become once again implicated in the social, economic, and political struggles of its moment. Thus, cultural liberalism as the final redoubt of liberal thought in an age of finance capitalism and imperialism simply becomes, at best, more and more refined, rarefied academic articulations of a philosophy imagined as grounded in one's own consciousness: "progressive development of culture, the exaltation of humanity, the perfection of personality," and so on; it thus has a strong immanent propensity to resolve in various religious expressions.[47]

But when forced to confront the actual moment of the 1930s, cultural liberalism is condemned either to ossify in the halls of academia with no relation to the conjuncture of the historical moment—again, a situation Tosaka shows can never actually, completely exist—or to accommodate itself to that moment in collaboration with reactionary elements whereby, *sono mama*, sentimental liberalism finds a narrow, literary, and cultural home *within* monopoly capitalism, imperialism, and fascist politics. Far from their self-image that it exists as reasonable middle between the ideological extremes of fascism and Marxism, cultural liberalism is at best nothing more than an intelligentsia's impotent plea for radical political credentials for their bourgeois melancholy (and its Japanese analogue *seimeishugi*) and, at worst, outright collaboration.

Unlike sentimental liberalism's purely personal and emotional differences with Japanism and fascism, liberalism's differences with materialism are grounded in theory—and a clear explanation for the historically observed phenomenon that liberals always "run right" when faced with leftist criticism in a crisis, as Tosaka notes in chapter 1:

That liberalism does not slide toward materialism is based on much more than personal or subjective feelings; it is based in theory.... Theoretically it is entirely possible for liberalism to become Japanism while remaining faithful to a liberal perspective. But for liberalism to become materialism requires not only that liberalism not remain true liberalism, but also that it become something completely other than itself. This means that liberalism absolutely is not the popularly imagined middle ground between Japanism and materialism.[48]

We are already a long way to discovering the origin of the confusion and casuistry of the postwar historiographical debate on Japan and fascism by noting that it comes from trying to elevate merely personal distaste of certain, more extreme elements of the content of fascist ideology and practice, while ignoring its form. Would-be, antifascist, sentimental liberals are doomed to always be searching for a bright line of "ultra" and "excess" between liberalism and fascism that simply does not exist, and so are forced, like Walter Laqueur, to construct a purely personal threshold in the crudest, theoretically incoherent, mystified, and thus politically useless appeal to his own angsty, mute interiority: "The search for definition and formulas belongs to the post-fascist age. Those who lived under fascism *knew (and know) in their bones* in what way this regime differed from others. Such practical experience with fascism is difficult to bequeath."[49]

The result of liberalism becoming independent of its original economic and political basis in the era of liberal capitalism is that though liberalism is still "thought," it has retreated from the actual world of economics and politics and settled within the much narrower world of literature, the world of "mere interpretation," the world of pure "meaning." As Tosaka shows throughout the text, it was the liberals' elevation of hermeneutics to the ultimate form of human "understanding" (*verstehen*) that prepared the ground for fascism.

In keeping with his rigorous historical method that requires any philosophy or "thought" to be embedded in its own historical moment, Tosaka traces the "modern form" of idealism in the global present of the 1930s. Unlike the constant repetition of a primal essence of liberal capitalism characteristic of libertarianism, despite the clearly changed social, economic, and political moment of monopoly capitalism and imperialism, the old idealism could not remain in its original Platonic or even (neo)Kantian form but had to respond to the actuality of the global crisis of capital accumulation. As he puts it in chapter 11, "Modern Idealism in Disguise: Foundation for a Critique of 'Hermeneutic Philosophy'": "Codes are changed during the course of war. And depending on whether it is on offense or defense idealism, too, changes its stripes. Now idealism has shed its old skin, and especially has stopped calling itself idealism. Those who are fooled by this ruse are not grasping the cicada, but merely the cicada's cast-off shell—but by then the cicada is already off singing in other trees." The name Tosaka gives to this updated, veiled idealism is another key neologism, "literaturism" (*bungakushugi*, 文学主義), a hermeneutic epistemology. While the term *bungakushugi* is translated in the text somewhat awkwardly in English as "literaturism" for syntactical reasons, it should be read very broadly and can be glossed as simply "literary theory" or even "the literary." Occasionally it is helpful to read it even more broadly as the more contemporary "textualism," as Tosaka's "literaturism" clearly prefigures contemporary poststructural and deconstructive literary theory's notions that are at times similarly hampered by the kind of idealism Tosaka is critiquing in the 1930s. The liberal elevation of literaturism to the apotheosis of all understanding signals a moment when a hermeneutics, though divorced from the political and economic spheres, has nonetheless become philosophy itself. This will result in what Tosaka calls "the literaturization of philosophy," meaning that philosophy has narrowed to the world of meaning and walled itself off from the world of the natural sciences and the materiality of production, undoing the *yuiken*'s project of producing Lenin's hoped-for antifascist materialism. (It is also the basis of an extraordinary three-chapter arc—16, 17, and 18—on the status and nature of the intelligentsia that culminates not in literary scholars, but in the industrial engineer.)

> Theoretically speaking, a general theory of categories dictates that it is not the case that science and philosophy are one series of particular categories, and against this, literature is another, different categorical series. Ignoring this rule to say that the categorical orders of philosophy and science are different from literature—that is categorically different, different at the level of principle—and that one has faith in only the categorical order of literature, recklessly using it for everything, is what makes something a "literaturist category" [*bungakushugiteki hanchū*]. (chapter 11)

INTRODUCTION

With literaturism as the privileged model of philosophy, the real, actual problems of contemporary events are ignored, or, at best, subsumed, and so neutralized, under a purely literary, aesthetic form of thought in which the question of freedom is reduced to personal "sad passion"[50] and real-world contradictions are replaced with the intellectual's "angst." At worst, they are "erased by the form of thought itself." Importantly, despite its real differences with earlier forms, this modern, "disguised" idealism is still "bourgeois philosophy," as bourgeois philosophy is consistently defined in *The Japanese Ideology* not based in the class position of its articulators but as a philosophy that responds to the specific needs of actually existing bourgeois society. This allows Tosaka to identify the key moments of idealism as bourgeois philosophy in a time and place where no one is still using the term and may even imagine themselves as actively fighting idealism. From here he traces the old-school metaphysics as it has morphed into Heideggerian, Nietzschean, Dostoyevskian, and the "philosopher of Angst"[51] Lev Shestov forms.

A key moment for the question of Japanese fascism occurs when this increasingly impotent and maudlin hermeneutic epistemology of literaturism is yoked to national history. With this move "literaturism" becomes the more reactionary "philologism" (*bunkengakushugi*, 文献学主義), or a "philological consciousness." Philologism in its social existence and active positivity now attempts to resolve current social problems based on the etymological and philological interpretation of words and texts based in the cultural past, as when Buddhist scholars mine the sutras in an attempt to resolve capitalist labor disputes.

Such an etymological and interpretive relationship between the imagined national past and the current crisis means that, politically, philologism resolves into a "restorationism" (*fukkōshugi*) centered on the "archaic":

> Explanation in terms of mere words (in this philological sense) makes *history flow backward* to some archaic thing. Thus such an explanation is unable to *actually* explain the thing. For those possessing this philological consciousness, bad faith or unintentional rationale somehow forces the argument to always lead back to the archaic. (chapter 2)

At this point, the production of the archaic in the capitalist present—restorationism—further develops to become, in another elegant Japanese term (*genshikashugi*) that is rather awkward in English translation as "primitivizationism": a "primitive" form of thought characterized by, among other things, totemistic and animistic aspects.⁵²

Here Tosaka's critique reveals the moment when a passive, negative liberalism undergoes a *dialectical inversion*—not a quantitative tipping point into "ultra" or excess—to become the active, positive, content-filled, idealist metaphysics of Japanism, "the Japanese form of fascism." As such, once it is imbued with archaisms of the national past, the broader primitivizationism is often best understood, and translated into English, as a "nativizationism":

> The root cause of the contradiction of restorationism reaction is as follows: Just as the historically specific stage of liberal capitalism imagines itself as a transhistorical category, projecting itself into an *infinite past*, as a special case of the present stage, restorationism is compelled by a pressing political necessity to create the new, antihistorical category: "the archaic [korai]." Though people will argue the details, this primitivizationist "archaic"—*though produced in the present stage of Japanese capitalism*—is arbitrarily retrojected back into a *finite past*. (chapter 8, additional emphasis added here)

Whereas *The German Ideology* held that Germany's relatively backward economic and political development meant German thought raced ahead of its material conditions, becoming purely speculative, *The Japanese Ideology* shows how the crisis of a developed industrial capitalism in Japan in the 1930s traces the reverse course, becoming philologist, nativizationist, Japanist, that is, fascist. Here we have another dialectical inversion: from Feuerbach's projection of a future, infinite, "universal man" in *The German Ideology* to the *The Japanese Ideology*'s Heideggerian and Japanist appeal to finite (yet reified), ethnic-national, clan-destined⁵³ "man" anchored to an archaic, folkic base that becomes the cathexis, the "zero-center,"⁵⁴ of all philosophy and history.

Liberal freedom of consciousness was orginally defined as that which was unsullied by the political and the social, it was thus, in Tosaka's words, purely "cultural." This lineage can be seen in its obsession with the development of the individual "personality," a personality that was not embedded within, but existed alongside, indeed imagined to exist above, the unfreedoms of the social, economic, and political spaces. (Tosaka locates the origin of "freedom," the concept, in the individualism of the Sophists. From there he traces it to the Renaissance and early modern Europe where it acquired aspects of artistic creativity, which allowed artists to imagine themselves as free because they were no longer mere "workers," before being yoked to a national culture and religion in Fichte, Schelling, and Hegel.)[55] This glorious isolationism had to change with the collapse of global capitalism in the 1930s. Culture would more than ever be the watchword of the decade, but now it must be a *compelled and policed* Japanese culture that imagined itself not "free from" the socioeconomic but identical with it. Here is where the general category of "primitivizationism" acquires a more concrete (yet still reified) national historical content to become the more specific, but still extremely vague, "nativizationism." This marks a move from liberalism's "voluntary spiritualism" to a "necessary [policed] spiritualism," the moment when a negative liberalism becomes tinged with the social positivity of Japanism. It is the move from literaturism to philologism, from liberalism to fascism, where actual, social contradictions that had been displaced into the passive, personal, liberal "angst," are now transformed into an active yet ultimately static metaphysics and a harsh defense of hierarchical power in fascism. As such, "freedom" has been restored, and even expanded, but the free subject has narrowed to "Japan," or "Japaneseness" alone.[56] Freedom would thus become the individual's self-comportment to the now "objective" manifestations of (national, cultural) freedom that appears in common sense and popular customs. The *tenkō* phenomenon would, in turn, represent an individual's "return" to the "objective" coordinates of this (national, cultural) "freedom."[57]

The contemporary production of the archaic categories of Japanism conjures the undead categories of the national past and makes them walk the earth again, but now mobilized to serve—and crucially, veil—the current needs of monopoly capitalism and imperialism that sought to solve the capitalist accumulation crisis through the historical materiality of Japan's colonization of Manchuria and beyond after 1932. Here Tosaka not only inverts the historical procedure of "palingenesis" but also reinforces Uno Kōzō's later creation of the neologism "feudality" (*hōkensei*, 封建性) to highlight the *active production* of feudal *affects* in the capitalist present, not a remnant[58] of a lingering Japanese "feudal *system*"[59] [*hōkensei*, 封建制]—the two words are homonyms in Japanese. This feudal archaism is not a historical *remnant* that impaired Japanese capitalism's achievement of full modernity, but a *revenant* conjured to address capitalist collapse, a revenant that could serve as a spur to future accumulation, that is, a nativizationist "feudality" that could jump-start a stalled capitalism in a fascist form. All contemporary history, culture, thought, economics, and politics must become a mere "expression" of this newly conjured, archaic element. Like the money form of capitalist exchange, the culture of the imperial house (not the emperor himself) becomes the universal form of value, the ultimate and infinite measure demanding endless, open-ended toil in service of a cultural debt that can never be fully repaid.[60] Unlike simple authoritarianism, fascism is ultimately an ideology of a capitalism in perpetual crisis:[61]

> When monopoly capitalism becomes imperialistic, it veils the domestic contradictions of imperialism through state power, while internationally it pretends it can solve those contradictions through force. Fascism is the political mechanism that takes advantage of the domestic and international anxieties of the petite bourgeoisie—the middle classes in the broad sense—those who have lost faith in both the dictatorship of the proletariat and the naked rule of the bourgeoisie. Fascism is the relatively expedient means creating the fantasy that it shares the middle classes' own interests, while, in fact, ultimately succeeding in extending the rule of finance capital. (chapter 10)

Given the necessarily vague nativizationism of thought centered on the archaic national past, and his rigorous method tracing out the forms of appearance of capitalist crisis in thought, common sense, and popular customs lorded over by "the Japanese ideology," Tosaka's potentially most controversial yet absolutely crucial category, "constitutional fascism," emerges as at once unexpected and inevitable. It also warns us to not merely look for fascism only in its fully developed institutional and state forms, but to pay special attention to the role of ideology and thought in the fascization (*fashōka*) of state and society.[62]

Constitutional fascism—"a type of fascism that has adopted a parliamentary system," (chapter 23)—shows that fascism is in no way reducible to simple "dictatorship." In fact, in many ways, Japanese constitutional fascism is a much more supple and expansive form, a more completely liberated fascism not limited by the historical personality of an actually existing Füher or Duce or party, but only by a usefully vague "Japan-ism." In

INTRODUCTION

this it represents the interests of capital itself, and although party fascism may wear "the mask of a fascism from below," fascism is always imposed from above. Further, fascism is a fundamentally ideological phenomenon, distinct from dictatorship or simple authoritarianism or totalitarianism, in that fascism's actual and ideal constituencies are "based in different social strata" (chapter 23, xx). This gap between ideal and real constituencies is what demagogy exploits. Fascism thus exists at the level of form (in thought and ideology, and common sense and customs) and orgainizes and mobilizes the social sphere regardless of whether it completely or spectacularly seizes control of the entirety of the state apparatus.

In 1930s Japan there were two competing major parties, the Seiyūkai and the Minseitō, who actually represented, respectively, landlords and industrial capitalists, but also had differing imagined constituencies in the "so-called farm villages" and "commercial and industrial workers." (Despite these differences there were "no real, important differences" in that both supported an expansionary fiscal policy and empire.) The nature of control in class-ridden, nominally democratic, capitalist societies is not an authoritarian imposition of thought control from above, a view that plagues theories of fascism that expand it out to totalitarianism. Rather, and much more supple, is "constitutive control." Constitutive control does not rely on a decree handed down from on high and violently enforced in all cases, though that form of control surely may exist alongside it. Instead, constitutive control veils itself by achieving control, not through naked expressions of power and coercion, but more indirectly: by the "production of a social antagonism," of course, all the while privileging one side of the antagonism. In the Japanist version, the fundamental social antagonism of Japanist idealism and proletarian materialism may be mystified to become the fundamental binary of East and West—with Japan standing in for the whole of the East as its messianic leader. The produced social antagonism between East and West replaces the necessarily class nature of socialism (materialism) with a national, ethnic—and archaic—folkic communalism, a procedure that underwrites the otherwise ethnically confused epithet for socialists employed by Japanists: the "Russian-style Japanese" (*roshiyateki nihonjin*).

The operation of this ideology, though produced through both liberal and fascist hermeneutic interpretation, exerts its power in the slippery social space as "common sense." Common sense is a nearly unconscious expression of a particular society's thought and is tied to the more academic questions of worldview, method, and logic. As such, it is something not easily locatable in the social space but nonetheless is always present operating as a "field of force" that may be uncovered through a materialist critique of ideology based in historical time (see chapter 3). Common sense is never the straightforward, neutral, or purely quantitative thing it is imagined to be, but always contains within it important, but veiled, qualitative aspects that allow it to operate as *simultaneously the ideal and the norm* of a given social space. Even bourgeois common sense harbored a contradiction between a banal, arithmetic average and an ideal representing the standard toward which it aspired. In the bourgeois common sense developed in the eighteenth and nineteenth centuries in Europe, this ideal was often borrowed from aristocratic tastes and mores. The presence of an ideal within itself—aristocratic for bourgeois and imperial for Japanist—also means that common sense is able to constantly act as a "Mephistophelean tempter" "soliciting" all toward its hidden ideal.[63] This Satanic seduction lurking within common sense enables Japanism to mobilize the gap between the ideal and real constituencies of both liberal and fascist common sense through demagogy: a demagogy grounded in a particular view of the masses as a purely quantitative entity without any inherent self-organization—the crowd, the mob—that needed to be ruled by a "spiritual elite." As largely *unthought*, but actively *lived*, Japanist common sense centered on national security could thus appear to be self-grounding, and fascism could present itself as the objective preservation and expansion of freedom.

In the case of constitutional fascism, after much tedious internal right-wing hermeneutic and philological disputes, some of them violent, the ideal of this Japanist common sense eventually settled on the usefully vague ideological slogan: "the clarification of the national essence" (*kokutai meichōshugi*). Under this banner the various forms and capitalist constituencies could be unified and further be yoked to the doctrine of national security. As partisan politics gave way to "national unity cabinets" after 1932, the bureaucracy, but especially the military, was useful for these purposes as they could appear to be above class self-interest and thus appear to represent the nation itself.[64] In turn, the ruthless expansion into the Asian continent by Japan's military could simultaneously be seen as the development of an "altruistic" Japanese spirituality.[65] Though the key metaphysical category in the case of Japanese fascism is "the East," *The Japanese Ideology* makes an important intervention in Marxist thought itself in refusing to adopt such a civilizational perspective, never taking the nation-state as the unit of analysis, but instead consistently viewing Japan as "a link in a global (capitalist) chain."[66] Thus the feudal affects of "the Japanese ideology" are merely the almost accidental content of a global form of fascism that only superficially distinguishes Japan from other fascisms in Italy, Germany, the United States, France, or the United Kingdom that take other nativizationist content, be they the Teutonic forests, Rome, forms of Christianity, or countless other possibilities.[67] Cathected by a nativist "sense of national history" located somewhere within "Japan's long feudal period" the specificity of Japanese fascism (Japanism) is a site where "*the general conditions of fascism* could be built upon the basic conditions of the remnants of feudal forces particular to Japan ... where *these feudal forces took the form of fascism*" (chapter 23, emphasis added).

As such, constitutional fascism is produced when the mere form of parliamentary politics became independent of, and subsumed under, the common sense of the "Japanese Ideology" and the archaism of the imperial house as the expression of "all things Japanese" (*nihontekina mono*). We should remember that Japan never suspended nor amended its constitution of 1890; the constitution remained in force throughout the war, only some of the supplemental, procedural norms surrounding it changed in any way.[68] In other words, the liberal, constitutional, parliamentary order was able to become a fascist body "as is" (*sono mama*).

While acknowledging the horrific conditions and the ascendancy of Japanese fascism, Tosaka ends *The Japanese Ideology* with a positive program in noting that the difference between the quantitative average and the qualitative level of common sense is dialectical and hides within itself a contradiction. Thus, any ruling ideology's common sense contains within itself a negative underside. This negation of bourgeois common sense is immanent to common sense itself as it must be articulated, if not always explicitly, as answerable to its own historical moment. In the negation of the positive content of bourgeois and Japanist common sense of the spiritual elites, mass, proletarian common sense still exists as the "truth of the streets" and must develop its own common sense based in its own historical and material "actuality." So while an idealist, hermeneutic—and in the case of Japanism, nativizationist—common sense seduces people to rise to the imperial ideal, a materialist common sense grounded in the everydayness of the working day also carries within itself a set of values located in the here and now. During the 1930s, the age of reaction in which he wrote, that proletarian common sense was on the retreat but could still be glimpsed in the critiques of the ruling ideology by the masses in humor, satire, irony, political protest, and labor actions. Despite the dire circumstances of what is called in Japanese historiography "The Dark Valley," and in good socialist fashion, like the conclusion to Marx's *Eighteenth Brumaire*, *The Japanese Ideology* closes with a call to action: not for a return to simple practical needs, let alone the end of ideology, but as the moment for a return to theory itself, theory as the development and organization of the materialist, critical common sense produced by the "everydayness" of the actually existing life of the laboring masses.

ACKNOWLEDGMENTS

Many groups and individuals have helped this project over the years, so many that I cannot possibly list them all; hopefully they will all know who they are and see their influence in the final result. Among these, special note must be made of my comrades and collaborators involved in *Tosaka Jun: A Critical Reader*, as well as my fellow panelists and audiences at Historical Materialism conferences (London), the Association for Asian Studies, UCLA's Trans-Pacific Workshop, Wesleyan University, Waseda University, the Modern Japan group at École des hautes études en sciences sociales in Paris, and the faculty and students of the Social Theory reading group here at the University of Virginia. Though parts of this project were completed at NYU, no thanks are due, and none offered. Finally, special thanks to Professor Tetsuo Najita, who long ago, in an offhand comment during a lecture, mentioned *The Japanese Ideology*, adding "someone should translate that one day." It took much longer than anyone would have liked, but I am grateful I was able to send him a draft of this book before it was too late.

THE JAPANESE IDEOLOGY

Words in ~~strikethrough~~ were censored in the original text.

PREFACE

This book is an investigation of contemporary Japanism and liberalism from various and ultimately, a materialist, perspectives. The book's title, *The Japanese Ideology*, follows Marx, who called his criticism of various forms of thought and their claims to truth and the resolution of social problems in Germany *The German Ideology*. This alone should indicate what I wish to say in this book. Of course, I know well enough my own weaknesses and do not presume to usurp Marx's title.

("Problems in Contemporary Japanese Thought" and "Liberal Philosophy and Materialism" are both new pieces. The others appeared in *Yuibutsuron kenkyū, Rekishi kagaku, Shakai hyōron, Shinpo, Dokusho, Chishiki*, as well as *Kaizō, Keizai ōrai, Gyōdō*, and *Bungei*, but have all been edited for this volume.)

For anyone wishing to learn more of the intellectual basis for what I say in this book, I would be happy if they would consult the works below—especially the second.

1. *Kagaku hōhōron*, 1929, Iwanami shoten
2. *Ideorogii no ronrigaku*, 1930, Tettō shōin
3. *Ideorogii gairon*, 1932, Risōsha shuppan bu
4. *Gijutsu no tetsugaku*, 1933, Jichōsha

5. *Gendai tetsugaku kōwa*, 1934, Hakuyōsha (revised edition, *Gendai no tame no tetsugaku*, Ōhata shoten)

June 30, 1935
Tokyo
Tosaka Jun

PREFACE TO THE REVISED EDITION

On the occasion of this revised edition, three new chapters have been added as supplements. As time has passed, I felt it necessary. For reference, other than those suggested in the first edition, I would add the following two works: *Shisō toshite no bungaku*, 1936, Mikasa shobō; and *Kagakuron*, 1935, in *Yuibutsuron zenshū*, Mikasa shobō.

May 1936
Tosaka Jun

SUPPLEMENTAL PREFACE TO THE REVISED EDITION

The revised edition has been reprinted several times. I do not have anything particular to add at this time, but only wish to direct the reader to four of my other books that have come out since the revised edition. These are *Dōtokuron* in *Yuibutsuron zensho*, Mikasa shobō, 1936; *Shisō to fūzoku*, Mikasa shobō, 1937; *Gendai nihon no shisō tairitsu*, Kyō no mondaisha, 1936; and *Gendai yuibutsuron kōwa*, Hakuyosha, 1936.

January 1937
Tosaka Jun

PART I
Foundation for a Critique of Japanism

Chapter One

PROBLEMS IN CONTEMPORARY JAPANESE THOUGHT

Japanism, Liberalism, Materialism

In Japan today we find nearly every variety of thought: Japanese, Eastern, Western, and, if we include all thought that has come down from some past thinker to the present, the list is nearly endless: Ninomiya Sontoku and Yamaga Soko; Confucius and Nietzsche; Dostoyevsky, Heidegger, and Jaspers; the list goes on and on. But all these examples, and many others, are really no more than opinions. None has yet reached any kind of social coherence in any broad sense to become "thought." Thought—the concept—is not simply some content worked out inside the head of some thinker. Which is to say that most thinking is not thought. Unless it also possesses some social force, some social objectivity, it is not thought. It is not thought unless it is deployed as a resolution of actual social problems.

Once we understand thought in this way, we are struck by the fact that the premier thought of contemporary Japan is liberalism. Now many out there are saying that liberalism has recently collapsed, so we must respond and explain just what kind of liberalism remains vigorous despite this popular sense of liberalism's demise. Clearly, liberal thought evokes hardly any positive meaning in the consciousness of the public. Since the Great War [World War I], the only examples of a self-consciously liberal movement are the democracy movement of Yoshino Sakuzō and a few others. And with the rapid rise of Marxism, we must acknowledge that a conscious liberalism has completely left the stage so that now we simply do not see any explicit attempts to promote liberalism. Still, we must not forget that on the other hand, ever since the Meiji Revolution [1868], the fundamental *social consciousness* of Japan has been liberalism.

Of course, in neither form nor essence can we say there exists a full and complete bourgeois democracy in Japan. Japan's current democracy has mixed with, compromised with, and been distorted by a host of feudalistic elements such as the bureaucracy, the military, and obedience to authority. Even so, it is important to acknowledge that a distorted democracy is still at its base a kind of democracy. Even if liberal consciousness in Japan today is rather unconvincing, it is still the foundation of our social consciousness. Indeed, precisely because liberalism has become common sense, and further, as it never breaks free of that basic common sense, cases in which a self-conscious "liberalism" would be explicitly announced remain rare and accidental cases. Today Japanism is ascendant, and it takes as its sworn enemy this very liberalism that exists as a diffused social consciousness. Now, this Japanist assault on liberalism alone does not especially prove the vigor of a *conscious* liberalism, but it does indicate that an *unconscious* liberalism remains the hidden basis of modern Japanese thought.

Now, notwithstanding liberalism's origins within, as it were, an economic liberalism—meaning liberalism and liberal consciousness—there is a direct connection between that origin and political democracy. But liberal thought is absolutely not reducible to the concept of democracy—liberalism encompasses a much wider field. Liberal thought is able to gather unto itself all sorts of other contents.[1]

Indeed, we should have fundamental doubts whether liberalism even exists as an independent and singular form of thought at all. It is quite unclear if liberalism possesses an internal mechanism of development, or if it contains the ability to clearly adjudicate antagonisms within itself in a consistent manner, or indeed whether it is even a living theoretical organization. On all these points we need to doubt if liberalism possesses an independence at all. But for the sake of argument, let's assume such a liberal philosophy has in fact been developed. Even so, any resulting *philosophy of* "liberalism" would not be confined to absolute fidelity to the totality of liberal thought. That is because all sorts of idealist contents have entered into it, and if such idealist contents were in fact to be organized into a philosophical system, there is no assurance that such a system would be compatible with the original "liberalism." Which is to say, liberalism's thought is quite liberal with the chaos of its idealist contents.

Surely we can say that one of the contents of *liber*al thought is freedom from, a *liber*ation from, social and political ideas.[2] And with liberation from social and political ideas, cultural liberation becomes the only issue. We can detect many understandings of the concept of freedom and liberation within today's liberals, but to take one example, the concept of cultural freedom becomes a religious consciousness, where it is further developed.[3] Mediated by, let's say, Christian, especially Protestant, theology, or Buddhist philosophy, liberal philosophy becomes religious consciousness, as the reader will surely agree. Many of today's *Bildung* intelligentsia have set out on the path toward religious idealism. This sort of religious consciousness normally stops here (to go further down this path would mean the whole project would become something else entirely). This move toward religious consciousness is one product of liberalist consciousness.

It is clear that religious freedom means to be free from political freedom. It means an escape from reality [現実]. As everyone knows, this is the fundamental premise and indeed the point of religion. So, as we clearly see in the current situation, such a move to religious consciousness becomes a way out—but not the only one—of liberalism's inability to resolve current contradictions. Instead of resolving contradictions in practice, those contradictions are resolved only in thought. Alternatively, these contradictions may be simply ignored or erased by the form of thought itself.[4]

Today we are witness to the intelligentsia's attempt to give philosophical and logical systematization to both the national and socially acknowledged "established religions" and the more derivative and heretical popular doctrines among the less educated masses. But without the frenetic work of an intelligentsia grounded in liberalism nothing can be expected to come of this project.

Further, we should note here that this so-called religious freedom inverts to become a so-called absolutism [*zettaishugi*]. Such a liberalism mediated by a religious consciousness is able to easily transition from this sort of religious absolutism to a kind of political absolutism. Religion has already begun to collaborate with political absolutism. For example, Buddhist exegesis has begun to claim that Buddhism is a manifestation of the Japanese spirit. Even Catholicism is urging the construction in Japan of an absolute

~~monarch comparable to~~ the religious authority of the pope. A Japanese ~~absolute prince~~ as an ~~object~~ of religious ~~veneration~~ has already become a real problem. We should be aware that this step out of liberalism into religious consciousness means we have entered into the realm of Japanism.

It is said that today Japan has begun to be ruled by a religious restoration leading to a religious worldview and religious thought. Leaving aside for now whether or not this means a "religious" truth-seeking movement, we cannot deny that this sort of religious thought is presently a significant phenomenon. And still, even if it were the case that this is a religious movement only, it does not mean that religious thought has been set up as an independent field of thought. For if it is not grounded in liberal thought, religious consciousness resolves in Japanism. It is through a particular relation to political activities that members of a society develop the capabilities of what we earlier called "thought." If we are talking about a purely religious religion then we are not talking about thought, but rather nothing more than a purely personal and private thing. But, of course, in reality, such a purified religious religion simply does not exist.

When it is organized into a philosophical system by means of a particular logic, and this is speaking of liberal philosophy in a broad sense—we understand, of course, that this nomenclature does not satisfy many—when such a system is organized, one of its fundamental characteristics is that the method of liberal thought simply becomes a refinement, merely a "hermeneutic philosophy of interpretation" (*kaishaku no tetsugaku*). In place of explaining the order of things in their actuality, it speaks only of a corresponding order of meaning. This is clearly the particular modus operandi of this shared philosophical method. For example, from the beginning to the present, the universe, the actual world, has been ruled by the time of physics. As is often stated, disciplines such as geology and astronomy have shown definitively that the earth existed long before the existence of conscious beings such as humans (or even animals). The hermeneutic philosophy of liberalism's logic does not problematize this order of things (the time of physics). Instead, it takes up the relation of humans to nature as a question of the order of things within human psychological time. Alternatively, it merely considers questions of the superhuman, the infinite, or the eternal. (Such questions only have any use in the world of meaning.)[5] In

PROBLEMS IN CONTEMPORARY JAPANESE THOUGHT

pretending to speak of the actual world and inform about material actual time, this liberalist hermeneutic philosophy speaks only of the world of meaning—and thus exclusively belongs to an idealist world. And so, *the world itself* becomes merely an object of interpretation.

Such a philosophy is nothing more than idealism, an idealism that has been taken up in a modern liberalist form and has merely been painstakingly refined by hermeneutic philosophy. It is by means of liberalism's camouflage that this brutal, idealist Death's Head has wrapped itself in soft liberal flesh. By dressing it up in modern garb, liberalism has normalized idealism.

The philosophical mechanism of this interpretive philosophy is adopted over an enormous field of inquiry—indeed, it traverses the entirety of philosophical idealism. Accordingly, as we'll see later, an exclusive focus on interpretation is absolutely not the womb of liberalist philosophy alone. Still, this focus on mere interpretation results in the most typical conclusions of liberalist philosophy, and this method is the theory of literary liberalism—a literary, hermeneutic epistemology,[6] "the literary" itself or, as it were, a literaturism [*bungakushugi*]. The specific result of such a hermeneutic philosophical method is merely a mechanism that functions as a sleight of hand that appears to dignify and give a progressive patina to cultural questions. It uses literary imagery to capture a phantasmic vision of present reality. Then, without any modification or mediation, these literary representations and images are deployed as philosophical and theoretical concepts. And so, in this way the actual order of things based on the *actual categorical organization* of reality—meaning [social] theory—is replaced with the linking of image to image adequate to their mere *interpretation as a categorical organization*—again, as [literary] theory. Such is the result of this method. Surely no more mystifying and expedient method exists.

Indeed, a current problem is that the majority of the literary liberals who make up the intelligentsia forming the current social consciousness of Japan are so "at home" in this literaturism.[7] And so when they discourse on anything, they unknowingly and unfailingly adopt the perspective of this literary liberalism and literaturism. In fact, more than anything else, today, as the intelligentsia is problematized by literary scholars themselves, we must remain skeptical of this sort of theory of the intelligentsia that appears to become nothing more than an ideology of the superiority of intelligence (see chapters 15 and 16). In any event, at minimum, this ideology of superiority is characteristic of literaturism built upon a liberalist philosophy. But the problem of the intelligentsia is originally focused on the *question* of intelligence. We must note in passing that for explaining the problem of intelligence, liberal philosophy is useless. Consider: Do the words "liberalist scientific resolution to the problem of intelligence" mean anything at all? Once again, we must note that it is already a mistake to say liberal philosophy exists as a completely scientific theoretical system.

Liberalism proper is a logical system built on the idealist interpretation of liberation, of freedom itself. Economic, political, ethical freedoms, these, too, are each problematized as instances of freedom itself, which means they are problematized as freedom in general. Thus the ensuing philosophy is a generalized logic of "freedom from." The result is merely a formalistic logic of freedom in general. While formalism is one necessary result of hermeneutic philosophy, we must acknowledge that from the start, formalism and interpretive philosophy are also two characteristics of metaphysics, which is to say they are characteristic of idealism.

We have already seen that the religious consciousness produced by liberalism, in due course, becomes the ~~absolutism~~ of Japanism. And it is at precisely this moment that we can see the parallel movement by which the interpretive, hermeneutic method of liberalism gives birth to Japanism. Seen this way we notice immediately that Japanist philosophy is in fact a product of liberal philosophy. At the very least, the method of liberal philosophy gives Japanist philosophy immense space to maneuver.

Earlier we noted that liberal philosophy's particular method, interpretation, was the reason it gave birth to literaturism. And again, parallel to this we now notice that this interpretive method also gives birth to a philological consciousness and the ideology of philologism, [*bunkengakushugi*]. If literaturism, as a hermeneutic epistemology, rather than being based on philosophical categories, instead founds itself on literary imagery, and then deploys these literary categories in a hermeneutic method, then philologism replaces actually existing things with the etymological interpretation of texts and literary sources. In the most extreme cases, words are cherry-picked from Japanese and then elevated to philosophical concepts. And really, is there no one who has not noticed just how extremely superficial such a "philosophical method" is? Yet this way of using classic texts without any adequate historical or scientific sense of the lived reality of the people who produced them somehow wins considerable confidence for its claims. It is precisely this reliance on the "interpretation" (or put another way, sophistry) of ancient literary texts that allows this philologism to become the literary, the literaturist "interpretation" of history. Nearly every instance of Japanists' "sense of national history" is founded on precisely this method.

An even more important point: Japanists aim at replacing the actual resolution of real problems with a philological interpretation of classic texts. One example is the resolution of current labor issues through the interpretation of Buddhist texts. It is not a question of passing through the actual history that produced those classic texts. It is only the archaic category that is transplanted and applied to the present. If archaic categories can be so easily transplanted into the present, then just what happens to the actuality that supposedly exists within our present reality? Of course, the present actuality is shuffled off into the development of the world of meaning through the interpretation of these classic texts. Surely there is no greater trick that instead of the order of things in their actuality, we get the order of meaning.

Of course, philologism, meaning a philological consciousness, does not necessarily have to become Japanism right away. Originally it cannot be understood as Japanism. It could become Hellenism or Hebraism, ancient Sinology (Confucianism) or ancient Indianism (Buddhism). Academic philosophers, Christian theologians, Imperial Way scholars, and Buddhist theologians all use these philological mechanisms to speak to contemporary things. But studying the classics is studying the classics—it is not the same thing as resolving current problems. Yet through this philologistical sleight of hand, ancient studies pretends it can solve actual present problems. And this union makes up the various forms of reactionary thought across the globe inevitably produced from within contemporary capitalism.

From the above we immediately see how philologism easily becomes an ideology of restoration, a restorationism [*fukkōshugi*]. Though present reality faces the future, with a conceptual inversion, restorationism invariably employs idealist concepts from the past to interpret the present situation. With its use of archaic categories, we can see how this method distorts the image of the present through this kind of interpretation. But we must not forget, it is somehow commonplace to accept the results of such an interpretation as a faithful representation of social development.

Philology finally becomes completely the tool of Japanism the moment it is applied to history. Though we initially called it a vague Japanism, it comes in many varieties. In general, there is Mussolini's kind of fascism, the fascism of the Nazis, as well as social fascism, and Japanism is thought to have the same interests as these other movements. Even so, all the generalized restorationisms, or spiritualisms, or mysticisms, all these run-of-the-mill reactionary ideologies, have taken on the hue of Japanism. Pan-Asianism and the Imperial Way are really species of Japanism. But a more precise meaning of Japanism is thought based on a Japanist "sense of national history."[8] Japanese spiritualism, Japanese agrarian fundamentalism, or again, Japanese Asianism (the ideology that places Japan as the leader of Asia), even these have a "national historical" Japanist content.[9] And so, all of them are without a doubt completely unified and must resolve in ~~absolut~~ism—which is in fact exactly what we are seeing today. As for the ~~emperor~~ himself there is no end to debate, but for ~~absolutism~~, we are talking about nothing less than the philologistic interpretive philosophical method applied to national history. This absolutism is the final endpoint of an active, positive idealism in Japan. In contrast, liberalism is merely the stability of a passive, negative idealism.

Though some may dispute it, Japanism is the Japanese form of fascism. If Japanism is not seen as fascist it is impossible to get a full understanding of this ideology as a link in a global chain.[10] It also becomes impossible to explain just how and why so much European fascist philosophy is used by Japanism. With varying nuances within totalitarian social theory (*Gemeinschaft*, absolute state, etc.) this totalitarianism [*zentaishugi*] happily uses the mechanisms of fascist philosophy. But in using foreign thought, Japanism surely is unable to do so in any coherent or rational way. For Japanism, then, the indispensable starting point must be the "consciousness" (?)[11] of the sui generis nature of national history itself.[12] (Positing the conclusion this way is a wonderfully convenient method of argumentation.) But in order to proceed, the essential philosophical *method* is not the particular categories of European totalitarianism, but instead it is none other than our already-stated philologism. But here, too, this philologism itself is not in any way particularly Japanese. Indeed, an explicit philologism is the premier representative of current German philosophy: just see Heidegger, for example. So what remains Japanese within Japanism is merely a Japanist national history. The result of our examination reveals that there's no philosophy left here at all.

Because its method is merely interpretive philologism, a consideration of national history by means of liberalism or liberal philosophy has therefore hardly any meaning at all. Only materialism or historical materialism can mount a scientific critique to oppose the Japanist historical perspective. To clearly make the point: liberalism does not actually oppose Japanism, only materialism can do that. The proof of this is clear when we notice that it was liberalism's hermeneutic philosophy that gave Japanism its "scientific"(?!) method and room to maneuver. What this means is that liberalism and liberal thought—just as it is and without breaking with itself [*sono mama de*]—easily becomes Japanism. Japanist philosophy is not limited to the philosophy of right-wing and reactionary groups. Outwardly liberal modern philosophy, which is to say also philosophies based in modernism and liberalism, can become models of Japanist philosophy. Professor Watsuji Tetsurō's *Ethics as Anthropology* [1934] is a good example. Today, the "study of man" and anthropology represent a particularly malignant liberalism. Both descend from our precious literaturism, and quite smoothly turn into representatives of Japanism. Here, truly, we encounter the family resemblance running through both liberalism and Japanism.

Professor Takahashi Satomi's theory of totalitarianism,[13] *The Standpoint of Totality* [*Zentai no tachiba* (1932)], alone must be counted as part of the genealogy of liberal philosophy. But we surely do not also need to point out that the category of totality is the indispensable and fundamental ideal at the base of Nazi social theory. Even if at first glance Professor Nishida Kitarō's "logic of nothingness" ["*mu*" *no ronri*, see chapter 11] cannot itself be labeled religious mysticism; if we objectively consider its fate, it exists as precisely the sort of religious consciousness aimed at the intelligentsia we discussed above. Nishida's kind of religious consciousness is tinged with a social positivity. In other words, it easily becomes Japanist. We've already mentioned how this works in the present reality. We can therefore see that liberalism is theoretically defenseless against a philosophy that uses liberalism's own logic and methods to break with classic factional fidelities and slides toward Japanism. That liberalism or liberal philosophy does not become Japanism has no basis in theory. It is merely a personal attitude or stance of any given author. But that liberalism does not slide toward materialism is based on much more than personal or subjective feelings; it is based in theory.

Normally liberalism is closer to materialism than it is to Japanism, or so goes the conventional political wisdom. But considered within the system of liberal philosophy, liberalism's fundamental principles place it in opposition to materialism, and thus it prepares the field for Japanism. Nevertheless, on the belief that liberalism and materialism may be allies, that is only true if liberalism were to stop insisting on its own liberalist standpoint and in fact become its opposite. Theoretically it is entirely possible for liberalism to become Japanism while remaining faithful to a liberal perspective. But for liberalism to become materialism requires not only that liberalism not remain true liberalism, but also that it become something completely other than itself. This means that liberalism absolutely is not the popularly imagined middle ground between Japanism and materialism.

At the start I said that liberalism was the latent social consciousness of modern Japan. However distorted or perverse, Japan is an advanced capitalist country, and so, it is natural to conclude as much. It goes without saying that today's liberalism, which is to say bourgeois liberalism, is based on capitalism, so liberalism is assumed to be the fundamental consciousness of capitalist society. Accordingly, if we take liberalism as the given social result of a developed capitalism, we must say that liberalism is in at least some way progressive when compared to other forms of thought which do not take liberalism as a given. For example, if we compare liberalism with the reactionary nature of various forms of restorationist thought based on the thought of medieval feudalism, liberalism is clearly progressive. A Catholic scholar has said he does not understand why more or less all social common sense is liberal(ism). But it is surely not necessary to demonstrate that, especially when compared with medieval Catholicism, liberal and Protestant common sense are in agreement with bourgeois social common sense.

PROBLEMS IN CONTEMPORARY JAPANESE THOUGHT

Further, in order to illuminate this liberalist bourgeois social common sense, Japanism (we should be careful never to forget that today we mean a particular reactionary and restorationist thought), possesses remarkable uncommonsensical characteristics. Japanism's inclusion of various uncommon sensibilities allows liberals to rebel against Japanist right-wing reactionary thought grounded in nothing more than personal or individual feelings. But that said, in reality, this also means liberals can do nothing to counter this uncommon sensibility of the trending Japanist thought when it seizes the less well-educated masses. When that happens, we once again see only a single common sense shared by liberalism and Japanism. We thus run head on into the problem of where the masses and public opinion (?) are located. And if we cannot solve the difficult problem of locating common sense,[14] any criticism of contemporary Japanism we might offer will lack all power.

In fact, Japanism has not only already become aware of its own particular common sensibility (?) [常識性]; we also see that it finally has adopted a policy of trumpeting it. Japanism is incessantly announcing it must enlighten (!) the masses. Incidentally, enlightening the masses is not a job any high-end liberal would take any pride in. These hermeneutic philosophers and philologists are all too busy constructing a metaphysics of meaning or polishing their individual consciousness (self-consciousness or self-reflection) and can't be bothered taking the time to consider society or the masses during a tea break. This means, then, that we need to talk about just how liberals are continuing to provide support to the Japanist Enlightenment movement (?).

As for liberal support for the Japanist Enlightenment movements, that happened in the early battles of the cultural fascism of the Cultural Unification movement [Bunka tōsei undo]. Japanists extend a hand of gratitude to the huge majority of today's liberals who raised hardly a peep of fundamental resistance to today's various cultural unification movements, making the relationship of liberals and Japanists one of support and thanks.

The third form of thought opposed to both Japanism and liberalism is, of course, materialism. Neither Japanism nor liberalism, but only materialism, is capable of a scientific critique of either Japanism or liberalism, either separately or in their relation with each other. And this is worth noting, materialism's critical ability is indirect proof of its superiority as a form of thought. The fact of the matter is that materialism, in seeking to resolve actually existing problems in practical terms, develops a consistent theory with an extensive and inclusive conceptual mechanism.

What I have tried to do above is offer some critique of Japanism and liberalism as well as identify the foundation of that criticism itself. In my view this is a major part of materialism's task today.

Chapter Two

FOUNDATION FOR A CRITIQUE OF JAPANISM
A Critique of Philological Philosophy

1. The Development of Philological Philosophy
2. Toward a Critique of the Philological Consciousness (文献学主義)

First, we must explain the meaning of the problem.

One of the tasks of materialism today is the scientific critique of the antagonism between the actual world and spirit (culture). This task is of course not the only one for contemporary materialism, but here we understand criticism to mean the overcoming of the object of criticism in both an actual and a corresponding theoretical sense. Now it is clear that overcoming something only theoretically is not the same as actually overcoming that object in reality. But it is also true that without overcoming something in theory we cannot say that something has been adequately overcome in actual practice. In popular usage, criticism is often set in opposition to actual proof, a view that sees criticism as a merely passive kind of intellectual labor, and this view of criticism in turn gives rise to the simplistic wisdom of positivism. Indeed, this common sort of armchair criticism of the mere observer—the fetish of such a so-called criticism—has absolutely no relation to the kind of fundamental criticism we mean here.

Our intended sort of criticism, meaning a scientific critique, means a form of criticism that employs unified and broad scientific categories (or, if you like, philosophical categories) to analyze an object. There is, strictly speaking, only one unified and comprehensive system of scientific or philosophical categories. To say that there is only one such system is also to say that such a system has the characteristic of being objective and scientific. Today, we call this unique system materialism (or to further designate it, dialectical materialism). Materialism is this singular scientific theory. In practice the outward appearance of the various fundamental concepts used by this theory are able to take on many external forms. Of course there is no other way for us to express ourselves than by linking analogies, humor, fantasies, or connotations—to use them in a literary or linguistic way (*bungakuteki*). For if we did not make use of linguistic forms there would be simply no way to produce either actual statements or thought. But in spite of this, indeed precisely because of this, all these floating aesthetic representations and everyday concepts must become materialist categories within a categorical organization.

As is surely well known, the general method of a materialist, scientific criticism is to render concrete, and thereby to render practical, by means of this general method, the conditions of the present situation. The various necessary and fundamental notions (the various foundations) of scientific criticism today are to incorporate the new techniques derived from this general method. For us, the particular task is to search for the foundations of a practical (*gijutsuteki*) scientific criticism against those so-called social and cultural foundations adopted by contemporary philosophical idealism.[1] Viewed as the big picture to this point, our theme has become a question, on the one hand, of examining issues such as journalism, everydayness, and common sense, and on the other, to see how far these concepts are able to combat both hermeneutic philosophy in general, and its more particular ideology of literaturism (see chapters 3, 4, 11, 14, etc.). Of course, both of these themes have the same foundation. And of course many more tasks remain.

Philology [文献学] (フィロロギー) aligns with the problem of literaturism and is a characteristic problem presented by interpretive philosophy (meaning a philosophy that ends with the mere interpretation of the world[2]). Which is to say that "philologism"—a philological consciousness—also appears here as a problem. Some have suggested that philology (*Philologie*) is literature and have therefore insisted that this so-called literature should be called "the arts," and there is a good argument for doing so. At

FOUNDATION FOR A CRITIQUE OF JAPANISM

minimum, viewing the problem from this perspective(?), we would do well to remember that the problem of philologism has an intimate relation with the problem of literaturism, or a hermeneutic epistemology (on literaturism, see chapter 11, "Modern Idealism in Disguise").

1

Philology (*Philologie*) is commonly understood to mean linguistics. But we must be careful here because linguistics is definitely not identical with philology. For example, according to Saussure, linguistic study began with the study of grammar in ancient Greece. But it is not until the second half of the eighteenth century with Friedrich August Wolf[3] and his followers that we have something called "philology." The explanation goes that this "philology" concerned itself only with ancient words and their interpretation, and because it was not concerned with living languages, linguistics penetrated this Wolfian "philology" (フィロロギー)[4] and was then developed [by Franz Bopp] as comparative grammar before eventually becoming scientific linguistics (which means it was already no longer Wolf's "philology" but was called *Linguistique*). This means that "philology" is definitely not completely unified with linguistics and also means no less that "philology" comes into contact with linguistics obliquely; that "philology" and linguistics share a zone of contact that traverses them both. We see then that philology is its own thing and that linguistics later was developed along a relatively different course. Which is to say, because this Wolfian philology is none other than a meeting of philology and linguistics, Wolf's philology[5] is translated as "philology"[6] [*bunkengaku*], or even "literature" [*bungaku*]. Here Wolfian philology intersects with more general theories of literature and belles-lettres. (For example, see Bernard Bosanquet's *A History of Aesthetics*, chapter 9). This is the reason that Wolf's "philology" is not simply linguistics.

For our consideration of the problem of philology it is fine if we neglect a full consideration of linguistics itself (this is because linguistics has no direct influence on the trends of contemporary thought). But we must not forget that philology is not completely independent of linguistics and must at some point intersect with it; this is an important point. In other words, whatever position we may take regarding how later and to what extent, the classics, or history, or philosophy itself became an issue or was developed by philology—however far we become divorced from the study of words themselves, broadly speaking—philology and philologism[7] present us with the difficulties that arise in the gaps between words and language, between thought and theory. In reality, cases where philological research and linguistic research become one are plentiful. We already have the previous example of Wolf, but there is no better example than the nineteenth-century thinker Wilhelm von Humboldt. In Humboldt's comparative linguistic research we see the problem of understanding classic texts linked up with historical description. He was able to create a continuity between classical texts and historical description precisely because he was simultaneously a particular kind of comparative linguist and a philologist.

When considering Humboldt, it is generally thought that the linking of philology with linguistics as the newly termed "philosophy of language" added certain characteristics to the entire project. And so by crossing a philosophical philology with an empirical linguistics the philosophy of language does develop its own particular course. We can see that there is an intersection between linguistics and philosophy of language, and compared to a Wolfian "philology," Philology itself did develop relatively independently from this Humboldtian philosophy of language. But despite all of these various lines of development, what is important here, and below, is to note that philology was never able to liberate itself from the problem of language.

At first this Wolfian "philology" qua Philology took as its task the reading of antiquity, especially classic texts. But in fact, the task was later expanded to encompass the contemplation of classical arts and to the understanding of contemporary texts and cultural representation in general. In this way philology was no longer restricted to an orthodox deciphering of language. As it expanded to become a general study of classic texts and a hermeneutic logic for decoding contemporary cultural representation in general. And here is the crucial aspect of [Wolfian] "philology," because with this expansion to representation in general, this "philology" was thus able to separate itself from what is called linguistics and the philosophy of language. Thus, in a flash philology was liberated from the restrictions within the problem of language and came to be thought of some sort of independent philosophical method—a method possessing a universality with practical applicability to the present. The process of expansion by which philology turned away from linguistic "philology" and turned its attention to the outside is what we now need to consider.

Reading a text is not merely understanding the words and sentences. It is understanding the thereby indicated thought and concepts [*kannen*]. Incidentally, because understanding is not possible in this empty way, the conceptual tools that produce understanding, while they are in fact themselves made of words and sentences, exist as alien to the classic texts as they are founded on rather specialized technical terms. To understand the usage of these tools themselves requires understanding the very tools of understanding. These tools of understanding and their attendant techniques are what is meant by "interpretation." Understanding thus always passes through interpretation. In a narrow sense, the discipline that develops the techniques by which the thought conveyed by words and phrases is called hermeneutics (*Interpretationswissenschaft —Hermeneutik*) [解釈学]. This hermeneutics is the philosophical core of Wolfian "philology." Why is this so "in a narrow sense?" It is because hermeneutics does not separate from its direct and explicit goal of explaining the meaning of words (and phrases). (If we use the term in the narrowest sense, hermeneutics means interpretation by means of the grammatical explanation of words and phrases.) Such a philology in the narrow sense, which remains tied to the direct explanation of words and phrases, is "the standpoint of hermeneutics." A representative example of this is A. Boeckh (A. Boeckh, *Enzyklodädie un Methodologie der philologischen Wissenchaften*; here the explanation of words—the hermeneutical method—is broken into four parts).

But placing hermeneutics at the philosophical core of "philology," that is, building up "understanding" as an independent function of human consciousness, means that the object of understanding and the appropriate field of inquiry of hermeneutics is already not limited to texts. Even less so is it limited to classic texts. And so, making philology the philosophical core eventually means that philology will not remain confined to the world of language. It will become a generalized hermeneutic theory, and from there it is then understood as a general theory of understanding (*Heremeutische Theorie, Theorie des Verstehens*). If we accept this radical conclusion, eventually such a philology will be unified with (an obviously idealist) philosophical science itself. Further, and this is the same thing, the philosophical method itself will have become completely philologized. Such is the result of this kind of thinking. The premier example of just such a trend toward a philosophical philology (?) is Schleiermacher.

Of course, Schleiermacher was Boeckh's predecessor, so speaking chronologically Schleiermacher's philosophical hermeneutics could be said to have once again regressed to the interpretation of language by Boeckh's hand. But now speaking from the standpoint of the development of the science of hermeneutics, Schleiermacher stands at the summit. He is the summit and the standard (but with Schleiermacher we do not yet see the wholesale application and philosophical acceptance of philology).

Now in fact both hermeneutics and "philology" existed in ancient Greece. It is said that alongside Aristotle's *philosophes* (philosophers, lovers of knowledge) there were also *philologos* (philologists, lovers of language). And in Alexandria there was already a philological school that went by that name. Turning to the Middle Ages (Averrös and St. Thomas), the interpretation of the Bible and ancient great texts was well known. But the key characteristic of early modern hermeneutics was its organization and scientific character, and accordingly—by not confining itself to the Bible and the Greek classics—its universality [*ippan*]. It is said that Semler[8] developed biblical hermeneutics into a science and Meier[9] took this and created a general, universal hermeneutic technique (see Dilthey, *Die Entstehung der Hermeneutik*). In other words, modern hermeneutics began after the Reformation. (When Luther was searching for a Bible in his university library, he found only a single Latin volume covered in dust. He reportedly said that it was only from this point that he could be said to have encountered the Bible. Apparently, it was then possible to be a famous theologian without ever having read the Bible.) As such it was the Protestant Schleiermacher who intimately linked hermeneutics and philosophy. (See Schleiermacher, *Akademiereden über Hermeneutik*. A predecessor here was Friedrich Ast's *Grundlinien der Grammatik, Hermeneutik und Kritik*, 1808; *Der Grundriss der Philologie*, 1808; and the previously mentioned Wolf, see his *Museum der Altertumswissenschaft*; see also, Joachim Wach, *Das Verstehen* 1).

But the philosophical depth of Schleiermacher's "philology" was never anything more than the depth of his theology. (In fact, much more than a philosopher, he is a theologian or a religious enlightenment thinker). Behind all his theology and philosophy lurks a yearning for the infinite. This yearning for the infinite is not the particular world of the Middle Ages nor that of ancient Greece. It is a retrospective yearning for all that has vanished from the world, a now free-floating yearning that settled in German Romanticism. Here the aesthetic appreciation of the world and interpretation by means of human feelings became the singular "scientific" project. At another time Schelling used this philosophy to erase reality and point the way to the world of free fantasy. We could say that Schleiermacher's aim was to replace Schelling's free fantasy with the historical past. Philology and hermeneutics were thus linked with philosophy. In fact, they became philosophy. We should be careful to note here that all such philosophies, be they Romantic, aesthetic, nostalgic, or contemplative, were but various forms of hermeneutic philosophy.

Regardless of how philosophical it is, or how philosophical it is made to be, we must not forget that Schleiermacher's philology (or his hermeneutics) completes the original line of development of philology (and hermeneutics). Indeed, through Schleiermacher, philology and hermeneutics were able to become a general method. Moreover, they were expanded to become an unfathomable worldview. But to the very last, elsewhere, philology and hermeneutics developed along its proper and original line: the grammatical interpretation of words and phrases—meaning that when confined to an orthodox philological and hermeneutical method, philology and hermeneutics were not expanded to reach beyond themselves to grasp objects above or outside their proper field of literary studies. As for the question of history, and we have already seen in the case of Humboldt, for philology to become philosophical, or—and this is to say the same thing—for philosophy to be made philological, it must break free, be liberated from, and eventually become independent of the course set out by philology proper. Philology's elevation to philosophy prepared the ground for literature to make a definitive leap and turn its attention to questions of historical description and a philosophy of history. And so here, now, for the first time, the theory of "understanding" within orthodox philology and the classics became independent, emerging as understanding in general, eventually declaring itself as the essence of all human consciousness.

The preparation for this leap can be found in Droysen[10] (J. G. Droysen, *Historik*). According to Droysen, understanding was the essence of the historical method. In fact, for G. Simmel's *Die Probleme der Geschichtphilosophie*,[11] "understanding" was historical consciousness itself, and this was already not limited to a historical method but eventually developed into a general philosophical system. It goes without saying that Dilthey developed these trends on a large scale when, on the one hand he incorporated the method of hermeneutic explication into his spiritual science (精神科学), and on the other, made that description of spiritual science the axis of his so-called Life [*Lebens*] philosophy: our lives are objectified and find expression in history and this expression is a true spirit. And it is only by first grasping this spirit that we can come to know ourselves. It is thus precisely by the interpretation of expression that we come to understand life. Dilthey stressed that philosophy was interpreting life as it was expressed in history, that this was in fact life interpreting itself and thus was a self-understanding. Philology and hermeneutics thus used the understanding of history as a stepping stone on the way to being elevated first to a philosophy of history, and then finally to the philosophical method itself. Whatever origin or lineage we may debate, for our purposes it is not necessary to explain the support given by philology and hermeneutics to "history" and "*Lebens* philosophy."

Dilthey has so far tentatively served as the representative of a philosophy in which philology was liberated from the problem of language and thus made interpretation "theory" itself. But if we look at it from the essence of Dilthey's philological philosophy, it was quite clearly a rich, historical description of spirit (culture or society). Further if we look at it from the perspective of historical description, it is the case that whatever else may be said about it, it clearly proceeded from a philological interpretation of texts (initially it was not necessary that Dilthey's hermeneutics become a historical methodology). Seen this way, the philological and hermeneutic essence of Dilthey's philosophy does in fact have some authority for actuality. And if we consider this philosophy as the foundation of a kind of historical description, that this philosophy was philological through and through, appears in no way strange. In fact, far from thinking it is a weak point of this philosophy to be considered merely philological, it is perfectly right and natural that it be so. In the end Dilthey's philosophy arrived at hermeneutic philosophy. It is not the case that if we remove the philology and hermeneutics Dilthey's philosophy is in fact pragmatically sound. On the contrary, any soundness is precisely thanks to the philological method itself. But when it separates from a particular system of historical description, philological and hermeneutical philosophy loses its grounding, and with just a bit of effort reaches its apotheosis. Heidegger's philological phenomenology is precisely this moment.

Heidegger was a successor to Husserl's phenomenology. Initially it was not simply that phenomenology had no relation to philology; in truth they were opposites. It is well known that Husserl countered Dilthey's *Lebens* philosophy with philosophy as a rigorous science. The concept of phenomena in phenomenology Husserl took from Franz Brentano's *Psychology from an Empirical Standpoint* [1874]. This, too, had absolutely nothing to do with philology. In fact, it was simply a way to denigrate Auguste Comte's positivism, which had completely removed phenomena from consideration. Modern philology was largely a Protestant project. It arose in opposition to a consideration of the totality of human feeling or respect for the organism, the humanism of Catholic phenomenology, with which it thus had little in common. Heidegger took this opposition and synthesized Dilthey's hermeneutics and Husserl's phenomenology. To be sure, late period Dilthey mobilized Husserl's phenomenological analysis, and Brentano himself was a formidable philologist of Aristotle. Still these moves were not merely a case of an abrupt change in circumstances ex nihilo. No, the problem lurks at a much more fundamental level.

First, we must stress that all phenomenologies are ahistorical. Hegel's *Phenomenology of Sprit*, or his description of the stages of development of consciousness, is not a history of consciousness, much less a history of the world. Such is clear once we arrive at contemporary phenomenology. Phenomenology's phenomenon, the appearance of its phenomena, always takes place on some particular hidden stage. Various names are given to this stage: consciousness, being, among others. And so, we can already see that with the synthesis of hermeneutics and philology, because the phenomena appear on some ahistorical stage, any inquiry into the historicity of hermeneutics or philology themselves must be a nonsensical question from the start. Indeed, the meaning of a phenomenon is always only considered as a question of the phenomenon's surface. In other words, the background or underside of a phenomenon is only problematized after being rendered as objects of this philosophy of surfaces, and thus background and underside lose their meaning. Superficialization is thus one with phenomenalization. And because this is the case, if we were to inquire into the background or depth of things in daily life, the meaning of these background things produced by hermeneutics or philology would be totally incapable of discovering or retrieving any meaning that had any sort of gap or articulation between the phenomenon and its background or depth.[12] This method has no way of discussing or measuring the depth of the surface.

Yet Heidegger sought to build just such an interpretive phenomenology. If we consider Heidegger's project objectively, it is exposed as a philosophical system that sought to remove the usefulness of history from hermeneutics and philology, and a system where historical consciousness is replaced with a sort of metaphysics of meaning (to be sure this is not the standard, so-called metaphysics). Because history was not able to be used for hermeneutics and philology, some sort of phenomenological something or other—such as "being"—would be used. It is no coincidence that this ahistorical philosophy broke through at precisely the moment when the worldview of German idealism (what most people conventionally call metaphysics) had reached a historical impasse. Indeed, it is also precisely this philosophical "system" by which the Nazi's general plan was able to charm the petite bourgeoisie and at the same time fascinate the German so-called cultured (?) [*kyōyō*] intelligentsia.[13]

Thus, hermeneutics or philology is liberated from its historical path and elevated to become "perfectly philosophical." With Heidegger, philology and hermeneutics escape their disciplinary linguistic and historical fetters to become the essence of philosophy itself: Because philosophy has now become philologism, philology in a narrow sense would no longer occupy the ultimate pride of place, while at the same time, there is nothing left that could trouble this liberated "philology." Thus, philology loses its original historical linguistic concreteness and necessarily becomes a caricature. In Heidegger, for example, the word "desevering" (*Entfernung*) is established by reaching out, taking wings, and removing the separation (*Ent*) from something distant (*fern*). Such an explanation is astoundingly silly, and to the extent that other words cannot be explained in this manner, etymology has lost all meaning. This cannot even be some kind of linguistic explanation. The path leading to such a phenomenology of language (logos), in this sense, is hardly more than the invocation of some sort of occult device. The fact that the substance of the interpretation has degenerated to such a philologic caricature is because hermeneutic science and philology have escaped the historical or linguistic elements that had been inherent in them. We should note here that if there is any truth in this method at all, it does not come from any scientific method of interpretive phenomenology, but rather it comes merely from some mistily invoked and monk-like "ideology" (Death · Anxiety · das Man).

By being rendered philosophical, philology was thus caricatured, and became philologism. And in the opposite sense, by being rendered philological, philosophy became unscientific. To be clear, there is nothing wrong with philology as philology. But the actuality of the world is also in no way a philological object. Any philosophy that treats philology as the august guest of honor is without a doubt a philosophy that must fear the invocation of present actuality. And any history that does not problematize actuality is meaningless.

To the point, Heidegger's hermeneutic phenomenology takes up the problem of being. It is thus an ontology, but the being at issue starts from human existence. So when the problem at issue becomes actual existence (*Existenz*), it means that ontology begins as an anthropology (*ningengaku*). Which means ontology or existence itself is a *self-interpretation*[14] of being.

The history of anthropology (人間学, アントロポロギー) is extremely diverse; even the term has many definitions. It ranges far and wide, from the origins of human thought to theories of humanity, to anthropology as various branches of humanity (*jinruigaku*), all the way to philosophical anthropology. But what we mean here is a particular anthropology distinguished from that more general discussion. The distinguishing factor is, it goes without saying, the presence or not of a basis in interpretation. So what we mean by anthropology here is none other than a hermeneutic anthropology. (Someday if given the chance I would like to provide a critique of the schools of thought in the various anthropologies.) But given this we must at minimum say that this sort of anthropology is not of the same kind as, say, Feuerbach's anthropological criticism of religious consciousness. The reason we call the anthropology under consideration here hermeneutic is that, as we have already mentioned in our discussion of hermeneutic philology above, this anthropology is one that has already washed its hands of historical consciousness so that all that remains is a metaphysical and, accordingly, some sort of spiritual material with which to build a new system. A good and direct comparison are the works of Kierkegaard. We need to parse these various forms of anthropology because in Japan all anthropology has been linked to Feuerbach, and so all anthropology is imagined to have some kind of relationship to Marxist philosophy. And it goes without saying that even though a hermeneutic anthropology is fundamentally opposed to materialism, its imagined vague basis within Feuerbachian and Marxist philosophy is enough to impart some fascination for our country's progressive (?) liberal philosophers. Such an assumed progressive anthropology is the imagined basis of all contemporary literary and other aesthetic humanisms. Indeed, "anthropology" has become a sort of shibboleth among the less sophisticated members of the intelligentsia. There is hardly anything that this term "anthropology" cannot attach itself to, and by doing so appear to impart some sort of vague progressive (?) sensibility to anything it touches: Buddhism as anthropology (Takami Kakushō et al.) and above all ethics treated as an "anthropology" (Watsuji Tetsurō) is thus imagined to impart some kind of modern progressivism.

The most exemplary instance of applying philology to anthropology is Watsuji's *Ethics as Anthropology* [人間の学としての倫理学] (see chapter 7). In fact, what Watsuji is doing here is not simply applying philology; he is deducing anthropology from philology. He is dropping a corpuscle of "being" into a philological solution and watching as anthropology (as ethics) precipitates out. By doing so, the application of philology is total. And in an even more totalizing manner, this anthropological method, derived from Heidegger's anthropology, completely removes the last dregs of the original phenomenology resulting in a purified hermeneutics (philology). In other words, the result is nothing less than a pure and purified Heidegger. Thus, it is enough if we, too, merely purify what we have already said of Heidegger's philologism.

2

The foregoing was based on philology developed as a science, and continued by showing how hermeneutic interpretation was modified to become a universal organizational method of philosophy itself. But now, rather than continuing to develop philology as an organized method, my goal is rather to consider a more fragmentary or, in a sense, a commonsensical way that philology is relied on when thinking about social phenomena. As such, the unsystematic application of philology to the present is the next question. Today in Japan this is a particularly important problem.

If we consider this philological turn as a particular social phenomenon, at first glance it appears on the one hand as extreme nonsense, and on the other hand as something extremely serious. As a social phenomenon the philological turn extends from the farcical thoughts and actions of all kinds of pontificators, including statesmen and all others in and out of government, to the lofty and esteemed research of the bourgeois academy (from full professors to associates and assistants and down to students). Now, when we consider the philosophical significance of this social phenomenon, the farcical nature of the popular pontificators is in no way less grave than any tragic gestures of the bourgeois academy. On the contrary, it is surely true that the more farcical this social phenomenon is, the more difficult it is to establish the foundations of a scientific critique. When an adversary is unscientific, it cannot be scientifically critiqued from within. In fact, in order to overcome this difficulty, we must feel keenly the necessity of the problem of philology.

On this point the proper distinction is between mortal sins and more relatively minor offenses. Above we said that this is not a question of farce versus tragedy. For example, the deductive method of Watsuji Tetsurō's *Ethics* is completely subsumed under lexical foundations. And though this is a grave symptom of such "pure" hermeneutics, if that were all, it would remain a relatively minor sin. People will easily recognize such an obvious caricature of philology. And so too the clumsiness of Kihira Tadayoshi's literary proofs are not the sort of thing that causes major problems. See for example his principle (理) = truth (コトワリ) = judgment (断) = partitioning (分割)—cf. Hegel's *Urteilen*.[15] Kimura Takatarō's theory that Japan is Greece is precisely such an unsystematic caricature of an already caricatured systematic philology. In the end, all these professors manage to show is just how high they can stack this nonsense. At this point there is hardly any essential distinction between a philological consciousness and a pathological psychology.

Importantly, uncritically adopting the classics and making them face the present realities is the real crime. Or to put it more generally, ripping out from the classics nothing more than a philological meaning and then using this as a basis to present a purely convenient resolution to current, actual problems is the bad faith or even unconscious assumption of this philological consciousness as a social phenomenon. Yet this social phenomenon extends from the streets to the hallowed halls of the bourgeois academy. For example we have Gondō Seikyō's *Minabuchi Text*, a great example of a classic text of the Shintoists, and it matters not whether it is an authentic text or a forgery, as either way the application of the text to the present is utterly meaningless. Messrs. Kihira, Kanagoki, Hiraizumi, and a host of National Purification School fascists all belong to this Japanist faction.

This philological consciousness is without limit: among Orientalists and China scholars there is Nishi Shin'ichirō's *Eastern Ethics* [*Tōyō rinri*, 1934], the writings of Sinologists and Asianists, Indian scholars, and the explanation of current events of the Buddhist priests. Further, for Western scholars, there are the bourgeois academic philosophers and their quasiphilological philosophical choices of exemplars like some German philologist or the serial quoter of Greek philosophical texts. They all imagine their philological ruminations will all somehow result in the resolution of some contemporary problem.

It is not necessary to criticize each and every instance of this problem. Of course, it is well and good to demonstrate the utter nonsense of each case when it comes to the actual world or actual moments, to chase down all the resulting absurdities of each and every confused point of emphasis. But the difficulty with this worthless philological phenomenon is that it is essentially endless and endlessly repeated. No, in the same way that we avoid the tedium of writing out each and every zero of numbers like ten billion by means of the formulation 10^n, when dealing with these myriad philological moments we must also appeal to a critical formula. Here I will offer four formulas in order to get at the fundamental mission and principles.

One. Explaining a word does not explain the object. In truth, understanding this thesis is the beginning and end of what I want to say. The words of each country or ethnic group currently in use naturally express the idea corresponding to each actual thing, but despite this, the gap between words and logic always remains a problem. Logic is the correspondence relationship between the concept and actual reality. It is perpetually developed as it passes through history, which is to say that logic is made increasingly concrete and is constantly calibrated. And because there is a fundamental gap between language and logic, with historical development there is a constant potential for this gap to grow larger. Logic is a living, dynamic mechanism, and indeed, language, too, has a social existence experiencing life and death. Language, as language, has its own development and something like a metabolic function. It is common to explain words, or to explain by means of words, by tracing back to the origins of the words. (If this is not done, we must then use a sort of social accounting to determine the "popular usage" [通念].) Once the word has been traced back to its etymological origin, this original meaning is adopted and used to explain the thing. As such, if in place of using contemporary terms to explain contemporary things the original etymological meaning is used instead, then the fundamental gap between language and logic has not only grown, but by adding a historical gap it has been doubled.

The mechanism of classical thought was built on an extremely intimate relation between language and logic (classical logic). For example, according to Ernst Hoffmann (1880–1952) in *Sprach und die archaische Logic* (1925), by means of *mysterion* (forbidden speech), *mystic* (unable to speak, [inexpressible]), *mythos* (to say / relate)—meaning story—*epos* (words), and *logos* (thought), a very tight connection between language and logic is established. Thus the prior series of the problem of speech and the later series of thought are directly linked by *mythos*. But the very goal of modern logic was to break free from this kind of system.

Therefore, this means that the more the thing to be explained is developed as a product of a given society, any explanation in terms of mere words (in this philological sense) makes history flow backward to some archaic thing. Thus such an explanation is unable to *actually* explain the thing. For those possessing this philological consciousness, bad faith or unintentional rationale somehow forces the argument to always lead back to the archaic. But...

Two. The "archaic" cannot be the basis for resolving actual, current problems. So, just what is meant by "the archaic?" (There is no relationship here between "the archaic" and classicism or the Greek classics.) We must, of course, rethink the natural science that appears in the classics, but for literature, philosophy, and social science there seems to be at least three different meanings and scientific uses of the archaic. (1) As a useful reference or precedent for a certain way of thinking and experience (including experiments); (2) as facts or sources for tracing the course of history; and finally (3) as a training tool or as a model. If we are talking of the first point, whether the classic text is now useful as a precedent or reference cannot be determined by the classic text itself. That is determined by the present circumstances. Merely quoting a precedent from the classics is not a proof of one's own argument, as any reference soon becomes obsolete. If we take the second case, historical sources do not themselves dictate how they are to be handled. The acceptance and goal of such an inquiry absolutely comes from the present circumstances—because a source is itself not a proof, sources can become material for a false history. And if we take the third sense, a model is simply a model; it is not a proof. So whatever it may be, the archaic can never be anything more than a reference. It does not have within itself the goal or mission to be the solution to contemporary problems. In fact, it cannot have that power.

We must not forget that the important thing about a classic is that it is something that has passed down through history to the present. If it had not been passed down, it would not be a classic, but merely some product of historical past. A classic is like a thread running through a tradition—if it is philosophy then it is the history of philosophy, if social science, then the history of social science. This means a classic is something that runs through and acts upon each age from the past to the present. And though this means that a classic cannot be a proof, it absolutely does mean that it is a point of reference. The classics must be critiqued in terms of contemporary problems and then either selected or discarded.

Failing to criticize (as cultivating/modifying or discarding/culling), meaning to unconditionally take the archaic as something useful, as if the word or text were completely transparent, is one of the fundamental characteristics of philologism. This holds even when talking of quoting the classics. Quoting the classics to impart authority to one's argument is not only absurd and useless, but by forcing all contemporary problems back into the archaic past it is also necessarily reactionary.

Normally this kind of procedure is called formulaic. But that is not entirely correct. In truth, a formula is something that is normally put to use. But a characteristic of a formulaic approach is not the use of previously derived formulas (science is not possible without using formulas); rather, in place of using a formula, what happens in quoting a classic text is that the formula is simply repeated once again, and this is somehow intended to demonstrate the solution of some problem. We may here interject: "Don't the classics also have some meaning as a formula? The archaic, as an archetype, doesn't it bear some similarity to a scientific formula?" In fact, no, it does not. It does not because the archetype or the ideal-typical is nothing more than the essence of a model we discussed in the third instance above. For even if we are able to use the archetype for educational purposes, it cannot be used as a tool to prove or produce anything. That is, if we were able to add color on top of one of Michelangelo's drawings, this might be considered a complete painting, but it is not much more than what is called plagiarism in literature. But the formulaic is not simply just used with training in mind. It is constantly invoked as a proof and considered something useful for—considered a tool for—creating new works. It is no longer a classic located in the past but is intended as a something close at hand in our present, a tool for idealist production.

Imagining the archaic as a practical and direct—a technically useful—formula of some sort is the result is of confusing the archaic as used in the *production* of something new, and the archaic as the *reproduction* of the ideal.[16] Distinguishing between these two uses of the archaic has tremendous importance for materialists. But for contemplative interpreters or the aesthetic appreciation of classicists (who are a subset of the philological consciousness), for them, these two senses are one and the same. It goes without saying that they are incapable of actually using the archaic as a technical tool, because from the start the archaic would never occur to them as a thing *to be used* at all. From the start, such thing is a classic; but contrary to this, if the archaic is a formula, not using it is out of the question and would be a waste. Undue respect for the authority of the archaic is one of the fates of a philological consciousness.

Three. An archaic model does not simply become a logic all on its own [*sono mama de wa*]. Searching for proof in the classics is nothing more than saying that archaic categories and categorical organizations may be logically applied to the present. Greek classics, Indian classics, Chinese, Japanese, medieval European, Arabic, all other classics, each has particular categories and particular categorical organizations—which is to say each possesses a particular logic. Even apart from the classics, nonmodern [未開] peoples have their own particular categorical logic. And incidentally these logics are not the same as the shared international [capitalist] logic among contemporary developed countries. To take an extreme example see Lévy-Bruhl[17] and his followers' research (nonmodern peoples have a particular logical and prelogical sense of group ownership or participatory ownership). Their research shows a definitive gap between the mechanism of thought of ancient Indians and today's international logic. A good example of this likely continues in the Buddhist logical tradition of *hetuvidyā*—the determination of right and wrong, a science of causes. (See also Ms. Betty Heimann's work, which occasionally appears in the journal *Kant-Studien*. In one article she argues that the difference between the mechanisms of European and ancient Indian thought are so vast they cannot even be considered analogically.[18])

But if a categorical organization is theory, and all of the developed forms of thought are grounded in the application of that thought to the actual world, in each of the various historical societies and ages, it is obvious that if that actual world develops, the thought grounded in that world must also develop. In order to develop a foothold, the categories making up the material that are the basis of the categorical organization must also be rebuilt. Because these are archaic categories, they must not be allowed to be casually imported into the present to deal with contemporary problems. Each age has its own historically specific categorical organization and logic. But the practitioners of a philological consciousness do not know that the categorical organization of a historical period is a logic, or they vehemently refuse to acknowledge its logical nature. For them, the archaic category *may be understood*, but it *cannot be used*.

Four. Archaic categories must be translated. But translation always terminates in translation. In a narrow sense translation is rendering sentences in one language into sentences in another language. But in a wider sense, translation means introducing a culture. The philological work is the same in both cases. Both meanings are present in Schelling's translations of Shakespeare or Carlyle's introduction of Goethe. Of course, this is the mission of philology. This is the sole contribution of philology to contemporary issues. But a translation is always just that, a translation. It is not the original. Nonmodern, ancient, classical texts and words, and even foreign languages of contemporary periods with the same level of cultural development, must be in some way translatable in language. (On the problem of this type of literary translation see Nogami Toyoichirō's *On Translation* in Iwanami Kōza's *World Literature*. For a phenomenological treatment see Ludwig Ferdinand Clauss, *Das Verstehen des sprachlichen Kunstwerks* 1929 and Husserl's *Jahrbuch Ergänzungsband*, among others, though this is not the most important issue here.) But, because in the wider meaning translation is the introduction of a culture, the problem cannot be limited to this kind of literary translation. The more important issue is the translation of categories and categorical organizations.

Translating logic across today's contemporary nations is not much of a problem. This is because as a result of the development of the world's *forces* of production, the techniques and mechanisms have largely become a shared global aspect. And these productive forces and mechanisms of production become the spur of the various countries' *relations* of production. This spur, we could say, appears as a global phenomenon. The logical mechanisms of the various countries are spurred on by this spear tip of production. This spear tip is everywhere because it is necessary to develop the institutions of international trade (imports and exports); and as a result, the international nature of this logic daily and increasingly becomes a lived reality. Translating the same thing into the same thing is not in fact translation. It is merely exchange or reception. Those who say that Japan has not fully digested European civilization or that foreigners are unable to understand the Japanese spirit are demagogues who do not understand the meaning of translating logics, yet these same people have no problem applying ancient Indian or classical Chinese logic to contemporary Japan. This we must not forget.

In fact, the real problem lies in translating ancient or classical logic into contemporary logic. For example, it is not sufficient to translate the linguistic content of primitive Indian Buddhist texts into contemporary Japanese so that it may be read by today's readers. If we do not interpret the cultural content of primitive Buddhism according to our current categories and categorical organization, such an effort would end without establishing any connection between that culture and our own. Even if this is enough to make the effort of interest to classicists, it is not enough to give the Buddhist text any current cultural interest. Now if for example we were to interpret it as Professor Kimura Taiken does, through the lens of Kantian philosophy, only then, through this sort of rediscovery, can we say that the ancient text is now reborn with some meaning as contemporary cultural material. Or alternatively, if we reinterpret the text from a phenomenological standpoint like Watsuji Tetsurō does, then it can become something that we can read theoretically. (See Watsuji's *Primitive Buddhism and Practical Philosophy*.)

But translation—meaning translating a categorical organization (a logic)—moves object A to object B. It is nothing less than a fraud to make the active, living associations of A also the active, living associations of B. Because there is an active logic within A, it must absolutely not be allowed through an act of translation to make A's particular logic now also active in B. In a sense, the logic that has been transplanted into B dies. Which means it is no longer a true logic. This A has an ancient, a classical logic, and this B has a present, practical logic.[19] Therefore translation is always translation. It is never the original. In other words, the philologist as a philologist is not one who uses a living logic—which is to say that a philologist is not a philosopher. *Philologos* is absolutely not *Philosophos*. These are the limits of the authority of "philology" and Philology. Ignoring these limits, either unconsciously or through bad faith, to equate the philological consciousness to philological philosophy is the fundamental mistake; it is the key fraud at the base of this philological social phenomenon.

This philological consciousness is one characteristic of hermeneutic philosophy (the injunction that one must merely interpret the world according to idealism). Of course, there are many interpretive philosophers who do not adopt the philological standpoint. But we must also note that this interpretive philosophy is not confined to highbrow hermeneutic philosophers. In fact, taking note of just how widespread both organized and fragmentary philological or hermeneutic philosophy is in Japan today is extremely important for a criticism of the many sorts of Japanism.

Chapter Three

AN ANALYSIS OF "COMMON SENSE"
Toward a Resolution of Two Contradictions
in Social Common Sense

The literary world has recently taken up the problem of everydayness (*nichijōsei*). According to some scholars, before addressing the issue of whether the anxiety of social life is an economic, political, or even theoretical one, the concept of anxiety so esteemed by writers today is one that above all must attack and cast doubt on the consciousness of everyday life. This use of anxiety is characteristic of the intelligentsia and in fact resides in their own explicit self-awareness. As taken up by these literary scholars, the everyday is contrasted with their own elevated, particular anti-everyday sense of anxiety.

Seen from the intellectuals' high literary and rhetorical perch, the everyday is the vulgar. Thus, everydayness is only considered to combat vulgarism, to defeat it anew. Now this way of thinking does have some sort of common sense about it. But when we ask these literary types what kind of thing everydayness is, we see in the end it means a vulgarism or philistinism unenlightened to the intelligentsia's concept of anxiety. Everydayness is thus simply the counterpoint to the intelligentsia's own particular sense of anxiety. No one seems to be interested in considering the issue beyond this. Following the lineage of this current common-sense view of everydayness as an unknowing counterpart to the intelligentsia's awareness of anxiety—an anxiety that is part of a particular theology and comes from a philosophy of their own private common sense—we see that the intelligentsia's concept of everydayness is the concept of the masses' empty, fallen human life, a life that has not been converted to the intelligentsia's own monastic, contemplative life. (This is the secret religious experience that today is manifested in the various secular miracles of political conversion to reactionary ideologies [tenkō].)¹ It seems then that the concept of common sense thus requires no more consideration beyond this simple fact. For the intelligentsia, the only thing necessary is that their own understanding of common sense oppose the degraded energy at the heart of the masses' vulgar everydayness.

But this attitude, this commonsensical way of seeing everydayness as nothing but vulgar, is itself rather banal. Accordingly, it is itself a rather vulgar common sense. In denouncing everydayness as vulgarism, this attitude takes no interest in the irony and paradoxes present within vulgarity itself. Without any charm or humor at all, the intelligentsia's common sense seeks only to denounce everydayness as vulgarity. It never bothers with asking if this everydayness might have within it a dialectical underside. But there is a powerful *principle of everydayness* within the concept of everydayness, one philosophically distinguished from a coarse, meaningless metaphysics. I have explored this principle elsewhere.² But as the intelligentsia's theory of common sense wants, and needs, to label all everydayness as vulgarism, it is laughably unaware of the significance of everydayness.

Immediately then, if we see that in truth the common-sense view of everydayness and vulgarism is in fact uncommonsensical, we realize that in general, common sense is not something that can be made to follow a straight path. In fact, in the case of everydayness and vulgarism, the irony of this common-sense view is not limited to literature (here I do not mean so-called Romantic irony). Irony runs through a whole host of concepts. The series "everydayness," "vulgarism," "common sense" is a sort of Mephistophelean, even Satanic, one; all these issues are concentrated in the problem of common sense. In fact, as Satan and Mephistopheles tempt and seduce,³ common sense has within it the capacity to test and critique science, scholarship, truth, genius, creativity, and so on.

Common sense, like everydayness, has been taken up by the literary world. If one says, in the end, commonsensical literary criticism never exceeds common sense, such a position could be countered by asking if that position is itself not uncommonsensical. Clearly a particular internal contradiction runs through the entirety of this relationship, but it seems no one

AN ANALYSIS OF "COMMON SENSE"

has paid any attention to it. In other words, conventional wisdom holds that common sense absolutely can only be grasped commonsensically. And so common sense is seen as merely a commonsensical concept. And this is not a problem limited to the literary world; today it exists unchanged throughout the theoretical and philosophical worlds. So we need an analysis of common sense that is scientific, and thus no longer commonsensical.

1

Seen from the intelligentsia's commonsensical perspective, common sense contains the following contradictions within it. On the one hand, it means a negative kind of knowledge: un- or antiscientific, un- or antiphilosophical, un- or antiliterary, and so on. But on the other hand, it also means a fully realized normal, popular social usage, or an actually existing kind of knowledge. The former meaning of common sense is an embarrassment whereas the latter meaning is thought to be a source of pride. These two contradictory meanings of common sense coexist within the concept of common sense, and just whether there is some sort of contact or compromise between them is totally ignored by common sense itself. Common sense itself is satisfied with a simple opposition between these two contradictory meanings. And stopping at this stage of analysis is simply the ordinary understanding of common sense. But it is characteristic of this ordinary attitude toward common sense to ignore these two contradictory theses and simply align them parallel to each other. Common sense thus appears to be in opposition with itself.

Philosophy, which in one sense is a literary science, always begins from the common sense given by its time. So when considering common sense itself, it is perfectly ordinary and normal for philosophical reflection to also begin from the historical stage of common sense of its age. *Doxa* in ancient Greece is a perfect example of this first step toward a philosophical concept of common sense. Seen from the perspective of true knowledge, meaning academic knowledge, doxa appears as the opposite of truth (at the Platonic stage of inquiry[4]). But as philosophy focused on the anarchistic essence in this view of common sense qua doxa, the concept was already no different than the ordinary, antivulgarism sense we saw above. And so, again several contradictory theses were present and ran parallel within this understanding of the essence of doxa. It was thus thought that a scientific understanding of doxa began with the tidying up of these contradictory theses within it. Even though Aristotle acknowledged a dialectic within his understanding of common sense, he nonetheless remained at this stage of conceptualization. Here, too, even if common sense (doxa) was the first step on the path to true knowledge, doxa remained opposed to full truth. Such a view was most likely a combination of seeing common sense as the more or less accidental intellectual fables or opinions of the natural scientists and, alternately, as the spontaneously generated popular wisdom of the democratic multitude [*minshū*]. It is thus obvious that this understanding of common sense was grounded in the aristocratic knowledge of ancient Greece.

Yet it is well known that the word proposed by Aristotle, common sense (common sense, *Gemeinsinn*), belongs to a completely different tradition.[5] In *De Anima* Aristotle argued that for each kind of perception there was a corresponding sensory organ that perceived it: eyes sensed color, light, and shape; ears perceived sound. But human beings also have the knowledge that the perception of color-light-shape given by the eye is different from the perception of sound perceived by the ear. It is not simply that we may know red is not the same as blue, but we also know that red or blue is part of a fundamentally different series of perceptions than high and low pitch. Furthermore, the differences between these series are themselves also perceived. They are not known through some extra- or suprasensical mental ability. That would require an external sensory organ outside the five senses that could compare and harmonize the perceptions of the five senses. Thus it was necessary to posit a sixth sensory organon beyond eyes, ears, tongue, nose, and skin. This shared, sixth sensory organon [共通感官] was the etymological root of what was later translated as common sense. But of course this problem does not end with the question of etymology. This sixth-sense concept of common sense cannot be one of the five senses, nor may it be a sensory organ outside the individual. Aristotle posited an organ likely located in the brain. Today we have entrusted this issue to the disciplines of sensory physiology or anatomy. Further, it is common for philosophical terminology to abstract this anatomical sensory organ to a psychological function. If we abstract this sensory organ out from biological anatomy, we are no longer presented with the problem of its location within the body, and now may talk about an organically perceived inner sense [内官] and an outer sense [外官]. Of course, this language of inner sense and outer sense as a philosophical concept has its limitations; namely, that while an outer sense clearly has no basis in the body, it is much less clear that an inner sense cannot be easily ascribed to some physical organ in the body. Thus the very notion of an inner sense must be considered to already be a philosophical abstraction. Which is to say that this inner sensory *organ* does not actually mean "organ" in the ordinary sense. And so we have come to think it better to call this an inner *sense* [内感] (even at this time such an external sensory organ that contrasted with an internal sensory organ [内官] was modified to be read as an external sense [外感]).

We can now understand the reason why *sensation* eventually came to mean *sense*. (This word, sense, will work even though philosophically it is now refined by the psychology of perception.) As the sensory organs were originally that which received sensations, even though a sensory organ and a sensation are not really the same thing, we can see from the above how both "sense" and "sensation" came to express the same concept. To wit, with the change from a shared sensation to a shared common sense we can see how the meaning has completely inverted. This inversion is clear in foreign languages: English, sense; German, *Sinn*; and French, *sense*. This further shows that we are not only dealing with the definition of sensations, but this "sense" is also at the base of the words "meaning" and "core" [*kokushin*] themselves. We should pay attention to this.

Thus, Aristotle's common sensation came to mean common sense. At this point the term "inner sense" not only first becomes clear, but this development is also the reason that inner sense also came to be the concept of an inner knowledge. As for internal sensation, or, as it eventually became, an inner sense, with just a bit of psychological reflection and analysis, it is clear that what is called inner knowledge is more concrete because its contents are more specifically delimited.

There can be some doubt as to whether this ancient tradition of common sense as limited to inner sense or inner knowledge was exhausted by early modern psychology, but it is inevitable that there will be various methods of delimiting the concept of inner sensations or inner knowledge. But important here is the more general point that this understanding of a common sense is considered an internal form of sense. If we had not done this investigation, it would be impossible for us to understand how this concept of a "common sense" as shared sensation [共通感覚][6] was the precursor to our current understanding of common sense [常識] as inner knowledge. It is no coincidence that the two terms share the same word. That is not the issue. For in fact, from its beginning in Aristotle's common sensation (*koine, aisthesis*), a common sense as an internal thing was directly tied to the concept of common sense developed by the Common Sense School of early modern philosophy.

The ancient concept of a common sensation and the early modern concept of common sense is mediated by the work of the Scholastics on a general sensory organ (even though this, too, returns to the question of internal perception). But our story is simplified with a single leap to the case of the Common Sense School of early modern philosophy.

2

The Common Sense School means the Scottish School of English philosophy, but for our problem here we will look to Thomas Reid (1710–1796). Reid is usually considered as opposing empiricism (the founder of which is John Locke). Locke considered the blank slate of the human mind [*kokoro*] to be an enigma, and as a result English philosophy adopted the standpoint of skepticism toward psychology, associative psychology, epistemology, and all various subjectivisms. Reid appears to have taken as his task to oppose skepticism's premise and conclusions. Without a doubt he took up the call not to doubt the authority of intuition developed in Lord Shaftesbury[7] and Francis Hutcheson's[8] aesthetic ethics, and so to oppose empiricism by making the question of the human heart the fundamental question of philosophy. But Reid absolutely was not an antiempiricist in the manner in which continental rationalism (à la Descartes) was intuitionist. Rather, Reid's intuitionism was arrived at as being a necessary consequence of English empiricism. He merely swapped empiricism's external experience for internal experience, so we must take note that Reid's system was simply an internal empiricism. Once again, the key point is this: Reid's empiricist "truth" was only considered truth because it was internal.

For Reid, external experience could not give any objective or shared (common) epistemological standard. And so, like Hume, Reid even doubted that external experience could provide any objective cause and effect in the actual world. And here, it was better to use the term "internal knowledge" because it limited the contents of that knowledge and thus allowed the problem to be specified. In this approach to common sense, and in order to protect the authority of experience, epistemology was necessarily sought in internal experience, in inner knowledge, in intuition. And so, for the first time, the human heart became something that must not be doubted.

Thus, by definition, this truth located within the human heart had no need to appeal to anything such as reason above it. This truth was self-grounding; indeed, being self-grounded was the very reason it was called truth. When Descartes's representation (idea) was true, it was a simple and clear rational basis, even if the only direct foundation of this idea was in intuition. For Reid, in place of this rational foundation, the truth of inner experience spoke for itself.

For this intuition based not in rationalism but in empiricism, this direct inner truth, thus has an empirical given-ness unique to and specific to the truth. Which is to say, the myriad contents of this intuitional content, under the name of truth, and without being based in rationalism, linked simple personal experience to "factual truth." As such, this intuition was by no means a single intuition. It was a specific process of dividing up concrete elements and, in that sense, possessed an articulation of theses and propositions. Further, because these propositions were arranged under the authority of truth, it became impossible to rationally deconstruct them, and the contents of these propositions, through the power of coagulation, necessarily became absolute. In other words —much like the concept of a priori in rationalism—these propositions became fixed and immovable to the point of becoming axiomatic. Put another way, these propositions became the ultimate elements and units of judgment for human life, used as-is at all times, making them impervious to deconstruction or irreducible to something outside themselves. Nonetheless, these basic units, while in fact quite complex, came under the aegis of, and attained the status of, axioms.

Of course, axioms are self-explanatory. That is, they are intuitively self-evident. Thus Reid held that the sole basis of human wisdom, as the power of understanding used by judgment, were these intuitively self-evident axioms, and human understanding was the instinctual acceptance of them. And, according to Reid, the instinctual acceptance of these axioms as intuited truth was the proper role of common sense. Further, the content of these axioms was the content of this direct human intuition and thus also the content of common sense. Common sense, then, as built from these particular and fixed aesthetic, ethical, religious, and theoretical theses, had now become axiomatic—which is to say acceptance and awareness of these axioms as universally employed objects was the starting point of consciousness, and in turn was the disposition and content of this consciousness.

The authority of common sense (as sound human understanding) was born not of external experience, but rather from internal experience. Here the point of contact between Aristotle's common sensation and Reid's (indeed the Scottish School in general) common intuition cum common sense is seen in much more than mere shared terminology. Of course, in Aristotle what is shared in common sense exists in between the perceptions of the five senses and the knowledge that exists above this. Opposed to this, Reid's shared sense as common sense exists in between individuals within a society. Here, though we must index it to an individual; in truth, in a way we really must appeal to an (abstract) average individual.

Yet Reid's elimination of the problem of the external for human sense organs in his *Inquiry Into the Human Mind on the Principles of Common Sense* deserves some attention. While it is true that human consciousness begins by means of a common sense shared among the five senses, if there is no unified human or individual sense, there cannot be built a shared common sense between individuals within a society. And so, in the opposite way, we cannot overlook the fact that common sense comes first from that which brings about a unity of varied individuals' consciousnesses. That which brings about the unity of an individual's consciousness is on the one hand, if seen as an individual psychology, this *koine* or *aisthesis*, while that same relationship, if the individual is seen as social psychological, the category is common sense [*jōshiki*]. Seen from the unity of an individual consciousness, meaning Aristotle's concept of a sense shared by the five senses, and Reid's concept of common sense, we clearly see the essential connection between the two.

We have already seen how Reid's concept of common sense used English empiricism as a stepping stone on the way to transforming empiricism into intuitionism. It goes without saying that Lord Shaftesbury and Hutcheson, in the style of Cambridge Platonists, ranged from Plato to Plotinus. Speaking from their motivations, they appear on the surface to be antiempiricists. But with Reid, their simple aesthetic, ethical, and religious issues were expanded and universalized to become arbiters of all knowledge before finally arriving at an empirical and everyday concept of common sense itself. Clearly opposed to continental rationalism, there is little room to doubt the empiricist essence of Reid's common sense. The function of this common sense is none other than to authorize all humans—as average individuals within a society—to form judgments based on their everyday experiences of beauty and ugliness, good and bad, true and false, and to do so without logic—that is, to form these judgments unconditionally and intuitively. It may be common sense that everyone experientially believes in the existence of the objective world. But with Reid, the foundation of this everyday experience is sought in nothing more than a prior internal intuition of the human heart.

3

Yet as everyone would imagine, Reid's conception of common sense contains many weaknesses. First, a dogma in the form of a particular thesis as an explanation of the axiomatic content of common sense is clearly impossible. Which is to say, were this the case—and speaking from the contents of this common sense (leaving the whole disposition to later)—this content cannot be an average popular sense held by social individuals; it must also specify some unchanging, eternal human understanding or capacity to reason. Though in rationalism human understanding and human reason is assumed to be unchanging and eternal, what is assumed to be unchanging is *only the active attitude* of understanding and reason. Rationalism did not claim that the *content* produced by that active understanding and reason is fixed and invariable. On the contrary, the content of this understanding and reason itself is refined and advanced by means of the judgment underwritten by understanding and reason. But for Reid's common sense—because in his common sense (that is, the content of understanding and the axiomatic understanding)—there is absolutely no advancement or progress; it is necessarily an invariable and conservative thing. Reid's concept of common sense, then, is merely the universalization of a historically specific English common sense, indeed, the universalization of a particular social stratum's common sense.

England at the time was in the midst of a politically reactionary period, faced on the one hand with Protestant revival movements in Ireland and elsewhere, and on the other hand, it was also directly confronted with the activity of the Jacobins in the French Revolution. The representative conservative thinker and leader of the Whig Party, Edmund Burke, famously opposed the rising tide of the French bourgeoisie with an anti-Enlightenment and reactionary attitude. But Reid was more than just a contemporary of Burke. Burke was also one of the soldiers of the Scottish School who built on the Shaftesbury School's aesthetics, itself founded on an invariant, aesthetic, emotional sensibility. While adopting the approach of English empiricism, both the Scottish School and the Common Sense School grounded itself in a respect for tradition that in many ways conflicted with empiricism itself; thus both the Scottish School and the Common Sense School were based on a particular aristocratic ideology upon which the rise of the English bourgeoisie was built.

Burke is to be counted among the theorists of the social contract. But while we could say that Hobbes's social contract—in being based in individualism and thus, in a sense, contained a kind of democratic principle—Burke, as a realist who emphasized historical tradition, held that in any form of government the people were the rulers, and so he can be seen as some sort of democrat; his vehement antipathy for the French Revolution is actually not a political but an ethical rebellion stemming from his liberalism. But he also unconditionally followed the erstwhile Whig Party's opposition to equality. Thus we can say that he was an extremely aristocratic, conservative sort of democrat. And Burke's aristocratic, conservative ideology is also amply reflected in Reid's concept of common sense. With Reid, the original democratic idea of common sense was immediately rendered a particularly English and aristocratic fixed sensibility and thus came to mean a past and unchanging set of conservative and eternal rules. Socially, Reid's common sense opposed revolutionary activity (the Jacobins), and theoretically it opposed the radicality, either progressive or reactionary, of Hume's skepticism. In other words, common sense was tasked with defending and preserving current roles against practical and ideological radical movements. Because common sense is not in general a problem, but using common sense in this way is, it must be said that the issue with Reid's "common sense" is not merely that it reflected contemporary English empiricism and English democratic style, but that it was granted authority by a particularly conservative and aristocratic common sense that lay within it. It is no accident that Reid's Scottish School descended from the Cambridge Platonists (Ralph Cudworth et al.).[9] The average individual posited by this understanding of common sense came to be the general masses necessarily modeled on the aristocracy. Reid's "common sense" then was merely a common sense already restricted by these several layers of conditions.

AN ANALYSIS OF "COMMON SENSE"

Because Reid's concept of common sense was occasioned by a historically specific and particular English aristocratic ideology, it was focused on the active aristocratic aspects and unsurprisingly ignored the negative common sense of the common people.[10] For these aristocratic ideologues, when it came to a question of the common sense of the common people, their common sense always culminates in simplistic common sense and never becomes anything more. Further, it is never considered that common sense may be contradictory. It is assumed that aristocratic common sense may be fundamentally and holistically resolved in its highest form. Which is why this philosophical concept of common sense is simplistic and monotonous, so debased that it doesn't even reach the ordinary, commonsensical level of today's concept of common sense. This is its third weakness. We started with the dialectical nature of common sense. But here at the end, by means of an empiricist and phenomenological English approach, the dialectical nature has been completely dropped. But today, even speaking in an ordinary sense, common sense harbors a few more contradictions.

4

The German "world citizen" Kant is rightly famous as an excellent philosopher of common sense, especially his historically momentous philosophy of "pure, bourgeois common sense." It is true that Kant was close to Thomas Reid's explanation of common sense, but naturally, we must pay attention to the ways these two conceptions of common sense contend with each other. But more important than this, Kant's human reason and human understanding were a Germanic conception of the faculty of human common sense in an age of Enlightenment bourgeois ideology. We can thus read Kant's critique of "pure reason" as a critique of "bourgeois common sense." This is because Kant's problem was: To what extent is human understanding (reason) complete or healthy, and from where do we uncover unhealthy contradictions? In the former case (this is analytical), healthy understanding is common sense. In the latter unhealthy case, it is "dialectical."

Proceeding this way, as to the a priori "intuition" of perception, the a priori "categories" of reason, and the consideration of their combination as an a priori "fundamental problem" (axiom)—for example, on the understanding of cause and effect—we will likely notice that these are all some sort of phenomenological (?) analysis of Reid's intuition-backed common sense. From this perspective, Kant's so-called formalism destroyed the fetters of aristocratic content in Reid's concept making possible the generalization and harmonization of formalism with bourgeois common sense. In opposition to Hume's skepticism, Kant replaced the Common Sense School's arbitrary common sense (axioms, dogma) with the critique of common sense.

We must say that Kant's critique of bourgeois common sense as a critique of reason itself was done according to a particular (German) bourgeois common sense. But a critique of bourgeois common sense by means of a bourgeois common sense, thus a "self-critique," ultimately remains within the extremely narrow limits of bourgeois common sense itself. In other words, what Kant himself calls the dialectic (for example, the antinomies), is none other than that which logically expresses the conflict of common sense with itself. What this shows, for better or worse, is the acknowledgment of a dialectical nonharmony possessed by bourgeois common sense. With Hegel the dialectic appears positively as a method of academic thought, meaning that bourgeois common sense—as an unscientific mode of thought opposed to academic thinking—has already left the stage and only the dialectic that opposed it remains. But it does not follow that all problems of common sense have therefore been eliminated. In fact, dialectical thinking for us today is a particular form of common sense that is no longer bourgeois, and further, it must not be bourgeois.[11]

The antinomies and dialectical nature of common sense do not end with the simple opposition of these two contradictory propositions within common sense. That was the limit of what Kant saw. But in fact, opposed to this, common sense itself is something that is true because it is common sense and at the same time is not true because it is common sense. This very antinomy is the fundamentally dialectical nature of common sense. Something extremely complicated lies hidden in this point.

As a means to resolve this contradiction we need to consider once again one of the properties of Reid's common sense. Because Reid's common sense was a particular and arbitrary thesis that appeared as a fundamental proposition (axiom), it meant, in that sense, the commonsensical *contents* of each individual. It was thought that the substance of common sense included each and every proposition commonsensically stressed. But because the validity of all these individual contents of common sense was underwritten by the healthy deployment of human reason, in addition to

AN ANALYSIS OF "COMMON SENSE"

each and every content of individual common sense, there was also another justification for this basic stance on common sense: the existence of a formal content to common sense that produced the individual contents. Hence, here a distinction is made between the content of individual common sense and the formal aspects of common sense that enable the individual content. These two aspects correspond to the content and form of common sense. Yet this is not only a relationship between content and form. So, as we consider common sense in this ordinary, commonsensical way, we notice that the single relationship between all these various contents of common sense—which have the form of a thesis, and the form of common sense—oppose each other, and more, are even inconsistent with each other. Let us develop this distinction a bit more.

According to a young officer I know, around the time of World War I when the military was not respected as it is today, he says that it was thought soldiers had no common sense and so were ordered by their superiors to study law and economics. Further, because of the form and content of common sense, regardless of whether lacking this kind of knowledge means that soldiers lack common sense, a lack of common sense is just a lack of common sense, so that no matter what sort of knowledge is gained, knowledge acquisition will not on its own remedy a basic lack of common sense, or so he thought. Indeed, if lacking knowledge of law, economics, and politics means no one can be considered to possess common sense; and although gaining such knowledge is one condition for elevating one's common sense, in an important way, gaining such knowledge does not automatically elevate common sense.

If common sense is thought of as the synthesis of various knowledges, then it would follow that knowledge acquisition would by itself increase the quantity of the contents of common sense, but it would not necessarily mean that the level of human opinions would also be raised. Qualitatively increasing and approaching a higher *level* of common sense is independent of the quantitative increase in knowledge of its contents. As everyone knows, knowledge does not simply and directly become judgment. The sum of knowledge is not opinion.

It is true that as knowledge becomes richer, that alone may raise the level of opinion. Thus if we think about it this way it seems to be the case—especially when we are talking about social scientific knowledge, a kind of knowledge that is itself grounded in a particular kind of view, or better, a kind of knowledge that is itself a particular view. Nonetheless, a view is not mere knowledge or the sum total of information. If we think about this for a moment, the sum total of knowledge—in the sense of an average or mean—can be seen as human opinion, but this average is no simple thing. The relation between common sense as content (as the mean of various knowledges and their sum total) and common sense as a level or standard (imagined as the general intellectual mean [知識の総和平均と想像されるもの]), does resemble the relation between an individual case and its statistical or collective average. But despite the substantial contact between the two meanings of common sense, for the time being they both still maintain an independence from each other. What may be said of one case cannot be transplanted as-is into the other. The simple fact that one may average all the individual cases already means common sense as a standard or level is independent of each standpoint of each individual case, meaning that average and that standard are independent of each other. Thus in the same way, we must distinguish between the common sense as the content of the individual cases and common sense as a level or standard.

Common sense as a standard, or the level of common sense, does not emerge from within common sense, thus indicating the independence of common sense. Common sense qua common sense becomes problematic if not reduced to something else. Therefore it is not a question of mere common sense as content, but rather a question of common sense as this standard level, because common sense considered as content is not true common sense—which is to say that common sense as content is merely the sum total of individual knowledge. Thus in truth, averaging various individual common sense does not give birth to common sense (as a standard level). Therefore, this average is not common sense (again as a standard level) but is merely the average level of knowledge. Such an intellectual level will develop to the academic level with regard to group or disciplinary knowledge, and more general knowledge will develop toward cultural standards. But neither of these will become what we are calling the standard level of common sense.

In general then, if common sense is measured according to these academic, technical, and cultural standards, meaning if common sense is not measured on its own terms, but measured against a scale based in knowledge—technical expertise, cultural and other standards—we would ignore common sense's independence and the distinction between common sense and all these other various intellectual, technical, cultural and other things. Which is to say that we would reject the existence of the very category of common sense. The necessary result that follows from this way of thinking of common sense would make common sense reducible to an intellectual, technical, cultural, or some other thing, and so common sense becomes merely an incomplete or degraded version of these other standards. Because if common sense is imagined as not having its own principle, it would indicate some standard below expertise. In other words, it is imagined that nothing is below common sense.

The result of considering common sense as a question of content is an intellectual and expert-centric one. It is a category of academicians. For contemporary Japanese academicians, common sense is viewed in this negative sense and thought of, for example, as the vulgarization and popularization of science and the arts. But if common sense is considered as centered on a standard or level, the concept needs to be completely rethought. This rethinking would reveal that common sense has its own internal standards of measurement, meaning that it is itself a particular standard. Here common sense (as something independent of intellectual and other standards) means a *norm* [*norumu*]. Incidentally, as a norm, all other elements are made to accord with this norm, putting common sense in a league of its own. Thus, common sense represents the pinnacle where nothing is above it.

Because common sense is considered to be untrue and at the same time it is considered true, then contradiction, antinomy, or paralogism is the very content of the concept of common sense. In other words, if we acknowledge the independence of common sense and its own particular principle, we verify its dialectical nature.

5

Common sense is derided for lacking creativity, meaning it terminates in a banal average. So in this case, a particular knowledge possesses a certain level given by a social average (this is not the level of common sense discussed above). Anything below that average is not considered, and nothing escapes above social average. Thus common sense is condemned to its negative fate. Accordingly, as a norm, this means nearly everything may be considered to be below, above, or at the level of this socially average common sense. In this view, knowledge that achieves a level above common sense is "creative." But it goes without saying that all knowledge is creative. This in turn means that the knowledge of this socially average common sense (see the example of the content of common sense above) is always an incomplete or immature kind of knowledge.

But regardless of whether knowledge is creative, independent of this issue the question remains: Is the level of common sense, is common sense itself, creative or not? We cannot ignore the fact that even this level of common sense finds its initial essence in the average (mean) of the opinions of individuals in a society. In these terms, it appears that the level of common sense as the average mean of knowledge (the content of common sense) and the standard of common sense as a norm are not two different things. But if we consider this a bit we come to understand that simply saying something is an average or somehow attaching the word "common sense" to it does not of itself make it a norm or a standard. For then the level of common sense is simultaneously the average of the opinions of individuals in a society and at the same time something above this average. And thus we have discovered yet another contradiction within common sense.

In order to resolve this contradiction, we must solve the puzzle of this social mean. Which is to say, we cannot solve the puzzle of the social mean with a straightforward and simple quantitative generalization of opinions of each individual in a society. Precisely because it is a social mean it *must be both a standard and an ideal*[12] (though it is not yet known how or where it is grounded). Reid's concept of common sense expressed this issue of the mean as healthy, as something that is both a standard and an ideal. (The concept of common sense expressed as *bon sense*, too, relies on a hidden ideal that secretly grounds its standard level.) Obviously, healthy is not an average between sick and well, but rather healthy is both a standard for each individual and also an ideal. Regardless, healthy is thought to be a person's normal state. Further, this language also conveys the sense of health as something to be maintained (unhealthy states are to be restored or renewed to healthy states). In other words, improving one's health and developing one's health are thought to be the human mean, the corresponding norm, and the normal state of human beings.

Thus, common sense, too, as the opinion of social individuals, now appears as something that develops and maintains itself, and the maintenance of this standard level of common sense becomes the normal state.

The total, mean average of social individuals strives to raise itself up to its own normal [healthy] level. So now for the first time, here the social average becomes normal—it becomes a norm, a standard. Thus this social average is in truth not merely a social average. Considered as a social average of the standard of common sense, this average itself is one that is constantly *solicited* to work to raise itself.

Therefore, the level of common sense does not mean the average of the opinions of members of a society at any given time. Instead, this average indicates a standard or an ideal to be striven for. We cannot locate this ideal line on a sheet of graph paper. Neither can we make its location a problem of inquiry. But wherever we encounter an average value, this ideal is at play nearby, acting like a force field traversing the whole of the social space. True common sense is a living thing that is thus constantly declining, disappearing, and dissipating, and this term "standard of common sense" then is something that is constantly encouraging common sense to develop and maintain itself. Just as with truth, as something that maintains and raises itself, common sense, too, is something that maintains and raises itself.

Because true common sense as the standard of common sense is not some simple average of the opinions of members of a society, and because it is also not some golden mean (中庸), it is thus something quite distant from what is called public opinion. The two concepts align only so long as public opinion is regarded as the average political opinion of the masses—and then only if those masses in fact share the same opinions. In general, public opinion is understood according to the principle of majority rule. But as for the principle of the majority, there is a basis for affirming and denying the rights of the majority. To the extent that we honestly honor the principle of the majority, in order to draw out the rights of those in the majority, in theory we must appeal to the actions and violence that exist above and beyond the simple act of existing as a majority. At one time in the Greek Assembly, the majority meant those with the loudest and strongest voices. In order to save the early modern bourgeoisie's concept of public opinion from these philosophical difficulties, it was necessary to reconsider the issue of public opinion within majority rule according to the "standard of common sense." (To connect this with our examination of Reid's common sense, this Greek example of public opinion—opinion, *Meinung*—can be tied to the concept of doxa above.)

But in truth we must be aware that the level of common sense itself has a political quality. We have already called the level of common sense opinion, distinguishing its meaning from mere knowledge (and in due course academics and culture). But the opinions of social individuals does not only mean the unification of individuals' intellectual wills. It also means the unification of intellectual will of each individual within a society that comes from having entered a mutual social relationship (mediated by material production). It is precisely this level of common sense that develops the social, political, and average value at work within this unification of political wills. Thus the level of common sense always possesses a fundamental politicality. Public opinion is this political common sense itself, especially in the narrow sense of political.

As a result, popularization and massification [大衆化] accompany the problem of common sense. But unlike what is thought of as ordinary social rules, it cannot be solved by means of average social values or majority rule. Massification [popularization] is not then *bringing the state of things closer to the given state of average social values*. Popularization by means of the standard (norm) of common sense is a means to bring *those that should be the majority to the state of things*. Thus people must be organized to become the masses, to become the majority.[13] Consequently, popularization's true meaning cannot be the organization of the masses. Here popularization corresponds to the power to develop and maintain common sense as a level or standard in the organization of the masses. So, popularization is a method that has no proper idealist content beyond this sense of massification. If it were to have another content this would merely be from its mixing with bad common sense (a common sense reflected in the level of knowledge).

To review what we have found so far: though common sense does initially have a relationship to the average value of the majority of people in a society, and though as a factual phenomenon, at first glance it appears to be merely the banal average of the opinion of that majority; both that majority and that average demanded investigation. As a result the level of common sense as an attitude is in truth not an average or a majority. Rather it is a kind of *idealist line of force that disciplines and develops the average and the majority*. Thus common sense, in the end, is not the majority nor is it the average, but rather is a minority who have approached an objective norm. Further, as a norm, common sense is, paradoxically, an exceptional common sense that has in fact escaped this average.

AN ANALYSIS OF "COMMON SENSE"

So, if common sense is in fact not merely some social average value, it would be meaningless to universally average the common sense of the various individuals in a society,[14] and in truth exceptional common sense is exceptional precisely because it has gone beyond that average value common sense. Therefore, those possessors of exceptional common sense (for example Edmund Burke, Kant, and we can also include Hegel and Marx) are absolutely not the majority—though there are many "commonsensical individuals" whose content of common sense does in fact stop at the level of common sense. But as even this number is clearly not a majority it is possible that they possess a common sense higher than the average intellectual. The truth is that there simply are not that many typical, average people.

6

Thus, common sense has finally been liberated from its original fetters as a social average of the majority. If we had not followed this line of investigation, that is if we had not forced common sense to reveal its own principle, we may continue to think that the concept of bourgeois democracy seems to find its principles in the mean and majority, but we would not have discovered that those quantities are not the principle of common sense. The fundamental principles of common sense are not to be derived from the concept of common sense of bourgeois democracy (and here we include the mechanistic positing of individuals in a society as having an abstract homogeneity and equality).

Where do the regulations of common sense go once liberated from this quantitative average and majority? They return to the already touched-upon principle of everydayness. In the popular understanding, everydayness—as both vulgarity and snobbery—is a life situation that has lost its principle, and everydayness is tidied up by reference to a quantitative determination. But that view itself is merely the result of a vulgar commonsensical wisdom. *The principle of everydayness* is independent of this; its principle is the principle of actuality (actuality) [実際性]. (In German this is called the "actual circumstances" [現実]—*Wirklichkeit*. Act = *wirken*). An analysis of the principle of everydayness is tedious, but I have elsewhere had occasion to work it out as best I can (see *Lectures on Contemporary Philosophy*).[15]

A simple way to think about the principle of actuality is to reflect on the example of the everyday function of newspapers. Who would search for the function of the newspaper within the research labs of the academics? Further, no one would think that a mere academic or devoted scholar is qualified to write a newspaper or edit a magazine. Precisely this journalistic function that opposes the academic function is proof that it comes closer to the principle of everydayness. Journalism, as the word itself suggests, is grounded in the worldview of the actual circumstances of daily life, and thus it is founded on the principle of everydayness. Thus this principle of everydayness is one that is likely not even imagined by the vulgarity of the representative academic fool.

Finally, criticism [クリテイシズム] (critique, commentary) founded in the principle of everydayness is one function of this journalism. Generally, critique and commentary on things always moves along the lines of the level of common sense (a given society's social and political yardstick). Yet what we want to say here is that common sense is not merely the shared sense of the society but is a social (and later historical) shared *everyday* sense. As a historical and social human instinct, common sense is a particular shape of intelligence of human daily life.

Furthermore, this human sense of the everyday, this common sense (that is, common sense as a standard level) is neither merely a social average nor a shared social currency. It is a norm, a standard. Thus it includes even those things that oppose the norm, indeed, an antinorm ironically must be made in the name of the norm itself. The Mephistophelian nature of common sense does its work in the gap between the emperor and the counter-emperor [*Kaiser / Gegen-Kaiser*]. The standard level of common sense is thus split according to the class antagonism. Just like the class nature (class opposition) of knowledge and science, thus also like the inescapable class nature (partisan) logic of knowledge and scholarship, common sense, too, has a class nature and a class antagonism. Common sense therefore also has an inescapable class (partisan) nature; what is called the "logic" of knowledge and scholarship corresponds to what is here termed the standard of "common sense."

So now two standards of common sense oppose each other, both sides insisting on the normality of their standard. From where is this opposition derived, and how is it to be resolved? Here we must once again aim at the relationship between the previously mentioned content and standard of common sense. We should take note that compared to an exceptional common sense, the standard of a lower common sense is likely to be more predominant and shared. In other words, this is proof that those who have this lower common sense are more in tune with social individuals' commonsensical knowledge standard. Thus, we see that the level of these inferior persons is only inferior relative to those with exceptional common sense, and that such a judgment is the result confusing the quantitative amount of the content of the ordinary level of knowledge that we called the content of common sense. Indeed, while it is natural not to expect excellence from any knowledge that completely stops at the ordinary level—which is not the "level of common sense"—even when comparing those who are at the standard level of common sense, the basic premise of an inferior standard of common sense is based on the content of knowledge existing below the ordinary level. In other words, this all returns to the known relationship that a lack of knowledge results in uncommon sense.

That today there exists a bourgeois common sense and a proletarian common sense is not only made clear from everyday experience. It is also clear from the antagonism between bourgeois journalism and proletarian journalism.[16] The concept of massification and public opinion are further evidence of this split. But, for example, the bourgeois understanding of massification is only spoken of as something like vulgarization or popularization. Massification as a bourgeois concept makes any further analysis impossible, and accordingly the original concept of massification leads to the posited conclusion of vulgarization and popularization, making any resolution too difficult to even attempt. It is thus common knowledge today that only the proletarian analysis of the idea of massification, as a concept, can be analyzed in a way that may result in a resolution.

We must say that public opinion also believes this concept of bourgeois democracy has completely reached an impasse. Public opinion today is in fact a private language that sputters from a corner of society that would be better called a bourgeois "publicuum," or it rains down from the stone steps of some *Gleichschaltung* "reformist" bureaucracy [*tōseiteki kanga*].

Common sense has disappeared completely from the world. Common sense is pushed into the cellar where it appears to have been suffocated. Yet this view of the lack of common sense is precisely the "common sense" (!) of the Japanists.

Thus, the results of our investigation: common sense as a level is determined by the standard of common sense. By clearly rendering these determinations explicit, the problems lurking within common sense—its contradictions, antinomies, and its dialectical nature—may be resolved. Within common sense generally live two contradictory theses: the affirmation and the negation of common sense, averageness and excellence, the class antagonism of common sense as a norm, and so on and on.

Yet we are sure several readers will pointedly ask, what relationship to actual problems does this analysis have? It is this: common sense itself, the unique principles of common sense, forms one of the cornerstones of materialism today. Why? Because it is within common sense that the principles of everydayness and actuality themselves appear. And these are none other than the principles that may defend mass thought from hermeneutic philosophy, and in that sense from metaphysics, and finally from idealism.

Chapter Four

ON ENLIGHTENMENT

The Meaning and Necessity of Enlightenment Today

1

Today the concept of enlightenment (*Aufklärung*) is split in two. There is cultural history's so-called enlightenment of the Age of Enlightenment, and there is also the more general, popular sense of enlightenment expressed in everyday speech. Of course, there is a fundamental relationship between the two uses, but as for the historical understanding of "Enlightenment," there is on the one hand an eternal and universal sense, and at the same time a sense in which the concept is confined and determined by its own particular historical conditions. Accordingly, today there is no single concept of enlightenment. Our goal is to historically, and thus theoretically, analyze the gap between these two meanings.

The precise details of the concept of enlightenment notwithstanding, the majority of people today likely already have some understanding of the term. But because most people, unlike academics, find the inessential details hard to easily intuit, they are unlikely to go on to produce fruitless, complex, and ultimately showy analyses. Thus, it is clearly possible for people to quickly get an intuitive sense of the essentials of the concept. Yet if today there are those who are unable to understand the everyday usage of the term, they likely do not feel the need for a concept of enlightenment under the present circumstances. Such people likely feel no benefit is to be gained from the concept, or they may even believe enlightenment to be a harmful concept. They would surely say that it was only during the Meiji period [1868–1912] when the more historical Age of Enlightenment version of the concept was essential, while those who feel that enlightenment remains an essential concept are likely then thinking of enlightenment in the everyday sense of the term. So, for us, we will ground our analysis in this everyday concept and our results will return to the everyday usage. This then becomes our goal.

The concept of enlightenment in Japan today is likely a translation of the German word *Aufklärung* and also possibly the English word "enlightenment"—or "civilization" [文明]. So, those who are to be enlightened [*aufklären*] must be those thought to be currently shrouded in darkness or fog. Historically this darkness referred to the irrational concepts or ideology that spontaneously developed from within the remnants of feudalism—that is the irrational as seen from the perspective of the Enlightenment itself. Of course, more than the development of economic and technical mechanisms, *Aufklärung* as "civilization" mainly meant a cultural development. When compared with England, and especially with France, Germany significantly lagged in both civilization and enlightenment. Kant, as the representative thinker of this kind of enlightenment aimed his critique at the rule of Frederick the Great, meaning not that Prussia was enlightened but that it was in an age of enlightening. When compared with England and France, Germany lagged in both productive capacity and cultural consciousness, so if we closely consider Frederick the Great's Prussia as an age "in the process of enlightenment," it is clear that this expression referred to the darkness and fog naturally and spontaneously produced from the remnants of feudal mechanisms. As the Meiji Constitution is said to have been written in accordance with the Prussian Constitution it can further be thought, and this is common sense among authoritative legal scholars and historians today, that *Aufklärung* opposed the remnant concepts that developed in Japan's extremely long-lived feudal system.[1]

This is more or less the historical line of descent of this so-called Enlightenment. But the current essential aspects of enlightenment, and accordingly the current meaning of enlightenment, completely differs from these historical conditions in a fundamental way. This is something we must pay close attention to. The fog that this current meaning of enlightenment is attempting to drive away is absolutely not the fog that developed within the basic conditions of Japanese feudalism. The current darkness is a *darkness intentionally introduced by the conscious adoption of the basic conditions of Japan's feudal system.*[2] Additionally, as this is not the complete darkness of a historical period; this darkness is more of a dim light. Even though it is the same dim light, and though it is the historical Enlightenment and the dim light of the "process of enlightenment," the current dusk is a type of intentionally blinding nostalgic melancholia—or perhaps like the sun hidden in the shadow of an eclipse. This alone is reason to understand that the performance and function of today's enlightenment must necessarily be a new and different thing. Today the concept of enlightenment must not only shine its light on the natural and conscious concepts of the feudal period, but it must also shine its bright light on the concepts grounded in the capitalist system that were themselves born of the historical Enlightenment. Thus the meaning of enlightenment today, compared with the historical Enlightenment, is gradually and continuously generalized while at the same time it is increasingly limited.

But there are more than a few well-informed people and members of the intelligentsia who even without tentatively disagreeing with what I have said to this point, and even without denying what I have said about the meaning of enlightenment today, would have little interest in this problem. We cannot deny this fact. They would respond, "Enlightenment is all fine and good, but we have far more important matters before us. For example, our research, reflection, personal anxiety, and the like are all much more important. Why do we not take up the question of enlightening people after these more pressing issues have been resolved?" Having such an attitude, these types of intellectuals first plan to enlighten themselves. Of course, that too is all fine and good. But what guides these intellectuals in such research, such reflection, or such personal anxiety? What actually leaks out from the mouths of these humble researchers, these dour contemplators, these self-*agonistes* is never more than some "philosophical," rarefied category of "totality," "experience," *gemeinschaft*, and so on. This is nothing more than contemporary mysticism and obscurantism founded in self-important pedantry. Thinking abstractly, they have decided that human experience is the ultimate victor, totality is better than piecemeal, respecting experience is better than ignoring it, and *gemeinschaft* is better than *gesellschaft*. As they speak in such a formalistic manner, whether or not rationally enlightened things enter into their content, or again if mystified confusions do, one hundred days of explication will likely amount to no more than a single fart. Those who feel no need at all for enlightened action do not even possess a personal enlightenment. And such is the situation in which we find ourselves today.

Now, enlightenment in the historical Age of Enlightenment appeared first and foremost as liberalism. Liberalism was its premier determination. Indeed, historically, the Enlightenment—that is, as a period of cultural history and as the ultimate category—cannot be thought of as a political category, nor is it an economic category. Here, then, liberalism is obviously not economic liberalism (free contract, free market, free competition) and further, originally it is also not political liberalism (representative institutions, constitutionalism, democracy). Emphatically it must be called cultural liberalism.

Still, this cultural liberalism (I will gradually explain what this means) was obviously distilled from economic and political liberalism. In truth, it was with John Locke, starting from a base in political liberalism, that the enlightenment of the Age of Enlightenment was first philosophically organized. It is not necessary to recount the materialist basis of individual economic liberalism within early modern bourgeois society. But when the concept of liberty corresponding to this economic liberalism acquired a cultural essence in place of the individual liberty of individual enterprise, commercial activity, contract, and labor—from this same individual liberty, what in fact precipitated from it, was a cultural aspect; that is, this liberty settled in the authority of an individual's personal understanding [悟性] and desires. And only then was it possible for this liberty to migrate to become political liberty. Incidentally, it was in this cultural moment that Locke was trying to seek out this liberty within understanding, that is to say, within human understanding (today we can just as well say reason [理性]). So today individual economic, political, and also cultural liberty are now all concentrated in one place under the name of the authority of human understanding. There is then nothing prior to human understanding; without this human understanding, there is no authority at all. The church, the aristocracy, the king, and so on—none of these things come before living, individual understanding; no pride is taken in anything absolute.

No doubt it was precisely this human understanding or human reason as a cultural mechanism that, as in the creed of the French Enlightenment thinkers, guaranteed the *liberté*—together with *egalité* and *fraternité*—of the French *citöyen*. But in Germany, Kant had the original idea that this authority accorded to understanding and reason, indeed that the freedom of understanding and reason, was to be sought within autonomy [自律]. In this case, freedom was not accepted as merely economic and political freedom, but rather the understanding and reason were seen as the individual's freedom, until this concept distilled into a fully cultural freedom. With Kant, by becoming the conscience of the world of the Prussian Bürger, liberalism was "philosophized." Freedom of political activity was replaced with freedom of philosophical speculation, and freedom within society was replaced with freedom of thought, becoming the founding moment of classical German idealism. In this way enlightenment was reducible first and foremost to a cultural liberalism. The particulars of Kant's own theory of enlightenment have been well discussed. He began his famous text "An Answer to the Question: What Is Enlightenment?" with a definition: "Enlightenment is the use of man's own understanding for liberation from his self-incurred immaturity." Here understanding is merely the active use of one's own freedom. It has the sole responsibility for ending the age of immaturity. It never meant that the use of understanding by responsible individuals would develop the relatively backward state of German capitalism. According to Kant, in a Germany in the process of being enlightened under the cultural reign of Frederick II, it also never meant the development of German capitalism through German unification or, as a result, the necessary progressive policies of Frederick the Great's struggle against the great princes. We need to take notice that Kant's enlightenment, by means of the free activity of the understanding, was limited to cultural activities between solely cultural individuals. Any free use of the understanding on the business or position of the citizen was not only not an example of enlightened activity, but under the reign of Frederick, such use was even a form of barbarism. From this we can clearly see that the space of opportunity for liberalism within Kant's concept of enlightenment is wholly confined to cultural liberalism.

This shows us that while Kant is a representative thinker of the Enlightenment he is also, contrarily, an example of a German critic and one who went beyond and rid oneself [啓蒙脱却者] of the Enlightenment. Indeed, from his own definition of the Enlightenment just quoted above, Germany was absolutely not an expression of the actually existing Enlightenment phenomenon in Europe or England. Instead, what he tried to grasp was an ideology of the universal, eternal principles of enlightenment. Kant had before him the famous Enlightenment philosopher Moses Mendelssohn, and Kant's teacher, Christian Wolff, preceded him as a philosophical organizer of German Enlightenment thought. Further, there were everywhere extraordinary examples of "popular philosophy." Kant took as his mission a criticism of all these commonsensical phenomena.

The philosophical—worldview or theoretical—foundation of English Enlightenment thought is without a doubt empiricism. In contrast to this English position and to many others, the characteristic philosophical basis of French Enlightenment thought was materialism (a bourgeois, metaphysical materialism). The foundation of German Enlightenment philosophy (the Wolff school) was the "philosophy of the understanding." We have so far traced the path of the German *Aufklärung* and from this philosophy of the understanding, from its rationalism, we can discern the second condition of the Enlightenment. Which is to say, historically the second condition of the so-called Enlightenment is a philosophical organization focused on the law of contradiction (Wolff was the first to build a "system" of traditional German philosophy).

But while we can say that this second condition is in truth especially characteristic of the German *Aufklärung*, it is also a theoretical mechanism shared with French materialism. The law of contradiction, with its opposite the law of identity, is the endpoint and the essential, unique foundation, the axis of thought; in other words it meant nothing less than the declaration of the adoption of a mechanistic logic. Within this philosophy of mechanism both so-called empiricism and so-called French materialism are one with the rationalism of the German Enlightenment. Regardless of their empiricist, materialist, or rationalist bases, a shared foundation in a philosophy of mechanism is the reason that all three systems may be considered equally metaphysical. In sum, the second condition of the Enlightenment was merely a condensing of the characteristics of metaphysics.

Thus, our next problem is the relationship of this historical Enlightenment given by the second condition, metaphysics, to the meaning of enlightenment today. To investigate this problem, we would do well to pay attention to the necessary historical movement between the former and the latter. As for the concept of enlightenment as a cultural category—cultural in that it is not an economic or political category—there was a reason for us to go through the development, changes, and rejection of enlightenment in classical German philosophy, a philosophy that felt no need to make any practical use of economic or political categories of enlightenment. It is said that Kant, already in his critique, was the first thinker who through criticism plotted a rejection of the Enlightenment, but such criticism appeared as a fundamental form in *The Critique of Pure Reason* as the law of dialectics.

Kant's dialectic (meaning his theory that the various antinomies of reason come from the mistaken use of reason) only plays an external, negative, and ultimately rejected role in his philosophical system. It was with Fichte and Schelling, and later Hegel, that theory itself attributed a fundamental and positive essence to, and then developed, the dialectic. It is not necessary to again recap that history here. The only important point here is that Hegel first rendered clear Kant's vague distinction and opposition between human understanding and reason. Hegel viewed Kant's reason as still stuck at the stage of understanding and as representative of metaphysics and mechanistic philosophy, and therefore saw Kant's system as opposed to a truly dialectical reason. Moreover, Hegel definitively criticized Kant's own critique of and flight from the stronger versions of Enlightenment philosophy's rationalism and the law of contradiction. Which is to say with Hegel, the second condition of the historical so-called Enlightenment was sublated.

It is hard to grasp the concrete meaning of this move by seeing it only from the standpoint of mechanistic philosophy, but in fact the real result is related to the recognition of history in this ill-fated, so-called *Aufklärung*. At the very least it was a characteristic of the German *Aufklärung* based on the understanding to pay scant attention to the concept of history. While Kant was one of the founders of a German philosophy of history and even a founder of a philosophy of universal progress, he was, nonetheless, unable to pay sufficient attention to the meaning of so-called historical irrationality (normally we can have no faith in this term). For Hegel this was because Kant based his thought on a metaphysics of understanding. So Hegel, basing his own thought on the dialectic of reason, became completely historical.

Now as everyone surely knows, both Hegel's concept of history itself, and his recognition of the so-called irrationality in history, have been exposed as fundamentally flawed. For us this is tangential to the main point; and further, given the point made in Schelling's later work, Hegel's thinking on history as the dialectic of reason and its development and the necessity of the manifestation of the ideal in history was nothing more than the idealization of historical rationalism. But the main characteristic of reason for Hegel was above all the originary self-realization of reason's own self-autonomy and freedom. This was merely a more philosophical organization of what Kant had been after, the first condition of the Enlightenment, namely the concept of cultural freedom. Thus materialism [*busshitsu*] (meaning matter as a philosophical category) corrected and inverted Hegel's reason and thereby overcame cultural freedom as the first condition of enlightenment in the historical Age of Enlightenment. This was now materialism [*yuibutsuron*].

Thus, it was dialectical materialism that in the end, today, overcame the two limitations of the historical so-called Enlightenment (the philosophy of understanding and the philosophy of reason—or again, metaphysics and absolutist idealism) to develop the content of a true freedom and a true rationalism. Readers will likely wonder if I have not just merely related a general history of philosophy under the nominal sign of the Enlightenment. But this is not the case, because only by following the course I did are we finally now able to historically derive the rational and general true appearance of the concept of enlightenment essential for today.

So just what kind of enlightenment is necessary today? If we were to express it rather quickly and haphazardly, liberalism would likely come to mind. (Moreover, this would mean a liberalism of cultural activities, meaning a cultural liberalism.) But the question of function is something else. At the least, speaking from within the content of the mechanism of enlightenment and the concept of enlightenment, the conditions of liberalism's enlightenment are already untimely. This is the point of my explanation. Kant's method of explaining the entirety of the Enlightenment—the free use of reason—is wholly inadequate for our enlightenment today; this is the historical age we have arrived at. Indeed, today there is nothing so confused as "reason" and nothing so unfree as "freedom." To recognize the history of some ethnic group it seems necessary for another ethnic group to have an awareness (as "reason") that understands absolutely nothing of the other; to extend the defense of the freedom of a nation's people it seems that those people themselves need to be completely deprived of freedom. Perhaps it was possible to exercise the free use of reason in a Prussia under a progressive Frederick II, but in todays' age of reaction, free use of reason is impossible.

The above has been an investigation of the *organized content* of enlightenment and the *concept* of enlightenment. But as to its active function—in other words when we ask, what sort of active form should enlightenment take today?—we enter into a new problem. Because originally enlightenment activities included, at a minimum, a kind of massificiation [*taishūka*]— the formation of common sense, journalism, and criticism—the problem of its active function is an important one. One we have to leave for another occasion.

2

As a supplement to section 1, let's review one more time.

Recently the literary world is abuzz with loud calls for Romanticism.[3] This Romanticism is thought to contrast with realism. But scientifically speaking it is not at all clear what contents are expressed by this word "Romanticism." According to most people, the contours of this discourse are given by the various conditions of German Romanticism. And sure enough, from literary history to cultural history more broadly, the German Romantics are seen as particularly characteristic of what is called the Romanticist movement. And this is not limited to a single literature. More broadly, it also runs through philosophical and even economic movements. Thus, as for what today's Japanese literary scholars think about and call "Romanticism," as a movement largely defined by German Romanticism, it is a direct fusion, and confusion, of the particular conditions of the historical movement and a certain movement today that is groping for those conditions: it is absolutely not a historical viewpoint. Because the word "Romanticism" names a particular historical movement of a specific historical period we must be extremely careful when using this word in the present.

We can say the same thing about the concept of enlightenment (*Aufklärung*). Indeed, the word "enlightenment" indicates a particular historical form: it names a political and also cultural ideal of the Age of Enlightenment of England and Europe in the seventeenth and eighteenth centuries. Today *Aufklärung* is a cultural ideal that opposes both classicism and Romanticism. Today Romanticism opposes the creative method of realism, but to forget that historically Romanticism opposed above all its predecessor classicism is dangerous. Indeed, both historical Romanticism and historical classicism opposed the features of the historical Enlightenment movement. But certainly today, when we say "enlightenment," it absolutely does not mean the enlightenment of the Age of Enlightenment. Today it is thought in cultural history that classicism and Romanticism immediately followed and replaced the bygone Age of Enlightenment. This now expired meaning cannot become a progressive goal for us in today's society. As for an enlightenment necessary today, while it must be something different from the "enlightenment" of the Age of Enlightenment, it must be nonetheless distinguished from that historical concept; it must be at once more general and also more particular. Even though we may draw out conditions of historical Romanticism that are themselves not wholly determined by the movement, such as an unlimited longing or the expansion of the world of the ego, or classicism's characteristic symmetry or proportion, we can also abstract out a general thing from the enlightenment of the Age of Enlightenment. This may not be limited to having meaning only for a necessary conception of enlightenment today, but if we were to proceed without it, we clearly could not hope for a scientific resolution of the necessary problem of enlightenment without these clues.

We can say Fukuzawa Yukichi is the greatest enlightenment thinker that Japan has produced. Further, in terms of cultural history, the first half of the Meiji period is the Age of Enlightenment in Japan. But by the Meiji period the so-called historical Age of Enlightenment was already long past in Europe. This therefore makes the meaning of Fukuzawa as an enlightenment thinker something more than, something other than, the so-called Enlightenment. So why then, despite these differences, is he labeled as an Enlightenment thinker proper? Likely it is because at least he does repeat some of the main conditions of the historical Enlightenment. So just what conditions are necessary for thinking of enlightenment today? To what extent are they the same as Fukuzawa or the historical *Aufklärung*? In what sense are they different—or better, in what ways *must* they differ? I do not think the majority of public opinion has an answer to these questions. No, Fukuzawa aside, there is no explanation as to what kind of activity the concept of enlightenment entails, let alone for what the meaning of enlightenment must be for today.

ON ENLIGHTENMENT

I have already looked at the problem of common sense [see chapter 3], and common sense has more or less become the problem of the literary world. But this concept of common sense has a particular historical meaning, and without referring to the "common sense" of the early modern Common Sense School we could not conduct a scientific analysis. But expressed in a broader sense of cultural history, these thinkers of the Common Sense School themselves are none other than a particular philosophical school of the so-called Enlightenment (especially the English Enlightenment). So, in tracing this relationship when we problematize common sense, we also must therefore problematize enlightenment. I think that this is what the behaviorist French literary scholars have done. Moreover, in a more concrete and clear sense—that is, by passing through materialism—we necessarily arrive at today's thesis. French materialism is already one representative form of enlightenment activity. If French materialism is considered without reference to enlightenment activity, would it not be a form of thought with little meaning and rather difficult to understand? Continuing in this line of thinking, consideration of the problem of materialism today must problematize enlightenment. But even without tracing this intellectual and cultural history, for materialism today there is no more important scientific mission than the analysis of enlightenment, which is something I think we all can directly sense. Materialism is not just some academic theory of a few scholars; it must be about truth—meaning the masses must understand it and feel it in their bones. The problem of enlightenment then comes down to scientific and cultural popularization, diffusion, education, and so on.

Most importantly, if Japan were not in the midst of an age of cultural barbarism, enlightenment might not be such an important term. But today the entirety of culture has lost all rationality, freedom, and actuality (materiality). Also, and we will see this later, it was precisely this rationality, freedom, and materiality that were the fundamental features of the Enlightenment.

I would like to consider the problem of enlightenment in more detail but cannot at the present time. For now, I will have to stop at this rather simplified sketch.

Enlightenment activity in the so-called Age of Enlightenment is thought to have begun in Holland and England. Now there was some precedent running through the Renaissance and the Reformation, but the essential period of the Enlightenment was the seventeenth century, especially with John Locke in England (now, in fact, if we talk of enlightenment as an ideal we could trace it all the way back to Francis Bacon). Locke's political liberalism, to borrow Harold Laski's expression, was based in economic liberalism, and this liberalism was concentrated in the free actions of the individual. It is also well known that it was Locke who first stressed individual freedom in free economic, political, and moral activity. At the time, this was a representative political ideology of the early modern bourgeoisie that sought the collapse of the contemporary feudal remnants: absolute monarchy and the authority of the Catholic Church. But of this ideology today it is necessary to note that Locke grounded freedom in the individual's freedom of thought, reason, and understanding. It was not only that Locke's *Essay Concerning Human Understanding* stressed a conception of human experience born of empiricism. It was also that this "understanding" itself was posited as the fundamental core of the human, of the individual. With Locke, the basis of an individual's political freedom emerged from within understanding—that is, within reason. This was because the individual's understanding itself was necessarily free. It was thought there was no other fundamental authority beyond freedom of understanding.

It was then in Locke that the first condition of the Enlightenment was precisely this linking of the understanding (or reason) to individual freedom. Following this condition, it was taken up in English religious philosophy and deism (rational religion)—it was from here that a kind of materialism, such as that of John Toland (1670–1722) emerged—eventually becoming the humanism of David Hume. Further, the Scottish School of Common Sense sought the recognition of the objectivity of the healthy nature of understanding here, too. This thorough-going human understanding was further famously developed by English moral science. In France, Voltaire, too, is counted among those who grounded recognition within a healthy understanding. But with Voltaire, contrarily, individual freedom was something to be denied by healthy human reason.

In German Enlightenment philosophy this relationship between understanding and freedom directly promoted a particular form. Kant, as the most representative example, on the one hand, and for the first time, systematized both categories by providing a distinction between understanding and reason, further holding that both understanding and reason had an external limit and, at the same time, an internal freedom (autonomy). Enlightenment for Kant was none other than the autonomy of reason. It was for this reason that in his text, "An Answer to the Question: What is Enlightenment?" (though this problem had already been taken up by Moses Mendelssohn) that Kant famously defined enlightenment as "the use of man's own understanding for liberation from his self-incurred immaturity." Such a definition is only meaningful if one first assumes that "self-incurred" implies that humans have an internal duty, in other words only if one imagines that human understanding is free. For Kant, the *Aufklärung* was human beings' determination and courage to freely utilize their own understanding in public speech and writing.

But understanding or reason, and the freedom of autonomy of both, is inadequate for a full understanding of the conditions of the *Aufklärung*. On the one hand, reason becomes merely the spirit to interpret the world, while on the other hand, we must notice that this freedom, as a contrast between the freedom of the will and humanity's god, becomes a sort of religious freedom. The understanding and reason of the *Aufklärung*, to the end, was necessarily a kind of rationalism, but the freedom of the *Aufklärung* must also retain its political freedoms. From here the two conditions of the *Aufklärung* were derived; one was its rationalism, the other its ideal of political reform.

Enlightenment rationalism is a characteristic of the German *Aufklärung*. Christian Wolff is the representative example. Wolff thoroughly stressed the rationalism in the thought of Leibniz and rationalized it. Which means that in rationalizing this aspect of Leibniz's philosophy, Wolff nearly completely ignored Leibniz's problem of factual truth—someting that can be rather helpful for the principle of the problem of history—and thus centered philosophy on the question of eternal truth. But at the same time, Wolff organized this philosophy of eternal truth that culminated in a decidedly academic way. Voltaire as the representative of enlightenment activity in France, as expected and appropriate for one who is thought to have invented the term "philosophy of history," is one of the pioneers of a scientific view of history from Herder to Kant and later even including historical materialism. But in Wolff, the problem of history is almost completely forgotten. Wolff's philosophy was a thorough-going mechanistic one (in other words, a formal logic of an ideology of the understanding). His philosophy made a formal logic of the law of contradiction (and this means as well the law of identity), the singular organon.

The thorough-going [doctrine of] mechanism is absolutely not exclusive of Wolff and the German *Aufklärung*. It was in fact the international logic of the Enlightenment period in England and Europe. An example that provides substantial ground for this logic was Newton. Indeed, Newton's standpoint was the same as Leibniz's in that it was not merely a dynamic mechanism in contrast to Descartes's mechanism. This is the story of Newton's differential calculus. That said, it did not escape the larger *mechanismus*. Newton theoretically personified the prevailing international technical level, and it was nothing more than a scholarly representation of England's forces of production. As examples like Fontenelle, Maupertuis, Voltaire, and others show, there was in France wide interest in Newton. Of course, the same was true in German Enlightenment thinkers as well. Here it will suffice to simply note how much Euler, Lambert, Kant, and others owe to Newton. Much of Kant's first critique was philosophically clarifying and critiquing the objectivity of Newtonian physics. Accordingly, as Kant was a critique of Newton, this fact alone means it included a critique of mechanism (as formal logic)—a critique of Newton is especially strong in Goethe and Hegel—and so this too indicates Newtoniansm was a characteristic aspect of the *Aufklärung*. The typical case of Enlightenment rationalism appears in Wolff's principle of the law of contradiction. Incidentally, for first systematizing and academicizing Enlightenment philosophy, Wolff is regarded as a famous rationalist.

Through Wolff, or at least through the Wolff school, many of the terms of German academic philosophy have been popularized—and it is clear that Kant directly received suggestions for his own thought from the terms and problems of Wolff's philosophy. (For example, it was Wolff who defined the word "ontology," and it is thought that Lambert, a major force in the Wolff school, was the first to use the term "phenomenology.")

But as for this academic refinement of Enlightenment philosophy, although it may appear there is something substantive here, in fact, Wolff's school is really the only example of a scientifically rigorous *Aufklärung* philosophy. Yet that said, though the Wolff school may have been rigorously and scientifically systematic, the resulting academicism, one divorced from the actual practice of political freedom and reason was likely the result of Germany's late-developing productive mechanisms, and so Wolff's rigorous academicism did not escape from an eclectic philosophy. As a result, German philosophy was poorly popularized, giving birth to a so-called popular philosophy. It must be said that this exposes one side of the coarseness of German Enlightenment ideology. But in the case of French Enlightenment ideology, even though it had a solidarity with this international movement (as the French Revolution shows), at the same time we must not forget that the enlightenment's role was fulfilled with the free use of official and popular language. Many of the French Enlightenment thinkers (and this includes many materialists and the so-called French *ideologues*) were not merely philosophical writers. They were also literary and dramatic authors and critics. Despite not being properly called eclectics, they were encyclopedists. This was the age of critical journals, study, and the salons in France—an age when there were many imitations and revisions of the so-called French *Encyclopedie*.

So, finally, we are left with the question of social reform coming from the condition of freedom in Enlightenment ideology. Obviously, this question was prominently expressed as the focus of the Enlightenment movement in France. No, even more, together with *egalité* and *fraternité*, French revolutionary ideology was nothing more than the incorporation of the French Enlightenment's concept of *liberté*. It must be said that French Enlightenment ideology possessed a political essence. In contrast, the German *Aufklärung* in general was a tutelary ideal based on human reason and thus fell into a merely cultural ideal of literary types. German Enlightenment ideology only has absolute meaning as a specific moment of cultural history. That is, it is nothing more than the cultural moment that preceded classicism and Romanticism. Kant clearly expressed this point. Enlightenment here was the public, not private, use of understanding. Private use here meant for example the civic and secular actions carried out by officials in observance of their official capacities. Enlightenment was opposed to this private use directing itself to the "public" or the "readership," and through the meaning in these shared texts, to conduct oneself as a scholar. Because it was thought that only here was found human progress, revolution was rejected in favor of a "gradual" reform. Kant thus linked the Age of Enlightenment—or rather not an *enlightened* age but an *enlightening* age—with the reign of Frederick II.

France and Germany are the two great instances of enlightenment, and the above nuances are the only difference between them. Thus we can conclude that both shared the philosophy of mechanism. Clearly this is the characteristic of the Enlightenment as a particular historical period. For the political and cultural development of the world that came after, we can say that it somehow cast off the mechanism of the Age of Enlightenment, but it is already proven today, both historically and theoretically, that it has not been able to cast off the resulting dialectic (materialism). Thus, the enlightenment necessary today is a dialectic enlightenment. Clearly, the goal today is a scientific cultural synthesis by means of the dialectic that does not lapse into eclectic or vulgar philosophy. Without such a cultural synthesis, choosing any concept of enlightenment or massification, or even political activity, is impossible. Here, for the first time, the meaning of being an encyclopedist of this new age will find its content.

The unitary relationship of the encyclopedist and the materialist in the French Age of Enlightenment has not changed one bit today. It is only that for enlightenment today, materialism has cast off its mechanism in favor of today's theoretical requirements. Only then can true rationality and freedom become a practical issue.

Chapter Five

A SCIENTIFIC CRITIQUE OF CULTURE
An Outline for a Critique of National Purification

It is evident that all concrete things have their own particular and independent existence. When compared with other nations, ethnicities, and cultures globally, the Japanese nation, ethnicity, genus (?), has its own particular economic, political, cultural, and global characteristics and independence. For the sake of convenience let's call these particulars the Japanese reality [日本的な現実]. Of course, as soon as we say this, we immediately call to mind a possible similar Asian reality or Eastern reality. We will leave the Japanese reality's relationship to these others for another time [see chapter 6].

For example, in May 1934 the journal *Shisō* [*Thought*] published a special issue on "The Japanese Spirit." This special issue referred largely to what we have just called the "Japanese reality." But why must the Japanese reality be a question of the Japanese "spirit"? It would not really be a problem if what is meant by spirit is an essence or nature. When the question is asked this way, "spirit" is what sets things in motion and gives life to things. Regardless of all other things, spirit here is that which breathes life into things, and so we talk of the "spirit of Christianity" or the "spirit of Greece" or the "spirit of capitalism." But here we already have a difficulty, for doesn't habitually anointing spirit the essence or nature of things unknowingly confuse the issue with a full-on spiritualism? But if that first use of the word "spirit" as a literary embellishment is taken seriously so that it becomes a logic, it has already become a spiritual logic. The "essence" of things becomes this sort of "spirit" due to its status as a concept of philosophical idealism.

Because Christianity, as a full "Christianity," is from the beginning a spiritual thing, saying that Christianity's essence is a spirit (*génie*) is probably not a problem. But as soon as we say something like the "Greek spirit (*génie*)" there is a whiff of a rather large and particular philosophical assumption. That is, is the Greek system of slavery a part of this Greek spirit? Does Greek slavery not run through the whole of the Greek spirit? As for the spirit of capitalism, if as Max Weber has argued, this spirit is found in Calvinism, it is probably fine to say that capitalism was a born of Protestant belief. But this method of christening capitalism's essence as "spirit" clearly has no simple meaning.

Naming the Japanese reality, specifically the Japanese spirit, or abstracting the Japanese present to be the Japanese spirit, is a symptom of surreptitiously mixing Japan with spiritualism. Because in general it does not deal with economic and political fields but mostly distilled "Japanese things" [日本的なるもの] from various cultural fields, *Shisō*'s special issue is more or less valid in calling "Japanese things" the Japanese spirit. But as a result, without explicitly doing so from the standpoint of Japanese spiritualism, without emphasizing this starting point, the very meaning of what is anointed the "Japanese spirit" is itself dubious. So even though the special issue contains many articles that participate in trying to deduce Japanese things or the Japanese spirit and discuss the particular circumstances of Japan, for critiquing Japanese spiritualism and the spiritualisms that lead to the various Japanisms, we must say that only Hirano Yoshitarō's contribution, "The Appearance and Social Meaning of Japanese Nationalism [国粋主義] in Mid-Meiji," even attempts this. This text is powerfully symptomatic of the very manner in which Japanese spiritualism's ideologues problematize Japanese things and the Japanese spirit without problematizing that manner itself. Therefore, the appearance of Hirano's text in Japan's premier intellectual journal is itself deeply meaningful.

Deducing Japanese-style things, or stressing the particular nature of Japanese conditions, can be problematized from two contradictory motives and interests. Showing the particularity of Japanese things alone is not conservative or reactionary. Such a project could in fact rather be a concrete, progressive one. But that said, placing particular emphasis on Japanese

A SCIENTIFIC CRITIQUE OF CULTURE

things without identifying one's motive—and simply imagining that one is proceeding in a purely faithful and practical manner of research [*Sachlich*], and is thus neither conservative nor reactionary—is simply not the case.

There are two fundamentally contradictory cases: one in which "Japanese things" are the explanatory principle for all others; and another where "Japanese things" are subject to concrete explanation by means of other principles. Beginning with the various proponents of "Asian particularism" and "socialism in one country," up to and including those opposed to the forced adoption of the metric system, this "Japanese thing" is not something to be concretely explained. Instead, it is thought that "Japanese things" themselves, now appearing as an abstract principle, become the principle of explanation. Japanese things here are not concrete links in a global chain.[1] Instead, "Japanese" is a prior, abstract thing that opposes the global. We can determine if stressing Japanese things is conservative or reactionary, and whether doing so is concretely progressive, by examining the relationship between Japanese things and global things. This is an important point.

Taking as a given that the Japanese current situation is isolated from and independent of the current global situation abstracts and subsumes the global question under the single principle of the Japanese situation. This is the logical trick of today's most representative social fascists and those who have renounced socialism for fascism [*tenkō fashisuto*] in that they share with the national fascists a method that abstracts the actual current situation of the Japanese present to become the Japanese spirit. Thus, first and foremost, national fascist philosophy returns to "Japanese spiritualism." This is why I take notice of the associations between the content and title of *Shisō*'s special issue and the social and national fascists. The principle and name given to Japan's so-called fascism, namely "the Japanese situation" or "the Japanese spirit" has not yet been systematically critiqued. But such a criticism is the urgent task of theorists today. Given the time, I would like to attempt a full critique of each (see chapter 6), but here, as a part of that larger problem, I would like to simply present the main points on how to criticize such an ideological phenomenon in general.

Of course so-called intrinsic or internal critique is not criticism. For example, when it comes to literary works, if criticism is limited to the author's subjective *idée*, "subjective" [*shukanteki*] in this case is often unhelpfully mashed up with the word "subjectively" [*shutaiteki*])—even including sympathy, antipathy, understanding, or structure—none of this constitutes actual criticism. Here explaining the techniques by which the idea is expressed is now a question of the "author" lurking behind the text, and it is not a substitute for a criticism to be presented before a general audience. In this meaning, then, for criticism to be objective and scientific it must fundamentally be thought of as an external critique.

In fact, people think of such external, objective, and scientific criticism as social criticism. Today everyone accepts that a theoretical criticism of context is insufficient, but many still have faith in a social criticism (especially a sociological criticism). As an example, Friche's[2] aesthetic sociology and Calverton's[3] sociological criticism are still widely taught today. As society here means historical society, unless society has somehow been abstracted out from history, we can say that social (and sociological) criticism includes historical and historiographical criticism. An example of this particular historical perspective is the critical method of Dilthey's hermeneutic philosophy. But as for "sociological" criticism or "hermeneutic" criticism, no matter how close it may come to a properly scientific ideological theory, in the end it is not an ideological or social scientific cultural theory. Therefore, we begin from the concept of ideological theory; that is, we criticize culture from the standpoint of a social scientific theory that requires a new confrontation between the previous internal critique and an external critique.

First, to the extent that the adjective "internal" has any essential meaning, it is evident that criticism must be an internal criticism. Accordingly, by somehow necessarily unifying external (outward facing and superficial) criticism with this internal criticism, we finally have something we can rightly call criticism. So, we should say that the function of a social scientific criticism is properly a unified internal and external criticism. But concretely analyzing the relationship between the internal and external is no simple thing.

Social science is the historical and social analysis of the contents of ideology. Which is to say, such an analysis must first ask how an actually existing ideological phenomenon is constrained by, and how it corresponds to, the relations of production. How is it constrained by passing through the given legal and political structures? Social control in a society in which monopoly capitalism has become imperialist is achieved through the

A SCIENTIFIC CRITIQUE OF CULTURE

mediation of ~~absolutism~~ born of capitalism's necessary ~~class nature~~. Furthermore, today's Japanese national fascism and other social fascisms are established from a capitalism whose feudal remnants have been quickly and *actively cultivated* and subsequently expressed in various legislative, administrative, and legal forms characteristic of capitalism's ~~advanced stage~~.

Second, of course, today's state of the relations of production, and the corresponding legal and political mechanisms, as well as their mutual interaction, are all links in a chain forged from the historical succession and development of each of those mechanisms. Because the current economic and political situation is achieved by means of the synthesis of the various results of past historical forms, fascism as fascist ideology is constrained by and corresponds to these materially and socially objective circumstances. Thus, the function of these objective circumstances is developed from the movement of history.[4] Clearly then, what is now necessary is to explain as cause and effect these terms "constrain" and "correspond." So here ideology is explained by means of the historical genesis, and transition and mechanisms, of the movement of this objective situation. In this sense, the function of an ideological theory lies in the explanation of that historical genesis and transition. Only through such an explanation can we see the particular characteristics of an ideology. For any ideology we must ask of both today and other historical periods to what extent it is, was, or is likely to be, influential; only then can we contrast and distinguish the characteristics of an ideology today from some specific ideology in the past. Moreover, at first glance, through this characterization, the content and structure of an ideology are nearly completely explained. (In, for example, explaining the contrasts between Hirano Yoshitarō's liberalism and Japanist nationalism; a good model of this kind of explanation can be found in Hirano's *Nihon shihonshugi shakai no kiko* [*The Social Mechanisms of Japanese Capitalism*].)

But explaining and characterizing the historical genesis and development of an ideology is not the same as explaining an actual state of affairs [事物], or of criticizing a state of affairs. Of course, in "explaining," it may be posited that it is natural for criticism or a critical standpoint to be part of this explanation, but this kind of criticism within an "explanation" is not yet a fully conscious, categorical criticism. Which is to say that at the stage of explanation, the high levels of internal ideology—that is, the object of criticism—is only made to correspond to the objective circumstances present in an external historical society, but these external circumstances and the internal ideology have not yet been unified into a fully concrete ideology. Thus, this stage is merely an external criticism.

Analysis of any given ideology (a particular thought, logic, emphasis), even one that includes naming the elements of its social mechanisms or its historical necessity, or the limitations given by its origin, must not stop at the stage of explanation of its genesis. For that leaves all sorts of further questions of whether the internal content of that ideology is widely accepted, or whether it contains truth; or of its veracity or falsehood; or again, of the popular circulation of its content, the level of faith in it, its explanatory power, or the possibility for consent. A logical or epistemological internal explanation of whether an ideology reflects (either distortedly or accurately) the objective structures of the current situation or truth is not given by a simple, external explanation of its historical and social emergence.[5]

By stopping at this level of historical and social explanation (the cause and effect of its constraints and correspondences), to the extent that it has not been consciously and explicitly tied to a logical or epistemological explanation, it cannot yet be said to be either historical materialist or social scientific, but rather is grounded in no more than the bourgeois "sociology" of intellectual sociology or cultural sociology. No matter how much such an explanation may stress its "class" nature, it is not able to make up for these defects. The problem of ideological criticism lies precisely in how the internal is taken up as a consequence of the external. Failure to do so means that this would not be a criticism of ideology, and that it would also fail as an explanation. Importantly, it is also insufficient to give a mere *account of* distortions and errors without also *accounting for* the emergence of those distortions and errors. We can only finally be satisfied when the particular demands of both explanation (external) and criticism (internal) achieve a mutual relationship.

If we are not constantly conscious of this mutual relation, we are presented with naive questions treated seriously like the Kantian question: Why does value emerge from mere existence? Whatever logic it may have, the fundamental negotiation of logic and history, which is the famous Leninist stage of philosophy, should naturally be applied to the "criticism" of ideology. Of course, we all recognize the error of methodism in

Deborinism,[6] and though that error stemmed from the logical "criticism" of ideology resulting in a rejection of Deborinism, the errors of Deborinism's methodism should not diminish the significance of the task of "criticism" itself. Logic and epistemology as weapons of a scientific criticism of ideologies right in front of us still have practical meaning. The direct and inseparable relation between "criticism" and "logic" was presented in categorical fashion by Lenin in *Materialism and Empirio-criticism* [1909, Jpn. 1927]. Unless such relations are centered on the problem of partisanship they can only be grasped obliquely.

(We should be careful to not limit "logic" to mean only science. Artistic, ethical, and indeed all cultural values, are also in this general sense logical.)

In short, as we proceed in the "explanation" of constraints and correspondences of the objective conditions of an ideology, we will in turn be addressing the logical truth and falsehood of that ideology.

In the very ideological nature of ideology it is discovered that the relation between the truth and falsehood of an ideology is organized by means of the historical, class, sectarian, and individual lived interests. The elements of historical and social structures (class, status, nation, region, and so on) are analyzed as representations of a particular set of shared interests of human life. From the standpoint of each of these elements of historical and social structures, the historical social totality, the objective nature, or the "objective present reality," is subjectively (the subject as mediated by practical activity) and partially reflected and reproduced. The constraints and the distorted nature of this reflection and reproduction (in the case of a mirror it is the refraction ratio of the surface and depth) are none other than this ideological nature that is the proper object to be criticized in an ideological "criticism."

In fact, here we have finally moved from "explanation" to "criticism." Moreover, at this stage we are able to not only give an account of errors, but also to account for them. This is not merely an explanation of cause and effect; it is already a logical explanation. But it is not yet a logical proof.

Ideology is not only that which is constrained by, opposed to, or a causal effect of the objective present reality. I have already stressed that ideology is also that which is a reflection or copy of that reality. But here I must also note that such a constrained object or reflected object possesses its own rules of development and maintains an independence from that objective present reality. By means of these unique rules of development, an ideological phenomenon and its logical function become a part of the contents of the objective, present reality and participate in the objective law of motion of objective reality itself, coming closer to a *refraction* than a direct *reflection*.[7] The problem now is the logical historical necessity (often this is insufficiently called a descent) that expresses this ideology as an ideology. Here we find the explanation of the emergence and foundation of the ideological nature of an ideology (its error relationship), but by genealogically returning to the origin by arranging the ideological characteristics of an ideology we can also use logic to digest and condense our explanation. In this way the logically condensed and digested object is demonstrated—the function of logic, with its generality and universality, is necessary to digest and condense the object—yet the proof that results from this process is not a pure, formal proof but is now a historical social (genealogical) explanation. The truth or error of contemporary ideologies thus returns to the classical origins of truth and falsehood. By means of this genealogy—the truth and falsehood of its truths and errors—its ideological nature is thus demonstrated. The "classical" has just this role in the problem of ideology. For example, quotations from Marx, Engels, Lenin, and others are only permissible in this sense of ideology (see chapter 2).

Arriving at the "internal" criticism from an "external" starting point involves the demonstration of the content of an ideology. This external/internal form of criticism can present proof or refutation of a given ideology. Here we must distinguish the particular characteristics of each of the three stages of ideological criticism offered so far. In other words, first, the antagonism between the truth of the present reality and the truths emphasized by an ideology (indicating the corresponding and constraining relationship between an ideology and objective reality). Second, criticism of the ideological system by comparison of the objective reality and an ideology's logical system (this corresponds to the explanation of objective reality as a reflected object or a model). Third, criticism of the use of categories (this is the stage of genealogical explanation as an indirect proof). In this way, the ideological nature of a given ideology, its truths and falsehoods, is given a logical persuasiveness against third parties (the social masses, supporters, or neutral parties) and opponents. This is an internal criticism as proof.

But as stated above, despite calling a simple demonstration a proof, such an "internal" criticism can never possess enough logical proof or persuasive

A SCIENTIFIC CRITIQUE OF CULTURE

power. What is necessary before a logical and persuasive proof can appear is a full accounting between this internal criticism and an external criticism (the emergence of the ideology, the emergence of its ideological nature, and genealogical demonstration of its ideological nature). Yet even in indicating the truth and errors, even while explaining the reason for the error, such a criticism would still lack explanatory and persuasive power. Such an unsympathetic criticism can never have any teeth. In this sense, the most concrete criticism, and the criticism that finally has a practical effect, should be first and foremost the object of criticism. The task of criticism is always to ask why something riddled with errors becomes so widespread. To dispel this contradiction in the specific ground, simple "explanation" or simple "criticism" are equally useless. If explanation is not developed to become criticism and also if criticism is not traced back to explanation, it is neither explanation nor criticism.

We must not overlook that taking on the task of this social scientific (historical, social, logical) criticism requires the majority of human knowledge and psychology. From its origin, social scientific criticism requires any and all of the humor and irony that may be derived from objective reality. This is because humor, irony, and the like grasp the dialectic in a literary way.[8] Marx's own particular techniques of expression hold great meaning even for the question of criticism. Further, surely many ironic phenomena—that is, logically nonsensical things that cannot be submitted to an internal criticism—may in fact be important objects of external criticism. It is not only because something has meaning that it is the object of criticism. Because something is nonsensical also makes it the object of criticism. The latter case is rather more plentiful as well.

Finally, we must note one more thing, especially when it comes to the criticism of nationalist ideology. We have already named the use of categories as the final stage of ideological criticism, but with Japanist ideology this stage possesses enormous usefulness and meaning. This is because, categorically speaking, there is no system as weak as Japanist ideology. The first weakness is that the preferred categories of Japanism (Japan, the people, Folkic spirit, agriculture, ~~The Way of the Gods, the gods, the emperor~~, and all its other various and sundry convenient terms) at first glance seem to be directly connected to the everyday lives of the masses. But, in fact, these categories have absolutely no connection to their actually lived everyday lives.⁹ Agricultural products or sericulture or animal husbandry themselves simply cannot exist if we remove the agricultural techniques and technologies of artificial selection. Furthermore, today there is no way to live a village life completely separated from industrial technology. Surely everyone would agree that it is impossible to live a life of production separated from productive technologies. Yet every one of the Japanese-style agrarian fundamentalists is an agrarian, antitechnology ideologue. The apostles of Japanese spiritualism and Pan-Asianism alike are all in complete agreement when it comes to an antitechnology stance. Speaking from the connection to actual practice, and certainly at least speaking from the standpoint of ideology, antitechnology marches under the flag of antimaterialism and appears as a shared movement of fascist reaction globally.

As for this antitechnologism, it can be chosen as a category *only because it is completely divorced from any actually existing technological life and practice*, which is why fascism can never escape from being a simple ideal object. This is also the reason that Japanist ideology terminates in mere literary phraseology.

But this antitechnologism is not limited to the ideologies of pure nationalism or even the wider field of fascism. It is also the final trump card of more or less fascistic capitalist and half-feudalist bourgeois philosophy. The weakness of the deployment of categories in Japanese nationalist ideology, it must be said, lies its use of the archaic (*Archaismus*). Because contemporary global categories (this is usually called imported Western thought) is rather inconvenient for constructing a nationalist system, great effort is made to use only archaic categories. These are nativist (*kokugaku*) and ~~absolutist~~ categories. But this archaism eventually derails and all nationalisms are restored to a distant, imported nationalistic thought. Sinologistic, Chinese-Buddhistic, primitive Buddhism-Brahmanistic, and others become categories.

The key feature of this categorical archaism is that its preferred categories stand in no logical or interpretive relationship to the categories used in actual, everyday life. Because having already ~~grown old and withered~~, because these categories only have philological meaning, they are reduced to performing ~~showy stunts~~ in the street. In world history and internationally, they are a plan for a coerced trade in incontrovertible notes.¹¹

A SCIENTIFIC CRITIQUE OF CULTURE

These weaknesses of Japanist ideology may be, and must be, criticized categorically.

For example, we should be aware that today much actual philological research is eventually linked up with these categories of archaism. Philology is essential to the study of Buddhism, Confucianism, and nativism. Philology and the archaic are a pair of arts that must be literarily restored. But if what emerges from that research is Buddhist philosophical concepts, or Confucian ethics, or Nativist legal studies, then it must be said that this exceeds the writ of philology. And thus, by means of this so-called hermeneutics (this is the aspirational name of philology), the logical distinction between the philological and actually existing categories will be prettily interpreted away.

A scientific criticism of culture should more or less follow the above plan. But because such an organized criticism is thought to be extremely hard to do in practice, even performing one piece of it must not be considered futile. Even one part, if it becomes scientific, and later even if common sense is incomplete, it may well still be possible that things more or less work out. On this point as well, our plan is decidedly practical.

Chapter Six

JAPANIST IDEOLOGY

Japanese Spiritualism, Japanese Agrarian Fundamentalism, Japanese Pan-Asianism

1

It appears as though some sprawling sentiment variously labeled Japanism, Orientalism, and Asianism governs contemporary Japanese life. We can see countless examples of social activities backed by this emotion everywhere; furthermore, such social expressions are reported in detail as if they have some extremely important meaning.

Our problem here is: To what extent is this sentiment grounded? Or alternatively, to what extent is it baseless? Whatever the answer, it is undeniable that this feeling is erupting everywhere, or at least is believed to be. If we consider this politically, which is to say, as this eruption is conceived of as political and can be politically exploited, it is undeniable that this problem is enormously important.

But emotions and the social activity built upon them remain sentimental and thus never escape the character and function of sentimentality, so that however widespread they may be, they never possess much rational value. Accordingly, if we consider this phenomenon theoretically, we must say that their importance is meager.

To be a good critic, such as when making human character an object of criticism, it is best to limit oneself to examining exemplary figures and to consciously neglect vulgar, gangster types [*yakuza*]. But this approach comes with limitations. No matter how meritless a person may be, when such a person achieves social influence in a time of crisis—either by accident or compelled by circumstances—no matter how foolish such a person may appear, regrettably, we must make them objects of theoretical analysis.

Thus Japanism, Orientalism, Asianism, and every other form of this sentimental phenomenon, even though they are not capable of being developed, are nonetheless subjected to our criticism. No matter how meaningfully these forms may declare themselves, in fact, when we consider their content, they are pure rubbish. Exposing this enormous yet banal tragicomedy, not just in Japan, but globally, is simultaneously a tedious yet urgent duty.

This is not the first time such a nationalism (or to be more accurate, an expansionistic nationalism) has flourished in Japan. Descended from the eighteenth- and nineteenth-century nativist movement [*kokugaku undō*] of the late Tokugawa period,[1] it first achieved prominence in the 1890s as a reaction to Meiji "Westernization." Next, using the Sino- and Russo-Japanese Wars as a pretext, this reactionary ideology expanded as it fought against the first instances of the proletarian movement, and later became more entrenched and insidious in reaction against the democracy movement surrounding World War I. This ideology has today merged with the crisis of Japanese capitalism as one link in the crisis of global capitalism, so that now with the trumpet blasts of the Manchurian Incident[2] and the Shanghai Incident,[3] it has spread out to touch every corner of contemporary Japan. Tracing it this way, we see that this eruption of nationalism is in fact an index of the crisis of this "nation" itself. It is simply the self-betrayal of nationalism by its own contradictory essence. This is the universal fate of all reactionary ideology. (There is a brief sketch of this nationalist phenomenon by Sakamoto Sanzen. See "Japanist Thought, an Exposé" in *Yuibutsuron kenkyū*, April 1934).

But the prodigious production and eruption of Japanism, Orientalism, Asianism and all the other "Nippon" ideologies—if you pronounce these characters as "Nihon" it is considered dangerous thought—into the popular, literary, and scientific worlds really belongs to just the last two or three years. It has developed alongside the establishment of Hitler's dictatorship in Germany, the nationalist movement in Austria, Mussolini's anti-Austrian actions, Roosevelt's unprecedented control of national production in the United States, the establishment of Manchukuo and the imposition of the [puppet] emperor [Pu Yi], and the endless and myriad muscular nationalist movements in our beloved Japanese Empire. It was only under these general global conditions that this recent and sensationalistic nationalism was able to achieve such dominance in Japan. Of course, aligning our august national movement alongside these international examples will upset some Japanese nationalists—those sorts who declare "Japanism is different; it is not Western fascism"—but the truth is not made for the comfort of a few people.

2

It is widely believed that Japan is at an impasse. While business leaders and some liberals may disagree, it appears that this impasse is also giving rise to various nationalist movements. Yet even if there is in fact no impasse, the emergence of these nationalist movements themselves creates an impasse. So, what is the cause of all this? These days the word "emergency" has lost its magical effects, but even if it had not, it would still be an inadequate word to explain the impasse. For if we inquire into the nature of such an "emergency" we find that its cause is the constant clamor of declaring an "emergency" itself.

For our Japanists it hardly matters what objective or theoretical analyses might be given to explain the emergency. Their only concern is that any explanation be easily grasped by the masses. For example, they claim that the impasse comes from the masses "not grasping the essence of the Japanese spirit" (see Takasu Hojirō, "Outline of the Japanese Spirit," *Economic Affairs*, March 1934). This may seem a plausible explanation as the prime minister and the Diet are also saying the same thing, but then the prime minister himself was called upon to explain the Japanese spirit in the House of Peers. But in any event, it is said that Japan's crisis is rooted in the Japanese people not grasping the essence of the Japanese spirit. In the same way it is said that the Chinese Communist problem and the Shanghai riots are likewise caused by those who fail to grasp the Chinese spirit.

So, what is the essence of the Japanese spirit? According to Takasu Hojirō, the "elements" of the Japanese spirit are that it is "life-creationistic," "centered and unwavering," "excels in cohesion and harmony," that it "optimistically progresses and expands," and "stresses the practice and actualization of The Way." It is imagined to encompass everything that is good. But as fine as these components may be, is this not also rather bizarre? It is impossible to know what is meant by life-creationistic. To take an example from philosophy, clearly Bergson's metaphysics would qualify; centered and unwavering would describe English political consciousness; German scholarship is a model of a spirit of cohesion and harmony; and US naval design or the "The Yankee Girl"[4] are wonderful examples of optimistic progress and expansion. Further, is not a focus on "the practice and actualization of the Way" the very spirit of Soviet Russia? It would be intolerable if the Japanese spirit was composed of all these foreign spirits.

So here Takasu delivers a coup de grace to these foreign anxieties by stating the Japanese spirit is "a consciousness of the Japanese national essence [*kokutai*]." It is unfortunate he didn't just say so from the start. For consciousness—of the national essence or indeed of anything—is not something one should be forced to accept or be duped into by some con artist. Achieving consciousness of the Japanese national essence is none other than a scientific knowledge of the actual history of Japan. Do Takasu and his ilk have some special "Japanistic" historical method? If so, they have a duty to the public and the world to make it clear.

Furthermore, it is unclear to me what motivation Itō Shōshin, the believer of "selfless love," had in penning his essay "The Essence of the Japanese Spirit" in *Yūben* [*Rhetoric*]. When we examine Itō's version, the Japanese spirit corresponds to a "self" called Japan, and that somehow selfless love and Japan's self-love become the "Japanese spirit," which "is a spirit that truly loves the nation of Japan, and by unifying nationalism and internationalism in a single Way, it both individually and nationally strives to develop Japan as a truly good nation in the world." As Itō himself says, this is not a Way only for the Japanese; it is a "universal way," open to Americans as Americans or Russians as Russians. Of course, this is exactly what one must say from the standpoint of selfless love. But just what is there in the standpoint of selfless love that requires taking up the Japanese spirit as a theme at all?[5] This is the part we don't understand. Could it be that once Japan has subjugated the entire world it will be revealed that the occult origin of selfless love was the Japanese spirit all along?

Yet, for these people, it does not appear that Japan is subjugating the world. In fact, according to Gakushūin professor Kihira Masami, the Japanese spirit flows forth from the spirit of "union and harmony with others" (see *A Consideration of the Japanese Spirit*). Today, as the bourgeois nations—the Great Powers—are unable to enact their colonial policies that still dream of carving up China, it has become common sense in foreign policy circles that "union" with others does not go hand in hand with "harmony." So obviously Kihira's words absolutely cannot mean Japan's subjugation of the world, for Kihira also states in his book that Japanese are a "peace"-loving people: in contrast to the Western system of "plunder" [とり やり] Japan practices "exchange" [やりとり]. According to Itō, this is another way that the Japanese can demonstrate their selflessness; clearly there can be no doubt that the Japanese people love their neighbors, love their neighboring countries. Indeed, just look at their friendship with China and Manchukuo!

What is it that governs the professor's "Japanese spirt" then? Of course, it has already been stated. It is the "self-consciousness of the Japanese people"—"I am Japanese!!" (Kihira, *The Japanese Spirit*). He continues, "The Japanese spirit cannot be defined" for "nothing can simply define the content of a three-thousand-year history" (*A Consideration*). Indeed. But there is a more fundamental issue: How is this three-thousand-year history (?) to be investigated? Unfortunately, we vulgar Japanese are still unable to understand this kind of Kihirian (?) Hegelian philosophy of history, so unless he can give us a scientific examination of that actual history, it is likely that this "three-thousand year-history" will indeed be most "simply defined."

Kinkei Gakuin professor Yasuoka Shōtoku's words appear to give another clue to this sense of Japanese history: "The true fount of the spirit of the Japanese people [*minzoku*] is found in the three imperial treasures; it shines with wisdom from the heart of the pure and clear mirror, it courageously wields the sword of righteousness, and encompasses the virtue of the cut jewel. Finally, it is the effort to unify the gods and the people and subsume the entire world within oneself." It is easy to understand why such a poetic and therefore abstract psychological depiction of Japanism is so easily amenable to the fascist new bureaucrats. But to put it bluntly, this is not history. This is nothing more than moral didacticism and flowery prose. Worse, even as moral didacticism and flowery prose it is rather primitive.

In truth, because this infantile literature is in no way separate from moral laws, it is in fact myth. According to Yasuoka, the three imperial treasures—mirror, sword, and jewel—represent wisdom, morality, and courage. Furthermore, the land of Japan is not merely that of natural geography; "The

JAPANIST IDEOLOGY

Eight Great Islands" were born from the eyes of the "nation-birthing gods" and so the "emperor and the Japanese people" relate to each other as older and younger brothers. Thus, the method of recognition of Japanese history is obviously "mythic," and the Japanese spirit is received as something eternally stopped in the mythic stage. The Japanese spirit never progresses or develops and we are forced to conclude that it is in fact the enemy of progress and development.

Accordingly, because "self-recognition as Japanese" is not equipped with any tools to deal with contemporary conditions, we can see it is no easy thing to actually practice such a consciousness. Yet it appears there may be a slightly more scientific shortcut to understanding the Japanese spirit. Professor Kakunoki Inshin calls it "neo-Japanism" (see *Neo-Japanism and the Philosophy of History*). The professor proves that it is not impossible to achieve a Japanese spirit. He believes that the spirit is present in the individual's "intentions." This individual-as-intentionality is a system produced by spatial, climatic, and regional differences, and so different national soils are able to develop various, particular national spirits. Thus, there is in Japan a unique Japanese spirit. Indeed, obviously. But as to whether the Japanese actually have such a spirit, whether such a "Japanese spirit" even exists at all, isn't this less a proof than a posited, self-evident principle?

Assuming for the moment that a spirit of the Japanese people has emerged, the problem remains just what sort of people the Japanese are. Incidentally, the professor attempts to make that answer clear by means of his "neo-Japanist" philosophy of history. The result of the professor's research is as follows: the natural world is the world of "events" [*dekigoto*] and the historical world is the world of "human actions" [*dekashigoto*]. The world of "human actions" is thus the world of actions, subjectivity, individuality, and heart [*kokoro*]. Therefore history must be a "consciousness resting upon subjectivity (spirit), action, and psychology [*kokoro*]." It seems his neo-Japanist philosophy of history hardly differs from what in the West is called "spiritualism" (?) [*yuishin shikan*]. Apparently then, the "neo" of this neo-Japanism is its Western flavor, and the "Japanism" is simply using *yamatokotoba*[6] so that in place of *Geschehen* we have *dekigoto*, and instead of *Tat* or *Tatsache*, we get *dekashigoto*.

But such a spiritualism is rather incoherent. The all-important individual-as-Japanese spirit is constructed by means of differences in material things such as space, climate, and geography, which is to say it appears to be determined by both "human action" and "events." In the West such a philosophy of history is not called neo-Japanism but rather "geographical materialism."

What is truly bizarre here, and what is totally unexplained, is just how this "Japanese spirit" built from this neo-Japanism, which is so close to Western geographical materialism, suddenly becomes an unchanging principle of life from when the first ~~emperor~~ [*tennō*] became the ~~sovereign~~, complete with the ultimate value being "dying in the shadow of the emperor [*taikun*]," and its motto found in the Chinese literati's much-loved couplet: "righteousness is the relation of lord to subject; human feeling is the relation of father to son." And so thusly has Kakonoki finally clarified (!) the "neo" of his neo-Japanism.

3

Above we have tried to appreciate various opinions of "the Japanese spirit." But from what we understand so far, this is not the Japanese spirit, but rather a Japanese spiritualism, and that spiritualism is theoretically bankrupt and incoherent. Further, we must acknowledge that there is to be no answer to the question of the Japanese spirit coming from the various Japanese spiritualisms. Despite the Ministry of Education's Research Institute for the Japanese Spirit, the journal *Culture and the Japanese Spirit*, and the Society for the Japanese Spirit's house publication *The Japanese Spirit*, we must admit the worthlessness of examining the Japanese spirit according to Japanese spiritualism. Japanese spiritualism then is not some true enunciation, but more the performance of a ventriloquist [*Bauchredner*].

So, is there perhaps a way of approaching the Japanese spirit from a different direction, one less (?) spiritualist? Say, for example, the case of agrarian fundamentalism?

The founder of the "patriotic academy" Aikyōjuku, Tachibana Kōzaburō, in his *Studies of the Agrarian Village* [*Nōsongaku*] seeks to explain Japan's unique economic, political, and social system, the "national characteristics of Japanese society" and "the characteristics of the rural village." To wit, Japan is not a "capitalist nation" but has instead an agrarian national essence [*nōson kokushitsu*]. For Tachibana, Marx did not know that agriculture and industry had different essences—that is organic and inorganic objects—and so Marx made a fundamental error when he treated agriculture, which takes organic things as its object, and industry, which deals with inorganic things, from the same perspective. According to Tachibana, because industry concerns dead "material," it can deal with them mechanistically, but the lifestyle of agriculture deals with living plants and livestock and so a spiritual aspect is essential.

Thus, for Tachibana the mechanization of agriculture is not revolution, but destruction. Even if some cultivation can be mechanized, the planting of rice seedlings cannot. This means that Marx's imagined industrial agriculture came from his ignorance of agriculture itself. (For Tachibana, this is because Marx only lived in London and Paris and never in a farming village.) According to Tachibana, this lack of contact with the farming villages meant Marx mistakenly ascribed the development of large farms in England and elsewhere to farming villages being destroyed by market competition and not, in fact, destroyed by the mechanization of agriculture.

This is especially true in Japan where because rice is the necessary staple of the Japanese, and rice is restricted to paddy fields where it is impossible to introduce tractors; therefore, for Tachibana, this fact alone shows that Japanese agriculture cannot be mechanized. Thus, there will never be an "industrial management of agriculture" in Japan, and the "actual reality" will be "the strength of the small farms." (We should note there is also the "actual reality" of embarrassed Japanese officials when a Soviet audience viewing a government-produced propaganda film burst out in laughter at scenes of planting rice seedlings by hand.)

From here Tachibana continues to say that "it is not industry that is subjected to the definitive, destructive, and crushing blows of capitalist pathologies... nor is it wage labor; ... it is the farmers of the agricultural villages. Therefore, if we wish to liberate our entire nation's socioeconomic structure from capitalist destruction, we must first, more than anything, save agrarian society." Here we have Tachibana's "fundamental thesis." Tachibana continues to say that urban society is an intellectual assemblage, but the agrarian village is a spiritual one, an assemblage in which the emotions of veneration of ancestors, nature worship, and reverence for everyday things are essential aspects. For Tachibana, a "welfare-ist society" built upon a "philosophy of the soil" that respects the land and nature must be the ideal toward which contemporary Japan must strive.

Here again we see that Tachibana's agrarian studies and agrarianism, which somehow and at great pains takes off from the "actual reality" of contemporary Japanese economics and politics, is nothing but one more example of the above "spiritualist" Japanese spiritualism. If we ask why agriculture is so great that it can become the singular principle capable of giving birth to Japanese agrarian fundamentalism, the answer is simply that agriculture and the rural village is originally "Japanese" in contrast to the "un-Japanese" quality of industry and cities, that agriculture is exquisitely "spiritual" in its essence. The rest of the explanation of agriculture and the rural village is merely an excuse and an apology for this original essence.

In contrast to Tachibana's agrarianism, which is literally a "farming village studies," when we turn to Gondō Seikyō, we get a "system studies." For Gondō, in *Jichi minpan* [A people's guide to self-rule], the particularity of Japan is first that it is a nation of "the communion of shrines and grains" [*shashoku taitō*].[7] Which is to say, the shrine indicates the gods of the land, and grains means rice ears, so the worship of the "shrine and grains" is the worship of the soil, and this is the first characteristic of Japan. Therefore "agriculture is the great foundation of the universe."

Thus, the agrarian-based society of Japan inevitably gave birth to an agrarian fundamentalist system. According to Gondō, this basis underwent a process of progressive recurrence as customs became everyday practices, practices became rituals, and rituals became a system and a code of conduct—and these moral and ritualistic practices of nature [道徳的成俗[8]] are its foundation. The condition whereby "hunger and thirst are the persistent lot of men and women; life, death, poverty, and pain are constant hardships, is from the beginning, the sign of the workings of nature, a sign that without exhortation or punishment one may be relieved of this lot and these hardships," for "the universe" is governed by natural, self-governance. As Japan's form has been from the beginning built from this naturalistic code of conduct, the ideology of autonomy becomes the final characteristic of Japan. So, because agriculture is the great foundation of the universe, communal autonomy traces back to the farm village. In the words of the recent Cabinet, the farm village is self-sufficient and self-renewing.

But we must pay attention to another point here. This agrarian fundamentalist autonomy in Gondō's "system studies" differs from other factions of Japanism in that it is definitively not an absolutist ideology [*zettaiseishugi*]. Emperor Uda[9] is reported to have said to Fujiwara Mototsune, "You are the subject of gods and the grains; you are not my subject." This is precisely the true form of autonomy. Compare this with the view that statism is inevitable given the inescapable conflict between public and private interests. According to Gondō, for the common Japanists in Japan today, such as those Japanist bureaucrats who wish to "reform" the Peace Preservation Law[10] into a punitive system, it is precisely that kind of bureaucratic, political Japanism that most harms Japan's original, communal autonomy. Gondō believes that the current impasse in Japan traces back to and is the fault of the bureaucratism growing out of the Meiji Ishin [Meiji Revolution 1868]. If this is the case, Gondō's *Jichi minpan* represents a slight departure from today's fascist context. Gondō apparently was prepared for his thought to be suppressed which only shows he clearly understood the implications of his position.

Gondō's thought is clearly not dangerous or evil. His political slogans are "Return to 'the model of the gods and the grains;'" make "the communal organization of the household" the "standard." But when it comes to socialism or communism (for him Marx was a socialist, not a communist), or when he is calling for some political policy, he states that any given people "can only follow their own customs and national emotions" (518). That is why an indicted rightwing defendant criticized Gondō, claiming he couldn't stand him. Gondō's thought is neither dangerous nor evil; indeed, it is rather quite healthy and good. Which is to say, he believes that today, rather than reforming the legal system, the more pressing problem lies in the renewal of people's hearts (reformation), because if people's hearts become responsive, any bad law or system can be developed along better paths. If, for example, landlords and tenants both reflected on this, they would have to reject practices based on coercion—for Gondō, a "recurrence" of the communal practices is what is important. The above recounts Gondō's agrarianism as a systems study, the character of Japan, and therefore the character of the Japanese spirit. Be that as it may, we must note that it is not another example of the Japanese spiritualism we have looked at so far. Even his idealist call for a recurrence of a communal code of conduct through the "reform of peoples' hearts" is not another instance of our previous practitioners of "Japanese spiritualism."

Yet, seen from a broader perspective this is in no way a good sign. Indeed, Gondō may be a scholar of systems, but he thinks exclusively in nationalist categories, so that should there appear on the scene a nationalist scholar of ethics or a nationalist historian who was to pursue nearly the same goals, one who has embraced philosophical categories, Gondō's problem would once again become an ideology of the "Japanese spirit." The only reason Gondō does not foreground characteristics of Japanese spiritualism is because he has not yet embraced the concept of absolute spirit (*Geist*) so useful in Japan today.

(As such it would be necessary to redo this analysis for Tōdai ethics professor Watsuji Tetsurō, who takes up these themes in *The Essence of Merchants*, *A History of the Japanese Spirit*, *National Morality*, and *Ethics*, and for Hiroshima Polytechnic University's Nishi Shin'ichirō in *National Morality* and *Treatise on National Morality and Filial Piety*, as well as Tōdai history professor Hiraizumi Noboru's *The Kenmu Reforms* and *The German Spirit*.)

4

It would appear from the perspective of either Japanese spiritualist philosophy or Japanese agrarianism, when compared with other nations and other peoples, that the defining trait of the Japanese spirit is its superiority over all others. Tentatively, all Japanisms may be reduced to a Japanese spiritualism. But what this Japanese spirit—meaning the essence of Japan—actually is, has not been theoretically or scientifically explained. This is as expected, for according to the Japanists, from the first the Japanese spirit, or "Japan" itself, is not an object to be explained. Rather it is nothing more than a method or a principle arbitrarily deployed so that all other objects are explained in terms of it.

Yet considered with even the tiniest bit of common sense, elevating the concrete geographical, historical, and social thing called "Japan" to a philosophical principle is bizarre. Indeed, if there were a philosophy of "Venus-ism" or "Daffodil-ism" no one would take it seriously right from the start.

Yet Japanism is thought to have no content and at the same time, to the contrary, any and all content can be arbitrarily ascribed to it. Those like Minoda Muneki[11] have recently in fact adequately demonstrated this point: "The way of the gods [*kaminagara no michi*] is a teaching that encompasses the teachings of past and present, East and West. It is the knowledge of all knowledge. Buddhism, Confucianism, Christianity, the entirety of Greek philosophy, early modern science, democracy, Marxism, fascism, national socialism, and the rest are all already subsumed within it" ("A Spiritual and Scientific Critique of Japanism," *Economic Affairs*, March 1934). Minoda is not making a joke about this terrifying principle called "Japan." He is simply savoring the deliciousness of the thought and emotions of Japanism.

Because Japanism has this ability to contain such an unlimited wealth of contents, it cannot be tidied up with one or two philosophical principles. Japanists themselves worry that an infinite variety of principles can be formed. This is a real concern. Aikawa Takaharu laments this very fact when he says, "What strikes us ... is why we who all share the same philosophy that takes Japan as the standard of thought are repeatedly split into so many factions" ("The Pure Japanist Movement and National Socialism," *Economic Affairs*, March 1934). As this is also a world with multiple gold standards, is it not too much to wish that the thinking around the Japan standard would not also be convertible into countless denominations? And finally, Professor Matsunaga Zai, too, is skeptical in the face of this problem: "The discipline of the content of Japanism is something to be organized in the future; currently we do not have the capabilities or the resources to do so" (*Outline of Japanist Philosophy,* [1933]).

Yet, what luck, Japanism does not stop at mere Japanism; Japanism has developed to become Orientalism (*tōyōshugi*) and Asianism (*ajiashugi*). This is not your standard Asianism—this Asianism is a developed form of Japanism. In other words this is Japanist Asianism.

Asianism's strength would appear to be that which begins from the reality [*genjitsu*] of Asia. Lord Lytton[12] is not for these purposes an Asianist, so, ultimately, he is unable to fully cognize this Asian reality. In contrast, there is plenipotentiary Matsuoka Yōsuke, who without giving the slightest outline of his thinking called for the abolition of political parties, but by virtue of being an Asianist, Matsuoka surely has no trouble understanding the Asian reality.

Professor Ōkawa Shūmei,[13] who until the May 15 Incident[14] was head of the East Asian Economic Survey Bureau, treats East and West as absolutely antagonistic objects. He states that without this conflict there would have been no history of humanity. "The true meaning of the words 'world history' is the summation of the history of conflict and competition between East and West" ("Asia, Europe, Japan"). But since the Great War in Europe, an "auspicious sign of revival" has emerged for an Asia so far ruled by the "whites" of Europe. But from here on, Asia will rule the world. Ōkawa finds proof of his vision in the anti-European rebellions in Egypt, China, India, and Indochina.

He further states that "on the surface these rebellions are political and economic" but also that the important point is that "what is running deep within is a total spiritual [rebellion]." Why is the form of these Asian rebellions spiritual? The answer is quite simple. He states: "It springs forth from the will of the soul of an awakened Asia." So, we understand from this that within the conflict of East and West there is the West that acts only through political and economic means, and against this there is Asia that opposes it with a spiritual soul. The West is materialism [*busshitsushugi*] (materialism [*yuibutusron*] or consumptionism [*gyūinboshokushugi*]), but the East is spiritualism. Such is the "reality" of Asia.

For the record, General Araki Sadao offers this apologist justification for Japan's conquest of Manchuria: "Now, when we consider the Manchurian problem, we must readily acknowledge it is a mistake to see it as a question of vested interests or a [geopolitical] lifeline [for Japan]. . . . So how should we view the Manchurian problem? It was the importation of Western materialism that degraded the Chinese people (could he mean Zhang Xueliang's[15] opium?), and ultimately so offended the Japanese spirit and Japanese morality that it sparked a response" (*Address to the Japanese People*). Why was Manchuria seen as Japan's lifeline? And why were the island mandates of the South Pacific Japan's "lifeline in the sea?" Because once upon a time the military itself expounded such "materialistic" propaganda. Clearly, Manchuria is not the West but the East, and so its soul announces the "proclamation of the Imperial Way" and "Exaltation of the National Morality" and "Establishment of the Imperial Way and Paradise," thus the Manchurian Incident is a spiritual one.

Kita Ikki, the inspiration of the young officers revolutionary movement, had already in 1919 declared as much in Shanghai; he scolds his compatriots with "Our seven hundred million comrades in China and India have no path to independence without our leadership and protection. . . . For those saddened by the deplorable state of our neighboring countries with their certain ill futures, how can they be satisfied with a basic socialism that clings to pacifism?" (*Nihon kaizō hōan taikō* [A plan for the reorganization of Japan, 1919]).[16] Kita's boisterous Asianism, which sutures chivalrous morality to a missionary zeal, is to its core Asianist, Orientalist—that is, spiritualist. He continues, "By unfurling the flag of our Asian union and seizing control of the inevitable world organization, we will proclaim the

Imperial Way to all the children of Buddha across the four seas, becoming the model of leadership for East and West."[17]

And so the crux of it all: As Asia is spiritual and thus Asianism is spiritualism, a true Asianism is nothing but the expansion of Japanese spiritualism. This is the true essence of Japanese Asianism. But obviously Japan is not the whole of Asia, so how is this Japanese spiritualism to be expanded to Japanese Asianism? Again the answer is extremely simple: Japan itself is to be expanded so that it becomes the East itself. Japan is to become the leader of an Asian league and through this embark on the subjugation of the world. This is the strategy and philosophy of our Greater Asianism. Asianism is based on spirit, and once we have come this far, it doesn't matter what material energy this form may take.

According to the economics professor Nozoe Shigetsugu there is a Turanian race that includes the Tungus, Mongols, Turkish Tartars, Ugric [Finns], and Samoyeds, as well as the proto-Turanian northern Chinese and Bulgans. The Turanian genealogy's homeland is Asia, the Middle East, Scandinavia, and so on—nearly the entirety of Eurasia (Pan-Turanianism and an Economic Bloc). Thus, against the whites who oppress our Turanianism, Pan-Turanianism aims to unify them and recover the ancestral homeland. For Nozoe, the Sino- and Russo-Japanese Wars and the Manchurian Incident are no less than Turanianism's declaration of war against the Slavs. Watsuji Tetsurō had previously said that the Sino and Russo-Japanese Wars were an exaltation of the Japanese spirit, but compared to Nozoe, it must be said Watsuji is on a much smaller, less ambitious scale.

Asian spiritualism is thus to be understood as the aggressive expansion of Japanese spiritualism. But what is its relation to Japanese agrarian fundamentalism? According to Asian spiritualism, the answer appears to be simply that Asian reality itself is agrarianism. In his *On the Establishment of the New Orient*, the "orientalist" Kuchita Yasunobu holds that the East (*tōyō*) begins with the family system in which extremely strong patriarchal social relations remain. For example, a relation of debt and gratitude between landlord and tenant,[18] like the *gemeinschaft* social structure studied by Tönnies, remains powerful. As such, the appropriate social organization is not socialism but "communalism" [*kyōdōshugi*]. Economically this would mean cooperatives or a cooperative movement (collaborative movement); politically it means autonomy, and culturally it means spiritualism.

For Kuchita, socialism must wait for the maturation of the individual, and only after that maturation may it emerge. But, [he warns], "In the East, individualism has not matured. The majority have stopped at the nonindividualistic stage of personality," and so a single leap into socialism is absolutely impossible. But the farmers stuck in the nonindividualist personality of the East, may "effortlessly don the mantle of communalism [*kyōdōshugi*]." Combined with Tachibana's farmer liberation and Gondō's rural self-rule, this a call for a farming village community [*nōson kyōdōtai*].

Of course, with its patriarchy and semifeudal system of agriculture, it is clearly true that the East or Asia still today possesses aspects of the so-called Asiatic Mode of Production. To ignore this fact makes it impossible to understand the form of economic, political, or cultural movements in the East. But if the so-called Asiatic Mode of Production is not in fact limited to Asia, then there is no reason to label it the Eastern or Asian mode of production itself. And if the present mode of production in Asia does not necessarily reduce to mean the "Asiatic" Mode of Production, it would further mean that the actual mode of production in Asia need not necessarily stop at the Asiatic Mode of Production.

Yet, for Kuchita it seems that the Asiatic Mode of Production is the immutable mode of production of the East. But why is this necessary? To put it simply, the concepts of "the complete and total people" and "harmonious national society" that appear in Tachibana's *Farm Village Studies* are merely a philosophy of "totality" à la Othmar Spann,[19] and that the "cooperative movements" in the villages invariably have an unconditional preference for *gemeinshcaft* social forms. But why must the "cooperative movement" be understood in terms of this confused European fascist philosophy? The answer is simply that this cooperative movement corresponds to the "Imperial Way" that "simultaneously rejects capitalism and Marxism." Here we have the "spirit" and "spiritual core" of every Asianism and every Japanism.

A final word:

Much like the meaningless varieties of fascist political factions, seen from a larger perspective, whatever spiritualist organization may be built, whatever agrarianism might be organized, makes no difference. What matters is that any actual thought or culture must be able to be translated globally within a broader meaning. If the categories of a nation's or a people's thought and culture cannot be translated as categories, they are not true. Indeed, just as true literature is "world literature," if a theory or a philosophy may only be understood by one people or one nation's citizens it is without exception a fraud. Further, even for those people and those citizens themselves, such thought and culture remain alienated; it is not thought or culture, but complete barbarism. (On this point see chapters 2 and 5.)

(Once again, it is necessary to take up the various forms of "national socialism" and "socialism in one country." If the totality cannot be explained from the economic base it is simply not true. Here I have only examined and classified sources close at hand.)

Chapter Seven

JAPANESE ETHICS AND ANTHROPOLOGY

An Analysis of the Social Meaning of
Watsuji Tetsurō's Ethics

The title of Tokyo Imperial University professor Watsuji Tetsurō's *Ethics as Anthropology* expresses not only the thrust of the professor's ethics and ethical thought but also his cultural and historical theory. Here we do not want to offer an introduction or a criticism of that text. Nor will we offer an examination of his thought more generally. Here, working from the contents of this "ethics" itself, built as it is upon a new, "academic" system, we simply wish to specify what significance Watsuji's theory might have for various aspects of the current situation in Japan.

Watsuji's ethics differs from previous, and rather demagogic, work in academic and moral thought by ethics scholars and moral training specialists. Which is to say, Watsuji's ethics exists at a relatively high academic level. And as it is also built upon an original intellectual foundation, it can serve as a foundation for current reactionary powers and their desire for a relatively elevated standard of reactionary culture. From academic research offices to more vulgar semi "academic" journals, the fans and consumers of this kind of "ethics" will probably be many. From now on, imitators of this ethics will be Watsuji's intellectual disciples, and *Ethics as Anthropology* will be an essential text. Compared with Professor Nishi Shin'ichirō's *Eastern Ethics* [*Tōyō rinri*, 1934], which uses only Eastern terms and quotations, and whose logic itself appears therefore to be Eastern, Watsuji's work is decidedly global and international. But the objective uses and significance of what both of these two professors are aiming at are largely the same. Still, Watsuji's more or less modern ethics is likely better suited than Nishi's for proclaiming the superiority of Eastern ethics to the world.

Watsuji's new foundation for ethics uses a clearly modern philosophical method. As we will examine this method a bit later, we can start by looking at the most immediate characteristics. At its most broad and basic, Watsuji's "academic" analysis of ethics begins by taking the meanings of ethical texts and terms as the key clues. As an example, for the question *What is ethics* [*rinri*]? Watsuji asks: What is this word *rin* and what is this word *ri*, as well as what is the result when we combine the two into *rinri*? The same method whereby we cannot understand the terms without going down the path of textual and philological explication applies to the words for "human" [*nin-gen*] or "being" [*son-zai*]. But we cannot casually accept his textual interpretation, and at the same time cannot ignore it either because, quite frankly, nearly all the marks of Watsuji's philosophical methods appear here in this textual method. No one with a more or less empirical or theoretical brain would think one can explain the actual thing indicated by a word simply by explaining the meaning of the word. In fact, we note that to do so would mean that this kind of textual interpretation is akin to a Buddhist priest or monk who believes it possible to explain social phenomenon through the interpretation of a sutra. Further, this kind of textual interpretation isn't even a literal one.

The true authority of textual interpretation comes from hermeneutics. In other words, according to hermeneutics a text expresses the idea (*idée*)—the spirit, the experience, and the way of life of the individual, the peoples—of the era that produced it; conveniently class seems to be less of an issue here. Thus through hermeneutics, that is by reversing the process and passing through these objective signs that have been inscribed or written down, we can gain access to the historical meaning of, for instance, the idea, spirit, experience, lifestyle of the individual, peoples, eras (and so forth) behind the texts. Of course, in concerning itself with historical materials and historical accounts, hermeneutics is a scientific part of the historical method, so hermeneutics is most trustworthy when reading on old document. Which is why this discipline originated and then developed for reading the Bible, and in the early modern period for Greek philosophy. In other words, because the issue in those cases was the old documents themselves, it was natural that the resolution of the problem would be textual and philological.

The problem comes when hermeneutics doesn't stop with one scientific element of the historical method—the textual interpretation of old texts—but instead comes to govern the whole of the historical method, when the authority and jurisdiction of hermeneutic interpretation is expanded, becoming independent of the general challenges of historical accounts, until, in an instant, the hermeneutic method becomes philosophy itself. Such is the present case whereby hermeneutics becomes the underlying procedure for the academic study of ethics. We have real doubts as to where the authority of textual interpretation comes from in this case.

This faith in hermeneutics is not limited to Watsuji. No one, ourselves included, thinks words are artificial or natural or divine. The representation of a people's or a nation's (and we need class here, too), or a region's history of human society is limited to their representation in language. Thus it is only by looking at language that we can see the lifestyles of the people who produced it. But we have real doubts that looking at language alone is itself sufficient to express a way of life.

According to Watsuji, however, language is the ultimate and fundamental characteristic. In Greek or Indian or Chinese thought, language is what distinguishes humans from animals, and so language shows us what is fundamentally human. Viewed this way there is nothing strange in claiming that the textual interpretation of things, as long as those things belong to human society, is the fundamental method of analysis.

We will get to hermeneutics' fundamental weak point or sleight of hand later. Our distrust here comes from how hermeneutics is explained and accepted as if it were a proof or had explanatory powers. Of course, even if Japanese and Chinese have invented the word *rinri* [ethics], the result of analyzing the word *rinri* itself is no proof that the word ethics describes the relationship of things themselves. Indeed, it would not be a proof of an actual ethical relationship unless the nature of the relations themselves were already "ethical"—not in this [hermeneutic] Japanese language sense, but as translated internationally. But with Watsuji, the scope of textual interpretation for explaining ethics as an ethical relationship—for Watsuji this means an active relation between individuals—is limited to analyzing the word *rinri* as a single citation, a single intuitive representation. Such hermeneutic interpretation of this representation is neither a proof of an ethical relationship nor an explanation of any particular method at all. This is because there is a theoretical gap here. The erasure of this theoretical gap with intuition by these so-called interpreters is theoretically significant.

As long as one accepts the authority of hermeneutics to be the entirety of scientific theory—that is, to the extent that one accepts the hermeneutic method in ethics, and that ethics begins with the textual interpretation of "ethics," "human," and "being"—it is not possible to utter one complaint. From the beginning, this ethics is not intended to prove or explain anything at all, but only to interpret the Japanese lifestyle, likely to simply justify it: to agree more and more with what we agree with, to oppose more and more what we oppose. Ethical or scientific criticism of morality, customs, social mechanisms—all that belongs to human society—is not part of Watsuji's ethics. The way we see it, this sort of ethics is not a critical ethics—it is an ethics that needs to be criticized.

But an extremely important point remains. The explication of an object subjected to textual interpretation by means of language means that the object is always restricted by a particular national tongue. In this method, *rinri* [ethics], *ningen* [human], and *sonzai* [being] are all Japanese words, and because they are Japanese, the explication of the actual things they indicate must not only be Japanese objects, but they also must be objects based on a Japanese standard.[1] This much is clear when we consider that the concepts, not just the words "ethics," "human," and "being," may all be understood globally. But if we integrate this global object and this Japanese object by means of textual interpretation along the lines above, it goes without saying that the interpretation must be based on a Japanese standard. The result is, for example, that if one interprets *rinri* as something that may only be expressed in Japanese, if it is literally interpreted in Japanese, the normal logic of hermeneutics would conclude that ethics isn't just Japanese, but that ethics itself is synonymous with Japanese-ness. Relying on the textual interpretation of Japanese words in this way will instantly result in "Japanese ethics" or "Eastern ethics." Of course it then goes without saying that ethics is best when it is Japanese. At the same time, as a conclusion, Watsuji's "academic," modern ethical theory is hardly any different than the aforementioned Hiroshima University professor Nishi Shin'ichirō's ecstatic *Eastern Ethics*.

The point for Watsuji is that ethics is the principle of humanity [*jinrin*]: humanity is the linked behavior between two people or between individuals.

In other words, Watsuji states that it is not the case that in the beginning there were separate individuals who then assembled and built relations, but rather that one should see that the space [*aida*, 間] between individuals was possessed of a human relationality. And just as the literal meaning of the Japanese word for ethics, *rinri*, would indicate, he thus concludes that Japanese society is from the beginning communal [*kyōdōtaitekina*]. As to why Japanese society is communal or why it must only be thought of as communal, such explanations or proofs fall outside this kind of "interpretation." All one need do is think hermeneutically about the phenomenon. This then creates a feeling, an atmosphere, an excitement that this communal Japanese lifestyle is a model throughout the world. For any of this to be true it is necessary that there already be a national essence [*kokutai*] unrivaled anywhere in the world.

So then, ethics is the principle of humanity. Put another way, it is the principle of being human. Luckily, the Japanese word for human, *ningen* [人間], is an extremely convenient word for Watsuji. That is, according to the dictionary, the word for human is made up of the characters for "person" [*nin*, 人] and "space" or "gap" [*gen*, 間],[2] so originally their combination as *ningen* indicated the "between-ness" the "within-ness," the relationality, the working together as an originary meaning that was later misunderstood (?) to indicate an atomistic individual [*kojin*]. For Western sociologists the distinction and opposition is between the individual and society, and they are at pains as to how to reconcile the two. But for we Japanese, our word for human, *ningen*, established a social relation between individuals that was not only later mistakenly inverted to be synonymous with the individual, but *ningen* also replaced the meaning of an atomistic individual with a "human" within a set of social relations. In other words, "individual" itself became a relation. On the one hand, the "human itself," was now a social relationship, and on the other, at the same time, the Japanese word *ningen* is the perfect word, a word that expresses within itself the high philosophical synthesis of the "dialectical unity" of individual and social being. Of course, in Watsuji's theory there is no such perfect word in the West, and so there is also no such lifestyle there either. But why is there no such lifestyle in the West? Why is the West governed by individualism? Alas, those questions fall outside of this "ethics" and this "humanity"—and "hermeneutics" has nothing to do with the answer.

JAPANESE ETHICS AND ANTHROPOLOGY

Watsuji further concludes that the Japanese words for "world" —*seken* [世間] and *yo no naka* [世の中]— are extremely good for expressing this relationality of the human. But here, too, these words are to be interpreted literally. Both terms for "the world" show the descent from Watsuji's pure truth to a looser popular usage while still indicating the "world of existence" (世) of Buddhist scripture. This descent into this customary use is the meaning of both words for "world." For example, "When people grasp society as this understanding of 'the world,' they can also simultaneously grasp its spatial, temporal, which is to say, climatic and historical characteristics." The Japanese terms for "the world" are therefore the ultimate expression of the truth of "society." The depth and height of philosophical truth is thus best expressed in Japanese. But as we have just shown, the occult mechanism that performs this sorcery is nothing but a tautology.

Thus, *ningen*, the word, indeed the thing, is the unity of the worldliness (the sociality) and the individuality of a person, both shot through with order, the Way, which is to say human relations; here being "human" is reducible to ethics. Such is the root of human existence. But just what is existence? For Watsuji the question is not, "Is being material or spiritual?" For him, the word "being" fundamentally means *human* being, which he claims can be known by simply looking at the word "being" itself. It goes without saying that existence expresses the sense of "being" [*aru*]. But "being" can be differentiated as "to be" [*aru*], "to be [defined as] something" [*de aru*], and "to be present" [*ga aru*]. The Chinese word *yū* [有] corresponds to this last sense, "to be present." Of course, in this case, the Chinese "to be present" comes closer to Watsuji's fundamental sense of "being" than the second sense, "to be defined as something," and so this third meaning becomes grounds for rendering ontology (*sonzairon*) as *yūron* [有論]. According to the professor, philologically, "to be" [有る] comes from "to have" [有つ] and this is meant to show that human relations lurk within the very word "being" [*aru*] itself. Thus "being" is a "possession" of human beings.

But if this concatenation ("to be" "to be something" "to be present" "to have") is reducible to a human possession, what way of being do humans themselves in fact possess? What humans themselves possess is the human way of "being." This is the word "being." Incidentally, let us consider the Japanese word for being, *sonzai*, with the first character, *son* [存]; the human subject is grasped in terms of temporal relations: "continuing [*zon*jiteimasu, 存じています]," "duration [*son*zoku, 存続]," "moment of life and death [kikyū *son*bō no toki, 危急存亡の秋³]," and so on. But with the second character *zai*, the human subject is grasped in terms of a specific spatial orientation: "residence [*zai*taku]" "reserve soldier / legionnaire [*zai*gō gunjin]," "absentee landlord [fu*zai* jinushi]," and so on. In other words, because the temporal *son* is individual "self-awareness" and the spatial *zai* is social, then "being" as *sonzai* is necessarily "human" being. "Being" for nonhuman entities, then, is only metaphorically derived from human existence.

And thus, because of this philological interpretation of the word "ethics," Watsuji's *"anthropology"* is "ethics." Though Watsuji uses the word "anthropology," his meaning is decidedly not the same as the so-called discipline of anthropology. This is because, here, according to Watsuji, in what is called anthropology in the West, the "human" is considered as a simple, abstract individual. For example, Watsuji criticizes Heidegger, for though Heidegger does theorize a person's self-aware existence, he overlooks that abstract individual's social and human relations, meaning it is not a "humanism" in the sense of *ningen*—that is, Heidegger's "human" is not the unity of individual and social aspects of their existence as described above. The theories of the mind-body relationship of both natural scientific (physical) anthropology and the metaphysical "philosophical anthropology" (in reality the philosophical anthropology of human differences) do not qualify for Watsuji as *anthrop*ology, because human, as *ningen*, transcends individual existence with communal [*kyōdōtai*] human existence. And so it is thought that there is born from this communal human existence a moral "ought" [*Sollen*] for individuals. The program and content of this kind of ethics can be devised by various means. But important here is that what Watsuji considers a proper ethics can only emerge from Japan, or possibly ancient China. Thus, Japanese ethics is the model of ethics itself. Watsuji's book of ethics is written to show precisely this. It was not written to simply elucidate ethics in Japan, and it was absolutely not written to criticize contemporary Japanese ethics and morality.

But there is absolutely nothing rare or strange about this "exemplary Japanese" ethics. In fact, far from it, it is identical to the basic thought of the leading lights of Western ethics (?). But to Watsuji, because none of them were able to cast off the inadequacies within their thought, they fell short of the summits of the proper anthropology of Japanese ethics. By confronting and connecting with Western ethics, Japanese humanism is shown to be the ultimate exemplar of anthropology, that is, it is the ethical example for all the peoples of the world. In other words, the conclusion is that the Japanese are the model ethnicity. Aristotle's *Politics*, Kant's anthropology, Cohen's "ethics of pure intention," Hegel's "*Sittlichkeit*," Feuerbach's "anthropology," and Marx's "species being," are all understood to be inadequate precursors of Japanese ethics. It is a current social phenomenon not limited to Japanese ethics or to professor Watsuji's mode of thought whereby paraphrasing Marx, something originally Marxist is made to run in a straight line to become something purely Japanese.

Again, what we just saw of Watsuji's ethics equally applies to the rest of his output: his historical climatology, his histories of the Japanese spirit, or primitive Buddhism, or national history, for example. While the aim of all of these is to stress the ethnic particularity, especially the Japanese and Eastern particularity, his method of investigation and his mode of thought is always governed by and based in Western philosophy. In his *The Practical Philosophy of Primitive Buddhism* [1932], against the majority of contemporary Buddhologists who employed European methods but stopped at the stage of high Kantian critique, Watsuji approached the issue from the perspective of "phenomenology" to arrive rather successfully at a relatively independent philosophical and cultural interpretation of Buddhism unattained by contemporary journeyman monks and professors. (Professor Ui Hakuju is an exception.) The aim of this ethics is once again, from the beginning, Japanese ethics—or rather *Japanist* ethics. Still, the method, which at first glance appears modern, is based in European "phenomenology," and so compared with other educators and Confucian scholars it possesses a significant, modern, cultural essence. But at the same time we must remain vigilant because there's a trap here.

Indeed, Watsuji's general method appears at first glance to be sparkling with genius, but we easily notice just how ideologically convenient it all is. While this philosophical method appears unique, because it is largely constructed of miscellaneous scraps, there is in fact nothing particularly special or of any pure essence here at all. Watsuji's hermeneutic ethics adopts and applies Nishida's philosophy.[4] But be that as it may, because it neither deepens nor concretizes Nishida's philosophy, people will see Nishida being merely parroted by Watsuji. And though Watsuji himself isn't clear on this, there is more than a little direct impetus from Miki Kiyoshi's "Anthropology" in the method of Watsuji's ethics. Further, it goes without saying that Heidegger was more original on these points.

Watsuji has clearly and often stated that he is following Heidegger's hermeneutic phenomenology. It is immediately clear that the way he takes up the analysis of language and his approach to the problem—seen above with "human," "world," and "being/existence"—is Heideggerian through and through. It is nothing more than expansion by analogy. Watsuji merely expands what Heidegger did with German, Greek, and Latin to Japanese, Chinese, and Pali. But we cannot conclude that the result is consistent with the basic thesis of Heidegger's so-called hermeneutic phenomenology. That simply could not be done. Or, rather, if it in fact could be done, the resulting ethics would be Catholic or German or Hitlerian. It absolutely could not be a Japanese ethics for a Japan in a state of emergency. Even assuming a social need for presenting a Japanese ethics, such an ethics would have a duty to critique and reconstruct several of Heidegger's fundamental theses along Japanese lines.

The fundamental characteristic of Heidegger's hermeneutic phenomenology begins from the problem of "Being" (*Sein*) [*sonzai*]. Which is to say that for Heidegger, the path to grasping being must begin with being as a problem first, as self-conscious human "being," or in his terms: Dasein. Dasein is the reason Heidegger said "anthropology" [*ningengaku*] or a "study of human 'being'" because ontology here simply indicates a method or means. Ontology is not in fact the subject of Heidegger's philosophy. This is the first difference between Heidegger and Watsuji's ethics.

If it were simply a question of different problematics, we would have a duty not to harp on the problems between the two methods. But the big issue is a question of results: meaning that the insufficiently worked-out assumption by which being/existence is exclusively human is the fundamental flaw. According to Watsuji the Japanese word "being" [*sonzai*] means the active relations of human beings. This in turn must make this Japanese understanding of "being" itself the most exalted concept in the world. But if this is true, even supposing a path from the problem of being to the problem of the human, neither this concept of being nor the human is Heideggerian. Human "Being," for Heidegger, who did not sufficiently link being and human, did not mean, as Watsuji does, a social, historical (climatic!) human community; instead, human "being" was taken up as a question of a person or individual. Thus the temporality that emerges within his single human being, "person," is not in fact the historicity of humans, nor can such a "human" have any social (or climatic!) nature. Both Heidegger's "being in the world" (*In-der-Welt-Sein*, *Mit-Sein*, and so on) and indeed "others" [*das Mann*] are related in terms of an individual's being, meaning that they are not subject to the strictures of actual human existence. This is the first flaw.

Treating human existence as individual "being" is the result of Heidegger's hermeneutic phenomenology, which makes consciousness (self-awareness) the ground of his academic analysis. Indeed, it is only when consciousness is taken as the path that Heidegger's (hermeneutic) phenomenology is worthy of the name. Ever since the Wolff School (Lambert), from Kant to Hegel to Husserl, phenomenology has taken place on the plane of individual consciousness. But Heidegger's is no "pure" phenomenology. Heidegger introduced hermeneutics, or rather modified phenomenology with hermeneutics. Dilthey chose to use the interpretation of representations as the method for interpreting history. For Dilthey, expression meant life, experience, and in that sense a particular consciousness. Here Dilthey did not cast off the significant psychological constraints. The method of a *Lebens* philosophy that links Dilthey's interpretation with the scientific rigor of Husserl's phenomenology, which is to say Heidegger's hermeneutic phenomenology, makes the phenomenological, or conscious, or in another sense, psychological, characteristics decisive.

According to Watsuji's critique, suturing hermeneutics and phenomenology in this way is largely impossible. While hermeneutics must pass through representation to pursue and reexperience the individuals, the peoples, the eras that lurk behind representation, unifying what lies behind these representations and the phenomena of phenomenology is an impossible demand. This is because the phenomenon as it exists in phenomenology is not one of true form or essence—phenomenology scientifically rejects such essences behind the appearance of the phenomenon. An object's true form is analyzed only as a phenomenon as it appears on the scene; thus the true form itself is that which has manifested (as a phenomenon). So strictly speaking, the word "representation" in phenomenology is nonsense, as there is nothing to be expressed that is not already manifested in the appearance of the phenomenon. Thus according to Watsuji's method in *Ethics as*

Anthropology, we must liquidate the Heideggerian phenomenological elements and move to pure hermeneutics.

We must say that we absolutely do not agree with Watsuji here. While it is true that the word phenomenon of phenomenology comes directly from Franz Brentano's *Psychology from an Empirical Standpoint* [*Psychologie vom empirischen Standpunkt*, 1874],[5] Brentano's philosophical perspective was a form of positivism. He adopted Auguste Comte's "phenomenon" for psychology. So, phenomenology itself is a phenomenalism and an empiricism, or, as it were, a Catholic form of realism into which has crept the superficial aspects of a phenomenon. It is clear and obvious that one cannot grasp "ethics" or "human" or "being"—the truth or significance (meaning) of all things—in this "phenomenology." It can be stated that interpreting things by means of this smuggled in phenomenal surface is too much to ask of this endeavor.

The above does not get to the problem of Heidegger's method, but that is not the issue here. But, when compared to phenomenology or a hermeneutic phenomenology, just where are we supposed to find the fundamental superiority of Watsuji's hermeneutics? The hermeneutic method itself is a particular, better a complicated, better still, an internally incoherent, phenomenalism and anti-essentialism.

As already stated, words such as ethics, human, and being are particular representations. Moreover, they are representations that fundamentally distinguish humans from the animal kingdom. This means that it is through this fundamental representation, as the path of the Logos, that the analysis of things may begin, as seen by Watsuji's ethics. But we have doubts as to the theoretical value of representation. Representation is the expression of living [*seikatsu*]. But the question is: How does that living pass through the actual and material process that finally produces representations? Explanation of the cause and effect of representation as it touches the historical and material foundation of society is not considered at all. It is simply enough to say that representation corresponds to a particular way of living that lies behind the representation. (Correspondence here is not meant as material cause and effect or interaction; it is merely mathematically assigned—*Zuordnung*). Interpreting this meaning was the goal of bringing the concept of representation into a philosophical system. This is not a question of the material relations of things, but the conceptual assignation of the "meaning" of things. This is the only issue permitted by "representation" here.

Indeed, a phenomenological phenomenalism wasn't even able to interpret the meaning of things or even meaning itself. But with the interpretation seen in Watsuji the "real" meaning of the material actuality of a thing is not interpreted. The object of interpretation here is a formal or mathematical assignation. It is even better to say that the meaning of representation is only an aesthetic, a poetics, the symbolic. Put rather extremely, this is to say that the relations of things are replaced with antirealist representations. Thus because of this substitution, hermeneutics is a particularly excellent phenomenalism—even an excellent phenomenology. Rather than a simple opposition to so-called phenomenology's motto, "Back to things themselves," because hermeneutics seeks to replace the "things themselves" with an antirealist representation of things, it is a more phenomenological phenomenalism than so-called phenomenology itself.

It is said that hermeneutic ethics does not ignore the material relations of production of historical society, for to ignore it would invite rampant falsifications in interpreting human relations. But if we inquire as to under what sign and in what sense does this ethics take up the issue of relations of production, to the last we get nothing more than that they are treated as a representation of human "being." Human "being" here does not pass through the cause and effect or the interaction of the relations of production.[6] In place of the structural relations of the material base, the conceptual relations of meaning are extracted for interpretation. The material base of a historical society is treated only as a particular social representation. The fact that social human relations are expressed as money means that the actual material practice of money expresses the cause and effect that produced the particular commodity called money. If this money is interpreted as a hermeneutic expression, in place of the ever-sharpening class conflict of capitalist society, we would likely get the "human being" discovered in Watsuji's ethics. Here lies the true nonsense of the hermeneutic method.

This hermeneutic method—whereby in place of capitalist society we get an extremely general and abstract "human being"—skims the aesthetics off the top of historical society until the result is, in a sense, simply ethics as ideology, or an "ethics-ism" [*rinrishugi*]. In other words, all historical and social phenomena—such as the base and superstructure—become uniformly flattened, superficial phenomena. The entirety of historical society is subsumed under a single, ultimate concept, the "human." And because this "human" has already been universalized and abstracted, the "human" means ethical human relations. Thus, all historical and social phenomena are reducible to ethical phenomena. Watsuji's ethics does not take up the supremacy of ethics because the problem at hand is an ethical one. No, his ethics is the inevitable result of the hermeneutic method, which consciously avoids beginning analysis with the actual, material mechanisms of historical society. This is the fundamental characteristic of Watsuji's "anthropology" [*ningen no gaku*], and more broadly, it is the basis of the much-loved "humanism" [*ningengaku*] of today's liberals and theorists who have converted to a fascist position in the *tenkō* phenomenon. This kind of ethics-ism is absolutely not the discipline of ethics. Ethics-ism is the origin; it is the "scientific" path one may walk in any and all directions all the way to economics, politics, or sociology.

Watsuji's ethics and all similar humanisms—themselves reducible to some form of ethics-ism—demonstrate the inevitable terminus of hermeneutics in Japan today. Here we have discussed in what sense hermeneutics is metaphysics and how that meaning within metaphysics is idealism all the way down. The question now becomes how Japanist is this anthropology and this ethics-ism? What sends Germany down the path of Hitlerism and Japan down the path of Japanist ethics-ism is the hermeneutics lurking within liberalism. In other words, Watsuji's ethics is strong proof of just how liberal philosophy inevitably becomes Japanist philosophy.

(Professor Watsuji has also worked on the problem of ethics in his *National Morality*. For primitive Buddhism, national history, and the history of the Japanese spirit, and others, see his work on climate and the essay "The Japanese Spirit." It would be interesting to compare these closely with Professor Nishi's *Eastern Ethics*.)

Chapter Eight

AN ANALYSIS OF THE RESTORATIONIST PHENOMENON

On the Familialism Analogy

For the sake of convenience, let's begin with the movement to abolish state-regulated prostitution. The Home Ministry clearly announced it would enact a nationwide ban on state-regulated prostitution in April 1935. (In fact, it did not happen that April.) Bans on state-regulated prostitution—meaning roughly the "pleasure quarters" or "red light districts"—are already in effect in Akita, Nagasaki, Gunma, and Saitama prefectures. Last year, the Metropolitan Police abolished the traditional system of spatial and administrative confinement for state-regulated prostitution, while at the same time maintaining a policy of some respect for allowing those working in prostitution the freedom to choose to leave the profession. Yet as a harbinger of the Home Ministry's current policy, it cannot be denied that these earlier statements appear to have somehow resulted in a great number of people assuming the inevitability of a total ban on state-regulated prostitution. Given the freedom (if only the formal freedom) to quit of 53,000 state-regulated prostitutes nationwide, the business slump of the 530 red light districts, and the loss of a three-hundred-year national tradition (?), one should not forget the great number of people behind this abolition policy.

Those brothel owners who quickly understood this great swell of public opinion and the new policy are hoping to pivot from room-letting to the restaurant business. But if the prostitution business itself had not slumped, the abolition policy would not have got off the ground. For example, it is said that 130 brothel owners in Suzaki were part of the petition movement. Of course, brothel owners' self-understanding of the slump is not the ministry's only motive, nor is it a question of guessing what the public will or will not be behind; still, such massive public support is never established without such a material foundation.

Accordingly, the central force behind the anti-prostitution movement, the "Abolish Prostitution Federation" [*haishō renmei*], disbanded in 1934, changing its name to the "Purity and Hygiene Association" [*junsui kansei kai*], signaled the advent of a new movement. But here we encounter a problem.

From the beginning, the urgent goal of the anti-prostitution movement has been the complete eradication of both licensed and unlicensed—public and private—prostitution. But that goal was always in the service of the much more general problem of social organization itself, and that is something that cannot be fixed merely by abolishing prostitution. To date, the immediate target of the anti-prostitution movement has been the extremely rare system of state-regulated prostitution that exists within a civilized country pledged to legally protect against the trafficking of women and children, and human trafficking more generally, because state-regulated prostitution's very nature must bring with it some kind of human confinement. It must not be forgotten how similar this position is to the situation of light-industrial female workers that Japan has repeatedly stressed at various international federations is based on the "particular circumstances" of Japanese labor and law, making it one more instance of Japanese particularity. In the case of light-industrial female workers, this position is explained by means of the result of the technical development of Japanese industry, the excellent skills of Japanese workers, and what will be important later, the beauty of the family and household nature of Japanese labor. But when it comes to prostitution, saying such things must be rejected as a national disgrace. The anti-prostitution movement aims only to suppress this national shame of *public* prostitution. And as the problem of *private* prostitution is thus not a *national* disgrace, but only the disgrace of the *proletariat*, it remains untouched.

The problem of private prostitution gives rise to the real problem. That is, near the end of the 67th Diet session [1934] a bill was submitted to the House of Representatives for the regulation of prostitution. The bill is worth noting because it was against abolition and in fact strengthened the system of state-regulated prostitution, and it gained a majority with the signature of 270 Diet members. As this was a House of Representatives that had never once seriously considered an anti-prostitution bill despite several proposals, there was no doubt that there were overwhelming numbers in favor of continuing prostitution in this pro-prostitution committee. If the anti-prostitution faction claims that abolition is the will of the public, the huge numbers of the pro-prostitution faction shout back, is not the majority of Diet members in favor of the bill strengthening the system of state-regulated prostitution in fact public opinion? This example is a lesson in just how well the House of Representatives represents public opinion. But the main basis of the argument for the pro-prostitution members was that the abolition of state-regulated prostitution would result in rampant private prostitution resulting in damage to public morals and hygiene.

I cannot get into a theory of private prostitution here. We must take note, however, that earlier some two thousand landlords from across Japan had arrived at the same conclusions as the pro-prostitution faction in the Diet. But the landlords' statement is more important still: "Statesmen enamored with Western civilization have recklessly ignored the nation's laws in encouraging private prostitution. We are absolutely opposed to the oppression of the brothel landlords and their long history of respect for national law based in the family system and allowing the evil of private prostitution to linger within the beautiful manners and customs of our national social life." This was no mere boastful rhetoric of the brothel owners. It was roar of their very livelihoods. This is simply more than the brothel owners finally saying with unabashed frankness what the pro-prostitution Diet members wanted to say. I do not think that the majority of Diet members have been bought by the brothel owners. In fact, I do not think that those members are acting out of love of prostitution either. I think it is simply that the Diet members, because they are unable to separate state-regulated prostitution from Japan's "family system" and "beautiful manners and customs," they secretly believe that anyone who has doubts on licensed prostitution is part of "Western civilization's" materialist (?) thought. This is because the idea that private prostitution is more harmful to public morals and hygiene than public prostitution is purely imaginary, a fact discovered even by those Home Ministry officials who were dispatched to the West.

What appears to be essential in the system of state-regulated prostitution is that it is a result of our country's three hundred, nay, three-thousand-year history of the beautiful manners and customs of our family system. I think this frivolous philosophy is surprisingly not far from the common sense of many. Of course, such a ridiculous philosophy is by itself insignificant. But it is important that the corresponding actions of that ridiculousness, surprisingly, tells a certain secret about the national ethnic spirit.

In essence, the problem of state-regulated prostitution is mainly the problem of the fetters of proletarian farmers. Today it is claimed that a harsh family system is one of the essential elements of the life of the Japanese folk. That is why the brothel landlords instinctively grasp for slivers of this unimpeachable ethnic social theory. Either for or against, the pro-prostitution campaign is simply one of the characteristic expressions of the concept of restoration in Japan today.

Indeed, there is no more expedient ideological framework for the interpretation of actually existing society than this invocation of the Japanese family system. This ideology's support for state-regulated prostitution has hardly been ineffective so far. And it is not only a matter of ideological support for low wages and containing the power of labor. More broadly, the family system exists to appear to alleviate the difficulties of the unemployment problem itself. Countless of the tens of percent of the actually unemployed in Japan are absorbed and treated as employed within the household so the household reduces the nominal and bureaucratically visible number of the unemployed. And in this sense, the truth of the ideology whereby the family system is the essence of Japanese society is now understood. So how are things going with this crucial Japanese family system?

According to the results of a survey by the Tokyo Statistics Division of 20,000 sixth graders in eighty elementary schools, 90 percent of the households consisted of only parents and children. Families that also included grandparents under the same roof made up only 10 percent of the total. That is, on the one hand, the survey shows that through marriage, independence, and other factors the number of family members who live separately is on the rise. In other words the ancient Japanese family system has collapsed and in fact is moving toward "individualism." At the same time it also showed that the majority of households in Tokyo were immigrants come to work from the provinces. According to the 1935 household survey by the police, the population of Tokyo grew by some 185,000, but two thirds of that number were people who had come to Tokyo for work. What we learn from these statistics is that the family system in Tokyo has collapsed and been given over to so-called individualism, and at the same time, too, the family system has collapsed in the farming villages and the regions. As a single-family household is built in Tokyo, those who remain generate a single-family household in the farming villages and the regions. Thus, even though the rate may vary—and here we need no fundamental distinction between urban and rural—nationally it is simply a statistical truth that the collapse of the Japanese family system has in fact become a great mass of people.

But for the ideologues of the family [*kazokushugisha tachi*]—a particular form of Japanists today, those who use the family system to interpret this actually existing society—the collapse of the family system is not acknowledged, or if it is acknowledged, it is acknowledged as the result of an evil individualism. In both cases they persist in attaching Japan's, and their own, hopes and expectations to the family system. The difficulties of unemployment and poverty are idealistically mitigated by means of the ideal family system. In fact, the actual collapse of the family system allows members of the family to be expelled from the family (household) into the ranks of the unemployed and those at risk of becoming unemployed.

This is the truth of female employment (and thus female unemployment), as women first gain independence by sacrificing a contented family life within the family system. In this case, does independence mean economically independent (employed), or having an independent status not economically independent (unemployed)? Of the nearly 1.5 million people who commute daily to Tokyo for work or school, some 520,000 are women. At minimum, this proves that the independence of the average woman is more a response to the collapse of the Japanese family system than the above concerns that the independent prostitute is destroying that system. Modern women have begun to cast off the ancient Japanese family system. It is an ominous sign that the familialists [*kazokushugisha*] (of various sorts) can never be at ease with these modern women.

A case in point: In his book, *A Modern Woman's Reader*, Ichikawa Kenzō, the famous women's educator and principal of Tokyo's First Higher School for women, advocated a new version of the ideology of "good wife, wise mother," or put another way, a new ideology of "good wife, wise mother" based on liberating women from their status as wives. But this is unlikely to lead to anything, as Ichikawa's book created a scandal in a Tokyo City Assembly filled with the possessors of familialist common sense. The book was banned from classroom use and there is a further move to ban it entirely.

According to the common sense of these family values assemblymen, there is all too much disturbing and pedagogically damaging individualism in the likes of Ichikawa and his ilk.

But the principle behind the thought and behavior of the family system as an anti-individualism cannot simply be attributed to some silly hobby or the lowness of education. In other words, it does not end in just any reactionary consciousness. It is further reducible to a current and explicit *restorationist* [*fukkōshugi*] phenomenon; more, familialism is the very model of restorationism. As such, this more general relationship, too, is important. Indeed, the antagonism between individualism and the family system (ideological familialism) is itself one example of the pure nonsense of contemporary Japanese consciousness. But through this opposition, the familialists show that the true intent is the antagonism between capitalism and the previous feudal system. Yet contemporary Japanese capitalism is already absolutely not some pure individualism. Quite the contrary, in various ways there has been a remarkable shift to an ideology of control, to a managerial capitalism [*tōseishugi*], in opposition to individualism. It is obvious that prior to monopoly capitalism, individualism was nothing more than the consciousness of the previous form of capitalism [liberal capitalism]. Thus the very act of bringing this former, but now defunct, capitalist individualism into conflict with the family system itself is already a retracing back to the prior form of liberal capitalism, and thus indicates the intention to *actively restore* Japan's long feudal era. By doing so it is easy to obscure the capitalist essence of today's developed monopoly capitalism and conversely give the illusion that monopoly capitalism is anticapitalist.

Yet, although the relevant term is restorationist phenomenon, it is always limited in the event to a reactionary phenomenon. Given the flow of history, there is no restoration that ever truly returns to the past. Therefore, this so-called restorationist phenomenon can only exist as some idealistic "-ism" or ideology, so whatever superficial consciousness or excuse there may be, if the ideology produces a practical and rational society, in that limited sense it can be said to have some progressive essence: the Meiji example of the so-called restoration of imperial rule [*ōsei fukkō*] would be an example, as would the Renaissance in Europe. But today, with the daily collapse of the actual family system clear for all to see, and turning against

AN ANALYSIS OF THE RESTORATIONIST PHENOMENON

the authority of rational social science, our family system ideology [*kazokuseidoshugi*]—and its incoherent consciousness—is a pretext for the continuation of a particular form of managerial capitalism [*tōseishugi*]. This pretext is easily and crudely accepted thanks to the vague, half-hearted nature of its content.

But even if we have understood that this familialism is a reactionary phenomenon, we have not yet comprehended why it is the very model of a reactionary, restorationist phenomenon. That is, why have the Tokugawa regulation of the pleasure quarters and the Tokugawa-era ideology of "good wife, wise mother" of the *Greater Learning for Women* [*Onna daigaku*, 1729] become *the* representatives of today's restorationism? Obviously, the family system is not a problem of the family or the household; it is a problem of society and the nation itself. Furthermore, the family system is not a matter of the actually existing *organization of* the social system or the state itself. Rather, as the endpoint of the family system, or better, as the precipitate of the family system, familialism is an *ideology that actively organizes* society and the state.

Now if we inquire into the individualism that appears in those like Principal Ichikawa's new ideology of "good wife, wise mother" as a problem of the state, it means we must note that it comes from the liberal theory of the state [*jiyūshugiteki kokka ron*]. That is, under the banner of the folk or the citizen, state and society are made into metaphors of a single family. And by so doing, the liberal theory of the state is rejected. Put more precisely, through a series of metaphorical moves whereby society is the state, the state is the folk, and the folk is the tribe or the clan, until all of these are rendered "the family," the liberal theory of the state is denounced and rejected. Within the consciousness of this denunciation movement, we must note that the reality of society and the state becomes a metaphorical family, and this metaphorical family itself doubles back[1] to become the reality of the state. Here we have the reason why familialism is the very model of the restorationist phenomenon.

But as for this prototypical restorationist phenomena, it is no longer adequate to call the invariable social consciousness hidden within familialism a simple restorationism: it is in fact a *primitizationism* or a *nativizationism* [*genshikashugi*, 原始化主義].[2] Indeed, even Rousseau's social contract theory, which corresponds to the bourgeoisie's civilizational consciousness, and which had a decisive influence on the concept of the state in Japan and elsewhere, was a particular kind of "primitivism" [*genshishugi*]. But as the very model of restorationism, nativization differs from Rousseau's natural law and naturalism, as it contains a more precise and necessary [nationalist] historical content. That is, first of all, it is now restorationist. But now regardless of its historical essence, this restorationism is radicalized to become nativizationsim. Why radicalized? Because once we take this step beyond simple restoration, instead of the history of human culture in general now appears the nonmodern, primitive barbarism of savages.

First, the feature that exposes today's familialism as nativizationist appears in theory. To adopt the imported distinction between *gemeinschaft* and *gesellschaft*, by setting up an opposition between the family system and individualism, Japan ideologues often hold that, opposed to the individualistic *gesellschaft* of Western society, Japan's familialism shows that Japanese society is *gemeinschaft*. And thus, the social psychology of the family system is unconditionally dominated by the organic sentiments of a parent's affection and the emotional relations between parents and children. And from such a perspective it is not impossible to see conspicuous examples of sentimental thought and behavior. Indeed, not coincidentally, the active logic of such a social psychology is mysticism. On the one hand, mysticism is irrational, is antirational; on the other it is an ecstatic, organic experience—a gut-level philosophy. Here lies the logical function of nativization. The logical analytical power must be familialist.

For example, in a family of two members with two minds and two bodies, we may have one mind, one body, or one mind, two bodies; because their feelings are not merely a question of analytical explanation, they must be intuitive and direct. Thinking of two separate individuals as directly and intuitively one is a symbolic and metaphorical logic. Thus the logic of familialism is nothing but rendering society a metaphorical family. This most practical application of this metaphor, and its "expression" ~~in the emperor system~~, is something not to be argued, not to be mocked. Familialism is a political product produced by a metaphor. And this metaphor is a logic produced by familialistic nativizationsim.

Second, mysticism is, in general, psychologically accompanied by religious feeling. The mysticism corresponding to a familial nativization, results in a nativist religious feeling. A primitive religious feeling or emotion corresponds to the emotions of the clan [*shizokuteki shūkyō no jōcho*], that is, it is an ethnic religion of the family. The problem comes as the nativization within contemporary Japanese familialism is not simply a logical one—it comes to appear in social representations, too. In fact, familialist, clannish, and ethnic religious thought is a political object in Japanese society. The religious feelings stemming from familialist mysticism are already not reducible to an individual's personal feelings but to society as a familialist religious system.[3]

The religious feeling and the corresponding religious system that emerges within familialist religion is a nativizationist religion. Put another way, it is a primitive religion, and from here emerges a particular totemism. Empirical studies by many sociologists have shown that totemism assumes certain forms of ancestor worship and the existence of prohibited sacred objects [taboos]. Furthermore, it also appears as a kind of animism. The creative powers of the earth, together with the life spirit of plants, can become the objects of worship, as they are when they are united in the animism of agrarian fundamentalism. In this way, familialism can begin in the home and be infinitely expanded out to the nation and finally to all heaven and earth.

If we consider a secondary phenomenon, the deification [神社化] of august individuals, we get a first sense of the concrete meaning of this familialistic primitive religion. If compared to a series of other social phenomenon such as a parade of samurai-helmeted children at a nation-founding festival, a cry for the restoration of Kamakura Buddhism, the banning of English in girls' schools, or the current fad for the crested kimono, it is understood that the meaning of this religious feeling is an extreme social phenomenon.[4]

The essence of various representatives of Japanism—ethnic nationalism, spiritualism, Shintōism [神道主義], and so on—lies within familialism as the representative form of restorationism. But we must not forget that even if it is a primitivized form of thought, the characteristic of the restorationist phenomenon that is nativization was in fact produced for the benefit of a highly developed modern Japanese capitalism; *it is a particular form of modernization.*[5] But in every case, the goal of further modernization does not appear in the form of historical reflection, retrospection, or "recognition" but rather, ultimately, appears as a form of ahistorical and antihistorical nativization as a feature of a reactionary restorationist phenomenon. The contradiction of restorationism whereby modernity is rendered primitive manifests itself by appearing to express history while in fact ignoring it.[6] Traditionalism appears as the destruction of tradition itself. The cultural traditions of the people are one by one destroyed by being nationalized.[7] This is the inevitable contradiction of restorationist reaction.

The root cause of the contradiction of restorationist reaction is as follows. Just as the historically specific stage of capitalism imagines itself as a transhistorical category, projecting itself into an *infinite past*, as a special case of the present stage, restorationism is called into service by a pressing political necessity to create the new, antihistorical category: "the archaic [korai]." Though people will argue the details, this primitivizationist "archaic," though produced in the present stage of Japanese capitalism, is arbitrarily retrojected back into a *finite past*.[8] The contradiction of restorationism arises from the conflict inherent in this theoretical move. For example, we must recall that due to the logic of restoration and the method of restoration, the classic texts of restorationism, the *Kojiki* and *Nihon shoki*—which the authorities of national history have placed in the seventh century—contain and are built upon this above contradictory, retrojective relation of "restorationism" in a broad sense. The establishment of the Meiji constitutional system and the current common sense of the national idea it is tied to were also products of this larger sense of "restorationism."[9] Even noting the current reactionary form of restorationism, in this broader sense, the Meiji national idea was produced by the same historical logic and method.

The secret of the reactionary nature of restorationism lies in the idealist primitivization of the [material] modernization of actually existing society. Because of the conflict in its temporal structure, reactionary restorationism is always mere ideology (intellectual, emotional). That is, it only appears as manifest in ideological, idealist interpretations of social objects, or deals only with the ideological aspects of social objects. The majority of today's restorationist reactionaries are *phraseologues* (interpreters of a set of fixed expressions, see phraseology); they are ideological idealists. It is important to note that this does not stem from the immaturity of their movement or by mere accident. Nativizationsim of thought in the service of maintaining and strengthening contemporary capitalism is the fundamental condition of today's restorationist reaction. Familialistic restorationism in philosophy, art, morality, law, and politics dominates present-day

Japan. At the same time, we have not seen a corresponding primitivization of industrial techniques, natural science, or industrial technology.[10]

Anyone who looks will surely notice that the restorationist phenomena of contemporary Japan are linked to various forms of chauvinism. But the mechanism that invariably unites both the current, actual needs of imperialism and the demand for primitivization of thought in these restorationist phenomena is none other than the ideology of the family system.

Chapter Nine

THE ESSENCE OF CULTURAL CONTROL
An Analysis of Various Aspects of Cultural Control in Contemporary Japan

It is obvious that the various invocations of "control" [*tōsei*] today mean political control: for instance, capitalistic administrative mechanisms necessarily give birth to a particular form of pure, economic control; the homogenization of commodities, standardization, the assembly line, and other aspects of the so-called rationalization of production are examples. But today these purely economic controls—which, of course, lead to many important political, social, and cultural implications—are not what is touted as control. Today control always means political control. This so-called political control includes all forms of control that take the nation as the unit, or the standard, for a means of governing. But even if it is imagined that these forms of control take the nation as the unit or the standard, for example, with the Japan-Manchukuo bloc or a Japan-China pact, already something beyond this exclusively national meaning of control has been brought into the concept. Thus we first need to recognize that the mechanisms of control are not simply political or limited to the mechanisms of governing by the rulers, for those are nothing but legal representations of the form of rule based solely on the ideology of a single, sui generis nation-state [*ikkokushugi*].

Japanese capitalism, as has already been stated, exists under bureaucratic and militaristic conditions. Which is to say, it quickly developed through urgent pressure from above. Accordingly, it has been from the beginning

THE ESSENCE OF CULTURAL CONTROL

dominated by a certain level of control, namely, state intervention.¹ But it is well-known that control was first and most effectively imposed by turning to the realm thought, namely the least independent aspect of society, the cultural sphere. Ideological control, straight from the playbook as the most general form of control and the role of governmental rule, is also the quickest and most obvious.

Thus the first proclamations in Japan were the great guiding principles for controlling and regulating education. As already stated, control is normally understood as corresponding to the form of governance based on the ideology of a single, discrete nation-state, and so naturally, the control of education was no different: it was organized around the singular particularity of Japan and its eternal, unrivaled history. Here we find one part of (economic and cultural) control in Japan. As everyone surely knows, control of education in Japan is extremely strict—the model for this control is, among others, the elementary schools (and extending into junior high schools). The authority of education comes not from Confucius's *Analects*, or Buddhist scripture, or Socrates. Even less is it found in Rousseau or Pestalozzi.² Thus, in place of a universal humanistic cultural authority, we must see how under immense pressure, education is violently organized around the authority of a sui generis nationalism [*ikkokushugiteki*] legally codified [*hōjiteki*] in a particular, national constitution. Such is the original essence of Japanese educational control; moreover, here is the ideal typical form of control in Japan. Here also lies the source of today's so-called cultural control.

At the same time, we should also note that the political concept of control differs in practical ways from control in other spheres. Though it is of course also a political concept, in Japan today the essence of the concept of control itself is not proactively interventionist. Though this concept of constitutive control may be in conflict with free initiative, free actions, and so forth—unlike the original interventionist form of "control" that sought to direct thought and behavior by infusing it with a specific, positive content—here it is not necessary to actively (positively) supplement or direct these free activities. In this sense, then, control does not mean actively denying any particular freedoms or actively opposing them. Rather, it means only that in cases where two freedoms coexist, the freedom most conducive to current purposes will receive priority—its essence is thus a rather negative (passive) one.³ As a philosophical concept, this negative form of control has been distinguished from "composition" or "organization." Representative examples include Kant's "control principle" [*tōseiteki genri*] and Hans Driesch's entelechy.[4] Here it hardly differs from the conventional wisdom of politics. As seen in the case of educational control, in Japan control was originally remarkably active and organizational. Though we can see that national history was "nationalistically" cognized as sui generis, and more or less completely organized from the moment educational control was announced, educational control is nonetheless a rare example of aggressive, constitutive content.

Educational control has spread out from elementary schools to higher education. Already, approved middle school textbooks are being replaced by nationally certified texts. In high schools and vocational schools, professors are also meticulously certified by the state. With the revision of the University Law, lecture content and objectives of each public and private university (Imperial Universities excepted) are effectively or nominally prescribed. But outside of elementary school, it might be supposed that the control of university and vocational education is not actively constitutive, that it differs from the original meaning of control. But we must note that a system of school inspectors has already been put in place in high schools. These are the assistant school administrators, but they are not there to assist the administrators. They are there to monitor the schools. This system may not be formally in place in universities, but even in the supposedly free public and private universities, any instructors who lecture on the "organ theory of the emperor"[5] are obliged to resign or correct themselves. This is likely no longer educational control in a narrow sense. It is rather the control of academics itself, the control of speech. At any rate, it is a problem that cannot be overlooked when discussing control in university education.

Though control of the educators themselves in the higher schools and the universities may be less meaningful, for educational control aimed at those being educated (and this is of course the aim of educational control) the relation is the exact opposite. Educational control by students themselves, by university and school administrators, government officials, and even civil society itself is a famous phenomenon in Japan today. One may think it strange that educational control is done by the students themselves, but as stated above, control as it operates in Japan today does not mean simply top-down control; it is instead a particular form of constitution, of organization. Thus, with tacit approval from the state, right-wing students

THE ESSENCE OF CULTURAL CONTROL

and others like them constitute just such an autonomous (?) mechanism of "control."

Beyond ordinary high schools and universities, beginning with a youth school in April 1935, various rural academies, youth groups, military reservist leagues, and religious groups have all directly and indirectly taken on the burden of controlling education. In the broader understanding of the educational world, these groups are the exemplary sites of control.[6]

Yet here we must add a difficulty to the question of the control of academics. Of course, education must take place under the banner of some educational ideal and proclaim a truth. But here, this idea and this truth is easily constituted by the plan of educational control itself. That ideal is simply the cultivation of good and loyal subjects centered on the nation. But in the academic world this plan is not easily done, for it is not easy to constitute an academic sphere, either on paper or practically, around some scheme of control.

That said, control as negative countermeasures against the original sense of an active, positive freedom can be achieved anywhere. In academics, negative control can be done by encouraging research with grants to certain research institutes, subsidizing research facilities with state funds, and any other number of methods of unequal treatment and prioritizing. Yet these alone do not lead to active, constitutive educational control. No informed person believes that an academic truth can be actively constituted even if we were to interfere in the lives of scholars and technicians as the Nazis do. But so far, no such academic truth has been defined. It is not impossible to present some kind of constitutive control of academic truth along the lines of the plan mentioned above, but the main point is the distinction between the outward appearance and the internal essence; and as all believe that the core of academic truth does not dwell in its outer face, the original problem remains.

At first glance it does seem that, today, just such a control of academics is becoming possible in Japan. Take the above example of the organ theory of the emperor. A large majority of contemporary constitutional scholars in Japan today accept this theory, and it is even the common sense of the majority of Japanese intellectuals. Outside academics, in government, the truth or falsehood of this theory is to be determined by the judgment of the Home Minister. Of course, the Home Minister has neither the qualifications nor the ability to make such a judgment on this theory, and his goal is not the determination of academic truth; rather, his is an administrative question. That said, because in both administrative and academic cases the content of the theory is the same, the government's judgment on the validity of the theory will also function as a mechanism for academic control.

The governmental authorities claim they have no intention to offer an opposing theory to the ~~organ theory of the emperor~~. (As long as the government is anything short of a mere ~~military junta~~ [*gunbudan*], explicitly banning the theory is impossible.) But we cannot overlook the fact that rejecting the theory or declaring it an error immediately implies the constitution of an academic counter theory. So here, too, academic control is extremely constitutive. There is no better example of this sort of constitutive control of academics than the research produced by the Japanese Cultural Spirit Research Institute [Nihon seishin bunka kenkyūjo]. The "research" produced by the institute, however, is not seriously recognized as such by academics, the press, or the reading public. Here is proof as to how difficult it is to control the constitution of academic truth.

Yet even with twists and turns, academic control, as constitutive control, is possible both nominally and in practice—especially in sociology, history, spiritual science [cultural studies], and philosophy. These disciplines are all characterized on the one hand as academic research, but they are also necessarily accompanied by questions of the nature of speech and representation themselves. Thus the control of critical and journalistic—journalistic in the original sense—academics emerges as the easiest shortcut to the control of speech. Initially the ~~organ theory~~[7] was, as it was intended, a purely academic issue (regardless of the bourgeois, bureaucratic, militaristic, and authoritarian currents lurking within it). The need to "politicize" the academy stemmed from the issue of controlling speech.

Whether the content is academic or journalistic, speech obeys the form of journalism (although journalism is not reducible to speech). Thus, because the control of speech is so tied to the control of journalistic speech, the old legal mechanisms of control of the press are used: publication law, newspaper laws, taxation, and others thus form a system of review. Understood legally, however, these forms of control are merely examples of the original, interventionist sense of "control" and do not rise to the example of our so-called constitutive forms. But the legal application of these legal mechanisms are themselves not legally determined; they are rather the concrete expressions of a particular political and cultural goal

THE ESSENCE OF CULTURAL CONTROL

for constituting and controlling speech. (The various *tenkō* confessions are a notable example, as is the ideology of "socialism in one country.") It has long been rumored that just such purely prescriptive legalistic measures for the control of speech are being prepared. For example, by merging the two largest communications companies, Rengō and Dentsu—which in fact means that the government acquired Dentsu—the military and the Foreign Minister brashly aimed at the control, unification, and constitution of the source of news, especially the source of news relating to Manchukuo, China, and the Soviet Union. It is rumored there are similar plans to establish a general office for newspapers as well. Radio is already organized by the state in this way, but it is debatable whether newspapers provide the same sort of fodder for such constitutive consolidation—for our purposes journals and pamphlets are distinctions without difference. An active, constitutive form of control over speech in any meaningful or adequate sense is nearly impossible, as it must be. This is because from the beginning, even if only nominally, the very concept of the freedom of speech itself always presents people with the possibility for doubt. To the extent that speech cannot be controlled by active, constitutive means, the original and ultimate goal of complete control of speech is never reached, a truth which is in no way strange.

So-called control is not the simple control of things; it means the constitution of things. And as a function of reconstituting an object before our eyes, it is always also the constitution of counter-objects and oppositions. Controlling national public opinion is neither the unification nor the standardization of public opinion; it is the constitution of two great antagonistic objects within public opinion. In other words, it is *the active constitution of an antagonistic public opinion*[8]—a national *contradictio in adjecto*.

The best example for proof that control must be an active, antagonistic constitution is seen in the control of literature. Take for example the famous plan of the Home Ministry's Police Bureau (albeit under the personal name of the director general) to consolidate writers of all stripes into a new Japanese Literary Institute [*Nihon bungeiin*]. On the heels of this plan there continued smaller second and third wave movements for a "literary institute" among right-wing writers (?). But though this movement still exists today, none of these planned institutes has never been actually built. Against this fascist literary control movement, the Artistic Freedom League, which should have been able to mount the most powerful protest movement, has nothing to show for itself, and today exists in name only. In this sense, it seems to be hardly any different than the unrealized plans for the Japanese Literary Institute. But recently the Police Bureau has plans to establish a copyright investigative committee in preparation for the enforcement of copyright protections, and it is reported that this copyright committee has taken this occasion as an opportunity to plan the creation of an auxiliary body variously named the Japanese Cultural Committee [*Nihon bunka iinkai*] or the Japanese Cultural Institute [*Nihon bunkain*]. All these endless plans well express the antagonistic and constitutive nature of cultural control.

The intention of the Police Bureau was to take all the various literary spheres and cultural groups and forcibly organize them under this Japanese Cultural Institute. The institute was to become the ultimate leadership mechanism for culture. For example, though one may be writing a novel, the literary groups imagine that an author would receive guidance and instruction from this leading cultural institute. Of course literary truth and national realities do not necessarily coincide, and so a fault line emerges within cultural control. But the important point here is that literary control is in fact the active constitution of a *literary antagonism*, so cultural control thought of as simply top-down control is in this case largely meaningless.

So, to conclude, if there is to be cultural control, if it is to be actually enforced, we are already not talking about simple control, but the production of a particular cultural antagonism. Accordingly, the phenomenon that appears with the dawn of "control" is not unification or standardization, but rather, as it creates two competing national literary groups, "control" means their very antagonism itself. This is not limited to literature; it is the very essence of what today is called "control." (This is also the essence of the problem of reforming the Imperial Art Institute.) The example of early Meiji educational control was all preparatory work for what today has become the model of the constitutive concept of control.

The constitution-as-antagonism of literature in Japan (what is popularly simply called "control") is also expressed externally—as seen in the plan for an International Culture Promotion Association. The imagined goal of the association is not simply to introduce Japanese culture or foster international exchange. In fact, when considered internationally, the cultural antagonism born of domestic cultural "control" is none other than an indirect yet grand Japanese plan of erasure and standardization for international cultural control. Furthermore, the subjective plan of the International Culture Promotion Association officials themselves is a secondary problem, but when Lord Lytton—of the Manchurian Incident Lytton Report—became the chairman of the Museum of Chinese Art in London and refused a request to include Japanese cultural treasures in the Chinese exhibit, these officials inadvertently yet objectively revealed the philosophical significance of their International Culture Promotion Association.[9]

Indeed, there is nothing so vaguely understood yet so skillfully deployed as this concept of "control." Which is to say that this control is not in fact control, but the exact opposite; it is "constitution," and further, it is not unification, but the exact opposite, the "production of an antagonism." Thus, this word control, characterized by a vulgar demagogy, reaches its summit in the control of literature.

Chapter Ten

THE FATE OF JAPANISM

From Fascism to the Ideology of the Imperial Way

Japanism is a form of thought born of the definite, particular circumstances of fascism. Strictly speaking, it cannot be seen as only some idealist object, for as this ideal infiltrates and is deployed in the economic mechanisms and material base of society, it forces itself onto those material social mechanisms. So, despite that fact that Japanism is fundamentally an idea that arose from particular material social conditions, it does not objectively reflect the material foundation that produced it. Thus, as a form of thought, and a disastrous form at that, from the start Japanism has a fundamentally ideological essence. Put simply, it is "The Japanese Ideology." Here I want to briefly analyze the various conditions and outcomes of this Japanism.

When monopoly capitalism becomes imperialistic, it veils the domestic contradictions of imperialism through state power, while internationally it pretends it can solve those contradictions through force. Fascism is the political mechanism that takes advantage of the domestic and international anxieties of the petite bourgeoisie—the middle classes in the broad sense—those who have lost faith in both the dictatorship of the proletariat and the naked rule of the bourgeoisie. Fascism is the relatively expedient means creating the fantasy that it shares the middle classes' own interests, yet all the while, in fact, successfully extending the rule of finance capital.

The general political, social, and economic policies of this fascism aside, in the case of Japanist fascism, we must pay special attention to a particular form that can arise from the imperialistic essence of fascism, namely a vague ~~militar~~ism or ~~militaristic~~ consciousness. This social consciousness arises when imperialism is faced with the necessity of conducting an imperialistic war. Of course, viewed as a general social consciousness, a militaristic consciousness need not necessarily be imperialistic, but conversely, given imperialism—meaning when the possibility of imperialistic war has some actuality (this is what we mean by necessity)—an imperialistic consciousness is always produced. Our problem here is when this imperialistic consciousness also possesses a fascistic character.

Of course, a fascist militarist consciousness is today a rather common global phenomenon. But in the case of Japanism, there further appears an ~~aggressive, militaristic~~ consciousness characterized by the existence and the consciousness of a privileged occupational group limited to Japan: the military. This characteristic ~~militaristic~~, imperialistic, fascist, and ~~militaristic~~ and ~~xenophobic~~ consciousness is a defining feature of Japanism. This is the defining characteristic of Japanism as the summa of Japanese fascism.

As people surely know, we must not forget that the ~~military~~ clique or the ~~military~~ authorities are not simply a social stratum or social group or an occupational organization, but in fact derive all their enormous power from the authority of the ~~emperor as commander in chief~~ [*tōsuiken*]. Here "military authorities" mean all professional ~~military personnel~~ whose social status is guaranteed by an economic freedom. Speaking from the social perspective of economic life (not their place in the chain of command), "military authorities" indicate all those but the unemployed ~~soldiers~~ and low-ranking ~~officers~~ excluded from the so-called ~~military personnel~~. Regardless of their previously mentioned relationship to the authority of the ~~emperor as commander in chief~~, considered as a stratum of civil society, this military, both formally and practically, indicates ~~military~~ bureaucrats with variously guaranteed social statuses, the majority of which are economically no higher than the upper middle class. If these bureaucrats are a kind of middle class, then the same must be said of "the military" as well. If fascism is generally supported by the consciousness of the middle class, then the fact that Japanism is supported by the virtually uniform consciousness nurtured by the military possesses an essential meaning.

But of course, it is absolutely no coincidence this sort of "~~military~~" has become the subject that underwrites Japanism's ~~militaristic~~ consciousness today. The emergence of this military, or rather its establishment, was the unavoidable and necessary result of opposing the oppression of foreign capital during the Meiji Ishin [1868]. Thus, both the historical necessity—and the militarist essence—of Japanism must be acknowledged. Furthermore, the establishment of such a military, seen even from the development of the Japanese military system, was one of extreme necessity. Today's common sense holds that Japan as a nation of soldiers is believed to be rooted in the ancient Japanese military system that restored the imperial court [ōsei fukkō, the Meiji Ishin, 1868]. Here we see a long-run necessity for a military-led militarist consciousness that became one of the essences of Japanism.

In treating the so-called ~~military~~ as a group of ~~military~~ bureaucrats, I have already provided a basis for distinguishing it from "~~soldiers~~" in general. Accordingly, saying the "the entire nation as soldiers" is absolutely not the same as saying "the entire nation as the military." From the perspective of the actual military system of universal conscription, all citizens are soldiers, but in terms of their professional social status, all citizens are not "the military." Yet these two different understandings are conflated in the ideal of an entire nation of soldiers.

Historically speaking, the gap between this organizational ideal and the realities of civil society too easily gives birth to the fantasy of a special link between today's ~~military~~ and the samurai class of the medieval and early modern eras. Put another way, today's military is thought of as a modern (nonhereditary) group of neosamurais. Thus, it is imagined that this ancient Japanese *bushidō*, "way of the warrior," which peaked in the Tokugawa era, courses through the blood of today's exalted soldiers.

The very fact that a distinct social ~~force~~ or group of ~~soldiers~~ called the ~~military~~ exists despite the reality of universal conscription, and that it evokes some kind of direct relation to the samurai class and *bushidō*, means that even at the ideal level, the military consciousness of this ~~military~~ must be a kind of feudal consciousness. This so-called *bushidō* has long been praised by foreigners for its uniquely Japanese character (a rare example of Japanism in the broad, international sense[1]), and today forcefully stressed by the Japanese themselves, is clearly the ideal of the whole of the Japanese folk (and Japanese citizens?). But *bushidō* as the ideal of the entirety of the Japanese folk only stems from a military system in which all are considered to be soldiers. If any other social reality is mixed in, *bushidō* becomes a feudal ideology of a particular social stratum.

THE FATE OF JAPANISM

Of course, the overwhelming majority of citizen-soldiers that are to be led by the military are farmers. Thus, for this militarist consciousness to have any actuality or any success, it must find its trusted base in the farmers. If the entire nation were indeed soldiers this would be a matter of course. At the same time, because an entire nation of citizen-soldiers as an ideal of the military system, and not the same thing as the social relations of economic distribution, when we say farming strata (or what are called the farming villages) we are not making an issue of the economic stratification within it; we instead mean those who live under the social order of the farming villages—in other words, farmers in general. Now the backbone of, and model subjects for, upholding the social order of the farming villages (mountain and fishing villages as well), and thus the people who most adequately represent the farming villages, are the various medium-scale farmers, or the rural middle class. The medium-scale farmers and this rural middle class are thus most representative of an entire nation of soldiers. They are the true social base upon which the ~~military~~ as the subject of a Japanist ~~militaristic~~ consciousness places its highest hopes.

That the rural middle class and the medium-scale farmers are the social foundation upon which the military-led Japanist militaristic consciousness places its greatest hope of success is little more than a particular instance of the general case that fascism is the consciousness of the middle class. Now, because in general the rural middle class and the medium-scale farmers are a reliable part of the present mechanisms of agricultural production, so much so that we call them the backbone of the farming villages, their daily consciousness can be described as *agriculturalism* [*nōgyōshugi*]. But if this consciousness comes into conflict with others, and when it is *linked to a national history*, the result is the so-called *agrarian fundamentalism* [*nōhonshugi*]. With this problem now linked to the history of the Japanese folk or people, this agrarianism inevitably slides toward a feudalist ideology [*hōkenshugi*] that looks to agricultural production as the basis of the feudal mode of production.

Thus the problem comes down to the difference between a historical *feudal system* and a *feudalist ideology* existing within actual, present-day civil society. As stated above, the Japanist militaristic consciousness arrived at an idealist, feudalist consciousness by passing through the military's conscious identification with the samurai class. Now we arrive again at a feudalist consciousness by passing through the realities of the farming villages. But the key determination of this feudalist consciousness lies in the concept of the "unity of soldiers and farmers" [*heinō itchi*].[2]

We say "the feudal system," but even if we focus on the era in which a feudal system most clearly took shape, we see that the feudal era is extremely old and long and includes many political variations. So we must acknowledge that what is popularly called a feudalist consciousness in Japan today is in fact nothing but a vague restorationism. Depending on the era to be restored, restorationism carries somewhat different determinations and drastically different meanings. But putting aside for the moment just what final determinations, and what final meanings restorationists today ascribe to their various restorationisms, we notice that our real problem is this vague restorationist consciousness. That is, this vague restorationism is clearly synonymous with a consciousness that tends toward the feudal.

Of all the current varieties of restorationism, the most fundamental and characteristic example—though restorationists themselves may disagree—is the emphasis on familialism. The family system itself developed as the keystone of the social order during the Tokugawa period [1600–1867], when the feudal system is thought to have been most complete. Therefore, the promotion of familialism must first and foremost correspond to the family system that reached its height in the Tokugawa feudal system. For some reason it seems no one looks for the historical basis of familialism in the family structure of the Heian period [794–1185]. Here, too, it once again turns out that restorationism is synonymous with the promotion of a vague feudalistic consciousness.

But Japanism's feudalist and restorationist intention of moving society toward a historical feudal system, one very different from the advanced era of monopoly capitalism in which it was born, means that it is a vague, haphazard restorationism; and therefore, this move toward a feudalist consciousness—restorationism—is none other than the *primitivization* of society. Of course, it is impossible to actually primitivize a society that has developed into advanced capitalism. But *primitivizationism* [*genshikashugi*[3]] may be conveniently achieved in the realm of thought, of ideology; and directly related to this, the very word "primitivization" itself allows one to remain in the material world while subjectively and ideally wishing for a feudal restorationist return. (Restorationist and feudalistic ideological

THE FATE OF JAPANISM

movements only make sense as idealist movements.) For example, while actual productive technologies cannot be primitivized or detechnologized, it is quite possible to wish for such an ideology, at least in thought. Furthermore, in pure thought, it is easily possible to link the growing global antitechnological view of "civilization" with an antimaterialism, an ideology that seeks the destruction of materialism.

While this all concerns the feudalization of consciousness in general, and a vague, haphazard restorationism or primitivism in general, as stated above, the key moment for Japanism's militaristic feudality occurred with the "unity of farmers and soldiers"—the merging of a nation of soldiers and agrarian fundamentalism. We must keep in mind that a military system lacking professionals and the domination of agriculture as the center of life are generally considered to be basic characteristics of primitive society. Even when we see this not as a historical feudal system, but as a "feudality"[4] that has had its main points abstracted out, it is clearly possible to bypass restorationism and make a single, direct leap to primitivization. Thus, when yoked to national history, in the end, this feudality is reducible to a nativizationism. At first, it seemed that monopoly capitalism, imperialism, ~~militarism~~, and the ideology of ~~military rule~~ all boiled down to feudality. But now we see they are all reducible to a merely slightly less vague nativist primitivizationism.

But we have neglected an important point. Up to this point in our analysis, the restorationist phenomenon has been some vague restorationism. But this is not enough to serve as a fulcrum for today's more advanced (?) Japanism. We will have to scrutinize primitivization a bit more.

That is, what we have called the primitivization of society has simply meant an idealist movement that pushes for or desires the primitive nativizationism of society; but a more important point remains. As this nativizationist movement takes place in thought, it naturally follows that it also results in the primitivization of those thoughts themselves. Thus, this conceptual primitivization, or the dominance of primitive ideas, is characteristic of those social strata that are either naturally or intentionally strikingly behind in both their logic and social consciousness. Once again, the social strata in this case are the inhabitants of the farming villages and the ~~military~~. For the farming villages this is surely the result of their lack of any wider intercourse; for the military it is undeniably the deliberate aim of their education. But more important here is that to become a form of social common sense,⁵ this primitive social consciousness must seize the minds of the class whose social consciousness is in turmoil: namely, this primitive social consciousness must seize hold of the middle classes.

Primitivization of the petite bourgeoisie appears under the banner of antitechnology, antimechanization, antimaterialism (?), and antirationalism, delusional religious consciousness, mysticism, occult beliefs tied to healing and fortune telling, and all other modern forms of primitive consciousness become an apparatus of capture for the turmoil within petit bourgeois, middle-class consciousness. Mysticism is the social consciousness of the middle class and the largely middle-class pacifist intelligentsia under Japanist fascism.⁶

Normally people likely associate mysticism with the ideology of the military. (It seems no one is too eager to promote a spiritualism of the farming villages.) But there is a very good reason why the military cannot go all in on a pure spiritualism: there cannot be a combat spirit that rejects mechanized infantry units. Primitivism is the natural common sense of today's middle-class citizens. But for this middle-class spiritualism to serve the interests of Japanism, it is linked to another "common sense" of the military. Here spiritualism cannot remain a simply voluntary spiritualism (such as European spiritualisms or Buddhist or Confucian spiritualisms)—it must become restorationist; that is, the general phenomenon of primivizationism becomes a [nationalistic] nativizationism. This means that by passing through spiritualism as the universal, global model of civic common sense, restorationism ceases to be a vague or haphazard, and becomes a social common sense centered around a specific political concept. That political concept is the Spirit of the Imperial Way centered on the imperial house [*kōdō seishin*].

Political concepts can never be established without a basis in civic common sense. Thus the military's promotion of a restorationism based on the unity of soldiers and farmers, on its own, is not yet a political conception. And the spiritualism of the petit bourgeois middle class is inadequate to any hope for a powerful material domination. But together, by merging the spiritualisms of the military and the middle class, the restorationism that dwells within Japanism may become the expression of the will of a fascist political power. Because this Spirit of the Imperial Way is precisely such a unification of the middle class and the military, it is the alpha and omega of Japanism. This is the ultimate, comprehensive conclusion of all we have analyzed thus far.

As space does not allow it, we leave undone the remaining task, to follow the reverse path and interrogate this essence of Japanist ideology,[7] now named the Ideology of the Imperial Way (note this does not mean the imperial house itself, but the ideology of the imperial house): How is it used as a current fascist political ideal? What are its political mechanisms? And furthermore, how does it serve the structure of the current, fascist form of capitalism?

PART II
Foundation for a Critique of Liberalism

Chapter Eleven

MODERN IDEALISM IN DISGUISE

Foundation for a Critique of
"Hermeneutic Philosophy"

There is absolutely no love within contemporary civic culture for the word "idealism." It is often easy to dismiss something with "that is idealism" or "that is idealist." And, indeed, there are particular, systematic connotations hidden within these accusations, so one of our jobs here will be to wash away those connotations. But for those attacked by labeling their thought idealist, the criticism does not always bite. They would likely respond, "My thought is absolutely not idealist. Isn't it in fact the very opposite of idealism? Your criticism that my work is some kind of idealism is nothing but proof that you know neither what idealism is nor what the main point of my thought might be."

Indeed, according to such people, idealism is an ideational ideology [*idea-shugi*], or an ideology of *ideals* [*ideeru shugi; risōshugi*]. To clarify, idealism for them is the belief that something is idealist only if it means some ideal has descended from the heavens and is imposed upon our present and made manifest, or that nothing truly exists but those objects with a perfect form in full relief, or again, that idealism means that the absolute abyss between reality and the ideal may be filled in by appropriate action (*Sollen*). In one sense this is absolutely true. But the problem is whether such people themselves are in fact secret agents of an idealism they purport to oppose. In so speaking of idealism we wonder if they are thinking of Socrates or

Plato or descendants like Kant. But merely opposing these figures is no proof that one is an anti-idealist.

Would Nietzsche be an enemy of idealism for destroying all moral authority and collapsing all its values? Or would Dostoyevsky, who in his later years had lost all faith in the ideal of socialist progress, be the true enemy of idealism? (On materialism see below.) According to Lev Shestov, the recently introduced philosopher of "anxiety" [*fuan*], idealism (and materialism, too!) are the enemy of the original philosophy of tragedy and nothingness. A new faction of contemporary theology believes it must protect theology from the romanticism of the Roman-ha form of idealism.[1] Nishida philosophy, presented as the premier case of Japanese and Eastern illumination, is in fact no different from the global phenomenon of bourgeois philosophy's self-criticism. (Bourgeois philosophy here means a philosophy that responds to the particular needs of actually existing bourgeois society rather than a philosophy unique to the bourgeoisie as a class.) Put another way, for these groups of people, idealism is merely a philosophy of "being" and thus because it is not a philosophy of nothingness, it is useless. At the same time, we can see just this intimation in not a small number of Nishida philosophy's practitioners: idealism must be buried, together with materialism!

It must be said, that in this time of capitalist crisis, the idea of condemning to death a particular instance of idealism as if it represented idealism in general is an extremely clever method of self-defense for bourgeois philosophy (in the above sense). "Idealism" is dead—but Nietzsche is part of the politician's skills, Dostoyevsky part of the literary conscience, and Shestov (rather, Kierkegaard with a dash of Heidegger) is in the minds of philosophers. All of these are not only perpetuating but in fact *restoring* idealism. In these sorts of thinkers, idealism purges all the disadvantages and impediments of bourgeois philosophy through the sacrifice of pure forms. With the current situation of Japan corresponding to the decade after 1905 in Russia, this situation is not just a self-defense of bourgeois philosophy; more likely, it is life-saving surgery. But that decade of the 1900s was also when [Lenin's] *Materialism and Empirio-criticism* [1909] had to be written.

Codes are changed during the course of war. And depending on whether it is on offense or defense, idealism, too, changes its stripes. Now idealism has shed its old skin, and especially has stopped calling itself idealism. Those who are fooled by this ruse are not grasping the cicada, but merely the cicada's cast-off shell—but by then the cicada is already off singing in other trees. Modern idealism has a habit of disguising itself. So to match its adversary, materialism, too, is no longer your run of the mill materialism. So just what is this idealism, this cicada and its cast-off shell? (A cicada that has shed its shell is still a cicada.) What is the true character of this new form which cannot be fully measured even with the older terms "idealism" or "ideals-ism" in Socrates or Kant, or the flood of idealist fineries in bourgeois philosophy? It is commonly said that the fundamental feature of idealism is that it is not the substance but the idea which is alpha and omega. But this word, idealism, is a poor one as it is extremely rich in content and too pregnant with meaning. Whenever such a vague idealism is put into practice, it is likely totally meaningless.

The word is useless unless it brings some *particular type* of idealism before our eyes. Even if the word is occasionally modified, activated, and adopted, such as Berkeleyan idealism or Kantian idealism or Machian idealism,[2] this alone is not the development of the word "idealism" itself, because the problem remains to grasp idealism from a *positive, active determination of the idea*, as something that is fundamentally prior to and replaces substance. Only once that understanding of idealism is put to use can this word "idealism" be made practical and active.

In current understanding, it is widely accepted that the first determination of idealism is found within metaphysics. Idealism's weak point is found in metaphysics; in contrast, materialism is antimetaphysical. Still certain refutations of Marx say that the Marxist philosophy within materialism is metaphysical and that this is its fatal flaw, by which they mean Marxism's supremacy of the material is merely an old metaphysics of matter, and it is thus unscientific and metaphysical to seek labor value or historical necessity or the kingdom of freedom behind phenomena. Which is to say, because it is neither an epistemology nor a positivism, it is a metaphysics. But "metaphysics" as a bourgeois philosophical category is not our problem here. According to materialist categories, metaphysics is nothing but a mechanistic way of thinking. Which means that metaphysics does not know how to grasp a thing in its associated movement, but rather is a method of thought that fixes thought into reified, discrete individual units.

But if we consider idealism from the various circumstances right before our eyes, we see that metaphysics as the sole determination of idealism is still not practical. As long as this determination is mainly what Hegel used to criticize Kant, and, of course, if it is thoroughly applied, Hegel's own idealism is itself metaphysical (though we must take care not to put the cart before the horse). In identifying idealism with metaphysics, the expression of this determination itself remains incomplete and will not necessarily land, because the same position from which contemporary bourgeois philosophy judges "idealism" poorly, also has no necessary love for "metaphysics." In contrast to countries in which metaphysics is commonly used in philosophy (France, for example), there are not many philosophers in Japan who would call their philosophy a metaphysics. Despite having metaphysics at the base of their idealism, they are not hesitant to reject metaphysics.

Of course this hidden metaphysics we are hunting here is absolutely not based on mechanistic philosophy. Indeed, the great majority of examples of it appear as condemners of mechanism. According to William James and Bergson, it is not isolated objects, but rather flow that is the true essence. It is said that as a long work on a single twenty-four-hour day, Joyce's *Ulysses*, is an example of a "realism," far from mechanism, and highly praised by "literary" realists. Furthermore, there are even those who think that they can progressively develop or ground this hidden metaphysics in the dialectic. Not only can we say that an idealist dialectic has not gone extinct from ancient times to today, but that today we have arrived at a true theological (!) dialectic, a source of pride for today's certain type of veiled metaphysicians.

So we must remember that at various points above I stated that metaphysics would require a slightly different determination. Thus, contemporary metaphysics, all of it—be it mechanistic or dialectic—is nothing but a "hermeneutic philosophy," a philosophy of interpretation [*kaishaku no tetsugaku*]. By being a philosophy of interpretation, the whole of contemporary bourgeois philosophy, superior and inferior both, is metaphysical. It is by being metaphysical in this sense that it is thought that purely interpretive, hermeneutic philosophy, specifically and positively, deserves the name idealism. Of course, designating metaphysics (and idealism) this way is neither new nor some rebirth within the history of materialism. As people surely know, just such a designation was promised in a few short words by Marx in *Capital*.

Thus we can here present hermeneutic philosophy as the second determination of idealism. If we do not so designate it, the fear is that we could not complete our investigation into whether bourgeois philosophy is actively idealist.

Of course, interpretation is the interpretation of facts [*jijitsu*]. If there is no fact, there is no interpretation in any sense of the term. It is also true that there is no fact without interpretation. Historical truth or falsehood will be decided by interpretation, as in the way we say that there is room for interpretation of the facts of an experiment. It is said that the place where one directly bumps up against truth is in interpretation. But if that is the case, as there is no such thing as a pure fact, such an individual interpretation is in all likelihood simply some isolated impression. In that sense, a fact is none other than something interpreted as such. Facts cannot be found where there is no interpretation.

It is all the more so when the problem is made philosophical. No philosophy can deal with things without recourse to or passing through interpretation. In that sense it is not too much to say that every philosophy is a philosophy of interpretation. Originally, the interpretation of a fact was the interpretation of the meaning that fact possessed, and thus a fact became a fact by means of the meaning it had (if not, such a fact is meaningless). For a philosophy to expose the unseen relations between the surface of facts, to *grasp their hidden unity*, to decide if a fact has any meaning, it is natural and necessary that this is found in the power of interpretation.

But within this interpretation itself, within this interpretation of the meaning of a fact itself, lies a problem. To speak of facts, in order to make use of and develop them themselves, and thus accordingly the meaning of facts, refers to the development and evolutionary course[3] of the facts themselves. Here there is an important point: the various meanings of various facts are ultimately the burden of the facts themselves. Accordingly, facts can first get their stability as facts by passing through their meaning and returning again to themselves. Meaning must return to the fact itself, with a responsibility to face again the original fact. Thus the interpretation of a fact is always the *practical* handling of the fact. Practicality is the only way to realistically change anything, or at least practically changing something must be the goal. As for the practical treatment of actually existing objects [*genjitsu no jibutsu*], it is thus imagined that the superior interpretation is always one of the meaning *possessed by* these objects.

But "hermeneutic philosophy"—the philosophy of interpretation—stumbles over this practical capacity of interpretation. Here the interpretation abandons its original role and forgets the original necessity and motivation for interpretation to practically deal with facts, and instead develops interpretation as interpretation for its own sake. Which is to say, the meaning of a fact is no longer the meaning of a fact, but is now detached, it has become ungrounded and free-floating "meaning itself." Thus, meaning replaces facts, and the facts of reality are now *produced by* this meaning. Meaning has now become independent of the actual fact that was the original womb of the meaning; it is independent of the fact's evolution and developmental course,[4] and we must note how it now becomes possible to rely exclusively on the mutual relations of meanings themselves, and thus construct a world of pure meaning. Despite the fact that the relations between one "meaning" and another "meaning" should have relied on the relations between facts born of various wombs, here the relations between meanings are radically, abstractly, ingeniously (?) short-circuited. And so, in place of reality is born "the world of meaning." The actual world is considered only after forcing it into "the world of meaning," and from there it is interpreted according to the convenience of meaning itself. This is the so-called mechanism of "interpretation" of hermeneutic philosophy. That which seemed to be an ingenious (?) imaginative power, a skill, a conception, or seemed to be an insight, is in fact, a frenzied, cheap juxtaposition of concepts. Moreover, it is merely simple, superficial, inferential thinking.

In a vulgar sense, such a precious weakness is easily recognized by all. Suicides in Japan have drastically increased in recent years, yet this has received no real interpretation in the newspapers. See for example, the philosophical artfulness, of the old, tired, yet at the same time most innovative, sort of interpretation in which a daughter commits suicide because her father joined the ~~Communist party~~. Perhaps because for newspaper articles any old facts will do, these articles, *as mere articles*, have a free-floating independent meaning unto themselves. But if this same weakness also lurks within the armory of philosophy, then the result is a hermeneutic philosophy and its defects are not easily done away with. There are solemn terms and a dignified tone. But if from time to time, and fragmentarily, there may be elements that come into contact with the ready-made wisdom of the reading and listening public, these sentimental clichés may be emotionally moving, coddling, and soothing for them. In place of deconstruction and argumentation, there is merely a series of emotional button pushing. This is one of the most characteristic features of hermeneutic philosophy, and through it, the practical treatment of actual things is warded off, sometimes through ecstasy, sometimes through tears. Idly standing by yet somehow still subduing the world by "interpreting" it in this way is surely a pleasant task. For these purposes, tearfully eating, or tossing and turning in angsty sleepless nights, is indeed a pleasant task.

It will shock no one to note that much of what is called *Lebens* philosophy is precisely this sort of hermeneutic philosophy. According to *Lebens* philosophy, interpretation is merely the self-interpretation of life. Thanks to life interpreting itself, this means that one is drawn into the world of pure meaning, independent of the facts. (The scientific significance of life is still a problem, however.) There is no need here to discuss the inseparable relation between this "philosophy of [mere] interpretation" and the "philosophy of history" or "hermeneutic phenomenology." It is enough to point out how both of these philosophies are based on, and have the flavor of, philology and its hermeneutic method.[5] The important point remains the same: the essence of hermeneutic philosophy both consciously and unconsciously tries to avoid the actual treatment of facts.

A hermeneutic philosophy is that which, under the name of philosophy, avoids practical problems. Thus current affairs have no philosophical meaning, for what is required by such a philosophy of mere interpretation is that hermeneutic philosophy's own principle problem be independent of actual problems. As for actual problems, when this principle problem does occasionally engage with them, the engagement is predetermined, and thus useless. Take the example of society: the *meaning* of society can be developed as exclusively founded in the ethical, meaningful relations between I and Thou, so that as society moves toward communism or fascism, we have an actual political problem, yet this hermeneutic philosophy of pure meaning completely fails to problematize it.[6] Hermeneutic interpretation is not abstract because it argues problems on a general scale or because it uses difficult terms; it is abstract because it abstracts meanings from facts and principles from actual problems, thus abolishing from its view the actuality of facts and their actual relations.

So the very nature of abstraction from the real world is clearly characteristic of contemporary metaphysics. Contemporary metaphysics' nonsense and silliness makes it absolutely impossible for it to deal with actual problems at all. This nonsense is also what makes today's academic and pedantic philosophy appear, like a school teacher, so earnest and sincere. And thus, this unreal, abstract metaphysics is the most powerful and popular form of idealism today.

It is thought wise that in order to intentionally avoid actual, practical problems, interpretive philosophy (metaphysics, idealism) frequently severs itself from empirical and natural sciences, or at least ignores them. "Philosophers of history" never forget to stress that historical things, which are according to them "philosophical" things, are somehow different from natural scientific things. For these "philosophers" anyone who looks at the common essence and mutual development of history and nature is someone who does not know history, to say nothing of being blind to human culture. Furthermore, when we come to "hermeneutic philosophers," the empirical and natural sciences have no philosophical significance at all. The scientific nature of philosophy—that is, its objectivity (from which comes its empirical and practical character)—is never problematized at all. Philosophy, they say, has its own, completely unrelated order. A certain faction of these Heideggerians insist that existence and wisdom given by the empirical practices of the world have nothing to do with an originary life of Heidegger's human "Being."

Such monkish antiscientism tries to evade the actual problem, for those problems are the inevitable result of such a rarified and purified hermeneutic philosophy—that said, the coarse scientism of Le Dantec[7] is nothing to be respected. Without stating its true intentions, through Kant down to the neo-Kantians—and in fact including Hegel as well—bourgeois society has recently begun imputing its own contradictions to problems within the natural sciences, so that for the first time the true nature of this philosophy has revealed itself.

But if we consider just what aspect of science, especially natural science, this "interpretation" resists, it is not in fact science's rationalism, its a priori restrictions, nor is it its nonhuman simplicity. In truth, this

MODERN IDEALISM IN DISGUISE

interpretation opposes the *demands of the material technology of production* based on the practicality of science. Hermeneutic philosophers fear that these material demands will seep out, penetrating the contents of their interpretations. But material technologies of production must be put to use and adopted *practically*—they cannot be interpreted away. For those who wish only to "interpret" the world, they must therefore invoke some problematic substitute. Thus, an ideology of antitechnology (better: an ideology with no respect for technology) is the true shape of the interpretive metaphysics' antiscientism above. Recently, the bourgeoisie has imputed responsibility for the various contradictions of capitalism to an inherent impasse within technology itself. And so, our age of capitalist crisis is precisely the moment when the bourgeoisie must conjure a philosophy of interpretation.[8]

Yet it should be noted that in order to become a full philosophy, interpretive philosophy (as metaphysics) must also organize itself into a particular categorical system. But, of course, the resulting system must be one of categories and a categorical organization conducive to the mere "interpretation" of the world. There is nothing more suited to this need than the most classic and archetypical logic of Judeo-Christian creationism [*sōzōsetsu*]. Creationism interprets the order of the world as a complete and holistic assemblage. If one may so easily explain the origin, course, and endpoint of the world then one could not wish for a more wonderfully appropriate method than the mere "interpretation" of things: The world is created by the good will of God, its creation is part of a plan, and it develops according to that plan, so that when the final judgment day comes, God's plan is realized. The actual, material world with its practical flavor and an order born of the natural sciences is replaced with a world order put there by a magnanimous emperor's boundless grace. Upon the surface of this converted new order is distributed an entire zodiac of interpretation's metaphysical categories.

I have called all of these types of categories theological categories. Because by its very nature a category based in another world order is of no use for supporting the actual, practical world, such a theological category can have no meaningful practicality, actuality, empiricality, or falsifiability. Such a theological category is necessarily a category that cannot be tested in a secular world ordered by material technologies of production. Thus,

I also label all these theological categories antitechnological as well (cf. "The Philosophy of Technology").[9] To summarize the argument so far: the philosophy of interpretation is founded on theological categories.

So far, I have said nothing that I have not said repeatedly elsewhere. But recently, we must note that in Japan the metaphysics of interpretation has begun to take a unique form. It is thus now necessary to designate the third positive determination of idealism. It seems that by examining this third positive determination we will be able to clearly establish idealism's second determination (hermeneutic philosophy) as well as the first (its metaphysical nature).

Let's first focus on the phenomenon at hand. It is said that Marxist campaigns have been in retreat for the past year. Exactly why is unclear, but nonetheless, it is true that recently there has been a remarkable public curtailment of Marxist supporters and Marxist sympathizers. And it is of interest to point out that this phenomenon is especially pronounced, and much discussed, in the case of literature. Even if we understand that though Marxist cultural groups have largely disappeared, it does not necessarily follow that Marxist cultural movements are extinct, and everyone knows that recently there has been a remarkable wave of disbanded cultural groups in literature. Left-wing literary movements have been dispersed into several editorial centers and so have no conscious affiliation or significance for a left-wing cultural movement. Some say that the urgent task is that, in the name of restoring the arts, literature itself must be developed, and thus these people stress that factional literary sympathies must be sacrificed to standardization and the constraints of current proletarian literature must be destroyed. Regardless of whether they do so under the banner of artistic revival, anti-Marxist authors or believers welcome this new development, either because they are good at it or out of some ironic revenge motive.

For both Marxists and other authors this phenomenon means, in fact, an ideology touting the ultimate supremacy of "pure literature," a literature for literature's sake, a cult of the literary, or even literature über alles [*bungaku shijō shugi*]. I think Marxist authors are more careful on this point, though, like many others, even I am wrong for positing—even for the sake of argument—that such a wholly independent literary realm actually exists. As the current literary world is no exception to the fundamental tendency of anti-Marxism of the current situation in Japan, this anti-Marxist ideology of "the literary" will be the most prominent feature of this larger trend. This is because the majority of "literary figures" believe that the fundamental thesis of Marxist literary theory was the joining of literature and politics, and that it is this connection to politics that has since been almost completely removed.

We must also notice that literary criticism has recently been radically "philosophized." Of course, this is the result of two causes. The first occurred by means of the general restoration of the veiled bourgeois idealistic philosophy I've already mentioned. The second stemmed from those authors and thinkers uneasy with the problem of the relation of literature to politics, a group that included even some leftist writers grounded in a scientific literary criticism based on historical materialism. These two causes fed on one another in the literary criticism written by these bourgeois idealists.

Thus, first from fetishization of "the literary" and second from the philosophization of literature, we get the third moment, the "literature"-ization of philosophy itself. Although philosophy and literature should have an inseparable relationship, and thus it may be perfectly natural, not unusual, or necessarily a bad thing, for literature (and literary criticism) to become philosophical or for philosophy to become literary, in this current case, philosophy becoming literary here clearly means that philosophy must become merely the ultimate instance of literature for literature's sake.

But while the cult of the literary may have some meaning within literature itself, and the relationship may be the same, the very words "literature über alles" [*bungaku shijō shugi*] is likely completely meaningless as far as philosophy is concerned. And it is not just meaningless. This term, "the supremacy of the literary," exposes the essence of the literaturification of philosophy. In fact, it may be better to call this phenomenon philosophy for philosophy's sake. Here we used the example of literature for literature's sake in literary studies to explain in different words philosophy for philosophy's sake. Because philosophy is not literature there is no fear that it could become this same ideology of literature for literature's sake. Instead, it is necessary to call the new form into which contemporary bourgeois idealism—metaphysics, interpretive philosophy—has fallen, a cult of the literary, a "literaturism," [*bungakushugi*], within philosophy. We can say that this literaturism itself is the third, active determination of idealism.

While we still need to explain the meaning of literaturism, no matter how literaturist a philosophy may be, beyond using a philosophical form, literaturism must make use of a categorical organization to explain things. But the categories of literaturist philosophy are literary categories. So then, just what does it mean to be a "literary category?" As long as literature is something dependent on the tools of language, literature is first established by being coupled with a concept. As for concepts, the tendency is to think of them as unselfconscious, abstract routines of an "idea." Using this word—*concept*—in such a simple, even vulgar way is wholly inadequate, considering that the word is a theoretical term. But of these various concepts within literature, the ones that are comparatively essential, mobile, and robust—with points of contact with other categories—may be further designated as fundamental concepts; that is, they are *categories*. But just because a category may come from and be used within literature does not mean that it is immediately a literary category.

With just a bit of thought it is clear that categories appearing within philosophy, science, and all other theories—that is, philosophical, scientific, and theoretical categories—are in the end no different from those categories within literature. Indeed, if the essence of an any given category were in fact unique as a matter of principle, then just how could we even have any contact, communication, agreement, or correspondence between literature and philosophy at all? It is well-known that if two things lack any relations—correspondence, agreement, commonality, and so on—we say that these two things are categorically different.

Thus the categories that appear in literature are normally not unique categories; they are the normal categories born from the same worldview as those philosophical and scientific categories, and they belong within a series of philosophical and scientific categories. Of course, there are many cases where a given category may be mainly literary and another more philosophical. Further, it is possible that the same word may indicate a category that has a different meaning in the philosophical or scientific worlds. In this sense, it is fine to say that a given literary category is different than a philosophical or scientific category. The problem, however, is not whether this or that individual category belongs to this or that world. If so many varied categories were present, it would be a serious problem for the logical demands of any given organizational order within that categorical system.

Theoretically speaking, a general theory of categories dictates that it is not the case that science and philosophy are one series of particular categories, and against this, literature is another, different categorical series. Ignoring this rule to say that the categorical orders of philosophy and science are different from literature—that is, categorically different, different at the level of principle—and that one has faith in only the categorical order of literature, recklessly using it for everything, is what makes something a "literaturist category" [*bungakushugiteki hanchū*].

The insidious nature of such a literary categorical order is that it often unfortunately, and confusingly, uses many of the exact same names as philosophical—normal—categories. It is a present fact that "reality" or "actuality," "truth" or "sincerity" are all philosophical categories, but at the same time, these terms are misused today by a certain type of literary figure as "literaturist" categories. Now if there is anyone who feels my so-called literary categories are, in fact, ultimately the same as philosophical categories; and further, that compared with philosophy these literary categories are treated as more or less extremely flexible objects and grasped in a finer, narrower way when compared to philosophy's treatment of larger issues of clarity and universality, such a resulting philosophy or literature would still be thought or written in unreconstructed literary categories, and it is this sort of conception that we sought to criticize here.

But unless we can explain why literary categories are so loved by literaturists, and why the insidiousness of this method isn't easily noticed, we could not grasp the significance of literary categories. The relation is that naturally, and as a matter of course, literaturists use literary categories *in place of* scientific and philosophical categories. Speaking of the actual method, the categories and fundamental concepts used in literature, philosophy, and science ultimately are all part of the same organization. But at the stage when one gives intuitive form to these concepts, that is, when it is a question of method for giving intuitive form to representing a phenomenon conceptually, literary phenomena are already no longer scientific or philosophical phenomenon—in fact they cannot be. Put another way, philosophy uses philosophical categories borrowed from philosophical phenomena, but in contrast, though literature may use the same philosophical category, it must borrow it from literary phenomena.

Yet, speaking from the perspective of everyday common sense insufficiently trained in theory, it is not necessarily an unforgiveable flaw if literary phenomena and concepts are treated as the same thing. In literature, there are various representations of an intuitive idea that are specific to literature. Authors can do fine work merely making full use of such intuitive representations. But when it comes to literary critique or literary criticism, literary scholars, indeed anyone, must search within literature for the invisible framework assembled through these representations and ideas. This is the time to seek out the concepts and categories within literature. Generally speaking, however, this is also the moment when those literary figures who have material grounds for advocating "the literary" as philosophy itself are exposed as being inadequately trained in philosophy. Which is to say, naturally one may excavate conceptual mechanisms in literature, but for that very reason literary categories will only be adequate to literary representations. Literary scholars thus imagine that by relying exclusively on literary phenomena they have the right to construct concepts and categories (not representations) unique to literature. And this is how they construct a "literary" categorical order. When these sort of literary scholars with their literature über alles turn to philosophy, they become "literaturists."

When it comes to literature itself, because literary *representation* is not the same as the *categories and concepts* within literature (or indeed literary categories), when I stress the philosophical interests of categories and concepts in literature, it is not to overlook the great literary value of literary representation. And so here, suddenly, we run up against the question of literature's creative method and worldview. And that is not all; the literary creation of timeless characters is absolutely not a conceptual or categorical problem. In fact, it is one of the treasures of literary *representation*. Philosophically, a categorical organization is a living aspect of literature, and so accordingly, at the same time, the creation of characters from Hamlet, Don Quixote, Bazarov,[10] Carmen, and others is, literarily speaking, the value of literary representation. Previously I had tried to theoretically synthesize concepts and characters, but I must now admit the attempt ran into some impossibilities, and further, there was the danger of being dragged into the quagmire of literary categories, in the above sense. (See the first chapter of *The Logic of Ideology*).[11]

MODERN IDEALISM IN DISGUISE

Today, the majority of the literary cultists secretly rely on literary categories in their literary activities, but this basis in literary categories is exposed when these scholars turn to literary criticism. While not rare, there is likely something to the fact that even writers who have produced excellent literary representations degenerate into foolish and silly critics when they attempt even the slightest bit of literary criticism. But this is not about literature; our problem is philosophy itself being based on these literary categories and how significant such a philosophy is in bourgeois Japan's cultural society. This point is especially easy to see, again, when these bourgeois idealist philosophers attempt any literary criticism as such a philosophy, when turned toward literary criticism, has all the merits and weaknesses of being "literary." What attitude is taken, or will be taken, by this literaturist philosophy against empiricism, the ideology of industrial technology, or rational logic more generally, is left for the reader to imagine.

We must also note that a philosophical consciousness or a consciousness of daily life appears not only as a literary consciousness, but also a political consciousness. Literaturism appears as a literary consciousness in the form of the primacy of the literary; literatureism's *political representation* is something we may call *literary liberalism*. We will examine literary liberalism in chapter 15, but recently it appears to be becoming a noteworthy theme even in literary circles. Originally, liberalism was a philosophical category, but now when it is exclusively supported only by a literary consciousness—the result of existing today within a different history and society for which it has no material basis—in a flash, liberalism itself has become a purely literary category. Literary liberalism is the word that expresses this remarkable phenomenon in today's Japan. Thus the large majority of writers in Japan today are liberals ("literary" liberals, that is). And so, because in Japan today liberalism does not exist in the world of politics, but only finds its support in the narrower world of literature, this situation tells us that we must acknowledge that the representative expression of liberalism today is a purely literary category. Thus, if one understands liberalism only in terms of literary categories, there are no grounds for understanding or interpreting such a liberalism as necessarily an expression of something progressive.

At first glance, it can be beautiful to speak of things using literary categories. But in the end, this results in a life rendered merely as a beautiful painting. Interpreting the world through literary categories makes the interpretation effortless and smooth. The cult of "the literary" is thus the perfect form of appearance of hermeneutic philosophy. It would have been impossible to achieve this type of "humanistic" charm simply using theological categories. So here hermeneutic philosophy turns its eyes from god to human beings, successfully developing itself until it reaches its apotheosis and becomes literaturism. By so doing, hermeneutic philosophy flees reality—unfortunately literaturists also love to use this word "reality." It flees the concrete reality, the practical problems, the principles dealt with by philosophical categories. For example, the prognosis, plan, and necessity of freedom in the actual material world are reduced to humanistic "passion," and real-world contradictions are replaced with human "angst." We could likely say that there exists no more riveting metaphysics than this. But such a cynical and moral (actually "moralistic") metaphysics is rare. ("Moral" for writers differs from morality in the actual world and is at base merely a literaturist concept). Recently, many have called André Gide the model of a moral writer. It is said that this Gide-the-moralist's "kind, literary heart" was pained when confronted with the structure of capitalist slavery in French sub-Saharan Africa. But if Gide were to offer an account of his so-called moral conversion [tenkō], he would likely have to confess that his moralism was unable to completely settle in a literary metaphysics, and so needed to call upon the practical morality of the real world.

Thus, first with metaphysics, then hermeneutic philosophy, and finally literaturist philosophy—all overlapping and supporting each other—we have before our eyes the model of an actively veiled "modern idealism" in Japan today.

Chapter Twelve

"THE LOGIC OF NOTHINGNESS," IS IT A LOGIC?

On Nishida's Philosophical Method

In my *Lectures on Contemporary Philosophy*[1] I offered my views on Professor Tanabe Hajime's philosophy. Since my aim in that piece was to acknowledge Tanabe's development of Kyoto School philosophy, I omitted any sharp examination of the differences between Tanabe and Nishida Kitarō's philosophy. But as Tanabe philosophy has been established, which is to say the very naming of it as "Tanabe philosophy" marks it as different from so-called Nishida philosophy, we must naturally make the differences between the two an issue. So it remains to take up Nishida philosophy here.

Of course, Kōyama Iwao, the commentary editor of *Shisō*, has already given readers a relatively generous, partial commentary of Nishida philosophy (February 1932), and has recently published an introductory text, *Nishida Philosophy*. But as neither of these texts come from any critical perspective, it seems to me that any examination of the original essence of Nishida's philosophy has been almost completely abandoned. Indeed, in his recent collection, *The Self-Conscious Determination of Nothingness*, Nishida himself has stated that this work represents a new stage in his research program. Thus, it would seem a good time to characterize Nishida philosophy as a whole. (I must confess a bit of a subjective reason for this, as elsewhere I attempted to characterize Nishida philosophy from without in my "Kyoto School Philosophy."[2] But as this piece was rather rough and the journal was not an academic one, it was not taken up within academia (?), and so I wish to elaborate on it here.)

Leaving aside my subjective wishes and motivations, we will problematize Nishida philosophy out of various objective and practical necessities. To wit, why is it so especially necessary to take up Nishida philosophy today? Apart from various conditions that we naturally should consider, Nishida philosophy's status today as a product of Japan or the world's most remarkable and powerful thought, or "musing" [*Grübelei*], is itself not a sufficient reason. Our present world is one in which all forms of fascist ideology strut about in broad daylight; a world where radio, newspapers, journals, and the like daily, endlessly, and so zealously embody nonsense and fraud that it surely scandalizes the ears of any philosopher who hears it. So, if anyone still believes that philosophers boldly promote "truth" here is evidence that such is simply not the case. Either consciously or unconsciously they all support fascist ideology, or at least that is their net effect. Such is clear once one sees that these philosophers view the antithesis of fascism—materialism—as the enemy. In short, these philosophers are bourgeois ideologues. I think that bourgeois philosophy is the essence of this bourgeois ideology, and today in Japan, the representative of bourgeois philosophy is clearly none other than Nishida philosophy. This is the main reason we must problematize Nishida philosophy.

Here already we encounter our first doubt. But we will disregard the objection that philosophy does not and should not have either a bourgeois or proletarian class nature. We can take up that issue once these people have done us the favor of reading a leftist text or two. Instead, our problem should be whether Nishida philosophy is in the end simply a generic bourgeois philosophy, or whether it is some other form of thought, such as feudal or fascist ideology in the guise of bourgeois philosophy.

There appears to be a basis for such questions when it comes to Nishida philosophy. Most Nishida devotees think his philosophy is Japan's uniquely creative philosophy, by which they mean that Nishida philosophy is a truly Eastern form of thought. Some have attempted to link it to Zen. (Of course, there are cases linking even Hegel to Zen.) Because pantheism, as opposed to a theory of a transcendent God, is generally considered to be Eastern, Nishida philosophy can be explained as pantheistic. In this sense its essence is non-Western, and thus should we compare it with Sōda Kiichirō's philosophy, Nishida can be thought of as having a feudal essence. Indeed, when compared to us moderns it is true that Nishida's is a cultivated Eastern philosopher (Buddhist or Confucian), and even feudal form of thought. It could be further thought that as it originates from a place with an especially strong feudal tradition—however inaccurate such an assumption might be—that Nishida would also be characterized by feudal traditions. But Nishida's mere inclusion of these Eastern and feudal elements in his thought does not mean that these elements are representative of Nishida philosophy.

While clearly pantheistic, Nishida philosophy's mysticism and religious thought, which are deemed Eastern and thus feudal, even these are absolutely not Eastern in the sense of being feudal. For example, Nishida philosophy is only Eastern in the same way that Plotinus is, or the way Augustine is Hebraic. Indeed, such Eastern-ness is an essential element of contemporary Western bourgeois thought. German thought is even shot through with mysticism, and so what we here call religious thought may only become the content of Nishida philosophy when combined with it. So first off, what are called the mystical and religious *contents* of Nishida philosophy are in fact absolutely not what is termed mysticism or religious *thought*. Nishida's method—and it is in method that a philosophy's character emerges—is not based on mysticism or religious thought. It lurks rather in the manner in which Nishida philosophy rationalizes that which lies outside of it or even that which opposes it (such as rationalism, criticism, or metaphysics). Even though Nishida's method is based on the Kyoto School's famous "nothingness," in the present discussion, that method is not the method of mysticism, nor is it a religious resolution. As this nothingness is invested with religious meaning, monks and priests imagine some kind of essential kindred relation between themselves and Nishida's philosophy, but that relation is in the religious *elements* within Nishida's philosophy, not in some *religious method*. (Of course, this must be the case as there is no such thing as a truly religious method.) Thus, the case for stressing Nishida's Eastern or feudal nature is inadequate.

So, what is the relation of Nishida's philosophy to fascist ideology? Since Nishida recently has come to take up the question of the dialectical method, it is said that Nishida's philosophy is a theological dialectic. Accordingly, it is said that this new theology agrees with Nazism and general fascist ideology on the question of actual problems. If that is true, then it would appear that Nishida somehow belongs to fascist ideology. But this assertion only works if one takes a lot of shortcuts; it cannot be made directly. First, it must be said that Nishida's philosophy is not a theological dialectic; second, even if, for the sake of argument, the dialectic used in Nishida's philosophy is largely the same as a theological dialectic, as we shall see below, because Nishida's philosophical method is in no way any kind of dialectic at all, what we actually have here is some other kind of method that merely explicates the dialectic but is not a dialectic itself. In the same way that Nishida's philosophy may, in certain circumstances, have a feudal effect, it cannot be said that Nishida's philosophy can never be linked with fascist ideology or can never have a fascist effect, only that those effects are not found in its essence.

Now, all that being said, objections likely remain. As a practical question, today's intelligentsia possessed of a progressive consciousness no longer have much of their previous enthusiasm for Nishida's philosophy, and we should wonder just how many progressive students are eagerly reading Nishida these days. In this sense, Nishida is no longer cutting-edge, modern philosophy, and Nishida philosophy is no longer popular among the new strata. It might then be asked, is this not proof of Nishida philosophy's feudal, and accordingly fascist, aspects? In fact, no, it is not. All this fall from grace shows is simply that Nishida's philosophy is an academic philosophy, not a journalistic one—or at least that it is losing its journalistic nature. Nishida philosophy once was journalistic (back before a theoretical journalism had gained independence from the academy), and it was then that it achieved its previous popularity. But recently, bourgeois philosophy has generally lost its progressive, journalistic appeal and retreated to the ivory tower. Bourgeois philosophy could only survive as a purely academic philosophy or as a secularization of the customs of the academy; and Nishida's philosophy is no exception. Thus, what appears to be Nishida's feudalistic or even fascistic aspects is nothing more than the philosophy of academia. In other words, Nishida philosophy's apparent links to feudal and fascist ideology is proof only that it is the perfectly proper philosophy of bourgeois society.

So then where do we find the specific, positive reason for declaring Nishida's philosophy a truly bourgeois philosophy? The reason lies in Nishida's philosophical method; a philosophical method must be determined by means of the conscious goal for which it is used. Proceeding this way our problem now becomes a question of method.

"THE LOGIC OF NOTHINGNESS," IS IT A LOGIC?

Examining Nishida's method this way, by seeing method determined by its conscious aims, looking at its recent effects, and despite the whiff of all its mystical and religious metaphysics, it seems to me that Nishida's conscious aim is simply a Romantic one. In this sense, it is a question of just how the fundamental concepts—the various categories—are actually organized and ordered within his thought by the conscious aims, and in what way the world is interpreted along these lines. This method—founded in interpreting the world as categorical organization—clearly begins with Fichte. (It was with Fichte that the idea of linking reality and philosophy within a general system of meaning was first actualized.) Passing through Schelling, this line of thought culminates in Hegel; the whole process is simply the birth and rise of German Romantic philosophy. (Fichte was the first representative of German Idealism viewed as German Romantic philosophy.) Nishida's philosophy is the completion of this conscious aim in its purest, most self-conscious form. This "completion" has in the present case some Nishidian particularities, but like another stage of completion in Hegel, what allows Nishida's philosophy to appear to be able to disassemble and reconfigure all philosophical systems naturally comes from its conscious aim within a systematic organization of the world as Romantic categories.

Thus, Nishida philosophy is the orthodox development of bourgeois philosophy, which is why it is giving form to orthodox academic philosophy today. (This is clear when it is compared with what is called bourgeois philosophy of the Catholicism of Heidegger and others.) Nishida philosophy's status as the natural endpoint of Romantic (bourgeois) philosophy is the reason it must become an issue for us.

So, let us here try to simply make clear the particular character of Nishida's philosophical method. The first and last issue for Nishida's method is how to think about "being." Here we must already be on guard, for the question is not "what is being?" for example, is it material? spiritual? or some synthesis of the two? Rather, the question is, if we think about being, *how* are we able to think about it? It is not a question of being itself, but a question of how to establish the categories and concepts of being. This is a fundamentally important point.

Modern philosophy considers "being" starting with the opposition of subjectivity and objectivity. Tanabe's philosophy tried to put an end to this opposition. Nishida's philosophy is more Hegelian, more Aristotelian.

Which is to say, it tries to grasp being from within the determination of judgment. Doing so means that all thought about being must be the self-determination of a universal [*katholou*].³ Such determination in judgment is the self-determination of the universal of judgment, and so, in general, "being"—as something that is thought—is a kind of universal, something that is situated in a place (*basho*). But no matter how self-determined this universal of judgment is, in the end, it can never arrive at the individual (person or entity) [*kobutsu, kotai*]. This is because the individual should not be wholly determined by its environment as it is able to move and to act within it. Thus this universal of judgment is inadequate to think the individual. (Here this individual is nothing more than a guide or ferryman for what is later thought of as the individual self). Thus, *to think* the "individual," this universal of judgment must be transcended and the individual backed by a new universal. This new universal is what Nishida calls a "self-conscious universal" and it is only with this self-determination that the individual is thought to have any meaning. In the same way, both the self-determination of the active individual (*noesis*) and the expressive individual (*noema*) can be thought. Now, the universal above is thought of as the self-determination of the universal below, but what determines the universal at the ultimate depths? It is called the final universal, but because it is a universal that is thought, it is still a determined universal that exists in a specific place, that is, it is the final "being." But such a universal "being" is still determined, and as that which determines, it must be thought. Thus, this determination then is no longer "being." At base there is nothingness [*mu*], but this nothingness must be determining, this determining "nothing" must be thought of as a self-determination of nothingness. *Basho* is the place of nothingness [*mu no basho*].

"Being" nothing while still determining is in fact the meaning of self-consciousness [*jikaku*], of consciousness [*ishiki*]. Here we approach the problem of subjectivity and objectivity. Self-consciousness and consciousness are on the one hand determined by nothingness. But on the other, it is because they are determined by nothingness that they can be said to "be," which means that both planes lie directly on top of each other. Nishida calls the former *noesis* and the latter *noema*. But we must not forget that using these terms borrowed from Husserl's phenomenology means that if self-consciousness—the concept—is not placed squarely within the horizon of phenomenology, it is entirely meaningless.

"THE LOGIC OF NOTHINGNESS," IS IT A LOGIC?

Accordingly, all of the various categories of "being" had to be organized into a system: "the self-determination of nothingness." This is why Nishida's philosophy had to become a system. And finally, this is why the title of that collection mentioned above, *The Self-Conscious Determination of Nothingness*, represented a turning point in Nishida's philosophy.

The majority of received philosophies all have come to contain some incompleteness or impossibilities. Nishida reflects on and honestly accepts all their philosophical demands to then expose the antitheses and contradictions within them. According to the professor, those things that cannot be joined together should not be, for example subjectivity and objectivity, the future and the past, history and the idea [イデー], and so on; it is their essential nature to never be joined. But in whatever manner these sorts of essentially incompatible objects have been joined in practice, they fall into difficulty when their unity *cannot then be thought*. That is, the manner of *thinking about* "being" is bad. In other words, thinking about "being" starts from the assumption that something exists which is then thought with a logic of being. Nishida believes this is only thinking of being on the plane of the *noema*. Thus it is necessary to think of being determined by nothingness; it is necessary to think being beginning with this nothingness. If not, Nishida believes that "being" generally may not be thought at all, and there is nothing to do but lapse into inescapable contradictions. What is required is not a "logic of being" but a "logic of nothingness." Thus, nothingness is a method (a mechanism), and as such nothingness cannot be considered as some metaphysical object; to think of it as metaphysical is to think of it as noetic. In other words, it is to think of nothingness as something that exists (a nothingness that exists in opposition to being makes nothingness merely another kind of being), which would ultimately mean that such a metaphysical nothingness is no longer nothingness.

But because Nishida's nothingness is a logical tool, it clearly does not have some kind of foundation [*Grund*] within mysticism (*Ungrund*, for example); it finds its direct source in our self-consciousness and consciousness. The logic of nothingness, then, is none other than the logic of self-consciousness.

The ultimate point of Nishida's philosophy is this method. As such we must examine the essence of this method, "the logic of nothingness" or a "self-conscious logic," a bit more. Specifically, we will look at what Nishida philosophy thinks is the essence of the dialectic.

According to Nishida philosophy, none of the dialectics so far conceived of in philosophy have been true dialectics. This is because contradiction was problematized in a way that meant it could not be adequately grasped. In the past, contradiction has been assumed to be something that arises noematically, but for Nishida, if something is grasped noematically, while it may simply be change, opposition, or antagonism, it is not a true contradiction. This is because contradiction is always an internal contradiction and this internal opposition is something that is established within noesis, not noema. Thus, both idealist and materialist dialectics treat some kind of noematic ideal or material located within "being" (existence) that then is seen to establish a dialectic, but such a "logic of being" cannot be thought of as a dialectical contradiction. In a true dialectic, being can only be thought of as directly and immediately nothingness, life-as-death and death-as-life. The dialectic can only be thought by means of self-consciousness.

So what is here presented to us as the dialectic or the *dialectic of self-consciousness* is essentially only a *self-consciousness of the dialectic*. But, contra Nishida, for us, there is a reason that the dialectic must be thought of first as a fundamental law of existence, and therefore that we must always distinguish between being and the consciousness of being. Accordingly, it is further necessary to distinguish between the dialectic itself and the consciousness of the dialectic. The problem becomes for Nishida's philosophy that it is only a self-consciousness or consciousness of the dialectic; it is not the dialectic itself. Thus for Nishida, the issue is only how one achieves consciousness of the dialectic—how the dialectic is thought—which is only *the meaning of the dialectic* (of course, as something conscious, conceptualized). The dialectic itself never becomes the issue. Indeed, the place (*basho*) where the meaning of the dialectic is established is consciousness or self-consciousness—essentially then it is established through nothingness. But must it necessarily be true that the place where the dialectic itself is established is within consciousness and self-consciousness?

Because the dialectic (of self-consciousness) is first understood in the logic of nothingness it would appear that this logic is a dialectical one. But what is elucidated here is not the dialectic itself, but only the *meaning and the significance* of the dialectic, so that the dialectic is absolutely not

"THE LOGIC OF NOTHINGNESS," IS IT A LOGIC?

something that is used. The effect of the logic of nothingness's problematization of the dialectic is the meaning and significance of the dialectic, the logic of nothingness is itself not a dialectical logic; it is not treated dialectically. The logic of nothingness is not a logic that thinks dialectically but rather a logic that interprets how one might contemplate the meaning of the dialectic. Thus, in practice, "the continuity of discontinuity" or "the rationality of the irrational" and the like do not demonstrate Nishida thinking these things dialectically. In fact, these expressions show that there is some sort of transdialectical mystical method at work here. (Nishida's method differs from so-called mysticism only in its use of nothingness as a logical tool.)

As Nishda thinks the dialectic as a function of *noesis*, and by using the logic of nothingness, meaning using a dialectic of nothingness, it is inevitable that it rejects the dialectic of actual existence. Accordingly, in order to treat being or existence, a dialectical logic (the dialectic of existence) is believed to be unhelpful. Is it then not the case that only the "logic of nothingness" (the dialectic of nothingness) remains? Because it says so much about the dialectic, "the logic of nothingness" (as method), appears at first glance to be a dialectical, logical method. But in fact, it is an outright rejection of dialectical logic itself. Nishida's philosophy accomplishes this corrupt interpretation of the dialectic by means of the logic of nothingness.

Already here we find the logic of nothingness's predestined relationship to the dialectic; namely, that instead of treating actual objects themselves, the logic of nothingness concerns itself with the meaning of those objects. But to the extent that without dealing with an object itself, it is impossible to adequately deal with that object's meaning, here the issue has become only a pure meaning, a meaning independent of the object. So, the issue is always only how is an object "to be thought?" It is not a question of what, practically, is this object or thing, but rather inquiry takes place only with the aim of asking what sort of "meaning" does this thing have? Thus, the problem is not what sort of things are society or history or nature, but what sorts of meaning do the concepts of society or history or nature possess? What position within a categorical system of meaning do these objects occupy? In this way, society only has meaning as a relationship between "I" and "Thou." If we were to try and pick out from *The Self-Determination of Nothingness* such phrases as "such and such is *thought of* as" or "such and such has *significance*" or "such and such is like such and such" the reader would be shocked at just how often these phrases appear. The logic of nothingness only problematizes the "logical significance" of things. (Ueda Jūzō has observed elsewhere that a reader may find just this sort of caricature of the hermeneutic method in the aesthetics of the Nishida school.)

The logic of nothingness is the perfect method for a logic that only cares for the interpretation of meaning. Any logic of being, no matter how idealist it may be, cannot avoid treating the concepts of being or existence. But for dealing with meaning and meaning alone there is nothing better than a logic of nothingness. Strictly speaking, as it wishes to stop at the mere interpretation of the world, the logic of nothingness is, to the bone, a pure metaphysics and a pure idealism. Indeed, precisely because it is neither "metaphysics" nor "idealism" it is the perfect form of both. In the same way that Tanabe's philosophy itself states, Nishida's philosophy is an idealism and identitarian thought, and thus it is a metaphysics. But rather because of this, it completely lacks "idealist" and "metaphysical" points. This is because Tanabe's philosophy is built on a logic of being. What deepened this philosophy of being was Nishida's logic of nothingness. But for us, logic must be a logic of existence. Hegel and Tanabe's philosophies are both logics of existence, though necessarily immaterialist ones. But Nishida's philosophy goes further and runs against this thinking rendering existence a logic of nothingness. But the logic of materialist dialectics is truly a singular, unified logic of existence, and accordingly it is a true logic. Thus the logic of nothingness is not a logic. This is because it cannot think existence itself; it can only think the "logical significance" of existence.

So, finally, existence, if thought of as the self-determination of a universal within the place of nothingness, as is done in this "logic of nothingness," we must note with some surprise that Nishida philosophy, which is constantly touting its speculative, religious, and moral depth, in fact reveals itself to be an extremely aesthetic, artistic, humanistic, indeed, hedonistic philosophy. Indeed, wasn't this originally the world's image of Professor Nishida? In truth, it is this aesthetic, artistic, humanistic, and once again, hedonistic character of Nishida's philosophy that made it famous and so popular. For without this quality such an esoteric philosophy could hardly garner so many amateur admirers. The meaningful images of Nishida the poet agreed well with the kernels of his readers' everyday feelings, finally sending those readers into fits of ecstasy. But just who were these readers? Romantic readers who until recently dominated Japan. Readers whose depth of meaning may have been commendable, but whose spirits were insufficiently moved by the material necessities of objective present-day actualities. Thus, the audience conjured into existence by Nishida's philosophy can be said to be Romantics. Indeed, recently Nishida philosophy seems to have lost some of its Romantic and aesthetic luster as a result of Nishida's attempt to establish a Romantic and aesthetic method—a way to organize the world as images of meaning. And it is this recent project that Professor Sōda has begun calling "Nishida philosophy." Professor Tanabe has called Nishida's philosophy a gothic cathedral, but I cannot agree with this unless it merely means that the Romantic impulse has retreated back into the Middle Ages. Nishida philosophy does not have that feudal flavor. It may no longer be the cutting edge of philosophy, but it is still a modern philosophy.

I have now outlined the ways in which Nishida philosophy has the character, and all the flaws, of bourgeois philosophy. That is, in essence it is a Romantic philosophy. Like all other forms of bourgeois philosophy, by including mysticist, religious, and metaphysical elements, Nishida's Romantic method, too, can have metaphysical, religious, and mysticist effects. Accordingly, and in addition, we cannot overlook a further point: it can serve as the foundation of a "metaphysical" and "idealist" image of the world. As such, all aspects of Nishida's philosophy possess the meaning of being an "Introduction to Metaphysics" (See Iwanami Kōza, *Philosophy*, no. 14 [1933?]). Thus, for the bourgeoisie, Nishida's philosophy must be a truly felicitous spiritual gift.

To sum up, Nishida philosophy does not proceed by means of a feudal or gothic method. Indeed, it has a modern, Romantic essence. One could not wish for a more appropriate method for supporting the cultural consciousness of the contemporary culturalists. It is in Nishida philosophy that contemporary individuals find their modern capitalistic cultivation and the perfect spokesman for their individual cultural liberal consciousness. Nishida philosophy is the philosophy of cultural liberalism—as opposed to economic or political liberalism. This is what accounts for Nishida philosophy's popularity. From here on, Nishida and all others are "free"[4] to put it to work in a reactionary "religious restoration."

Chapter Thirteen

THE SORCERY OF "TOTALITY"
Takahashi Satomi's Philosophical Method

In the previous chapter, "The Logic of Nothingness: Is it a Logic?," I characterized Nishida philosophy. There are some who say that Nishida's is an academic philosophy and others that it is journalistic—but the problem does not lie in that question. The essential point is that while the meaning of various philosophical problems and relations may be resolved with the professor's "nothingness," whether philosophical or not, actual problems, practical problems, cannot be resolved from such a metaphysical standpoint and method.

Nishida Kitarō's standpoint and method of "nothingness" may be opposed with a standpoint and method of "being"—and the representative of a philosophy of being in Japan today is Tanabe Hajime. Professor Tanabe believes that through his "absolute dialectic" (that is the Real-Ideal-Dialectic) he has been able to arrive at a synthesis of a so-called idealist dialectic (Hegel) and a materialist dialectic (Marx). I have touched on this characteristic of Tanabe's philosophy in *Lectures on Contemporary Philosophy*.

Incidentally, to say "dialectic"—be it idealist, materialist, or indeed absolute—is to situate oneself in relation to the standpoint of movement and process. In general, the dialectic method is necessary to grasp the movement of things, the world, and meaning. But precisely why it is necessary to grasp "being" as a movement or process is an extremely important and decisive point; for to actually and practically resolve the question of being or existence, it is necessary that one choose a dialectical method. This necessity does not stem from the dialectic as the most complete standpoint, nor from the fact that its method has the fewest weaknesses; it does not come from any of these subjective, idealist reasons, but from the fact that materialism is the only way to deal with "being" *practically*.

In lecture halls and seminar rooms it is a respected common practice to casually separate practical problems from "fundamental problems." Practical problems are entrusted to the realm of "applied philosophy." And as applied philosophy is nothing more than the mere application of some principle provided by pure philosophy, if one first studies the fundamental principle this principle may be applied to some practical problem whenever necessary—or so "philosophers" believe. Of course the philosophers who stress this focus on fundamental principles, and those who have this thoroughgoing self-image know very well that the day to take up practical problems and seriously turn to "applied philosophy" will never come. And so this possibility of applying fundamental principles to practical problems is in fact practically impossible. Now for this fundamental philosophy—all philosophy studies principles, but here we mean a philosophy that *only* studies principles—in such a fundamental philosophy, there are in fact no practical problems. A practical problem here merely means a particular instance of a fundamental problem and the fundamental principle's application. There is at root here a fundamental optimism; for as there is no difference between a fundamental and a practical problem, by merely refining the fundamental problem, the method and prescription for any practical application will simply follow as a matter of course. And this is why this sort of fundamental philosophy, as a matter of principle, forever banishes practical problems from its purview.

Here then possible problems and practical problems are confused. The result of this confusion is that possible problems and practical problems are forever separated from each other. Thus when one considers the manner of grasping existence, in place of the standards of actual realities, this philosophy employs some arbitrary standpoint and method from the realm of the philosophy of possibility. Is there anywhere from within the merely possible that requires taking up the standpoint of the movement and process of existence (being)? (Indeed, in the same way, the necessity of an actually existing problem has no necessity as a problem of the merely possible.[1]) Furthermore, according to this sense of possibility, it is easily possible for a stilled, static whole to subsume both movement and process themselves, thus transcending all movement and all processes. And so in this method, from this standpoint of the possible, and accordingly from within the method of the possible—from the standpoint of the philosophy of the possible—it is in fact able to arrive at a complete and untroubled position. The representative of this kind of bourgeois philosophical world that stresses the philosophy of the merely "possible" is the Tōhoku University professor Takahashi Satomi.

Professor Takahashi's philosophy is hardly well-known and thus his name does not ring out. His published output is too small when compared with Professors Nishida and Tanabe. (But his publications are not small when compared with other philosophers, for in Japan there are many philosophers who show hardly any signs of work outside of the classroom.) But I believe we must note that Takahashi is a philosopher who belongs alongside both Nishida and Tanabe. The most striking aspect of the professor is the relentlessness and sharpness of his analysis, his fidelity to what phenomenology calls the "thing" [*Sache*], his fastidiousness and thoroughness with respect to compromise, in not cheating or distorting the "thing." Formally, his philosophy displays a reliance on a credible scienticity. Yet even from such a foundation, we are tempted to criticize the professor.

That said, in a sense, a criticism of the professor's philosophy is at present impossible. By this I mean that the characteristics of Professor Takahashi's philosophy are largely found in his collection *The Standpoint of Totality* [*Zentai no tachiba*, 1932][2]; and according to the preface of that work, it would seem that the standpoint of a systematic whole that emerges in the collection is no longer the current standpoint of the professor. As he himself explains in the preface, he now stands in a position of absolute nothingness, or that his "totality" [*zentai*] is "a whole [*zentai*] that, as a pure whole, includes systemicity itself." As the contents of the book are from a position between the standpoint of ordinary, finite mortals and this standpoint of absolute nothingness, his new standpoint of absolute nothingness is impossible for us to clearly understand. The professor does not give any detailed explanation of his current standpoint, nor does he present any resolutions to any problems from this new standpoint. Thus, beyond this collection, the professor's writings include "On Epistemology," "On Temporality" (both included in Iwanami Kōza's series *Philosophy*), and "Husserl's

Phenomenology"—none of which is appropriate for learning of his final standpoint of absolute nothingness mentioned above.

Thus we have no choice but to criticize the mode of thought that appears in *The Standpoint of Totality* and through this criticism also critique the professor's current way of thinking.

As the title states, the concept of "totality" is the most important and indispensable thing here. Takahashi elevates it to a singular principle: "the principle of totality" (7). In any philosophy, when a concept has been elevated to a principle, that principle has the quality of a logic. Nishida philosophy's nothingness was developed into "the logic of nothingness," and so, here, too, we can see totality as the development of a logic of "whole [*zentai*]—part." In other words, in dealing with things philosophically—possible versus actual, contradiction versus synthesis, nothingness versus being—philosophy employs various logical and intellectual mechanisms. In place of these mechanisms, Takahashi's philosophy has chosen as its fundamental relation, the relation of whole versus part. According to Takahashi, this choice is what makes his first "concrete, total method" (11).

Indeed, there is likely no one who believes that when they think a thing, that they are thinking in an especially partial manner. And there is hardly anyone who in thinking does not think they are thinking from the "standpoint of the whole." In that sense for anyone at all to say, "concrete standpoint" or "pure standpoint" is meaningless, and in the same way, "the standpoint of totality," too, has no meaning. But with Takahashi's "standpoint of totality," he does not mean this obvious and, of course, indispensable general claim. What he means is a particular form of the whole-part relation that has been refined to become a logic. So, though the word "totality" is attached to his "standpoint of totality," for now there is no guarantee as to the whether his standpoint is itself a total one. Just as humanism is not limited to the humane, readers and indeed Dr. Takahashi himself, should never be deceived by this term "totality."

So the fundamental question becomes whether this logic of whole-part can be used as a logic. According to Takahashi himself, it seems there is still some doubt on this fundamental issue. For as the whole obviously already includes the part, why must the part be separated from the whole at all? Indeed, if this whole includes the part and is also completely separate from it, then the whole is enough on its own, and so dealing with the separate part is logically a little odd. On this question, Takahashi states that it does not come from some strange motive, but that this is an extremely fundamental "terrifying, awesome question" [*orsorubeki toi*]. That said, the question remains unanswered.

For example, a room is included in the totality of the interior of a house. Spatially this is no problem. But when this whole-part relation that is only guaranteed spatially becomes a logic, is it not natural that some doubts may arise? Even if one uses the category *Nebeneinander* [arranged alongside] (as opposed to *Nacheinander* [in sequence]) the situation is not promising. Is not the fundamental excitement around his logic of whole-part in some way coming from the "awesome question" or again "awesome doubt" that variously excited philosophical youths and Meiji philosophers who wished to grasp the philosophy of human nature—or, again, to how his word "totality" is also associated with the excitement in German literature for the word "*Hen Kai Pan*"?[3] In truth, in order to be a true "totality" we are required to think anything and everything. But in the relations of things, even if there are contradictions and exclusions, if looked at truthfully, the mutually contradictory object and the mutual excluded object both must enter into an intimate relation with each other. Which is to say that holism, totalitarianism [*zentaishugi*], itself must also include partialism [*bubunshugi*]. If Takahashi-ism does not also include anti-Takahashi-ism then it cannot be Takahashi-ism. So it follows that the *singular* standpoint of his so-called standpoint of totality cannot be Takahashi's philosophy.

In reality, because a person's position and standpoint always ceases at a relative totality, a relative whole, "the standpoint of totality" cannot be said to be a true absolute, complete totality. Thus it must be said that the total standpoint only emerges from the progress and development of a relative standpoint. If we remove this process then we can never truly say anything about totality or wholeness. The category and principle of totality are themselves things of the dialectical method. In other words, we must understand that when it comes to dialectical logic, it is only active when it is used, and that it itself cannot be made the partner of some other part or achieve any independence as a logic. If we lose sight of this inevitable relationship, the relation between the whole and the part appears in the form of Takahashi's "terrifying question" of whole-part logic. But the relation between the part and the whole is actually one of the uses of dialectical logic.

THE SORCERY OF "TOTALITY"

Takahashi's thought has been refined by Hermann Cohen's method, and further, in confronting Cohen, Takahashi's thought has gone beyond Cohen's. According to Professor Takahashi, Cohen's foundation is not a true principle. The foundation of Cohen's thought has it that according to Cohen's transcendental method, that method is the origin, the beginning of all (*Anfang*).[4] According to Takahashi's own principle, *Anfang-Prinzip-Principia-Anfangsgrund*, totality is not just begun from the beginning but must be present in its totality at the beginning. Thus the development from A → B is not independent of B → A, and so all processes (movement, change, development, etc.) are in that sense "reversible" [*kagyakuteki*]. So it is necessary that the whole contain both A → B and B → A and thus naturally the whole's essence must be one of silent stasis [*seishi*] (Takahashi, 75).[5]

The whole is stasis. Of course, this stasis does not mean that movement has been banished from it; movement and stasis bustle up against each other, and only in this way—that is, partially—is movement related to a more foundational stasis, making stasis the true whole. Fair enough, let's go with it. But what in reality becomes of the movement and stasis of existence when it is sought by means of this magnanimous standpoint of stasis in liberalism? It is of course, as stated, motion and stasis together. But to what end? Was it necessary to put it into Pandora's box in order to view it? (According to the professor's system "taking out" would of course also mean "putting in.") Is this necessary for a "philosophy of principles"? So when this philosophy wants to deal with principle problems, anything goes: For are not the actual movement from A → B and its interpretation as a conceptual movement [*kannen undō*] from B → A, already in fact the same? If they were not, Takahashi would likely say that the actual movement A → B itself cannot be understood. Individuality [*kosei*], too, is first understood as true individuality from this standpoint of the whole. Indeed, so it is. But what is actually accomplished by pairing the *real movement* from A → B with the *conceptual movement* B → A? In the end, by simultaneously pairing the movement of A → B belonging to the order of reality with the movement of B → A under the aegis of the order of interpretation, reality will fall away; the principle of actuality will be lost and become reducible to the principle of interpretive possibility. In this case, the result is that the given actual problem is not the movement A → B. Instead, and quite conveniently, according to the wishes of this philosophy of totality, it is again a question of stasis. This seems to be the only work that it persistently does: it reproduces the principle of wholeness, totality, itself.

Movement and stasis are not rescued by this higher form of stasis so loved by the professor. It is rescued by some relation between this movement itself and stasis itself—a relation we call the dialectic. Some may ask, is this relation not a static one? No, as I just stated, no reified, isolated stasis is necessary, for the question is one of the relations between motion and stasis. If one were to think this higher-level motion and higher-level stasis, it would be the unity of the actually given motion and stasis and their relation itself. If the problem weren't considered from some presupposition of stasis from the beginning, it wouldn't be necessary to think up so many instances of stasis (and movements). Someone who likes the number 1 may attach it as much as they like, say, to the number 5: $5 = 5 \times 1 \times 1 \ldots$ but the number 5 will never increase. Indeed, even if 5 is multiplied by 1, 5 never becomes 1. The problem is not the interpretation of actually working, moving individual objects. Interpretation here is simply an operation for practically dealing with objects, and it is a something that is necessarily erased once it produces a result. No matter how meaningful (*Sinnhaft*) a thing is—*because it is things that possess meaning*—meaning itself does not become a thing. The trouble comes when the meaning of things is replaced by the interpretation of meaning when dealing with a meaningful object.

But let's now problematize the professor's clear love of a philosophical system in which it is necessary to take a position from this "total" "stasis."[6] He makes a rigorous distinction between method and system, and against a methodism he consistently opposes a systemism. Of course, this system must be a static one (an emancipatory system or a dynamic system are, for Takahashi, nonsensical) and so this system has no contradictions with totalitarianism [*zentaishugi*]. As stated earlier, Takahashi is unsatisfied with today's watchword "systematic whole," and so he continues past it to the totality of "absolute nothingness." Even though we have made the system our problem, it might be thought inappropriate so say so here, but as this absolute nothingness increasingly includes myriad entities (*Sein*), of course, it is a systematic whole. Thus, as with Takahashi's systemism, indeed even more so, all this is infertile ground for any method of dealing with actual problems. So in order to see this last point, we will make a concession and consider his much-loved "system" in place of "absolute nothingness."

But if we think about this carefully, those who love systems should naturally create them. Hegel is the best example. Even those who don't like systems create them. But so far Takahashi has not. So far, in place of a system he has just stressed a systemicity, a systemism. But the outline of the system he is after, in other words, the system that he would likely build, has at some point already definitively been decided. A "system" of, say, the example of Takahashi's "totality," is nothing more than a word that describes something from the internal organization of its contents. This totality is an "experiential" totality, however, and a totality "that can be made conscious" within which are "the rights and capabilities of 'being'" (95). In other words, it is almost absolutely certain that Takahashi's totality will result in the construction of an idealist system. It would be unimaginable if such a system built of conscious ideas alone could be anything but an idealist system. But Takahashi's system is never built; it remains a "standpoint." It makes an outline of a philosophy, but not an actual philosophy. Thus we cannot say what form this idealism will take, but we at least may be sure that by means of the sorcery of the above "stasis" that this "standpoint" will place any and all actual things into this Pandora's box and seal them with the curse of pure possibility. So as a system it might best be called a "metaphysics" of "stasis." And whether we agree or disagree, it is the fate of all to be swallowed whole by this "standpoint of totality." This Leviathan is every bit as powerful and gluttonous as today's state power.

If Takahashi were to bring this logic of the "standpoint of totality" to bear on social problems, it would likely give birth to a truly terrifying social philosophy such as the philosophical foundation of absolutism. A concept of the "totality of experience" would have no trouble linking itself to the concept of national citizenship or the folk. Well-intentioned and academically conscious as he is, Professor Takahashi has no plan to attempt such a rash project. Takahashi's philosophical interests are the above problems of a "standpoint"—consciousness, time, mathematics, physics, and the like—and he seems to think that social problems have hardly any value for (pure) philosophy. In my view of the problem of continuity, the theory of discontinuity (dialectics) is said to lead to the "revolutionary theory" of the "extremist faction," and against this a theory of continuity (the continuity of a systematic totality) is said to correspond to milder social theories; these are the only two options. The philosophical system of "totality" is not then a system of existence, but rather a system of "consciousness."

Because Takahashi's "totality" is a system of "static consciousness" ("experience"), the dialectic must naturally be deeply problematic. And so it is not difficult to imagine his response to it. But unlike Nishida and Tanabe, who struggled mightily to overcome materialist dialectics, Takahashi is only interested in the dialectic found in Hegel. Perhaps he felt that neither Hegel nor Marx escaped the dialectic process itself, so the only choice for him was to focus on the "philosopher" Hegel.

With regard to the fundamental problem of Hegel's dialectic, Takahashi gives an ingenious and very suggestive analysis. Normally the fundamental problem of the dialectic is the identification of the beginning [端初] with the origin [始元]. But Takahashi takes up the issue by distinguishing between Hegel's "dialectic of the origin" from a "dialectic of contents," and examining the relation between the two. Thus for Takahashi when Hegel asserts that pure being (*reines Sein*) is immediate and abstract, the two dialectics are confused. In other words, Takahashi states that though a truly immediate object should have an unmediated immediacy, by thinking of this immediacy as abstract, it becomes a mediated immediacy. This is because something may only be called abstract by means of having been mediated by the action of abstraction [*chūshō sayō*].

Normally, the true meaning of Hegel's dialectic is thought to be the fleeing from the original dialectic of the philosophical origin and adopt the dialectic of the contents. But according to Takahashi, by means of this dialectic of content, it cannot be understood in any unified way why the opposition between being and nothingness must be made one again. In order to understand this, both pure being and nothingness must be thought of as the same sort of abstractions placed within the same "action of abstraction" itself. Takahashi stresses that this action, "abstraction," is itself the true first origin, and the second origin is the self-limitation of the first. In other words, it is none other than the origin chosen by pure being itself. Accordingly, pure being is decidedly a category which is the product of the action of abstraction of consciousness and the idea (*idée*). For Takahashi, Hegel had thought, however incompletely, that there was some sort of prior immediacy that underwrote all this and so his dialectic appeared from the outside to be mystical and paradoxical. Thus, Takahashi believes that Hegel should have grounded the dialectic of content in the true dialectic of origin, that is, in the dialectic of abstraction itself.

Of course, as the result of being mediated by abstraction, the abstract and immediate origin of pure being is already not the origin. The corresponding category of abstraction must then instead be becoming [成]. Because becoming is thus the true origin, being and nothingness is now merely a mediated differentiation. Thus, this becoming corresponds to the previous "totality." If we think this way, we can understand Hegel's "dialectics of being" as a "dialectics of becoming" in a unified way.

In fact, just as before, though totality includes both stasis and movement, the result is a priority for stasis; here though, while becoming includes both being and nothingness, there is a priority for nothingness. And this nothingness is not merely nothingness, it is an originary nothingness, so in this case it is called the "dialectics of nothingness" (287). Here the professor hopes to show that the "totality" of this dialectics of being and the dialectics of nothingness is the true meaning of the dialectical method. And thus everything is subsumed under the "dialectics of totality" (302) and everything is systematized by the "dialectic of the system" (305). But what is the result of all this? It is not merely that contradictions are unified all on their own within this systematic totality, but because of the originary nothingness, "being" continuously and gradually comes to be "becoming" and development. Thus, contradiction is no longer the essence of the dialectic, but rather Takahashi holds that infinite difference is the essence. Indeed, it is thought that if the system is not eternally continuous it cannot be total.

But according to the professor, to the very last, his "dialectic of the system" is not one of dialectical movement. This is because without transcending the "viewpoint of process" nothing may be called a totality or a system at all. Thus, all motion and movement results in being completely "sublated." But with Takahashi, this "sublation" which is normally merely one process of the dialectical method, here achieves a unique form of absolute and total "sublation." In other words, stowing away something in Pandora's box is true sublation. So here, by the hand of Professor Takahashi, the dialectic method becomes completely and totally undialectic. His "dialectics of nothingness" is in truth the "nothingness of dialectics." It is thought that dialectical movement is necessary for the practical resolution of actual problems, but if we were to ask the professor about this practical application of dialectic, he would respond by saying that the very act of asking the question of practical problems is itself already an error.

The important point is found in Takahashi's answer to the following questions: How can Hegel's pure being be immediate? Accordingly, why is it in an unmediated opposition with nothingness? Further, how is it mediated? Takahashi unified the contents of thought be means of the conceptual tool of abstraction. As the unity of two concepts this is fine, as far as it goes. But what demands attention here is that being or existence, when divorced from all sense of objectivity, these concepts lose perhaps their most important instances of being useful. Being's origin, or put another way, being as the origin, is not something that comes from the operation of the concept of the totality of experience or abstraction as in Takahashi's philosophy. It clearly comes from our everyday experience, from the world in which we actually live. The origin of "being" is not due to some concept; the origin is founded in "materiality."[7] Indeed, in this case, even if it is called an idealist dialectic, as for the relationship between the concept and materiality—that is, matter transcends the concept in the physical world—we must grasp this transcended, nonidealist materiality. As we are now caught within this idealist tragedy, the relationship is simply tidied up by abstraction, but this is not a solution—is there any better falsification of the real problem than this? And if anyone says this problem is actually the beauty of the concept, then there is really no way out.

The reason why bourgeois philosophy is idealism is not only that on the one hand it is founded on a idealist, spiritualist system [唯心論]. It is also because it finds it necessary to employ metaphysical categories and a metaphysical logical method. This general situation of all bourgeois philosophy is manifested in professor Takahashi's "the totality [zentai] of experience" and "the whole [zentai] and the part." In my view it is this concept of "experience" through which today's idealism most ingeniously expresses its concepts. Further, the relation of part to whole in today's metaphysics—all various formalisms—is a new focus for idealism (we all know of Husserl's analysis). Which is to say that Professor Takahashi currently can be seen as insisting on the logic of the whole-part totality of experience to combat the widespread dialectic that has been baptized in Marxism.

THE SORCERY OF "TOTALITY"

Still, the professor has been thinking on this a long time; his "standpoint" was not developed in a single day, but it appears to have been on his mind for his entire working life. That said, the desire for this "totality" is not only direct but must be said to also be rather primitive and undeveloped. Normally, if not swapped with another form, such a primitive demand cannot be fulfilled all on its own; yet the professor, from the beginning, does all his work under the aegis of this same, original "totality" and appears to develop it completely unmodified. Because this is, as it were, a civilization developed from an unreconstructed primitive base, it is not too much to say the professor appears to secretly love Eastern (indeed, Japanese) thought. Finally, it doesn't appear that the details in our professor's mind are an especially rich vein of thought. When it comes to display his intellectual perspective, it appears to be no more than that of some fan of old-time philosophers, or perhaps that of a young theology student. But to harp on the class nature of such an undistinguished liberal professor risks making a mountain of a molehill. The philosophical method of the professor's "totality" is like Pandora's box, a liberalism which accepts anything and everything. But we must be careful, for this vague inclusivity does not mean Takahashi's standpoint of totality is useless for today's global fascist social theory or social philosophy (that is, "the total state" [*zentai kokka setsu*]). For even more so than its own world of philosophical abstraction, the essence of this philosophy is clearly more objective when it is applied to and deployed against actual social problems.

Chapter Fourteen

LITERATURE AND PHILOSOPHY IN AN AGE OF REACTION

On the Delusions of "Literaturism"

Is making rhymes in meter enough to call something poetry? Or again, is the defining characteristic of poetry simply the use of special words and deviations from standard syntax or line length? Surely even if the resulting lines rhyme, such a construction definitely would not be what is essentially meant by poetry. In the same way, simply labeling something "literature" is not enough for it to be one with the essence of literature. It is no different with philosophy: simply calling something philosophy is not enough to actually make it philosophy.

Furthermore, in the same way that for those who think merely labeling something as philosophy is enough to make it philosophy—meaning, in fact, those who feel not the slightest necessity of philosophy—those who think something is literature through mere fidelity to a particular traditional or customary literary form is sufficient, they too have no sense of the necessity of literature itself. Accordingly, such types approach this "literature" from what lies behind it or at its base, that is from a lifestyle or desire, which are then taken as the original sources of literature. Pushing this line of thinking a step further, and despite the fact that "literature" is usually a concrete work with a particular form and an actual literary object, this actually produced work is not what is being called literary here, but rather it is the background, the context of the just-stated lifestyle and desire that is considered the truly literary.

It is all the more for philosophy. Today, for a certain sort of literary artist (*bungakusha*) who detests epistemology and metaphysics like the plague—I feel no obligation to define these terms here—such an artist does not also in turn also think their writing has no philosophy, nor would such an artist feel ashamed to find philosophy appear in other writers. Thus, as used here, philosophy is not a logic, but a worldview. Truth then, philosophical truth, is not in the publishing of actual philosophical works one after the other but is simply some philosopher's personal thoughts.

In general, the fundamental discourse between literature and philosophy can be understood in the above relationship. For literary works, if only the work's form is considered—novels are novels and poems, poems—then just as the word "form" says, this is just a formal way of considering them. Thus, even if these works include some literary techniques, there is still obviously no thought happening here. Such "literature" is completely independent from philosophy. Further, if it's just a question of some philosophical premise or mechanism, such a philosophy has no thoughts on literary objects. Such a philosophy cannot have any relation to literature. But in fact, there is no such purely independent philosophy or literature; indeed there cannot be. If one is said to exist, it cannot be done without reducing philosophy and literature to caricatures. This is the point we need to stress here.

The reader is likely at a complete loss as to why I started my discussion this way. I believe the answer eventually will become clear, but I would add that the first thing that emerges with such an inseparable relation between philosophy and literature is criticism. But before we get to criticism, we need to be careful. Speaking strictly as a matter of credentials, critics are not authors [*sakka*]. Because critics do not produce literary works, if the previous essence of literature lies in the production of a specific literary form itself, then critics are not literary artists [*bungakusha*]. There are both many authors and many critics who therefore claim that critics, aside from following meekly in the footsteps of literary artists, have no "literary" abilities.

Yet this same critic, when facing the readers of literary works (indeed even more so for those who do not read literary works), is thought to be an indispensable introducer of literature and thus someone who has excellent literary qualifications. And this is not all. Critics also must give guidance, support, and make demands on literary works, all aimed at the artists themselves. In fact, these critics may not be authors themselves; nonetheless, they are not only expected to intervene in the intent and results of a literary work but are also expected to speak to an author's literary qualities. (I once expressed this same idea as the "potential literary work" [*kanōteki seisaku*].) To resolve this contradiction in the literary qualities of the criticism we must search for the essence of literature (and in the same way of philosophy) not within the literary work but outside of it. That is, criticism first emerges at their point of contact, in the space between philosophy and literature. Literature and philosophy are mediated and unified in criticism.

To cut straight to the conclusion, criticism itself—literary criticism or philosophical criticism, any criticism at all—must be simultaneously literature and philosophy. Criticism proper is neither an artisitc literary work nor a treatise. Critics must be artists and philosophers in a particular sense, tentatively neither an author of literature nor a professor of philosophy. But because criticism must subsume the whole [*pin to kiri*] of literature and the whole of philosophy, the essence of criticism is a doubling of disciplinary wholes. Though just what exactly deserves the name "criticism" cannot be decided from this general theory alone.

So what are the characteristics of criticism in Japan today? Put another way, this question means: What is the current *relationship* of literature and philosophy in Japan today? Here we must once again repeat our warning: criticism itself is neither simply literature nor philosophy. In the same way that literary criticism must be relevant to literary qualities, as philosophy it must not be allowed to have no relation to the logical system of philosophy. In other words, even literary criticism must have a relation to the logical system of philosophy. If a literary criticism does not maintain a relation with a philosophical logic because it is claimed that some given criticism is a literary and not a philosophical criticism, then it cannot be a true criticism. Such a criticism does not mediate literature and philosophy, but in fact seeks to insulate literature and philosophy from each other, making them each independent and absolute. By so doing, such a criticism caricatures both literature and philosophy.

Indeed, in Japan today there is much that goes under the name of literary criticism. Put more extremely, we could say there is hardly any criticism that is not called literary criticism. But in this case, this is literary criticism only in the most commonsensical meaning of the term "literary criticism": it is criticism concerned only with the literary arts. Such a criticism should not be thought of as either a literary or a philosophical criticism of the literary arts. For example, as I have been saying for some time, even though recently there has appeared a popular literary discourse dressed in philosophical garb, the question of whether or not this is literature or philosophy is not a question of outward trappings but one of substance [*jisshitsu*].

So, the question is: What sort of purpose is indicated by those literary figures [*bungakusha*] who seem to think that true criticism is that which concerns itself exclusively with the literary arts? Why is it that criticism, which should be simultaneously literary and philosophical, only turns its smiling face to the literary arts (especially the scholars [*bungakusha*] favorite, "literature"), while casting an icy stare in the direction of philosophy? For example, why is it so common for this so-called criticism to be extremely cold to modern science when science is one of the most important contents of thought (philosophy)? As a proper [criticism]—that is, a simultaneously philosophical and literary criticism of science—has no relation whatsoever with this recently popular "literary criticism," in some cases these "literary critics" seem to think that a criticism of science is itself pointless.

Contemporary Japanese scientists are in general remarkably ignorant of the function of criticism (real and bogus)—natural scientists are especially thick on this point. In contrast, as long as Japanese literary figures are unnecessarily anxious about receiving criticism, it is not unreasonable for them to do so in such an unbalanced and self-serving way, and because the conditions of existence of science and literature are different, there is in some sense a necessary aspect of the above phenomenon. But for a criticism that is literary, meaning that it should also be philosophical, there is no excuse for this situation. (Recently, through a few scholars who have begun reflecting on the relationship between literature and science, *a critique of science* has begun—but this is absolutely not the same as *a scientific critique*. Further, this situation is only progressing in the face of extreme opposition of so-called natural scientists.)

Of course, the false belief that criticism simply means literary criticism stems from literary scholars' own personal and angsty worldview. (Here scientists offer passive agreement.) In this they have only lightly touched the "literary" part, merely the smooth skin of the giant elephant that is actual criticism, so we get only a criticism limited to their own literary interests and likely of no interest to anyone else. Such is "literary criticism" [*bungei hihyō*]. In fact, the majority of today's "literary criticism" is nothing but an expanded version of purely academic criticism. More than this sort of criticism, if it is at its base a criticism that does not treat topical events, and in that sense, if it is not a criticism of the times, such a criticism would definitely not have the characteristics of actual criticism. Criticism must be explained in relation to its social and journalistic function. The problem is that we don't find any such criticism of current events, but only rarefied academic criticism. Which is to say, the particular unbalanced and self-serving worldview of the literary figures has completely won out. The current expanded form of their personal, angsty worldview has its source in their desire to pursue some sort of actual or potential social life as a decidedly particular and unreconstructed ivory-tower "persons of letters" [文壇人]. Thus, even if it perhaps includes a bit of other things, literature is invariably criticized from within and largely in terms of this private, academic "literature." In the end, this expansion results in not just literature but everything being criticized "literaturistically." And thus, for example, any criticism of literature from outside this "literaturistical" worldview is blasphemy, a sin against "literature." In this case, the majority of these bellelettrists—that is, today's Japanese literary figures—all seem to have the self-delusion that literary criticism is *the form* of criticism. This delusion holds that criticism, and according to them then, literary criticism, finds its reason for being in the service of the activities of the writer. And in conjunction with, and like the literary authors, the delusion also holds that literary critics exist in the service of the "literary artist" as deserving respect and deference. (The debate on "The Impossibility of Criticism" [批評不能] is a good example.)

The fact that this same delusion may be seen in so many natural scientists can be counted as an interesting phenomenon in the contemporary cultural landscape. A famous physicist has stated that philosophers (we would call them critics) have made various demands of science but that because scientists are so busy, they don't have time for such chattering. The literary types at least had to consider the issue of whether the critic had any capacity vis-à-vis the writer as an open question, but according to this natural scientist, it is natural that the critic does not have this ability, and there is no time to even ask the question.

LITERATURE AND PHILOSOPHY IN AN AGE OF REACTION

We must notice how literature, natural science, and of course philosophy may appear as mere caricatures if we don't properly grasp criticism. According to natural scientists, critics should not intrude on the work of specialists. According to the literaturists, even though critics should speak to an author's works, it is ultimately futile, because in this understanding the critic is not a literary artist. So then just what becomes of the critic? And so, not only literary scholars and natural scientists, but critics, too, are now fodder for caricature.

Many literary figures believe that literary criticism exists for the benefit of the artist, and all criticism is in the service of literary criticism, so at times it appears that in order not to fall into perversion, life itself must exist for the benefit of literature. The utterance of the relatively useless slogan[1] "literature = life" is thus obviously terrifying in its awesome implications. As said before, the problem is that because literature is its own sort of unity [*pin kara kiri made*], then in the present case the question is just what is its connection, or not, with philosophy and science (which themselves have their own sort of unities)? If the above sloganeering, "literature = life," is true, then just what sort of thing is this life for this literature? If life here means literary life, then it's obvious that there is nothing to life beyond the literary, and so literature becomes life itself.

In contemporary Japan, this "literaturism" largely differs from an idolatry of art for art's sake [*geijutsu shijō shugi*] and aestheticism. We must be wary of this difference. With art for art's sake, the arts and "literature" were explicitly independent of life and reigned above it. In today's literaturism, on the contrary, the whole of life itself is explicitly unified with an unmodified literature. Aestheticism said no more than that emotions had precedence over intelligence and will, meaning its claims alone are not enough to become today's literaturism.

Indeed, in the orthodox tradition of artistic criticism, art for art's sake previously occupied an important position. But today's literaturism does not come from this orthodox line of artistic criticism. More importantly, literaturism's content is not merely "profound" but simply "true," which means that at first glance it can appear to be unaesthetic and even seem to deny an artistic form. This already goes beyond some basic devilry [*akumashugi*] to become, quite honestly, a gangsterism [*akutōshugi*]. Literaturism's form of appearance is no longer "literature" but a caricatured "philosophy" or, indeed, a theology.

But today's literaturism did not come into the world as some useless fad. Herein lurks a deep plan of the hidden hand. The problem is related to the history of criticism, especially the recent history of criticism. Readers may wish to recall the recent so-called Artistic Restoration [*bungei fukkō*].

Of course, art must always be restored; if art's ultimate oppressive ~~fetter~~ is ~~politics~~, then ~~contemporary politics~~ must be toppled and the arts must imitate ancient Greece. It is unclear just what authority today's "Literary Restoration" is toppling, to what classics it is returning, and from where it intends to rebuild. But it is clear that what must be restored does not include science or productive technologies, only literature [*bungaku*] now called "the Arts" [*bungei*]. This is interesting in light of our storyline here.

Accordingly, literature must be reborn as "the Arts." Hardly anyone would have any reason to oppose these terms. But why then, in the same way and at the same time, is it unnecessary to also restore science? The usual answer is that the mechanistic worldview of modern natural science that is the basis of the bourgeoisie's particular thought has at every important point reached an impasse—this isn't a relative problem of Japanese "literature," however, but rather a major issue globally.[2] Thus what is reborn out of the crisis of natural science is not science but religion, theology, metaphysics, and mysticism. So, as for those critics who appear under the banner of Artistic Restoration, which of course includes the restoration of "literature," we don't forget to number among them, most of all, those who earlier restored religion, theology, metaphysics, and the like. With the apparent sudden movement of an "Arts" restoration, why was it that only science appeared to be left behind? Indeed, more than this, science was not merely left behind by this movement; indeed, science was the old authority against which the restoration of "Literature," religion, theology, and so on rebelled.

Here we can offer no comfort to Leonardo da Vinci, whose own self-reflections such as "In knowing how to dig canals I am also learning to build castles" were all too nonliterary. The problem is why has this sort of literaturism appeared today? Why have literary arts been reborn as "the Arts" and literature as "Literature?" For a large portion of recent criticism (or we could say the critical spirit), though it may don the guise of the "philosophical" or the "literary," the result of this movement is, in fact, unphilosophical and thus also unliterary. I previously stated that if criticism self-destructs in this way it only results in a caricature of both literature and philosophy, but here we must add that this literaturism is the most appropriate form of the caricature of literature. Originally, a cartoon was nothing more than that which abstracted and exaggerated some particular feature.

In Japan, the function of philosophical and literary criticism was only firmly established when post–Great War Marxist philosophy began to dominate the strata of intellectuals. These philosophical and literary critical functions were characterized on the one hand by a scientific criticism (not a critique of science), and on the other by a social criticism. The unification of these two functions—in general meaning the essence of Marxist philosophy—newly established the value of criticism. This was because now, for the first time since the beginnings of Japanese literature, philosophy and literature were directly mediated; scientific knowledge and literary representation were destined to be comprehensively related. This was because the above relation between politics and literature became a problem. This moment likely brought with it many evils. As a result, much in the same way that Galileo's science was chastised by the pope, "literature" had to be admonished by this "criticism."

But this evil is not the heart of the issue. The real problem was not that this criticism was too philosophical or too literary, but that it was not philosophical or literary enough. Thus, this situation was likely not the reason that this sort of criticism must be self-destructed. Though now, from the outside, it does in fact appear that this criticism noisily collapsed. And here is our exemplary literaturism. For this beloved literature, things like partisanship are not a problem, and like a smokescreen a singular, undifferentiated literature is all that lies before our eyes. Most readers will surely accept that this becomes a situation in which literature does not exist for life, but that life exists for literature.

But even this literaturism did not appear out of nowhere. The tradition of Japanese bourgeois literature may be fairly called a literary liberalism. Of course this literary liberalism was not cognized as a literary consciousness grounded in political liberalism. Rather, because liberalism was consciously grounded in a "literary" consciousness, more than calling it literary liberalism, it is more appropriate to call it liberal literaturism [*jiyūshugiteki bungakushugi*]. Thus from the very start literaturism belongs to the previous tradition of Japanese bourgeois literature. Moreover, we must see, too, that there were a huge number of Marxist authors and literary theorists who had within them the makings of this liberalist literaturism; it was in an age when progressivism was on the retreat that this literaturist movement showed its true colors. Thus, from *bellelettrists*, liberals, and leftists, all may be brought together and harmonized, subsumed under a shared "literature." And it is in this sense that "literature" progresses. It may even be the case that "literary" progress is expanded *tout court* until it becomes progress itself, but this sort of statement is why literaturism is literaturist.

With various highs and lows, and several nuances, the literaturist movement within contemporary Japanese cultural phenomena is spreading to various strata of the masses—the dividends of the god of war; Mars's plans are for fascism among the petite bourgeoisie and the petit bourgeois lower intelligentsia, and literaturism among the petit bourgeois higher intelligentsia. Significantly, the particular shared characteristic of today's so-called liberalism and the progressivism (?) based in it is literaturism. As for the false belief that this literaturism and the particular form of Japanese fascism are objectively coming from completely different places—well, that is the defining delusion of the literaturists.

Finally, let's consider one of the most characteristic forms of this literaturism. This is none other than the literaturist delusion that our period, a period in which criticism is self-destructing, is in fact the golden age of criticism. One instance of this phenomenon is the belief that as literature and philosophy have in fact fallen apart, it is believed that literary criticism has finally become philosophical. In the same vein, and at the same time, as we have recently entered a reactionary age, we see there has been a remarkable increase in the number of literary critics, and also the "philoso"-fishy [「哲学」臭い] literary critic. But we can see just how troubled this sort of "philosophy" is by noting that it is in fact merely the pedantic and academic extension of literaturism's "literature." (There are many examples of this, but I have previously written on the case of Kobayashi Hideo.)

Together with the call for an unreconstructed "literature" to be quickly extended until it is philosophy itself, there is on the other hand, the corresponding phenomenon that allows "philosophy" to be "literature-ized." As European, especially German bourgeois philosophy—meaning a philosophy appropriate to the current situation of bourgeois society—has abandoned empirical science and its own scientific bona fides, it has lost the resulting philosophical categories that emerge from the ground of everyday verification, and further, has lost any standards of categorical arrangement.

Thus the only thing that can be relied upon—going under the various names of theology, psychology, humanism, and the like—must be called literary categories (and further, literaturist categories). Philosophical categories are replaced with literary categories. (When literature uses categories properly, it freely uses philosophical categories by means of literary *representation* and absolutely never replaces philosophical categories with literaturist categories.) When it does replace philosophical with literaturist categories, "philosophical" literary criticism and "literaturist" "philosophy" emerge one after another.

For example, let's look at the category "reality" [*genjitsu*]. This category, as an original philosophical category (which is the only true category), has a historical, social, and so economic, political, conceptual, and cultural "existence." But as a literary category, it is obvious that this merely endlessly intoned yet empty word "reality" is nothing more than some rarefied Dostoyevskian "reality." Similarly, with the strange category of "anxiety," social anxiety and concretely grounded anxiety end up becoming [Lev] Shestov's rootless, free-floating anxiety. Today metaphysics has realized that all other paths have been closed off and so plots its final escape into these literaturist categories. This is why metaphysics must make an ally of literaturism.

I think that readers must take careful note that the confluence of the giddiness and the philosophical-sounding nature of today's literary criticism is a reactionary plan for "literature" to pillage philosophy (and thus also true literature). And yet all of it took place under the banner of that particular consciousness: literary liberalism.

Chapter Fifteen

THE ESSENCE OF "LITERARY LIBERALISM"
The Progressive and Reactionary Nature of "Liberals"

A literal interpretation of the word "liberalism" would be an extremely foolish one, yet shockingly, given liberalism's current popularity, it seems just such a literal definition of liberalism is the unspoken understanding for many of today's liberals. Which is to say, they would have "liberalism" [*jiyūshugi*] simply mean making a "doctrine of liberty" [*jiyū o shugi to suru*], and accordingly, this understanding of liberalism makes it an ideology that simply opposes illiberalism, opposes an ideology of unfreedom. Such types would thus hold that whatever else may be said of liberalism, by definition, liberalism cannot be a bad thing. Of course, while likely no one would state it so baldly, I would wager that there are many whose definition of liberalism would, in fact, be based on no other, deeper understanding.

In particular, given idealist philosophers' unconditional reverence for the central problem of freedom in German idealism, and literary figures' love of a transcendental, free-floating, and escapist freedom, it is easy for those with the above simplistic definition of liberalism to believe that those other groups' fidelity to these other concepts alone are enough for both of these groups [idealist philosophers and literary figures] to be allies of liberalism.

But here we come to an important point: the concept of freedom [liberty, *jiyū*] was not born from within philosophy, nor does it come from literature. In the same way that to say "practice" immediately conjures thoughts of human ethical activity, say "freedom" to a philosopher and they will immediately think of "freedom of will"—both are mistaken beliefs coming from within the philosopher's own subjective thoughts. And while it is unclear whether the majority of literary figures have thought seriously about just what freedom is—I have my doubts—in essence, for them, freedom is a decidedly natural phenomenon, and though they know, feel, and think about the knowledge of freedom, they do not feel any *practical necessity* for freedom at all—because all they ever do is talk about it. Originally, before philosophers and literary scholars, the necessity of freedom was felt first by entrepreneurs and politicians. Thus the philosophers' and literary scholars' concept of freedom comes from this so-called economic and political concept of freedom.

It is a historical fact that liberalism was born of "economic liberalism" and then, similarly, became political liberalism. If we exempt for now socialism or other examples of political philosophy, I do not know exactly when this philosophical or literary liberalism began. Even today, the idea that a complete liberal philosophy has yet to be formed is not a strongly held opinion. But as we shall see, even now, a complete philosophy of liberalism is likely something that can never be established. Though liberalism is thus an economic and political category, and originally not a philosophical or literary category, it is common knowledge in Japan today that when philosophy and literature says "liberalism," the term indicates no relation to the problem of political freedom. Today, liberalism as a common-sense term is no longer a political category; it has become a wholly literary one. Which is to say that cultural liberalism is now the sole home of liberalism itself.

If we do not pay attention to this point, we will not be able to pass any appropriate judgment on "liberalism" or "liberals" in Japan today. If we consider liberalism only as a political problem and not as a literary, ideological problem, we will not be able to expose the minds of today's liberals.

It has been said that once the power of communism retreated and even the power of fascism had crested, the world became a liberal one. But while the movement of bourgeois political action and thought that stresses the necessity of bourgeois party politics—or talk of the deterioration of parliamentary politics—may be a movement of bourgeois democracy, this alone is not enough to make that movement also the movement of liberalism. Democracy is a movement that belongs completely to a politics or political worldview in the service of bourgeois political freedom. Accordingly, democracy can, depending on the circumstances, become a petit bourgeois, proletarian, or rural political ideology. In contrast, because liberalism today belongs to a cultural ideology of the petite bourgeoisie—the intelligentsia and bourgeoisie—these liberals are absolutely not constrained by some necessary relation to bourgeois political freedoms.

In light of this phenomenon, it cannot be said that we are seeing a restoration of political liberalism, and so in this sense it must be said that politically, liberalism is not necessarily a laudable thing. What appears to be being restored is bourgeois democracy—or its den of thieves; it is absolutely not the restoration of political liberalism.

What is being restored within liberalism today is not political liberalism, but literary liberalism. Literary liberalism is what runs through and represents the essence of today's liberalism. We can see this sort of liberalism raise its head in the broad sense of the "literary restoration." Starting with today's "artistic restoration [*bungei fukkō*]" which for authors and literary scholars is limited to "literature"—in fact the result of thinking on this term reveals it to mean a "Restoration of 'Pure Literature'" [*junbungaku fukkō*]. The result is that from this literary restorationist base, "philosophical restoration" or religious restoration, or the chorus of all the other attendant restorations, all of these unexpectedly become the *actual contents* of liberalism; which is to say that today's liberalism is a literary liberalism. And this is why so many literary and quasiliterary ideologues who are not interested in, or even have any opinion on, political movements are so enamored with the [mere] *word* "liberalism."

For literary scholars who have no sense of the literary or philosophical realities of actual culture and nature, they easily, casually, and consciously throw themselves into the reactionary camp without any trouble, because for them, the singular, original element that can render peaceful human sensibilities is this *term* "liberalism" that has fallen to us from Heaven. Thus, without exception, everyone is happy to be, and to always have been, a liberal.

Many people have expounded on the progressivism and reactionary nature of liberalism. I will do so now myself, focusing on an analysis of the liberal mind. As we shall see, analyzing liberalism from the perspective of liberals' consciousness is an extremely appropriate method.

THE ESSENCE OF "LITERARY LIBERALISM"

First, let's start with the commonplace notion that liberalism is individualism; in other words, a liberal is an individualist. But the word "individualist" may be defined in any arbitrary way, so we must determine the meaning of individualist for the individualism within today's liberalism. Today's liberals who come from and are brought up in the petit bourgeois and bourgeois strata, and who have passed through the "cultivation of personality," are definitely not and need not be economic exclusionists; neither are they absolutely required to be moral egoists [*dōtokujō no rikoshugisha*]. Depending on the circumstances, it seems there are many instances of today's liberals being extremely social and not self-regarding aristocratic ideologues.

The truth of the individualism of today's liberals appears most purely in their literary and philosophical points of view. They think of things as centered on the individual. Be it society or history or nature—indeed any and all of their value judgments—it is the existence of the individual that is the standpoint from which flows all judgment. Liberals who have well understood equality do not limit their understanding of liberal to only themselves, but to their own individual selves and another individual; and this means their selves relate to another individual, not to some supraindividual objective thing.

But this notion is extremely hackneyed and stale. For the problem must progress to asking what is the actual content of the standpoint that takes the individual as the standard of judgment. It is common practice for liberals to grasp their individuality as their personality. Though the term is personality, because we are told by liberals that it is not an ethical, moral concept, it is the "individual" that ties together everything from the logos to pathos, from ideology to pathology, and physiognomy to "characterology,"[1] so that personality as a "humanist" category becomes the problem at hand.

This humanist "human" is however not explained in terms of nature, history, or society. The opposite is true: nature, history, or society themselves must be explained starting with the individual human. Liberals believe that the latter method has more literary fidelity and philosophical depth. We would do well to note that nearly all of today's (literary) liberalism is in truth humanism. (Previously there was something called "character-ism" but we can see that it was a precursor of today's humanism.) According to the champions of the "literary restoration," apparently planting one's feet solidly in humanism is the "restoration" of literature (?). Is it not a vulgar, comical assumption that research on humans (*ningen*) must begin with humanism, (*ningenshugi*)—in the same way that a study of freedom (*jiyū*) must be based in liberalism (*jiyūshugi*)?

So these literary liberals who have appointed themselves the guardians of all things human love the very word "human" and so also love the word "anthropology" (*ningengaku*), which all seems to conclude in an ideology of anthropology (*ningengakushugi*). Logically speaking, this sort of assumption is exceedingly humanistic. Here we encounter one example of the humanistic, self-congratulatory nature of liberals' logic.

But it is necessary to recall that this ideological anthropology was none other than individualism. From this individualist perspective, the liberal must here stoop to an "anthropological" observation and start to speak of an "atomistic synthesis" between individuals when dealing with practical problems. Because this liberal, as an enlightened centrist, is beyond all partisanship and factionalism, this alone also means a liberal is an individualist, and cannot allow any internal connection or union between individuals. Here an individual is a complete interiority so that any connection or combination can only be considered as something exterior to the individual. Thus, as all factions are necessarily and absolutely external things, they must be of secondary importance for the individual. Liberals judge all "humans" individually, for to do otherwise would be a partisan or factional judgment that is by definition an artificial and external judgment. This is what liberals call "equality."

On the other hand, as literary liberals have hardly any relation to economic or political liberalism, their "equality" must be different from the interests of "equal opportunity" or "human equality." So, because their individualism cannot terminate in a completely atomistic individual, it naturally requires some particular form of connection between individuals. Once again, this individualism feels the same needs as the anthropology above, and so the form of connection between individuals it adopts is a humanistic one: here arises "pathos" as a connection between individuals. Thus, according to the liberal, particular human individuals only enter into a particular connection with particular other human individuals. If we inquire into what this connection is, we get an armchair anthropological judgment that these favored members of humankind form a particular

THE ESSENCE OF "LITERARY LIBERALISM"

social connection. Incidentally, here we need to call this social connection a sect.

Indeed, liberals are beyond factionalism. (The old truth that "postpartisan" is, in fact, a truly excellent form of partisanship is, of course, out of the question.) This is because for them, there exists no external, objective standard linking individuals. But because they are postpartisan, they are sectarian. Why? Because, as they tell us, there is nothing but subjective, internal bonds between individuals.

But when there are no objective criteria linking individual to individual then in any true sense there is no politics. This is the source of the general dislike of and disinterest in politics for today's literary liberals qua individualists. But we must investigate the deeper, fundamental reasons why these liberals do or do not disdain politics.

According to liberals, a political connection between individuals can only have a subjective foundation. This is because any objective relations between individuals are not fundamental actualities of human existence. Thus, according to them, politics means nothing more than human (or anthropological?) haggling and machinations of the mind. For their part, these liberals hate objectifying or targeting this human mind, so they naturally detest politics—in fact they come to feel it is their duty to despise politics.

But these literary liberals with their fundamental sectarian tendencies, of necessity, feel the need to tie politics *in a subjective sense* to their own sectarianism. It turns out that this is, in fact, extremely easy to do. At that moment, it is also extremely easy for this literary liberal to then emerge as the ultimate, ideal, and authentic sectarian. A sectarian's politics is always opportunism, and other than opportunism, a literary liberal knows nothing of "politics."

These inevitably sectarian literary liberals are postpartisan in the sense that they have no partisanship, but it is necessary to get a better grip on the essence of "partisanship" itself. The inescapable opportunism of the liberal is first a result of liberalism's theoretical incoherence. In fact, when it comes to theoretical partisanship and factionalism, these must at least in part come from theoretical coherence. A theory having coherence, a "logic," is one of the important causes of the partisan nature of theory. Even so, as theory and logic are not limited to problems of thought and language, but rather also govern actions, to say the partisanship of theory immediately implies the problem of the partisanship of actions. As for (literary) liberals as opportunists—because they are opportunist in their actions, their theory must be illogical. Their "postpartisanship" then in fact means their "illogic."

Because liberals cannot have any partisanship, they then also cannot have any logic, and so no matter how much philosophical wordplay they try, they cannot have any "philosophy" in any fundamental, meaningful sense. And it is doubtful literature is even possible absent any fundamental philosophy.[2] Anyone who expects some sort of liberal philosophy from these (literary or philosophical) liberals, is someone who is merely confessing to everyone that he feels no actual, personal need for philosophy at all. A socialist without philosophy, or without a real, felt need of philosophy, easily ~~defects~~, becoming none other than the unceasing believer of ~~expediency~~, the opportunistic liberal, where even if one wanted to have a philosophy, one cannot.

When it comes to the question of liberalism's progressive or reactionary nature, if we take the so-called literary restoration as a litmus test and don't forget the existence of the wide range of literary liberals in Japan today, it's clear there is nothing so disingenuous as liberals' progressivism. It is all but meaningless to argue that this position or that person is progressive; such questions must be considered under some sort of critical conditions: For the cultural situation in Japan at precisely this moment we must ask what is the real interest of the literary liberals that goes under the banner of literary revival? (It is a good idea to look at what is being recovered from.) For these liberals, literature is something to be "revived" [復興] meaning to be "restored [復古]"; they never say it is something to be developed or created.

That literary liberals may appear progressive, if we ignore their cultural restorationism, comes from nothing more than their personal, subjective "antipathy" to fascism and feudalism. But even this antipathy comes first and foremost from their general dislike of the partisan thing called politics. What they actually need to do is reflect on the countless instances when they have been much more "progressive"(!) in ~~oppressing~~ the proletariat than in fighting fascism. This is all clearly the result of the (literary or philosophical) liberal's literary or philosophical "illogic."

Chapter Sixteen

THE CONSCIOUSNESS AND CLASS THEORY OF THE INTELLIGENTSIA

Against the So-Called "Class Theory of Intelligence"

Japanese literary and academic circles have once again raised the problem of the intelligentsia (customarily called "the intellectual class"—here we need not deny this is an inconvenient appellation). The intelligentsia problem once again has reared its head and not simply because for the intelligentsia themselves they must be endlessly problematized as fundamental, which is to say that the intelligentsia are fated to be eternally self-problematized. Rather, however fundamental or fated this problem may be, mere repetition of the problem or simple rehashing of the problem is meaningless, and we do not think there is much possibility that such a meaningless phenomenon actually occurs. Without determining the reason why the intelligentsia is, once again, being problematized, there would not be much that we could say about the problem of the intelligentsia at all.

When the intelligentsia was problematized in the past it was under conditions suited to intellectuals themselves as a rather pessimistic matter. With respect to themselves, it seems that the problem of the intelligentsia and all its self-doubt, anxiety, and even self-deprecation were all psychologically motivated. Because intellectuals have a natural tendency to take pride in the superiority of knowledge or intelligence—knowledge and intelligence are not the same thing—their natural, spontaneous intuition is to believe that society is first categorized by means of the distinction between intellectuals and nonintellectuals. In that case, when the superiority of knowledge or intelligence is tied to the ruling relations of society so that knowledge and intelligence come to share the same interests as the ruling class, the superiority of knowledge or intelligence almost immediately implies a special social position. Further, as both knowledge and intelligence have value in overcoming opposition with universal applicability and the ability to recognize universality, this special ability of the intelligentsia itself easily, and all on its own, indicates a transcendental and privileged social class. If we are speaking as social science, "The intellectual class" is an unscientific, vulgar concept, but because it is nonetheless often deployed to explain this special class position, here it is a particular form of self-delusion, which believes that the knowledge or intelligence of the intellectual class imparts some form of the special right to govern society; such is an example of their inborn pride. But the impetus for the most recent problematizing of the intelligentsia is that now this pride itself has somehow become suspect.

As both experts and intellectuals, the intelligentsia is of course confident in its right to rule in contrast to the nonexpert, nonintellectual vulgar masses. It is the source of eternal happiness that the intelligentsia rests content in the knowledge that even if the vulgar, mundane ruling powers are held by the rich and the politicians, they, the intelligentsia, alone hold a spiritual, aesthetic, scientific, which in this case means a *cultural*, right to rule. But according to the fresh lessons that social science teaches us, the new ~~leaders~~ of society are not the intelligentsia but must be the ~~proletariat~~. Indeed, social science teaches that the ~~proletariat~~ should not make up only the vulgar leaders, but that political opinion and cultural ~~control~~ should be placed in the hands of the proletariat, where even the intelligentsia themselves would study, learn, and teach.

For those who take great pride in themselves, when that pride betrays you, it is easy to overestimate the situation. It would be extremely natural for pride to thus turn into humility. And this is why that it was here that the profound (?) anxiety of the intelligentsia began for the first time. (Today literary critics seem to be struggling with this "anxiety" of the new intelligentsia, but it definitely also indicates the atavistic genealogy, the ancestral return, of the melancholy of previous intellectuals.) Thus the vast majority of these bad-faith, malignant [悪質] intellectuals wallowed in their historical impotence, and in place of something that should have been criticized, reformed, and used, they completely and easily accepted and shallowly internalized this impotence, so that once this standpoint metastasized, the intelligentsia's historical impotence was inverted to become a particular special ability and source of pride. The lamentations of the armchair intellectual have in fact come to indicate a sort of intellectual manifesto. Which is to say, when it comes to a question of being unhappy, the unhappy person is in a privileged position over the happy one.

However much this is an exaggeration of the passive weakness of the intelligentsia, this habit for exaggeration itself is the intelligentsia at its foolish worst. In the end, all cases of pride or self-deprecation are habitual self-exaggerations with no desire for resolution, and all with a focus on a present that doesn't actually exist; indeed, as they are, in fact, grieving their own selves, they cannot bear to cast away their grief. All of this is a negative position, yet as always, even this angst terminates in a kind of perverse pride of the self-satisfied intellectual—and it must be said this angsty terminus displays a self-satisfaction. If we ask why don't such angsty, worthless types simply wash their hands of this label "intellectual," more than anything it is because being an intellectual now means precisely this sort of first-rate sensitivity to suffering insults as intellectuals.

Apart from such foolishly malignant intellectuals, there are those who have a touch more self-awareness. In place of the self-deprecation, insults, and despair, they have been able to form a new, more "intelligent" sense of pride and anticipation. However much this word intellectual has been separated by lies and truth, at any event, for those who now ~~join~~ the proletariat and proceed according to the proletariat's ~~interests~~, when compared with the self-rationalization of the above malignant intellectuals, these new intellectuals come much closer to the truth. Back then, some of my young friends, in an effort to reform their apparent rarefied lifestyles, got upset and made a point of selling off the expensive books they had accumulated as students—none of this came from the self-destruction and self-abnegation of the anguished intellectual.

But here we are snagged on a fundamental problem. Without question we must once again pay attention to the issue of the above vulgar conception of "the intellectual class." Of great importance here is the intellectuals' own everyday commonsensical intuition, a sort of self-awareness. "Are we not a kind of special social class? We are neither the proletariat nor the bourgeoisie; this is because we are educated and thus when compared with the politician and the businessman, we are much more cultural." And from here it is not a great leap to imagine themselves as somehow opposing both these classes. Despite the quick absorption of social scientific knowledge, or rather due to the particular deployment of that knowledge, we can see how this self-image developed. This is because most of the intellectuals belong to the petit bourgeoisie and there is no place more effective for exaggerating intellectuals' impotence and centrism [*chūkansei*], or conversely the transcendence and superiority of its historical role, so that soon this thinking seems to provide a basis for considering intellectuals as a social class called the knowledge class. In this way, an unconscious plan unfolds beneath the nicknaming the intelligentsia the "intellectual class" so that just as the name says, their self-image unknowingly reveals the intelligentsia's hubris in speculating on its social historical role as some sort of demi-urge.

Of course, in whatever sense it is understood, the "class" in the "intellectual class" is not a social scientific category. Now if it is a question of bourgeois social science, a science that invariably classifies social relations as flat and even, in this limited sense we might say intellectuals are a class; but this only proves that bourgeois social science remains stuck at the level of vulgar common sense and is scientifically worthless. As everyone knows, as a scientific form of representation, the intelligentsia is not a social class and so, accordingly, the vulgar, commonsensical "intellectual class" is clearly inappropriate; So amazingly, at precisely the point when the concept needed some concreteness, "intelligence" was and continues to be absent from the heads of the "intelligentsia." This is an important point.

Broadly speaking, intellectuals take a stand as belonging to an intellectual group that has a kind of group consciousness (and as I said at the beginning, this is what allows them to eventually give birth to their self-image as a class). As such, they already feel some sense of pride so that when that pride is lost, it turns to self-abnegation and humility, yet because from deep within their hearts, while humbling themselves, humility itself cannot help but become a new basis for their pride.[1] Yet to the very last, there is absolutely nothing grounding their self-image as some sort of privileged historical actors with some fundamental social power beyond their deep desire to have one. For such bad-faith intellectuals, this always results in swapping the problem of *intelligence* for the problem of the *class nature of intellectuals*. And this move is not limited to bad-faith intellectuals, as the very confusion as to whether the intelligentsia is the same as the petit bourgeois social stratum gives birth to a vulgarized social scientific vocabulary.

Indeed, in the same way, when one says fascism in Japan, a similarly vulgarized vocabulary makes it easy to think of fascism as something feudal.

But the way in which intellectuals are taken to be some kind of intellectual class is absolutely not limited to malignant intellectuals. When they stressed the active aspects of the intelligentsia and spoke of ~~joining~~ the proletariat or ~~forging solidarity~~ with the proletariat, even the previous theorists of the scientifically meaningful "Theory of the Intellectual" presented the problem as: Should we intellectuals ~~support~~ the proletariat? ~~Support~~ the capitalists? Or go *our own* way? Meaning the problem had become, given that the intellectuals are a discrete unit of the social class structure, how should this unit cast its historical vote? In this way, the intellectuals naturally are assumed to be holding some sort of deciding vote. Emphasizing the weakness, powerlessness, and dependence of the intellectuals, is nothing but emphasizing the small numbers of a minority as a performance, which in no way prevented a spontaneous, unconscious plan for this minority to use the antagonism within the majority and to take the lead. This is the inevitable result of appealing to the fundamental premise that the intellectuals are first and foremost some sort of particular social class.

Indeed, the theorists of the intelligentsia are often intellectuals themselves, and so the problem is presented as a problem of the "self." Thus it becomes convenient to make this a question of the social subjectivity of the intellectual stratum. But in fact, the more acute problem of subjectivity in the case of the intellectual lies in the problem of intelligence [*chinō, interijensu*]. The intelligentsia may tentatively conjure the image of intellectuals as a particular social stratum, but we must take note that the intelligence invoked here is nothing but an empty signifier and has no definition whatsoever beyond being a mere sign. For the intellectuals themselves, the construction of the problem of intelligence both personally and socially makes it easy to understand the problem as first: How do we best use our collective intelligence?

Malignant intellectuals who have never tried thinking about how their intelligence can be improved or used from a social point of view—which is to say for them intelligence itself is actually malignant, and leaving aside a discussion of how intellectuals' constant despairing over the pallid nature of intellectuals has invited a dramatic debasing and dumbing down of their intelligence itself—such intellectuals are thus intellectuals who consciously ignored the special capabilities of intelligence itself. The above examples of the antiacademic intellectuals and those earlier intellectuals who fretted over which class they belonged to, when considered as a problem of collective intelligence in society and the problem of social class, show that both these groups belong in the same camp.

In truth, class ~~conflict~~ is the foundation of the whole problem, because capitalist society is always a ~~conflict~~ between the capitalist class and the proletarian class. This is axiomatic [*kōshiki*], and because it is an axiom, it is not necessary to prove it over and over again; it is instead a thesis that should be kept in mind at all times. (On this point, we should say a word about the many who oppose such "formalism" [*kōshikishugi*]: Because you [*shokun*] don't want to use the formula for a triangle, and because you must then in fact start with the elementary proof, and thus also prove the formula for a triangle each and every time—this is rather an excellent sort of axiomatic formalism. In the end, if you do not prove the elementary parts, it is impossible to scientifically prove more developed theses.) So, taking a stand on this formula (and not forgetting it), the problem becomes: For the intelligentsia as a group of possessors of intelligence, what class role do they have? Presented this way, the mindless and abstract problematization of asking just what class does the intelligentsia belong to, or is the intelligentsia neutral, will disappear. Instead we will have: What role does the intelligence of the intelligentsia play in the bourgeois camp? And what role results from the intelligence of the intelligentsia within the proletariat? This all represents a step forward, and so we may now work to solve the problem more clearly and easily.

Today, both the new stage in the problematization of intelligence and the return of the problem of the intelligentsia, when compared with the previous problematization, are motivated by somewhat more positive circumstances. Thanks to a general ebbing of, for example, the liberation of "literature" from politics and political surveillance, a group of literary scholars have suddenly noticed these more pleasant circumstances, and intellectuals have become courageous enough to examine the problem of the intelligentsia once again. Here it must be remembered that this summary of the loosening of restrictions on literature describes none other than a regression of the actual power of the proletariat. Thus, for example, today's intellectuals, be they literary critics preaching "angst," or former Marxists-turned-anti-Marxist [*tenkōsha*] and their "anxiety posturing," neither this "angst" nor "anxiety" has any real tragic sense when considered in toto; in contrast

CONSCIOUSNESS, CLASS THEORY OF INTELLIGENTSIA

to the previous iteration, their "angst" has become a sort of pure, prideful anguish, their "anxiety" is rather a deep conviction and belief in the ideology of anxiety [*fuanshugi*].

Whether advocating for the self-confidence of intellectuals, or the older intellectual self-doubt, in both cases what is being problematized is the active subjectivity of the intelligentsia, which is a development (?) or at least new feature of this latest era of the problem of the intellectual. In this sense, they speak of the "rebirth of the intellectual," that anxiety is the eternal true face of human life, that the intellectuals themselves exist within this anxiety, and other similar pronouncements. Whether intellectuals actually have intelligence is in fact counted as one of my own fundamental doubts. Further, that anxiety is the essence of the intellectual or that anxiety is the fundamental ground of human existence are both lies; they are nothing more than a favorite monologue of malignant intellectuals.

But all that aside, even if the problem is a question of the positivity of the intellectuals' subjectivity, it is not permitted to make it a problem of the intellectuals egotistical jabbering within society. As for the source of intellectuals' subjectivity, it always had to come from their intelligence as viewed collectively. Furthermore, even if intelligence is the issue, this may not become an ideology of the supremacy of the intellectual class or the supremacy of the skills based on that class, or again, a transcendental academicism. In pursuit of the problem of the assertive positivity of intellectuals' subjectivity, if we fall into some kind of class explanation of intellectuals—"intellectual supremacism" "literaturism" or, "mobilizing" the intellectual class with say a "rebirth of the intellectual" or "anxiety" or "expertise" [*senmonka*]—in essence the result of this new theory of the intellectual is merely a rehashing of the old theory, and not just a rehashing, but it is the intellectuals' version of Intellectualism (a class definition of intellectuals), one that emphasizes and even develops its malignancy and stupidity. I think I would like to generally define this phenomenon—these sellouts abandoning actual social problems in favor of idealist musings—as "*tenkōshugi*."[2]

The subjective and positive problem of the intelligentsia must be first theorized starting from the role of intelligence within the proletarian class. This must become the intellectual consciousness of all progressive intellectuals today. All other theories of the intellectual are reactionary deviations [*tenkō itsudatsu*].

Chapter Seventeen

DOUBTS ON THE THEORY OF THE INTELLIGENTSIA

Is the Current Problematization of the Intelligentsia Mistaken?

Recently a great number of social and literary critics have debated the problem of the intelligentsia; so much so that at first glance it seems as if there is no room for anything new. But in fact, this is not true. We need to raise serious doubts about how the intelligentsia problem has been problematized.

As everyone knows, broadly speaking, during the heyday of Marxist thought, the main theory of the intelligentsia was viewed from a largely negative perspective: in a capitalist society ruled by class antagonism, how powerless are intellectuals, or to what extent are intellectuals aware of their powerlessness? And this negative perspective seemed to become "Marxist" common sense and spread to the mainstream.

From the intellectuals' perspective, such a pessimistic theory of the intelligentsia, such a problematization of the intelligentsia, was of course motivated by specific circumstances. Which is to say, for Japan and other late-developing capitalist societies, intelligence is the cellular form, the intellectual element—a decent translation of the intelligentsia—of the first and main subject of any progressive social consciousness or social movement. Accordingly, these intellectuals are in that sense also the leaders, manifesting as the surface phenomenon of social progress and development. And even if this were not so, these intellectual elements are, generally speaking, leading members of society, and this alone was enough to permit them and others such an assumption. And so now, the intelligentsia's Marxist

DOUBTS ON THE THEORY OF THE INTELLIGENTSIA

progressivism, largely linked to this ideology of intellectual leadership itself, unwittingly, comes to diminish the original and fundamental perspective of Marxism, namely the proletarian perspective. In order to prepare the ground for this tendency to diminish the role of the proletariat, it was natural at that time for a negative theory of the intellectual to rise to the surface and become a point of emphasis.

On the other hand, warning of the antiprogressive nature of this negative theory of the intellectual is not simple scare-mongering when we note that the various intellectuals' theories of despotism and dictatorship (?) were derived from theses of antiproletarian thought and antiproletarian politics. But emphasizing such danger, would, of course, not be to admit the unconditional and complete powerlessness of the intellectual; for the intellectuals, all this was merely to indicate the inherent social impotence of the intellectual. Thus, lurking behind this negative theory of the intellectual is a hidden assertion of the positive activity of the intellectual. But common sense is a vulgar thing that never knows the underside of things, and in that sense never gets the joke. So, though all the while being called an intellectual, this element completely failed to develop intelligence (intelligence here understood as one of the basic human aptitudes). And, to be brutally honest, this element further became devoted followers of the unconditional pessimism of the intellectuals until it constituted a Greek chorus. But the worst part? This negative theory of the intellectual was sung in Japan as if it were some sort of Marxist thesis.

So that now, when it is commonly said that Marxism's "popularity" has begun to decline, this pessimistic explanation of the intellectual also had to wither. And corresponding to a series of former ~~Marxists' conversions to right-wing ideologies~~ (*tenkō gensho*)—it is a pity I cannot discuss that in detail here—what must be called the inherent but hidden positive theory of the active intellectual was revived. Indeed, if it was common sense that the negative theory was Marxist, it was only natural, and became common sense, that this positive, active theory was non-Marxist or even anti-Marxist. And such a superficial common sense view would surely appear legitimate if one merely danced upon the surface of social phenomena.

But to the extent that the "negative" theory of the intellectual is not in fact Marxist, the common-sense view that a "positive" theory of the intellectual is non- or anti-Marxist is also not true, for what appeared as two opposing theories—negative and positive—is in truth, the passing through antagonism and alternation that should naturally be manifested in history. Only then will a truly Marxist theory of the intellectual be developed.

The Marxist issue of the contemporary intelligentsia should be: Where today would we look for the positive, active nature of the intelligentsia? The "Marxist" doctrine that society's intellectual element is merely negative and passive has already been dispensed with, or at least is something that is easily dispensed with. But as to the apparently dispensed-with non- and anti-Marxist "active theory of the intellectual," it in no way does away with the true positive and active nature of the intelligentsia.

2

The intelligentsia is usually translated as the intellectual class, and regardless of whether that is an appropriate translation, at least it is interesting as a symptom of the mistaken way we problematize the intellectual in Japan. It is fair to say there is no one who doesn't know that translating the intelligentsia as the *intellectual class* makes it a category of social science and that this intellectual class has a corresponding direct social coherence with the social mechanisms of production, a "class" in the same way as the bourgeoisie and the proletariat. Nonetheless, whatever the story, this term, the intellectual class, is telling us that the intelligentsia is imagined by analogy to be a class in some sense as the above social "class." Today there is a need to focus on this fundamental point.

The two "classes" [*kaikyū*] of Marxism also become four—or two and two—social strata [*shakaisō*]: the capitalists and landowners on one hand and the proletarians and farmers on the other. These social strata indicate a particular social status, and thus also name an occupational position in society. But, and this goes without saying, a stratum or occupational position is not the same as a class. So then, there is also the category of petite bourgeoisie as a middle stratum between the two social strata; because people usually say this petite bourgeoisie is limited to the small producers, this category of the middle stratum is a term meant to express a stratum between the bourgeoisie (and landlords), as a social stratum, and also proletariat (and farmers), also as a social stratum. Others also contend that the intelligentsia belongs to this same petite bourgeoisie as a middle stratum.

Indeed, a social stratum is not a social class. But nonetheless, sociology holds that social strata is, in fact, the same as social class (a stratum is not the same as a class in social science). This "sociological" perspective, which proceeds not from the fundamental relations of production but arbitrarily from the given social phenomena, easily and without hesitation, renders these phenomenal class strata on the surface of society as bona fide social classes. In so doing, the problem of "intellectual class" is not merely a question of semantics but touches on the essence of the sociological perspective. Even if the intelligentsia is a middle social stratum, calling it the Intellectual class is a symptom of sociology's errors.

But the language used doesn't really matter. More important than the name is whether the intelligentsia actually belongs to the middle stratum of the social strata. According to some, the intelligentsia is a wonderful, newly discovered middle stratum (Ōmori Yoshitarō[1] is an example of this view). Is there any group seen as a more mass [*taishūteki na*] middle strata than the salaryman? The salaryman is something other than a "contemporary" intelligentsia. As a social phenomenological category, it is unclear to what extent the salaryman is actually a question of a social stratum (common sense would seem to indicate bank employees or clerks and officials beneath middle management, but I would like to inquire as to how this works "social scientifically"). Most likely, this "newly discovered middle stratum" could be explained with a term like "knowledge workers." But saying "knowledge workers" doesn't actually tell us anything new, and we are still unclear on the meaning. If the monthly salaried bank employee who handles cash at the teller window is a knowledge worker, then is not the bus driver who has to constantly repair the engine to drive the bus also a knowledge worker? (The driver even exists within the masses.) It would seem that salaryman translates to "paid monthly" and as the driver is paid daily [hourly] he is neither a salaryman nor a knowledge worker. Wouldn't this strictly mean that those officials who are paid a yearly salary are also not salarymen? (Here, too, even the bank clerks belong to the masses.)

Speaking analytically, as an actual social stratum, these common-sense terms like "knowledge worker" or "salaryman" are absolute nonsense. Can we say that there is any basis at all for calling them representatives of the contemporary intelligentsia? For someone graduating from technical school or university, just why do the "knowledge class employment agencies" find work for so few unemployed graduates or actually end up finding them jobs as day laborers? The strange tale that the salaryman is the representative of the intelligentsia probably comes from the view that the intelligentsia stratum—assuming such a stratum exists—is a particular occupational position in society, and if so, *unemployed* intellectuals do not have the credentials to enter the intellectual social stratum. My guess is that this myth came from the readership of the criticism journals, a readership understood as a social stratum. But this readership "stratum" has a very different meaning than it does for the social stratum of "salaryman" or "knowledge worker." It was the "sociologist" [Gabriel] Tarde[2] who discovered this readership as a social stratum; here, at least, we are not ashamed of counting this discovery of the salaryman within the intelligentsia as an achievement of the sociologists.

In other words, because the common-sense category of the salaryman is insufficiently analytical to express or indicate a social stratum, the salaryman is simply the salaryman; it's probably some sort of social occupational position or social status. As such, the intelligentsia belongs to some other basic and particular tradition of social determination, and so its story is a very different one. In order to "discover" a representative of the intelligentsia, the intelligentsia itself must first be thought of as some kind of delineated stratum [shakaisō] of social occupation or social status. Assuming for the moment that the intelligentsia is a particular social stratum, it becomes sutured to the social phenomenon of salaryman as some kind of similar social strata, and without this suturing, this whole idea does not work. That is why the thesis that the intelligentsia is a social stratum is not proven at all but shows that it is nothing but a self-repetition.

But why go so far as to deliberately misidentify the problem and posit the intellectual as a particular, fundamental social stratum? The answer is simply that because if one starts from the perspective of sociological phenomenology, the intelligentsia had to be an intellectual class as a matter of course. But from this same perspective you could just as easily deduce a "delinquent class" as the sociological summation of juvenile delinquents, or a "suicide class" from the group (?) of suicides, and so on, and so on.

Thus, the important point is that this thesis of the intellectual social strata itself becomes a kind of thesis of the intellectual "class" (which everyone knows is wrong). Today, sociological phenomenology exists to completely overwhelm the essential perspective of social science. With sociological phenomenology things are not taken up from the perspective of the social relations of production, but rather in relation to the "bosom" [懐ろ] of the occupational status of high society. In place of historical materialism [*yuibutsu shikan*] is born the pocketbook view of history [*pokketo shikan*]. This could be called the "salaryman ideology."

So, of course, both this salaryman ideology theory of the intellectual and the sociological phenomenology theory of the intellectual are incapable of understanding the true social positivity of the intelligentsia. Indeed, who today would expect any intellectual positivity from the salaryman?

3

Alongside the social phenomenological theory of the intellectual is the culturalist theory of the intellectual. Here, in place of the salaryman, we have the literati, writers, critics, and others who, as possessors of (in some sense) higher levels of intelligence, are considered the representatives of the intelligentsia. Because for these types, confidence in their intelligence has grown recently, and has even taken a formal shape, it may now be seen expressed in behavior, and the resolution of the problem of the positivity and activity of the intelligentsia must be sought within this intellectual element. From this perspective, the intelligentsia is definitely not thought of as the intellectual stratum or the intellectual class. It is more individual, more individualistic—in that sense it is an internal perspective—and so the intelligentsia is thought of as a single "intellectual" [*chishikijin*]. Here the theme of assertiveness and activity is considered from the unique perspective of "the intellectual."

But there are several fundamental doubts here. First, even if we say "assertiveness and activity" that comes from the unique intellectual perspective, this assertiveness and activity itself is not unique to the intellectual world, which makes this "unique" perspective a smug intellectual self-image or something created in the dressing room of the theater of the intellectuals. Accordingly, this perspective would not only have no objective meaning but it would also have extremely weak meaning for the intellectuals' subjectivity itself. Therefore, the assertiveness and activity of the intellectual must, in the end, pass through the subjectivity of the intellectual to extend to a particular objective relationship to society (it seems that the theorists of the intelligentsia have not yet considered what concrete influence this relation may impart). Thus, the intellectual's assertiveness and activity must be in their relation to society. So, it is now possible to see how this relation gave birth to the misleading statement that the assertiveness and activity toward society is something unique to the intellectual.

As such, there are no restrictions on what concrete form the intellectual's assertiveness or activity should take toward society, and so the social stance of this intellectual stops at some carefree, general, abstract result. The uniqueness of the intellectual's assertiveness and activity is now also unfettered by anything. Accordingly, as a function of the uniqueness of the intellectual's general and abstract attitude toward society, this perspective brings with it the above mentioned right to rule as passed through the intellectual's "supremacy of the intellectual" [*interi shijōshugi*]. In this sense, then, what was the uniqueness of the intellectual becomes the social independence of the intellectual. In other words, it becomes the intellectual's transcendence of social class and social strata, until finally it is transformed into the idea that the intellectual should dominate society. I don't think this is some baseless fear.

But if this is the result of a theory of the intellectual—and if we haven't actually made it this far today, it is only because the movement has not yet fully developed—but if this is the result, we would have an extremely primitive class analysis of the intellectual that considers the intelligentsia a fair, unbiased, nonpartisan, that is, a third, middle *class*. If we view things from this assumed perspective, the intelligentsia does appear to have a particular capacity for anxiety, and it appears to be rich in doubt, just as the vulgar contemporary common sense would have it. In other words, the natural conclusion would see the intellectual as the most promising class, a fair and impartial third subject, equally dissatisfied with the bourgeoisie and the proletariat.

Discovering an objectively average social phenomenon within the intelligentsia—like the salaryman theory—not only results in a social class theory of the intelligentsia, but, even if the intelligentsia is seen as a collective concept that subjectively and oligarchically gathers together a group of individuals, we would still fall into all the evils of a class theory of the intelligentsia.

That is not all. The second fundamental problem is that to look for the representatives of the intelligentsia among the literati, writers, and literary critics is to assume that the literary arts are the highest standard of human intelligence. Bourgeois society assumes that so-called culture [*bunka*]—which is different than civilization [*bunmei*]—as well as cultivation or

DOUBTS ON THE THEORY OF THE INTELLIGENTSIA

Bildung [*kyōyō*] is the essence of human intelligence. But in fact, this "bourgeois ideology" version of intelligence was born of the medieval and feudal era when the priestly class had a monopoly on intelligence. The belief that literary labor is a higher form of intelligence than the labor in material production means "literature" is merely a modern form of this medieval monasticism. Because the assertiveness and activeness of the intelligentsia is seen in a small number of literary scholars, the claim that the resolution to the problem of the assertiveness of the intelligentsia and the problem of the intelligentsia itself comes out of nowhere.

This culturalist or literaturist theory of the intellectual has the same essence as the above sociological theory; this is important to notice. One of the fundamental flaws of culturalism or literaturism is that it fails to pay attention to the significance to the actuality of the form that—if they are not suddenly born sui generis, or if cultural and literary forms are not just "there"—behind all social phenomena and literary beliefs lie the material productive mechanisms of society. Seen from the material production perspective, culturalism and literaturism are a particular (culturalist and literaturist) social phenomenology. Compared with the phenomenology of the sociological theory of the intellectual, we see that it shares exactly the same essence as a phenomenological view of social phenomena.

4

The intelligentsia straddles all social classes; it is dispersed. We call this dispersed intellectual element the intelligentsia. Thus, in fact, the intelligentsia is a collective concept expressed in terms of the myriad intellectual elements and the corresponding quality and standard of the intelligence they possess. Thus, in order to analyze this collective concept of the intelligentsia, deciding which group to focus on and begin the analysis is more important with this problem than any other. Of course, in place of the phenomenology of the sociological and literaturist perspectives, we must begin from a social scientific one.

The problem, then, as always, begins from material relations of production within society. The intellectual element here is neither the salaryman nor the man of letters. It is the industrial engineer. Because the industrial engineer is the basic intelligentsia, intelligence must be a technical or technological intelligence directly linked to human productive activity.

Intelligence, as even [Hyppolite] Taine saw, is a sensory intelligence [感能] directly linked to human sensations. (The belief that intelligence or intellect is independent of sensation is a bourgeois and Scholastic superstition.) For example, we must view the worker's instinctual and analytical perception of his or her social class's interests as fundamental intelligence itself. In the same way that the mere knowledge and erudition of academic education are not identical with intelligence, the nonrealist consciousness of the literary scholar, and the free-floating sensations of the salaryman, are not particularly intelligence. We should say that intelligence is the instinctive competence within human practical consciousness. That is, the meaning and content of mental faculties are lost when separated from human productive life. Beneath social group, social stratum, social class, and further, family, individual, and social conditions, the one who has laid the groundwork for all this intellectual activity, what we should call the intellectual element here must first and foremost be the industrial engineer.

Starting from this industrial engineer, our concept of the intelligentsia can be gradually expanded to an organizational order including the general scientist, artists, politicians, educated persons, and so on. We should note here that this intelligentsia must be grasped as an order of things different from social status, lifestyle, occupation, social stratum, social class, and the like. After establishing this particular status of this intelligentsia and connecting it to social status or stratum or class or any other discretionary groupings, then we must, and only then are we able to, analyze the chosen grouping.

Here it will likely be asked just where these technical intellectuals who represent the contemporary Japanese intelligentsia display their positivity and assertiveness. But first let us at least acknowledge that when compared with authors and literary scholars, the engineers have much more self-confidence in their intelligence. A cult of intelligence has been the main object of worship for engineers and scientists since long ago. Confronting the contradictions of bourgeois productive technologies as one outcome of the contradictions of capitalist society on the one hand, and more recently the artificial fomenting of the munitions industry on the other, they seem to be increasingly awakening to their sense of their intellectual competence. But they have very little unified ideology, and if they do, because there are few plans or occasions to announce one, this only means

DOUBTS ON THE THEORY OF THE INTELLIGENTSIA

they don't explicitly talk about the assertive and active nature of their intelligence (but even this lack of a felt need to trumpet themselves corresponds to a strong faith in their own intelligence).

Certainly today, under the capitalist system, is the first time that the active and assertive nature of intelligence is guaranteed. Accordingly, as a result, such a consciousness is even supported by capitalist ideology. But on this point at least, this confidence is hardly different from the self-confidence of the literary intellectual. The problem is how does the assertiveness and activeness of intelligence under capitalism become independent of the capitalist system? (This is not the same as becoming independent of capitalism's class ~~antagonism~~.) The problem of the assertiveness and active nature of the intelligence of the literary scholars was likely here as well (if not, then there is need to fundamentally correct the criticism). So, the problem is first and foremost, how to make the abilities of the engineers and technicians under capitalism independent of the capitalist system?[3]

We do not believe we can expect the construction of a socialistic society from the intelligence of the literati or the salarymen. So, in general (not just in Japan), the role of the positive and active nature of the technical intelligentsia—within the limits of the resulting governing social organization—becomes the positive and negative poles of the society's intellectual element, the intelligentsia.

In the Marxist theory of the intelligentsia, from the very beginning, the essential nature of the intellectual as either active or passive lies in the basic structure of society's productive mechanisms. In Japan, this basic fact appeared as a series of theories of the intellectual either rejecting or supporting passivity or activity. By resolving the contradictions between these various phenomenal forms, the essence of the problem has manifested itself; meaning this must be the objective meaning and impetus for the recent phenomenon of theorizing the intellectual.

Chapter Eighteen

THE THEORY OF THE INTELLIGENTSIA AND THE THEORY OF TECHNOLOGY

A Reexamination of the Theory of Technology

To the bourgeois mind it is conventional wisdom to problematize *gijutsu*—technique[1]—as first and foremost in the form of "technology and economics." Which means it is mainly a question of industrial, agricultural, and other productive technologies and techniques. Thus, accordingly, the content of the problem of "technology and economics" is a question of industrial economics or agricultural economics. In framing the problem this way, it is also possible to tie this to kinds of commercial and managerial technologies and techniques. If one expands the concept of technology this way, it may be extended all the way to legal technique, administrative technique, and we could likely also make it all the way to things like literary technique. It is obvious, however, that given such a naive method, there would be no concrete or systematic relations between all these various "techniques." Any necessary and fundamental doubts on this conception are just barely avoided only because "technology" is used in such a vulgar and banal way.

The reason this question remains open is that the social requirements necessary to have a *social category of technique* have not been adequately organized philosophically. As the category of technology or technique itself is an extremely important philosophical one, nearly everyone has an implicit understanding, and it is therefore assumed that everyone already shares an understanding of the category. Such an assumption is also why even the technological and technical economic mechanisms of society are discussed in such a loose manner.

Second, technology is often discussed as a fundamental problem in bourgeois philosophy and the bourgeois worldview, not only because it is a particular social domain by virtue of its direct relation to the economic mechanisms. Technology is also often discussed as having some particular themes unto itself. Especially as the recent global situation encounters economic, political, and cultural crisis, the fundamental importance of the problem of technology comes to be felt everywhere. In particular, today the philosophy of technology and the attendant civilizational theory [*bunmeiron*] have a kind of special purchase. But in this case, the concept of technology remains in a form that is very difficult to grasp scientifically. It is likely right here that the category of technology should be grasped in its broadest and most fundamental sense, yet in the end this bourgeois "philosophical" concept of technology is nothing more than some learned adornments gracing what is at base the prior commonsensical conception.

Now then, technology itself is one of the things that touches upon a decisive and fundamental problem for materialism in general. In Japan, materialism's theory of technology has recently shown some development, and we could say it has at least succeeded in clarifying two crucial points. First, despite the universality of technology as a philosophical concept of broad and comprehensive meaning, materialism's technology theory has analyzed and synthesized the general concept as a systematic totality of primary and secondary elements. The theory holds that technology in general must be concretized as something that bifurcates after stemming from the fundamental line of material technology of production. Clarifying this bifurcated relationship, which at first glance was self-evident, but whose meaning was in fact hardly noticed by bourgeois conventional wisdom, is the first big achievement of materialism's technology theory.

The second achievement lies in distinguishing between technology on the one hand and technical skill, techniques, and technical methods on the other. Technology in its proper sense (*puropaa*), that is, *the material technology of production*, means the objective, material base of society that from the very first must be strictly distinguished as one aspect of, but different from, the specificity of the skills of the laboring subject who deals with this technology and the techniques and methods that may be seen as extensions of these skills.

But none of this is yet a sufficient materialist clarification of the nature of this primary technology—in the strictly "proper" sense.

On this second point we would do well to recall Aikawa Haruki's "Key Points in the Recent Debate on Technology" (*Sociology Review*, no. 1).[2] Here, Aikawa summarizes and discusses his views on the theory of technology as well as the debates among materialists. In this piece, we could say he offers a consistent and fundamental criticism of one of my own earlier articles on this subject, my "Philosophy of Technology."[3] As for my idealist deficiencies and any errors in the piece, I agree with his criticism. On these points, I myself hold his essay in high regard. That said, I am unable to dispel some fundamental doubts about his positive positions presented in this piece.

Technique, according to Aikawa, can be nothing but the system of the material means of social labor—at a particular stage of development—of the material forces of production in human society. That is, technology is primarily the organization of the means of labor. The materialist approach, he insists, is to limit the concept of technology to the above sense. In fact, all of the determinations of his technical concept begin with and are concentrated in this definition. It would seem that what is rather casually called technology includes technical skills and methods on the one hand, and immaterial techniques and technologies of production on the other. In the common-sense usage, technology is definitely not thought of as only referring to an organization of the means of labor (machines, tools, factories, transportation facilities, and so on). Common sense would likely hold that technology refers not to the organization of the means of labor itself, but to some idea of technology at the base of that organization. (Here "idea"[4] is a particular and expected result of an analysis.) Thus Aikawa must explain for what reason he chose the everyday word "technology" to express the "organization of the means of labor" instead of using some other term; on the one hand he would need to explain why the common-sense usage of the term is unscientific, and on the other, how his understanding of technology is able to force a critical reflection on the current everyday usage of "technology." Without doing so, in place of the determinations of technology, his usage would terminate in a simple "definition" so loved by bourgeois science, and "the organization of the means of labor" would mean "technology" or "technique" as a mere arbitrary definition and academic jargon. In which case, as always in this bourgeois method, "technology" is

THEORY OF INTELLIGENTSIA AND OF TECHNOLOGY

mere terminology; it is mechanical and arbitrary, and so we can expect no true development of the concept.

We can speculate that Aikawa is taking his definition of technology from Marx's writings, but I have yet to find the specific place and cannot recall anyone else quoting the passages, so Aikawa's textual basis in Marx must remain mere speculation. To the extent that Aikawa is citing Marx, he gives no specific passage where Marx used any similar definition of technique.

The main source of Aikawa's argument is Marx's explanation of "technology" (*Technologie*). He states: "Any who doubt whether or not technology is the organization of the means of labor should reexamine Marx's thesis (which Lenin extracted in explicating historical materialism in his *Karl Marx*)." This statement by Aikawa is placed between two quotations of Marx's thesis. The first, appearing before the above passage, states "Technology reveals the active relation of man to nature, the direct process of the production of his life, and thereby it also lays bare the process of the production of the social relations of his life, and of the mental conceptions that flow from those relations."[5] The second quotation of Marx comes after Aikawa's passage: "a critical history of technology ... [the formation of] ... the productive organs of man in society, of organs that are the material basis of every particular organization of society."[6] These are the passages Aikawa says Lenin pushed to the fore.

Here Aikawa concludes: "As the object of the study of *Technologie*, 'technologies and techniques' are none other than the particular—which is to say particular to the material basis of society at a specific level of historical development—'productive organs' which are in turn the means of production, and especially the means of labor." Aikawa further claims that what Marx elsewhere called "the technical basis of society" is identical to the above "material basis of society."

It is immediately clear, however, that Aikawa's conclusion that technology is "the material base of society" comes, at best, if at all, only from Marx's second thesis. In contrast, the first of Marx's thesis would likely produce the opposite conclusion, for there Marx states that technology is "the active relation of man to nature" ("the direct process of the production of his life"); and consequently "the process of the production of the social relations of his life, and the mental conceptions that flow from those relations," meaning that the "technology" that Aikawa has so far been searching for must be found within these quotations. So then why must not only the formation of relations of production, but also the mental conceptions based on "the active relation of man to nature" be thought of as "the organization of the means of labor"? It would seem, quite contrary to Aikawa's conclusion, that Marx here is explicating technology as something explicitly not limited to the organization of the means of labor. And we must note that Marx continues: "Even a history of religion that is written in abstraction from this material basis is uncritical," and further, that "to develop from the actual, given relations of life the forms in which they have been apotheosized" is "the only materialist, and therefore the only scientific" method. In other words, what Marx refers to here as "material basis" or "material" means nothing like Aikawa's "means of labor," but simply indicates the general starting point of a materialist view of history.

We must also say that Aikawa's reasoning concerning Marx's second thesis is rather weak. For although Marx does equate the "productive organs of man" with the "material basis of every particular organization of society," deriving "the means of labor" from a combination of these two statements is a rather dangerous reading. In Marx's original, the expression the "productive organs of man" is simply analogous to "the organs of plants and animals, which serve as the instruments of production for sustaining their life." If this analogy is read as based on the external similarities, it merely implies "the active relation of man (and plants and animals) to nature" as a function of the material organs. While Aikawa wishes to insist that the organs as instruments of production imply the means of labor, Marx simply wishes to say that the organs of production are not passive, but active. Further, if the intended analogy is a more literal one, then the so-called productive organs of man (the material basis of society) are a material basis more literally like organs—as the nervous and muscular systems are also organs—and not merely the organization of the means of labor. Elsewhere Marx explained this tautologically (from our perspective) as the "technical basis." Further, if Marx did indeed make an essential analogy between technology and the productive organs of plants, animals, and humans, this would indicate that technology is not simply limited to an objectivist [*kyakkanshugi teki*] (or even mechanistic) definition as the organization of the means of labor, but that the historical origin of technology is found in the organs of living things. Thus, it would then follow that the meaning of the analogy of the productive organs indicates both the organs themselves

THEORY OF INTELLIGENTSIA AND OF TECHNOLOGY

as the "organization of the means of labor" and the subjective sensory and kinetic functions.

That said, not only can Aikawa's "organization of the means of labor" not be derived from Marx's two theses, but also, if we were to think about it a bit more naturally and on a more sophisticated level, we would have to conclude that Marx's statements are antithetical to such a mechanistic [*kikairon teki*] definition. Now I have no intention to embark on a philological exegesis on whether such and such does or does not come directly from Marx's own words; I only wish to say that my reading of Aikawa's two Marx quotations tends in the opposite direction from his.

Of course, Marx's own words are not the only basis for Aikawa's reading. It seems that his own system of thought required him to think of technology in this way. But it goes without saying that a thinker's own systematic necessity is not always an objective necessity. It would not be scientific or appropriate to offer a theory that in place of critiquing and transcending common sense is completely divorced from common sense, yet still using the same word, technology, shared by common sense. To be sure, it is not in the least necessary to respect the claims of common sense, but unless the theory is able to redeem common sense, it cannot be said to be scientific, and certainly would be a theory unable to be held by the masses of society.

All this is not to say that one may not proceed in thinking this way. But as it is inconvenient to take a colloquial word like technology and make it scientific, one needs a completely new and independent scientific concept, and only then may tentatively call the new scientific concept "technology." But in that case, one should call the new concept something like "technicity" or the "technical basis." Regardless, there would still remain just too much of a gap between this new term and "the means of labor" to understand why the new word was chosen. In other words, the "means of labor" is already clear and does not need to be rendered as "technology" or some other term. Indeed, as no one, including Aikawa, would feel the need to identify the means of labor with technology if they were absolutely two unrelated things, it is clear that there is a necessary something linking the two. But no matter how intimate that connection may be, the two can never be unified as one and the same. This is especially true as there are times when equating these two concepts is itself problematic for more substantive reasons.

Strictly speaking, the unmodified colloquial term technology likely cannot become a scientific category. But an analysis of this everyday term would have to be derived from various categories of theories of technology. As the moment of technological phenomena, "the organization of the means of labor" would surely be necessary as one of those categories. But if this category is isolated from other categories that express other moments of the phenomena of technology, it becomes meaningless and loses its usefulness as a category. So what sort of category is being imagined here? A category that is well expressed and measured by means of the system of the means of labor would surely need to be something like the "technical standard of society" [*shakai no gijutsu suijin*]. So can't we imagine that what is popularly called "technology," is captured as one moment of this category of the technical standard? For now, this concept of the technical standard remains in the imagination.

Of course, even if we posit a technical standard, this act alone will not make it a particular visible form. In that sense, it does not have the materiality of something like the means of labor does. Nonetheless, it would have materiality in exactly the same way that the social forces of production do. Compared with both the means of labor, or their organization, the technical standard is a much higher social abstraction, and by that alone it belongs to a more abstract social mechanism. But it is only through this category of the technical standard of society that the so-called organization of the means of labor and the corresponding skills belonging to labor-power are initially and actually combined and conceptually unified. Thus, the technical standard is also able to satisfy the demand to conceptually incorporate skills and techniques within so-called productive technology.

The technical standard as abstracted from the organization of the means of labor is measured by the organization itself, but at the same time the skills belonging to that organization are measured by the technical standard. Even if one says that the particular skills of labor-power within a particular society correspond to the organization of the means of labor, this merely expresses an expected result. But in fact there exist continuous interactions between these skills and the organization of the means of labor. For example, if there is no standard, no socially average level, there could be no design for the driver's seat of a tractor. The scale by which this socially average level of skill is objectively measured is the technical standard of society.

THEORY OF INTELLIGENTSIA AND OF TECHNOLOGY

The practical interaction between the means of labor and the actual skills of labor-power first occurs when they are converted into a technical standard that serves as a sort of *technical equivalent* [*gijutsuteki tōkabutsu*].

Although at times Marx appears to use technique [*gijutsu*] and the science of technology (*Technologie*) [*gijutsugaku*] interchangeably, the two must be distinguished scientifically. Indeed, as a science of techniques is definitely not identical with a science of technology as such, we should also not say that the object of a science of technology is directly and solely technique. The study concerning technique is absolutely not the same as "technology" and could, for example, likely be economics or sociology or the like. Further, in the introduction to his *A Contribution to the Critique of Political Economy* [1859], Marx called the study of the particular branches of production "technology," and he distinguished it from the study of general production or generalized production. (Thus Aikawa's explanation of Marx's science of *Technologie* and his assumption that "technique" designates the object of that science is already problematic). If one differentiates the science of technology from so-called technique, what sort of thing is this science of technology? Here is where the category of the technical standard is useful.

As I have already said, the science of technique is not simply the study of technology. The science of technology is in fact a technical organization of assumed techniques (expertise and knowledge based on hands-on experience and skills). It must therefore mainly be the means of labor and its system of organization. So, what is meant by the development of the science of technology? It means, as an ideology, a rise in the standard of subjective skills of engineers in general on the one hand, and, on the other, a rise in the objective technical standard of society. If the objective technical standard of a society may be seen in the level of engineers, there would be some reason for why popular usage would rather loosely use both *Technologie* and techniques to mean the same thing. And here we can also see a further reason why common sense would expect to find the main moment of so-called technique within the technical standard.

So, the social technological equivalent that mediates the organization of the means of labor and the skills of labor-power is something like this technical standard, upon which we may now for the first time construct a broad, unified, and hierarchical totality of techniques. If we do not use the sort of social abstraction expressed by this technical category, any philosophical or worldview or cultural theory concerning technology would be complete nonsense. Marx's insistence that even a critique of religion must begin from the standpoint of technology would also become impossible. The relationship between the problem of technology and cultural theory is mainly a problem of the relation between technological development and human progress. In the primitive age, before the means of labor and the skills of labor-power were not yet physically separate, in Marx's metaphorical expression above, the technical standard was represented by the function of the organs as productive instruments. Here the technical standard was simply the degree of development of humanity's biological intelligence. We can consider the category of the technological standard as one descended from the primitive, undeveloped stage to today's developed social organization as a standard moment of "technique as such," and say that it remains a category to measure the fundamental development of human society. If this understanding of technology is the basis of material society, the content of "technology" may be grasped by assuming the "standard-ness" of the technological standard. If this is not done, one would have to appeal to a system of the means of labor, machines, instruments, and the like. This is literally the first step toward a mechanistic philosophy [kikairon].

Of course, Aikawa is not the only one who assumes that technology is "the organization of the means of labor." Indeed, there are today many materialists who rely on this assumption. But I believe that this reliance is worthy of a ruthless materialist reexamination. This essay is one attempt at such a reexamination. While my personal views on the technical standard remain a hypothesis, nonetheless, there is no escaping a materialist interrogation of the current "materialist (?)" definition of technology. Readers, what say you?

Finally, I must touch on my immediate motives for raising these doubts on the current theory of technology. I believe that the recently much discussed theory of the intelligentsia seen in literal and academic circles has, in fact, something to do with the doubts I have raised here.

The present debate on the intelligentsia appears to have two flaws. First, the debate has a tendency to ignore the subjectivity of the problem of the intelligentsia—that is as a question of the intelligence of the intelligentsia—in favor of grasping the intelligentsia simply as a particular stratum of society. But the progressive task for the intelligentsia today must lie in the

THEORY OF INTELLIGENTSIA AND OF TECHNOLOGY

question: "How will the intelligentsia use its subjective intelligence in a progressive manner?"

The second flaw is that the problem of the intelligentsia lies in the tendency to arbitrarily begin the examination with the analysis of the literary and philosophical problem of intellectuals, completely severing the intelligence of the intelligentsia from the question of technology. As human intellect and intelligence is born of, and conditioned by, the active practices of social humans vis-à-vis nature, generally treating intelligence as severed from technology is none other than completely ignoring the original and fundamental principle of materialism. This is an extremely careless and idealist conception of intelligence. Amazingly, such self-evident points do not appear to be in the field of vision of today's progressive intellectuals. Without a clear focus on this issue, the question of the actual intelligence that constitutes the subjectivity of the intelligentsia becomes meaningless, or it is raised in some perverse form such as "the active *spirit* of the intelligentsia." And asking the question this way condemns it to a dark and dire destiny.

Of course intelligence is simply one of the skills of labor-power. This is why the problem of the intelligentsia is presented as a question of the relationship between intelligence as the skill of labor-power and technology as such. But the problem is unsolvable unless one knows what technology itself is, and what practical and technical relationship it has with skills. If one considers technology as the organization of the means of labor, the question of intelligence—and thus also the question of the intelligentsia—is overlooked or even destroyed. This is the reason I ventured to designate technology as "the technical standard" of society.

From this, it can be concluded that the problem of the intelligentsia can never be solved outside a materialist standpoint. Which is to say, it can never be answered in a simplistic way as a liberal question for liberals.

Chapter Nineteen

LIBERAL PHILOSOPHY AND MATERIALISM
Against Two Types of Liberal Philosophy

In a recent newspaper, Dr. Gorai Sosen says that the true enemy of Japanism is materialism. It is not immediately clear just what is meant here by Japanism, and still less by materialism. Whatever its status as a behavioral phenomenon in contemporary society, from a theoretical standpoint, Japanism cannot be said to have any true theoretical independence whatsoever. There is simply no way it can be seen as a theory that can stand on its own. As proof, if one tried to endow it with any sort of adequacy to make it relevant to society in general, Japanism would have to be backed up with any number of foreign philosophies. There are very few instances of such a manufactured and finicky philosophy developing into anything more than some sort of vulgar philosophy. In contrast, materialism has traditionally been seen as a system possessing a singular, independent, and comprehensive theoretical organization. Thus, theoretically speaking, such laziness as aligning materialism and Japanism on an equal footing and calling one the true enemy of the other must inevitably invite ridicule.

I could not help but laugh when perusing a certain journal of criticism attempting to introduce various factions of contemporary thought only to see that materialism sat alongside all sorts of confused and bogus thought such as that of Heidegger, Scheler, and Jaspers. Of course, when one ignores relative historical significance and arbitrarily compares whatever recent phenomena happen to appear before one's eyes, the results are often laughable. The stupidity of such judgments is due to their total lack of equitable objectivity, and there is nothing as ugly as these sorts of lazy, impressionistic, and subjective opinions.

Compared to the simple juxtaposition of contemporary materialism with the ethereal philosophies of Scheler and Jaspers, it is much more fruitful and important to juxtapose it with contemporary Japanism. Though as I stated above, while Japanism cannot stand on its own as a question of theory—of course, in a way, a nontheoretical theory (?) may always stand on its own—from the perspective of an actual social force, it is probably true that materialism is a powerful opponent of Japanist philosophy. And from materialism's perspective as well, Japanist philosophy is an irreconcilable opponent. Whatever else it may say about itself, Japanist philosophy is the philosophy of Japanese fascism; and materialism takes fascist philosophy in general as its ultimate antagonist.

Now it would seem that the recent social situation in Japan has momentarily focused the public's attention on the problem of liberalism. The editorial pages are all proclaiming that liberalism has fallen, but just where had this now fallen liberalism been all this time? The simple truth is that up to now there had only been small amounts of freedom, and all that has happened is that already limited freedom is once again being repressed. Consequently, we could say that liberal consciousness, that is, an interest in liberalism, has in fact recently been stimulated, and in some aspects has even risen to the occasion, or such was the actual power of recent or so-called liberalism following post-peak Marxism (?). Whether liberalism has fallen or been reignited, the recent events are neither a fall nor a quickening of liberalism.

In any event, what must be made clear is that whereas materialism had been the original antagonist of Japanist philosophy, what is happening now is that liberalism is forced to awaken to the reality of what it means to find oneself in an antagonistic relationship with Japanist philosophy. While this appears as obvious to everyone, this perspective has not yet been pursued by liberals to the extent it should. As it does not share the same theoretical interests of materialism, liberalism has no footing in a fight against Japanese fascism. The current situation demands a choice between materialism and Japanism. Further, liberalism must seek to find its own footing within materialism.

Of course, both habitually and emotionally, liberals are loathe to agree with this recommendation. Liberals are constantly assuming and stressing that liberalism is a unique, autonomous philosophy. We therefore feel a necessity to criticize and overcome this liberal philosophy, for if we did not, we would not be able to make the most of liberalism itself. If liberalism does not rid itself of this liberal "philosophy," it has no chance of critiquing or overcoming Japanism. And this is the issue we must turn to now.

We say liberalism or liberal philosophy, but today these words are used to denote an enormous number of very different meanings. They might simply mean a doctrine (?) of loving freedom or "antifascist" sentiments. They are also code words for "anti-Marx," and the examples of such vulgar concepts go on and on. But it is necessary here to recognize that liberalism has at least three parts or aspects. First, liberalism first emerged as economic liberalism. This economic liberalism began with the physiocrats' and later classical economics' rejection of the state intervention of the mercantilist state. Second, as a theory of economic policy of free trade and free competition, economic liberalism eventually gave birth to a corresponding political liberalism. Liberty and equality as the social status of citizens, and the political idea of democracy (bourgeois democracy) built upon it, make up the content of this political liberalism.

From within, or perhaps based on, or corresponding to, this political and economic liberalism emerges a third aspect of liberalism. For the sake of convenience, let us call it cultural liberalism. In place of economic and political consciousness we can think of a more general, higher level consciousness called cultural consciousness. Cultural liberalism is liberalism within this cultural consciousness; it is cultural behavior as a social activity built upon this particular cultural consciousness. Many have noted this cultural aspect of liberalism, like Aono Suekichi's[1] "liberalism in literature" or Ōmori Gitarō's[2] "spiritual liberalism." Not only do both of these examples have no comparability with the other aspects of liberalism, but Aono overly privileges this cultural aspect while Ōmori dismisses it as having no value at all. Regardless, we can say that many assume this cultural aspect of liberalism to have special importance today.

These three aspects of liberalism have a certain independence from each other, and so we must not lose track of any of the individual parts. Just as a planned economy in no way directly contradicts the political liberalism of parliamentary politics or party politics, the "fall" of political liberalism may in fact lead to an exaltation of cultural liberalist consciousness. Indeed, we can see how the fall of political liberalism (which in truth is due to the same causes as the current waning of Marxist cultural theory), has led to a "restoration" [*fukkō*] and a flourishing of a particular form of cultural liberalist consciousness. Examples in literature include: the active spirit, the cult of anxiety [*fuanshugi*], Romanticism, various forms of humanism, and others.

As such, even if economic and political liberalism both fall, a tenuously independent cultural liberalism may actually be able to thrive, at least momentarily. Thus, in general, if it is axiomatic that anything labeled liberal is something to be protected, then in those cases when economic and political liberalism are in a largely unfavorable situation, cultural liberalism naturally must become the last resort of liberalism in general. A great many of today's cultural liberals [*bunkajin*], Aono Suekichi included, are searching for the positivity of liberalism exclusively within the confines of this cultural liberalism. It is safe to say that many of these generic liberals are liberal in only the most vague and sentimental ways, and while they may have no liberal economic opinions or democratic intentions in politics, they all privately believe in cultural liberalism. We can then say that it is precisely this cultural liberalism that today is the newly active and influential form of liberalism.

From within this cultural liberalism has emerged a particular liberal philosophy. But before we look at it, we must first note one more thing: namely that the category, the fundamental concept of "liberalism" contains two different types. Generally speaking, any category that indicates a social phenomenon uses the same word to indicate both the particular historical form and the transhistorical general form of the phenomenon. For example, the word Romanticism indicates a particular period in German cultural history that followed classicism and more generally also indicates antirealist movements of any age. We could say the same about the Enlightenment. Liberalism is no exception. As a historical category, liberalism was an economic, political, and cultural ideology of the rising bourgeoisie of the seventeenth and eighteenth centuries. But even so, we must not ignore the fact that the word "liberalism" is also used to express a transhistorical, universal humanistic category free from the historically specific ideological constraints of its historical form—Hasegawa Nyōzekan calls this sort of universal form "a moral category." Of course, as a historical category, liberalism is simply bourgeois ideology, a product of capitalist culture. But when liberalism becomes a moral category, it can be thought of as having already been liberated from its particular class nature and its particular ideological character. As a moral category, liberalism assumes an extremely accommodating form, able to absorb any specific contents at its own convenience whenever the need arises. It must be said that for those generic, unremarkable liberals who will worship anything liberal, liberalism as a moral category, as the latest, the final stage of liberalism, will present itself as the only place to go.

What matters here is that it this "liberalism" as a moral category is cited as direct validation for the above cultural liberalism. Put another way, liberals who place their ultimate trust in cultural liberalism base that trust in thinking that their liberalism is one founded in liberalism as a moral category. In other words, they argue that it is this moral (universal, humanistic) liberalism that gives cultural liberalism its authority. If this argument were correct, then cultural liberalism would necessarily be the last and highest stage of liberalism.

But there is a subtle mistake lurking here, one that gives rise to great errors. No matter how "cultural" cultural liberalism may be, and thus no matter how transeconomic, transpolitical, and in that sense no matter how antirealistic a liberalism it may be, none of this means that cultural liberalism is an example of a transhistorical, "moral" category. It should not be permitted to think that cultural liberalism, which was only one aspect of liberalism, is the same thing as liberalism itself—liberalism as a moral category—reigning over the whole of liberalism. If forced to think in this way, one would have to change what is called *liberalism as a moral category* into something more like *moral liberalism*. Such a moral liberalism would be the same as cultural liberalism. But if we make this move, then both the freedom from the historical fetters within liberalism as a historical category, and the "freedom" that the moral category had, are no longer guaranteed to moral liberalism.

Continuing along these lines, we would have to conclude that if cultural liberalism were something to be newly established today, because such a cultural liberalism would be identical with the moral category, a category whose legitimacy cannot be denied, then the establishment of cultural liberalism would be the establishment of liberalism in general, and economic and political liberalism would both be built upon cultural liberalism. In other words, economic and political liberalism would both owe their authority to being based on a moral foundation. And this would in turn mean that opponents of political liberalism would be accused of being immoral. But that is not all. Such cultural *liberalistas* would start to think that they possess the sole right to true and general liberalism by simply adhering to this cultural liberalism and ignoring any problems of political (or economic) liberalism (or freedom). And this is how we get cultural *liberalistas* arguing that political freedom does not really matter because what is really important is a robust self-consciousness.

Cultural liberalism has the bad habit of using liberalism as a moral category to pass off its own liberalism as liberalism-in-general and transplanting everything into moral liberalism; and so cultural liberalism degenerates into moral liberalism. It is already no longer a liberalism of culture but has become a culturalist liberalism [*bunkashugi teki jiyūshugi*]. As we can often see the traces of this form of culturalist liberalism among literary figures in a broad sense, I have previously called this form a literary or philosophical liberalism (see chapters 11 and 15).

And so now the "literary" philosophical system of liberalism has been finally established. Cultural liberalism had been but one part, one aspect of liberalism, but now as this one part has declared its independence and has begun to unify the whole of liberalism, cultural liberalism comes to mean a specific ideology, a specific philosophical attitude toward liberalism in general. And here we have for the first time a "philosophy of liberalism" a "liberal philosophy"—though this is only one of two forms of liberal philosophy's emergence, see below for the other. This new liberal philosophy will make use of literary categories in place of philosophical categories (see chapter 11 for more on this phenomenon). This is why it is a literary epistemology, a literaturist, liberal philosophy, that is a liberal philosophy built on a hermeneutic literary consciousness. This is also why, for example, all the varied types of humanism in literary criticism are secretly based in this liberal philosophy, and if they have any political implications, those political conclusions would be entirely obvious and predictable. The reader will perhaps have guessed that this philosophy is the pillar of those liberal literary figures who have converted from progressive to reactionary ideologies (*tenkō bungakusha*).

We must note that this literary liberal philosophy, which now has become liberal philosophy *tout court*, is a system of thought not limited to being deployed only in so-called literature. In fact, today this liberal philosophical mechanism lurks within much of bourgeois philosophy. See, for example, the way in which Nishida philosophy evokes some sort of liberalism in its readers [see chapter 12]. And if it does so, it would mean that this liberalism is our unreconstructed literary liberalism, which is to say a moralist liberalism, and thus Nishida's philosophy, is one kind of liberal philosophy. It is interesting to note just how many bourgeois philosophies in Japan can be classified as this type of literary liberal philosophy. Indeed, this is how various cultured, *Bildung* philosophies with apparently no relation to political liberalism still may be traced to this liberal philosophy and its literary consciousness.

For liberal philosophers of this type, it is no coincidence that no matter what more or less rational and progressive political common sense they may derive from their cultural education, and despite their relative respect for the theoretical importance of Marxist cultural theory in intellectual history, all, without exception, oppose materialism. Their opposition is prefigured in the choice to remain within the limits of cultural liberalism. Material forces such as the forces of production and powers that are the foundation of society have no purchase whatsoever for this type of liberalism. From the very start materialism was totally unnecessary for this philosophy. From this starting point it takes only the slightest nuisance for such a philosopher to become an opponent of materialism. The above remains true even for those literary types with their literary consciousness who are the representatives of the cultural intelligentsia.

So far, we have considered the birth of a type of liberal philosophy grounded in cultural liberalism; now we will examine the emergence of a different type rooted in political and economic liberalism.

Generally speaking, literary liberalist philosophy appears not to speak of liberalism in any way at all; this is explained by literary liberal philosophy having never been a liberal philosophy in any adequate sense.

It is likely inevitable that a liberalism that resulted from fleeing the original economic and political liberalism to suddenly rise up as a cultural liberalism would not produce an adequate liberal philosophy. A genuine liberalism worthy of the name must begin from an economic and politically grounded liberalism. From this base, a cultural liberalism may be automatically incorporated into this field.

LIBERAL PHILOSOPHY AND MATERIALISM

This second type of liberalism is in no way common in Japan today. Its most remarkable form appears in the efforts of Professor Kawai Eijirō. I say "efforts" because according to the professor himself, a philosophy of liberalism has yet to be adequately established, and it is those academics like Kawai who are working to bring it about. (See "The Intellectual System as a Principle of Reform" in *Chūō Kōron*, 1935, no. 5, among others.)

According to Professor Kawai, liberalism is an ideology that arises from the birth of capitalism. But just because this was the case in the beginning it does not mean it will remain true forever. Further, for Kawai, most people, and especially Marxists, rashly assume that because of its capitalist limitations, liberalism can never escape social reformism, but Kawai believes this is a premature conclusion. As he cautions us: "The current stage of liberalism has deviated from social reformism and developed itself into socialism." Of course, socialism indicates the antagonist of capitalism, but Kawai continues to say that given the special circumstances of countries like Japan and Germany, the principles of their contemporary social order are not a pure capitalism and its corresponding bourgeois liberalism because Japan and Germany are both characterized by the large number of feudal remnants within their social order. Thus, according to the professor, the current stage of Japanese liberalism simultaneously has two enemies: capitalism and feudalism. Against feudalism it must become an antagonistic "liberalism"; against capitalism it must become a socialism. So Kawai's current Japanese liberalism is an organic unity of liberalism and socialism.

For Kawai liberalism is socialism. But what kind of socialism is this? According to the professor, the current stage of liberalism qua socialism results in idealism [*risōshugi*]. Marxism as a materialism is not only not an idealism; it is the opposite of idealism, and, as the professor would have it, it is a materialism because it negates "ideals." So at minimum Kawai's "socialism" must oppose Marxism. Just where is this current stage of liberalism that opposes feudalism, capitalism, and even communism (Marxism) headed?

Professor Kawai bases his explanation for this current stage of liberalism qua idealism within the history of liberalism. According to the professor liberalism developed from *natural law* to *utilitarianism* before finally arriving at the current stage of *idealism*. Kawai's idealist liberalism is likely modeled on Thomas Hill Green's ethical liberalism.[3] Kawai has thoroughly studied this Kantian, un-Anglo-Saxon ethicist Green. But as Green died in the 1880s, I am not sure he is the appropriate model for the current stage of Japanese liberalism in its state of emergency. We must remember that this attention to Green illuminates liberalism from a rather surprisingly ethical perspective for an economic liberal and parliamentarian such as Kawai.

Professor Kawai's liberalism, which is also of course his idealism, aims at the social development of individual personalities. Of course, a solitary individual cannot single-handedly develop their personality within society, nor would this be desirable. The desire to develop everyone's personalities through feelings of empathy such as "for the public good" or our "unfortunate brethren" would of course at the same time socially develop one's own personality. An idealism that expresses these ideals must be first and foremost a "moral philosophy." From there, in the sense that these morals have some concrete content that realizes these ideals, it must then become a "social philosophy." Which is to say, this liberalistic social philosophy, indeed this sociophilosophical liberalism, politically would be a doctrine of antistatism and also be parliamentarian; economically it would mean freedom from the coercions of capitalism (whereas the older bourgeois liberalism meant freedom from the coercions of the state).

The professor's liberalism is an idealism because it possesses the moral ideal of the free development of the individual personality (Green has an extensive analysis of this in his *Prolegomena* [*to Ethics*, 1883]). This liberalism is thus an ethics [*rinrishugi*]. And so here, this hard-earned economic and political liberal philosophy is completely unchanged from the earlier moralistic liberalism of the literati and the cultural philosophers. In fact, today, this sort of ethics is a trick shared across all bourgeois philosophy. For them all political and economic mechanisms are reducible to the ideals of ethics and morality. And from this ethical base is born "social philosophy" or "political philosophy" or "economic philosophy." Take the similar reductive logic for example: because the expression "a nation of soldiers" [*kyokoku kaihei*] holds that all the nation's people are reducible to soldiers, the generals and colonels who are the "soldiers" represent "the people." Can this really be a serious logic?

"Ethics"-ism as a trick has the exact same structure as another one: "ideal"-ism. If having an ideal meant idealism, then Marx himself would likely have been the ultimate idealist. Regardless, he adopted materialism in place of idealism (also translated as *kannenron*). This was because his socialistic ideal—we should not forget this meant the true freedom of the people (see *The German Ideology*)—this socialistic ideal was to be reached through material, actual means, a materialist consciousness of the problem and a course of action coming from it. Contrary to the worries of Kawai Eijirō, Koizumi Shinzō, and other ethicists and philosophers, Marx did not have to theoretically confuse an acknowledgment of the necessary laws of matter with a practical course of action, nor did he have to consider them separately. The transformation of reality into logic and fact into value is the materialist dialectic itself. Which is to say, logical relations and value relations are reality and facts abstracted to the level of principles by human historical experience. If we forget this point, we would have absolutely no way of understanding any of the contemporary scientific critiques of culture. But in Marx the two elements of material means and idealistic goals are neither separate things nor are they simply made into one. It is only in this way that one may know a particular means will be adequate to the particular goal. But for Professor Kawai's idealism, the means must be idealist because the goal is ideal. For example, the means for attaining freedom must be a free "parliamentarianism." We cannot understand why a means in general would become unfree if it does rely on the bourgeoisie's so-called parliamentarianism, but in any event, secretly confusing means and ends is the trickery of "idealism."

The professor claims that we must oppose Marxism because Marxism's confusing of means and ends results in Marxism making material means the ends themselves—yet this confusion of means and ends itself is characteristic of the professor's own "ideal"-ism. Idealism can only have meaning as an ethical stance—this kind of human sentiment or that kind of attitude. (Kiyozawa Kiyoshi believes liberalism to be just such an attitude.) And so if this "ideal"-ism were to become a philosophical system it would be an idealist one. I have often written of the fundamental flaw of idealism as a general philosophical system; and here these tricks of idealism serve as perfect examples of this.

Suppose there were a person who constantly said, "Truth, truth!"—truth explains truth, and truth defends truth. That person would surely be tagged as a "truthist." Which is to say people would recognize that this person's "truthism" is not the truth. It is necessary for both ideals [*risō*] and freedom [*jiyū*] themselves that we do not do the same caricatures with "ideal"-ism [*risō-shugi*] or "liberal"-ism [*jiyūshugi*]. It would be wonderful if an "ideal"-ist and "liberal"-ist such as Professor Kawai were not the one to discredit ideals or freedom. Marxists also value the freedoms of speech, assembly, association, parliament, the body and all other freedoms—Professor Kawai calls them the "formal" and "practical—as means to achieve the ideal of human freedom. But only "liberals" believe that installing freedom as a goal and respecting freedom of behavior is immediately a doctrine of freedom, a liberal-"*ism*." Just where exactly is the guarantee that such moral or ethical emotions and intuitions of freedom directly and immediately become a philosophical theory called liberalism? It was materialism that had the habit of being cautious toward the very human danger in believing that emotions become a system in one stroke.

If a love of freedom alone guaranteed an independent philosophical system called liberalism, then shoe salesmen would have a shoe philosophy and barbers a hair philosophy. (Indeed materialists probably love freedom more than anyone, and more than anyone, despise the obstacles to freedom.) The rich sentiments of liberalism become a cold, barren theory when they attempt to organize themselves into a philosophical system. This proves that liberalism itself was never a true image of a doctrine of freedom. It is thus not mere bad luck that Professor Kawai must lament the incompleteness of liberal philosophy.

Certainly those most interested in the so-called fall of liberalism are not the materialists but the Japanists. That said, up to now any sort of theoretical criticism of liberalism by the Japanists has been quite rare. Fujisawa Chikao's "On Liberalism" (*Social Policy Newsletter*, May/June 1935) is probably the most noteworthy.

But as a political scientist, Fujisawa is only concerned with political liberalism. According to Fujisawa, today political liberalism has completed its task. Further, the liberal theory of the state is constitutionalist—the rule of law—and as much as possible it separates the state from society and subtracts from the state as much social and ethical meaning as it can in a consistent attempt to leave the state with nothing but legalistic and administrative functions. As such, for Japanists a liberal state knows nothing of the ethical authority of society—even the Japanists are ethical! But, Fujisawa warns, even in Europe this constitutionalist liberalism has played out its role and has been subsumed under a new manifestation: the idea of the total state [*zentai kokka*], in which the whole of society is the state, and every

LIBERAL PHILOSOPHY AND MATERIALISM

member of society is only human once qualified as a member of the state. The state function infiltrates every aspect of society. It seems that this means the private affairs of individuals in this society are not allowed.

Thus, the total state recovers its original (?) social authority. Here authority means more than mere power. Liberals generally only know power, so they think that any lack of power is "freedom." (This is true of those like Professor Kawai.) But according to Fujisawa, such freedom is only passive, negative freedom. True, positive freedom, far from being incompatible with power, is unified with it. This "authority" is the unity of an active, positive freedom and power.

Fujisawa is introducing and parroting Nazi theorists of the state (Carl Schmitt among others), so it is enough to recall the phrase "our Führer Hitler" to know the true nature of authority, power, and positive freedom. But Hitler is not a sufficient concept of authority for the Japanese Fujisawa Chikao. The true authority of the state requires the necessity that comes from tradition and bloodlines. Which means that the Empire of Japan becomes the very model of the authoritative, total state.

From here, Fujisawa descends into the etymological and philological punning common to nearly all Japanists. The only thing worthy of our attention here is that the organ theory [of the emperor][4] is a liberal and leftist theory of the state, and against this, the theory of imperial monarchical sovereignty is a rightist theory of the state, whereas only Japanism is a state theory that unwaveringly walks the middle road.

Because this means that liberalism is becoming of the same nature as materialism, materialism finds that it has fallen into the breach and is forced at great pains to mount a defense of liberalism. Materialism must do so through a "scientific" study of the history of the folk—that is, through a materialist and historical materialist study of Japanese history. I suspect that materialism is much better qualified than liberalism for a such a materialist analysis of history. In other words, the most radical defender of liberalism is not liberalism but materialism. Now, as to how the liberals with their subjective sentimentality will react to this conclusion—there are no guarantees.

Chapter Twenty

CONTEMPORARY JAPANESE THOUGHT

The Superiority of Materialism for the
Question of Thought

It is common knowledge today that the world of thought is divided into right-wing, centrist, and left-wing. These are in turn popularly divided into various instances of fascist, liberal, and Marxist thought. But this common sense is built upon an extremely superficial conventional wisdom: even among examples called Marxist, if the essence of the thought is considered, there are a huge number that may be counted as social fascist, and not a few that are very close to liberalism. Similarly, among liberals one may find those without any real liberal qualifications, the majority of whom are nothing more than warmed-over social fascists and fascists. Thus it would seem that while these popular labels—Marxist or liberal or fascist—may be convenient, they have little fundamental meaning. At the very least, it would be the height of foolish common sense to be a liberal because one believes that liberalism opposes both fascism and Marxism.

Of course the classifications of fascism, liberalism, and Marxism as separate ideologies are derived from their relation to the current state of class ~~struggle~~. At the end of the day, the class nature of the ideologies should not be ignored, for without this ultimate standard we would be unable to say anything at all about todays' intellectual universe. But when it comes to questions of what is fascism, liberalism, or Marxism, not only is there no consensus within conventional wisdom or in the ideologues' own understanding, but it is also plainly true that there are many fundamentally distorted self-understandings. For example, contemporary Japanese fascists are constantly explaining that their own thought is in fact antifascist, and liberals understand liberalism [*jiyūshugi*] as nothing more than the pursuit of freedom [*jiyū*]—which in fact results in liberalism opposing liberalism. And self-proclaimed "Marxists" believe they can be moderately Marxist by attacking Marxism.

These complications and perversions are not resolved by distinguishing them as ideologies of particular cases of socially objective phenomena, which indicates that we must not take up these issues under the subjective conditions of the fascist, liberal, and Marxist ideologues. Such a method would result in a "world of thought" being built on an unbreakable relation to the personal thoughts of thinkers. The above complications and perversions are born of the discrepancy between a thinker's own subjective embrace of their thought and that thought's objective meaning. Thus, as the above popular common sense classifications are sometimes coming from the side of the subjective self-worth of a thinker, and other times from the side of the objective meaning of that thinker's thought, common sense can't help but be unstable and confused. To the extent that common sense simply states, "that is Marxist" or "that is fascist," it is like saying, "that is the Seiyūkai and that is Minseitō"[1]; it is like sticking a stamp on a letter, and as it is simply stamped on the exterior surface these common sense labels are not to be taken seriously. But the meaningful point here is the attempt to clearly understand the particular characteristics of a social phenomenon by classifying the ideology by means of its politics. In grasping thought as an ideology under specific social conditions, it is absolutely not allowed to separate that thought from its political ideology. That said, ultimately, we should not forget that an ideology's political nature itself is merely a striking and more direct and immediate feature of any given thought. Which is merely to say that all ideologies' fundamental characteristics lie deeper, and their various political ideologies may be directly or indirectly attributed to their more fundamental natures. Thus, if one only looks at a thought's resulting political ideology, it is not uncommon for the ideological character of that ideology to fail to come to the surface. Good examples of this are certain philosophical ideologies and natural scientific ideologies. Simply looking at "fascist physics" or "liberal mathematics" would result in almost nonsensical characterizations. This is why the "sociological" common sense whereby thought is an ideology of the left, right, or center, does nothing to resolve our issues. Thus, it is not possible to draw a map of the intellectual world in this way. This is because when one tries to place any thinker on the map in any concrete way, it not only will be wrought with difficulties and go poorly, but the resulting sketch would resemble a haywire, a confused thicket.

So, in place of a sociological map of the intellectual field using left, right, and center—or fascism, liberalism, and Marxism—I must construct a map built on more rational contents. That is, we need a more philosophical map. Thought is the unification of a worldview and an intellectual method; since ancient times thought in this sense has been classified as idealism or materialism. In fact, this time-honored classification is the best and most useful standard for a social mapping of today's intellectual world.

In speaking of the antagonism of idealism and materialism, it can appear that slick common sense once again has this covered. But not only does common sense not understand the meaning or the contrasts of either type of thought, it has also never grasped the actual meaning of the two terms in any practical way. Furthermore, the current social significance of this concept has not been sufficiently grasped in any practical way by a basic outline of idealist philosophy, or even materialistic philosophy programs. As we carefully and concretely examine this issue, we would not be wrong in thinking that the popular understanding of idealism and materialism is unaware that these two types of thought are not only two different worldviews, but those worldviews have two corresponding logics. These errors come from the common sense belief that thought is simply something like an idea; but in fact, thought is not simply holding some idea or bandying it about—if you look closely at the actual situation, thought means promoting an idea *by deploying it*. "Thought" means the organizational mechanism of the development of the idea. Broadly speaking this organization is called the "logic" that runs through the thought's virtues, realizations, completeness, and factional nature. Hegel and others expressed this with the term "inference [推論]." The categorical organization is therefore the tools of logic. Thus it is the case that there is no "thought" without the incorporation of everything from the worldview to the categorical organization. Thus a proper thinker [*shisōka*] is one who has taken on this entire construction; a child or a madman may simply have an idea. Idealism and materialism both have this basic form of thought and so they are not simply two worldviews but are also two logics. Was it Tomomatsu Entai (and not him alone) who tried to evade this problem of the aspects of thought by stating that the idealist or materialist question was all just frivolous theorizing? Such questions are what disqualify people like him from being considered thinkers. The contrasts of idealism and materialism do not only provide a mapping of thought and the intellectual world, but awareness of these differences also implies criteria for determining whether or not one is, in fact, a thinker at all. Of course, as we shall see, even those who lack these qualifications of actually being a thinker may exist *socially* as "thinkers."

Especially when it comes to a popular understanding of materialism, recently there are many who hold particularly bizarre ideas. People will often say this is a materialist thing or that is materialist thought, but just what that means seems to be totally unclear to the person saying it. Though such nontheoretical, intellectual gangster-like understandings cannot become a serious interlocutor, it nonetheless surprisingly agrees with a part of the general public. In Japan today, such a commendable understanding is bandied about in the House of Peers and the House of Representatives, so splendid is this ~~idea~~.

In Japan, current materialism is called dialectical materialism. This thought, according to a fair historical consideration of philosophy, is in fact, a current outline of world philosophical history. The various problems of so-called idealism (for example the problem of the subject, the individual, consciousness, freedom, and others) should be critically resolved by means of dialectical materialism, but today dialectical materialism itself is understood in all sorts of distorted forms.

The first distortion is one where materialism is understood as objectivism. Here it is thought that the problem of the subject is not taken up as a problem of the subject. Those like Ōmori Gitarō do not take up the problem of the intelligentsia from the subjective conditions, the intelligence, of the intelligentsia but only as a question of the intelligentsia's "objective" social stratum and social class. This is only one example of such an objectivism, but even this materialism hardly differs from the vulgar popular understanding of materialism as a form of thought in which even the human spirit is an object like a stone or water. Originally today's materialism was social; it was the thought that belonged to the proletariat and the farmers. But in the present example, materialism could probably be seen as traceable to the salaryman or "students" in a broad sense (as readers of the so-called journals of criticism), or even to the bureaucrats. This is close to the understanding of those like Sakisaki Itsurō.[2] When materialism is conceived this way, it is already less "thought" than the social tastes and preferences [*shumi*] of the salaryman.[3]

There are countless cases like this when materialism becomes objectivism. That said, the opposite is also the case. It is a very common intellectual phenomenon whereby materialism becomes subjectivized. Among these there is the specific case where dialectical materialism is thought of as historical materialism—in which Marxism is converted [*tenkō sarareru*] into another philosophy of history. The most accomplished (?) of these thinkers is Miki Kiyoshi.[4] It was through his materialist philosophy of history that not a few among the many students and scholars he influenced tried to make compromises between materialism and their own idealist tendencies. I was one of them. As was Oka Kunio. Today both of us have abandoned our youthful philosophical convictions. Funayama Shin'ichi has just recently rid himself of this philosophical hobby and the comprehensiveness, elasticity, and practicality of his thought has made him an honor student of materialism. Today the few remaining literature students who are close to Miki's position do not pose a problem. Nonetheless, from then to now Miki's influence appears in various forms and in unexpected places. Professor Tanabe Hajime is one of materialism's supporters who does not acknowledge the original meaning of the natural dialectic, and this too is related to his special feelings against what he sees as a materialistic ideology of historical materialism. Of course, Tanabe has never been a materialist in any way. It is clear that such materialist philosophies of history like Tanabe's are thriving vulgar, academic materialisms (?) produced by infusing materialism with the philosophical and literary tastes [*shumi*] of Japan's "cultured" middle class.

The eternal falsifier of materialism is of course idealism. As such, we must transition to a section on idealism. But first we must take note of an unexpected case. Dialectical materialism is, so to speak, proletarian materialism. Yet in one sense it must be considered as a development of French bourgeois materialism. There is basically only one representative of this bourgeois materialism in Japan today, but it is the extremely famous Hasegawa Nyozekan. In Japan bourgeois materialism was once represented by Fukuzawa Yukichi as enlightenment philosophy, as French materialism by Nakae Chōmin, and as German materialism by Katō Hiroyuki. The first has been reduced to the daily practices of the Japanese bourgeoisie, the second passed into the anarchism of Kōtoku Shūsui[5] and Osugi Sakae and has lost its intellectual power (only the writer Nii Itaru lingers as a memento mori), and the third tradition seems to have ended with the recent death of Ishikawa Chiyomatsu. Today only Nyozekan remains as a relatively comprehensive and familiar example of English bourgeois materialism.

Hasegawa claims his intellectual attitude is extremely "materialistic" because he acknowledges no other philosophy beyond positivist common sense. He does not like to abstract out his thought's organizational structure, as his type of philosophy seems to hate theory. But there is always a particular and striking organization in the habitual manner in which Hasegawa talks of his ideas; a consistent character that anyone is able to see. We are convinced that a simple conscious development of this logical organization would fall into some sort of idealist situation. Hasegawa's materialism does not acknowledge the practical utility of the dialectic and so accordingly this is the reason it does not become dialectical materialism. Nyozekan's materialism is in no way a perversion of materialism; it is simply an incomplete materialism that has been put to work as is. But this incomplete materialism results in various idealist deviations. As for the fate of bourgeois liberalist thought (not necessarily bourgeois democracy), today there seems to be no other path. But Nyozekan is the only thinker to have given us an organized intellectual foundation for such a fate.

Or take the example of Professor Kawai Eijirō's advocacy of liberalism. Simply removing the opposition of idealism and materialism only to arbitrarily render liberalism's economic, political, and cultural ideologies as fundamental principles (Kawai's thought stems from an economic ideology), and then build a philosophy is like inventing a "cobbler philosophy" or a "barber philosophy." Even if one has an idea, this does not make it "thought." It is no accident that in Japan today liberal philosophy still has no actual existence. It is the same for "liberalists" Baba Tsunego and Kiyosawa Kiyoshi, who, because they have no clear worldview or logical organization, cannot in any meaningful sense be counted among the thinkers [shisōka].

So, if we ask what sort of person a truly materialist thinker is, strictly speaking there are very few.

This is not the case simply because so few people have managed to truly take dialectical materialism to heart, but also because those materialists who do, become, at best, academics or specialists, and do not enter the wider intellectual world as thinkers. Doing so is not impossible, however. Materialism gives shape to a materialist intellectual system by concretely analyzing and comprehensively unifying according to a materialist worldview and a materialist organization. Unlike the case of idealism, this is not easy. Indeed, there are a great number of materialist social scientists. For example, Hirano Yoshitarō, Yamada Moritarō, Kobayashi Yoshimasa, Yamada Katsujirō, Ōtsuka Kinnosuke, Hattori Shisō, Hani Gorō, Inomata Tsunao, Tsuchiya Takao, Sakisaka Itsurō, Arisawa Hiromi, Ishihama Tomoyuki, Sassa Hirō, Ōmori Yoshitarō, and we could include others. There are noticeably fewer materialists among philosophers and literary theorists. In top-level philosophy there are Saigusa Hiroto, Oka Kunio, Funayama Shin'ichi, Nagata Hiroshi, Akizawa Shūji, Honda Kenzō, and others. In literature there are Kurahara Korehito, Miyamoto Kenji, Moriyama Kei, Kubokawa Tsurujirō, Miyamoto Yuriko, and Aono Suekichi, among others. Materialists are extremely rare among natural scientists and mathematicians. At most we could number Ogura Kinnosuke and once again, Oka Kunio, among the ranks of materialist natural scientists. Surely among the above names there may be several for whom it is a problem as to how deserving they may be of the materialist label. And not only that, but as they are all academics and specialists, much as we said of journalists and critics, they cannot yet be said to become proper "thinkers". The more materialistic, the higher the qualifications are to become a thinker.

That said, we must not forget that today materialism is the most comprehensive, unified, and objective worldview, and the most practical organized logic. In fact, contemporary materialism is the thought most well suited to the fundamental characteristics of basic "thought." Currently, without relying on this materialism we cannot have an actual, unified, organized thought with any scientific critical abilities. As for the names given above, nearly without exception, by virtue of all being critics, journalists, or encyclopedists—and if we dispense with the standards of general thinkers—we can tentatively call them thinkers. As materialism itself can be thought of as more advanced when compared to other philosophies, the requirement that to be a thinker is to be a scientific critic can be made very strict. If one ignores even the vulgar common sense of the public, I think it is not too much to say that materialism will be the only basis of proper *thought* going forward.

As proof of the superiority of materialism, let's examine the various types of so-called idealism (even if a particular example does not see itself as idealism or even considers itself anti-idealist) and test its qualifications as "thought." The reader will surely see that like a kaleidoscope, there is nothing within the colorful scene that would merit the status of "thought."

We dare say the majority would agree that the most creative and excellent thinker in Japan today is Professor Nishida Kitarō. Indeed, if it is a question of the greatest mind and the deepest contemplative powers, we must rank the professor at the top. But we are engaged in neither a heroic narrative nor questions of psychological genius. Our problem is the question of Nishida's thought and philosophy, and mind and thought are not the same thing. Nishida philosophy is extremely original and likely forms an epoch in the history of philosophy, but none of that indicates the excellence of Nishida philosophy as thought. We will quickly understand this if we first ask just what understanding of society is in Nishida philosophy. The ultimate clue to Nishida philosophy's social theory is found in the I-Thou relationship. In general any thought that explains historical society with such an individualistic, ethical, and humanistic shibboleth, rightly or wrongly, is definitely not an excellent from of thought. Further, it is a thought that absolutely cannot explain the character, contradictions, or tendencies of contemporary society. In that sense, it must be said that Nishida philosophy almost completely lacks any social thought at all.

The many fans who praise the excellence of Nishida philosophy are merely enamored with the common sensical humanistic truths that regularly appear in the professor's writings; they hardly touch the fundamental points of Nishida philosophy at all. The same is true for those readers who dabble in Zen, as there is also a fair bit of Eastern mysticism in Nishida. The essence of Nishida philosophy is in fact the so-called logic of nothingness. Therefore, the Nishida school should first try to use this logic of nothingness to judge whether Nishida's logic is effective in the formation of thought. I think Professor Tanabe Hajime is the first person to try this. Tanabe uses the logic of nothingness to form a hypothesis of the ideal of the state behind the current class rule of the "class state" [*kaikyū kokka*].[6]

In other words, by grasping the state, the actually existing "state of being" [yū teki kokka], as underwritten by the "state of nothingness" [mu teki kokka], Tanabe is able to rationally interpret the ideal meaning of state and society without contradiction.

Indeed, because actually existing society is interpreted though the colorless, transparent medium of nothingness as a social ideal, actual reality will be reproduced as is, without any trouble. But realistically that is where it ends; reality is in no way realistically changed by any of this. All that has happened is that present reality has been interpreted to be backed by an ideal. This is all hermeneutic philosophy, the mere interpretation of the world.[7] The logic of nothingness is probably the unrivaled and most thorough, organized logic for such a hermeneutic philosophical interpretation of the world (this is also what idealism considers "thought"). By discarding the crucial actuality of thought capable of actually changing the real world, and simply constructing the meaning and order of the "idea" that envelops reality is the tell-tale sign of metaphysics.

Today, idealism is generally called metaphysics, which is shown in the concrete contents stated above. In other words, because it is an intellectual mechanism that aligns not with earthly order but a heavenly order, it may be fairly deemed generally theological. It is no accident that Nishida philosophy is linked to dialectical theology or that Tanabe philosophy attempts to match a bodhisattva.[8] (Since it was first introduced to the theology department of Dōshisha University, Nishida philosophy has been a pillar of current academic religious restoration and the restoration of Christian theology.) Generally, interpretive philosophies like Nishida's are for the most part supported by liberals (these generally interpretive philosophies are different from the special form of interpretive philosophy discussed later). But should this general philosophy become a theological ideology [shingakushugi], speaking from the standpoint of objective social value, it is then already no longer a philosophy of liberalism.

The hermeneutic philosophy (idealist thought) built on the logic of nothingness, just as the word "nothingness" says, includes no special mechanism in its logic. But merely interpretive, hermeneutic philosophy can accommodate various mechanisms within itself. I think we can call one case of these supplemental contents a literary consciousness or our previous literaturism [see chapter 11]. This means the phenomenon in which philosophy is rendered literary at its base. Accordingly, in general, this indicates that thought itself is no longer a scientific critical capability but devolves into a literary monologue.

Of course this thought is not merely so-called philosophy or some logical framework. It is also not simply a collection of scientific knowledge. In this sense, thought always appears in the form of literary expressions and literary representations. And precisely because this is so, we think that there is a concrete form to thought not only in science and philosophy, but also within literature and the arts. But it must be stated once more that thought is not merely an idea. A literature that expresses an idea does *not directly* make literature the expression of "thought." As thought requires an intellectual mechanism, a literature that lacked such a mechanism would be nothing but a "thought-less" literature. Incidentally, literature always expresses the contents of thought with a combination of concrete literary representations. This is obvious, and whether this is good or bad, the point to notice here is that a representation is not the same as a concept. In other words, just because one borrows a literary representation does not mean that the concept expressed is a literary one. Concepts (logic is the functional organization of various fundamental concepts) are ultimately scientific, philosophical, that is, practically objective. But at least in the case of literature, only the *representation* of the concept is allowed to become literary. Yet today's idealism, metaphysics, and the various schools of hermeneutic philosophy replace the mechanism of a scientific and philosophical organization of fundamental concepts—materialism—and then make a logic out of a literary organization of fundamental concepts mediated by literary representations. Only then can one imagine that one has rescued one's thought from materialism.

A good example of this is Lev Shestov. Through Miki Kiyoshi's recent position as editor of Shestov translations, the "philosophy of despair" is a model of the literatur-ification of thought [*bungakushugika*]. This comes out in Nietzsche translations, too. But whether it is Nietzsche or Kierkegaard, the key thing to notice is how the special character of their thought is located in the contrivances of literaturistic philosophy. The problem is clearly not only that the literary expressions and styles of the thought are literarily sophisticated, but rather that the more the thought is rendered literary, the more the public's vulgar common sense comes to view literary representation as thought itself.

In the literary world, the intellectual phenomenon of idealism is linked to the cult of the literary [*bungakushijōshugi*], and in social theory it gets linked to the cult of intelligence [see chapters 15 and 16]. This is the fatal flaw of someone like Kobayashi Hideo who—though one of the "philosophers" among bourgeois literary critics—though he absolutely does not empathize with Miki or Shestov, is nonetheless compelled to use literaturistic theory. Furthermore, speaking from a social-phenomenon perspective, it cannot be overlooked that this literary consciousness has an essential relation to the fascist conversions [*tenkō genshō*] of a group of literary scholars and authors. Whatever the case of political or social activities within so-called fascist conversion, the fundamental changes brought about by fascist conversion of a materialist literary consciousness is none other the conscious or unconscious use of the mechanisms of literaturism.

A literary consciousness originally corresponded to one instance of literary liberalism. As the original role of modern Japanese literature was an idealistic criticism of feudal morality, once liberalism became mainstream, but for special exceptions, the majority of artists may be counted as liberals. Toyoshima Yoshio, Hirotsu Kazuo, Kikuchi Kan, Sugiyama Heisuke and many others seem to consciously be liberals. And to be sure, the literature of despair group and the more positive faction of the "active spirit" are also liberals. Moreover, here "liberalism" itself means literary liberalism; it is a liberalism that must be divorced from the political activities of liberalism (that is, divorced from the necessity of pursuing democracy). In fact, here even political liberalism means only a supra- or transpolitical literary concept of liberalism. Unexpected as it may be, this kind of literary liberalism contains a path to fascism. Though nearly everyone is warning of the dangers within the so-called active spirit literature, the literature of despair, too, through its "conscience" and "humanity" has already attained a moralistic religiosity. And in every sense, the role of current religion is absolutely and objectively no longer liberalism.

Apart from their ultimate objective effect, speaking from their direct interests, the above two types of hermeneutic philosophy mainly succeed by appealing to the intelligence of the cultural intelligentsia. And as the content of this literary model, thought is founded on the interests of the middle class; it must appear as either an escape from social reality or the inaccessibility of social reality itself. The only difference between the two types of hermeneutic philosophy is that those with a relatively theoretical intelligence prefer Nishida's brand of interpretation, while those of a relatively more emotional intelligence prefer a philosophy built on a literary consciousness.

I believe, however, there is one more form of interpretive philosophy called philologism—a philological consciousness. The vast majority of academic philosophy in Japan is trying to build a structure to resolve actual current social problems by piecing together bits of etymological and classical knowledge. This is nothing but confusing German or Greek philology with philosophical inquiry. Of course, such "philosophy" is unworthy of the name. But the place to glimpse this philological consciousness is actually within a scene being rocked by practical needs. An ideology of philology and a philological consciousness are perfect for connecting the historical reality (?) of the Japanese Empire to some sort of enabling intellectual foundation.

Being not only limited to Japanese nativism, this philologistic interpretation aims more broadly at using nativist, Confucian, and Buddhist classic texts to critique and establish the intellectual products of civilization in contemporary Japan. Despite the fact that the *material mechanisms* of Japanese capitalism are completely divorced from the historical categories found within these Eastern classics—actually precisely because they are wholly untainted by capitalist material forces—these classic texts had to become the *ideal mechanisms* of Japanese capitalism. Under ordinary conditions the spiritual mechanisms that would arise from Japanese capitalism would be rejected out of hand as Western or foreign or materialist thought; so then the space in which to construct Japanese or Eastern thought or spiritual civilization is wide open—thus, it can only be drawn from the classics, from a period with historically specific categories completely different from the present. The sloganeering of the ideologues of the Japanese spirit, agrarian fundamentalism, or greater Pan-Asianism are all instances of this degraded philological consciousness. Soon this philologism will likely become the method of constitutional interpretation. Among this type, but without such an overt and degraded philological consciousness, would be Watsuji Tetsurō and Nishi Shin'ichirō. In contrast to Nishi who is absolutely a practitioner of this philological consciousness in an academic form, Watsuji has distilled philologism to hermeneutics and migrated to anthropology so if one is not careful it is easy to miss Watsuji's philologism. In fact, Watsuji appears to be closer to a variant of the literary consciousness mentioned above. But this apparent closeness has other significance, as we shall see.

Most philologistic idealism results in true Japanese fascist thought. Which is to say, it results in the unity of church and state of the tutelary religion [*shashoku shūkyō*]; that is, it results in the restoration of a religion of the Japanese folk and Japan as the nation of the chosen people. Thus, if the Japanese folk is the model ethnicity for all humanity, then must not Japanese philologism become Japanese anthropology? This is precisely Watsuji's Japanese ethics = "anthropology" [see chapter 7].

But a more radically idealist form of interpretive philosophy has even abandoned interpreting the world. Even more, it appears to be no longer idealist. That is, it appears as a physical pragmatism of the individual body. By absolutely prizing the stomach over the mind, the person over knowledge, belief over theory, thought itself has become something to be forged in the dojo just like judo, kendo, or Zen. Such is the meaning of practice [*jissen*] in this pragmatism [*jissenshugi*]. And so political activity must take the form of direct action. Thus, this idealism becomes, as it were, a Hinayana religion: the body is the problem. Indeed, all possible problems are the "four inevitables of human life": birth, aging, sickness, and death. Buddhist revival, myriad heretical (?) sects, folk medicine, and the inherent holism of good and bad fortune, as well as the various physiognomies—which was an important part of Nazi philosophy—all this idealist rubbish does nothing but play a mute Sancho Panza to fascist thought. Thus, the social ground from which bona fide Japanese fascism emerges needs no further explanation here.

From what we have seen so far, it is easy to understand that the majority of today's influential idealism has little hope of possessing the necessary qualifications to be considered "thought." Further, if we include those various schools of thought that have since lost their influence, idealism has quite a number of forms. More, we also need a different approach to classification. For example, among the neo-Kantians, we must not forget philosophers like Kuwaki Genyoku or physicists such as Ishihara Jun—note that both are clearly liberals. But it is absolutely true that such liberalism of individual intellectuals does not make a trend in the intellectual world at large.

Finally, one more problem remains. I'm sure many a reader would likely say that thought is the thought of some thinker, and that if that individual thinker's thought is unique, for example even if that thinker does not belong to any school of thought, can't we see such thought as influential? Alas, no; this just isn't so. A truly representative thinker is always part of a larger trend or school because within that thought there is some sort of objective intellectual mechanism that is used by many other people. For example, though both are now deceased, it should be said that the Sōda school of thought was established by Sōda Kiichirō, but can it be said that the Fukuda school was the result of the influence of Fukuda Tokuzō? From this I think we can make a formal distinction between those who are thinkers [shisōka] and those who are not. In the ordinary sense Kawakami Hajime[9] was definitely not a creative "thinker," but it is common knowledge that as a representative of Marxism, Kawakami gave birth to many intellectual disciples. He does not lose his status as a representative of Marxist intellectuals.

It is in this sense that I hesitate to follow popular opinion and count Sugimori Kōjirō as a thinker. Indeed, he has many worshippers. But if it is a question of worshippers Tokutomi Sohō probably has more (Tokutomi was not a thinker, but perhaps at best a historian, or if not, a mere demagogic writer). In other words, as a speaker and a rhetorician Sugimori is a superb ideologue, but not a thinker with an intellectual mechanism. And what about Murofuse Kōshin? He is, as a so-called journalist, a critic of civilization or alternatively an introducer of civilization, but he is not a thinker. This is because his charm is absolutely not in the coherence of his thought but is constantly renewed by various thought from the outside. The late Tsuchida Kyōson was also not a thinker in this sense.

The meaning of the word thinker may be freely decided. But the question is what sort of thinkers can be expected speaking from the assumptions of various thought? In this sense a thinker is not a mere scholar or expert, a debater or a hobbyist, a writer or an artist, a journalist or an essayist. A thinker is also not a thought "broker" or a possessor of stereotypes. A thinker is a scientific critic of the world. And in that sense hardly one single thinker may be found in the idealist camp. Common sense will likely find this statement doubtful, but it is really not so strange. Originally, materialism was the weapon of scientific critique, that is, materialism was the weapon of thought. But it must be said that today even within materialism there are few thinkers, meaning thinkers who take the initiative as an original, critical, materialist thinkers. But this current situation shows only that the path of materialism is steep, not that the qualifications of materialist thought have been shaken. In fact, if it is to be actual and practical, there is no royal road to science.[10]

PART III
The Masses and Socialism in an "Age of Reaction"

Chapter Twenty-one

THE CURRENT MEANING OF "PROGRESSIVE" AND "REACTIONARY"

"Civilization and Enlightenment" [*bunmei kaika*] was *the* slogan that symbolized the new thought of the first year of the Meiji period, 1868. Taking more or less random examples from that first year of Meiji we find publications and collections titled, *Civilization & Enlightenment, Gateway to Enlightenment, In Praise of Enlightenment, Enlightenment Dialogues, Enlightenment Explained, Civilization: A Down Home Dialogue, On Enlightenment, Poems from an Enlightening Japan*, and so on. These all already appeared in the discourse on Civilization and Enlightenment in the *Meiji Culture Collected Works* and can also be found in Miyaki Kaikotsu's *Civilization and Enlightenment*. Thinking on it now, there is no other intellectual slogan in modern Japan that can compare.

I said the slogan or motto that "symbolizes this thought," but of course, back then it was not "thought" in our social sense, but mere thinking or contemplation. So-called thinking or contemplation are themselves already the result of the abstraction of a more concrete, material thing—in the past, abstracting out from certain practices was considered a kind of philosophy. Thus, concrete thought is in fact built upon a base of systematic customs and products of civilization which makes them things with an extremely important internal essence. Look at the beginning of Katō Suekichi's *Civilization and Enlightenment* of 1873 and you will find pieces on hairstyles, hats, shoes, dwellings, and meat eating; Such customs are themselves the most concrete forms of thought, and when thought becomes everyday common sense, thought *is* customs.¹ When the social structure is relatively stable, tastes and customs can appear to be mere representations of an individuals' diversity with no intellectual value at all—but in moments of great social change, even tastes and customs come to appear as objects of hard intellectual cohesion and pressure. In general, if something called "thought" does not reach this level of common sense and customary practice, then it really cannot be called living thought. I will touch on this point at the end but wanted to preview it here.

Today a symbol of contemporary thought comparable to Meiji's "Civilization and Enlightenment" would probably be "progress" [*shinpo*]. Of course, it is not that there was no word in the so-called Civilization and Enlightenment era for progress, but it was not as prevalent as it is today, nor was it as necessary to understand it as it is understood today. As the phrase "Civilization and Enlightenment" was abbreviated to "culture," this motto of 1868 was later diverted to express the "cultural" consciousness that emerged after World War I in Europe. As one could already see in people like Abe Jirō, this modern concept of "culture" was already founded on a theory of individual character. Further, "culture" was a function of 1920s postwar socialization, and it took on a more or less social viewpoint. From there, finally, the concept of culture was generalized to the historical activities of society that we use it to mean today. But in Japan this word "culture" has not completely rid itself of the odor of high German idealism's philosophy of culture. Be that as it may, this "culture," the one that originally corresponded to "Civilization and Enlightenment," was, as that slogan says, absolutely a concept of the Age of Enlightenment [*keimōki*]. Which is to say, this case of the word "enlightenment" [*keimō*] (which mostly corresponds to the German *Aufklärung*) itself means not simply "Civilization and Enlightenment [*kaika*]," because the determinations within the concept "Civilization and Enlightenment" that illuminate and clarify humanity are decidedly not carefully woven into the concept in a historical sense. (This Enlightenment as *keimō* was also a favored expression of 1868). But when it comes to "progress," this is a concept that originally and clearly stands as a historical concept.

"Civilization and Enlightenment" was a motto of a rationalism of the Age of Enlightenment, but with "progress," though we definitely do not call it historicism, it is a motto that is built upon grasping historical *movement*.

MEANING OF "PROGRESSIVE" AND "REACTIONARY"

Enlightenment as *Aufklärung* is the thought (*shisō*) of the overthrow of feudalism and the various changes characteristic of a ruling bourgeoisie (at least it is in Japan). In contrast, Enlightenment as "progress" is the thought of the overthrow of capitalism and the various changes characteristic of emerging forces. In terms of the meaning of the words themselves, it is not the case that Civilization and Enlightenment, or progress, cannot be used for the intellectual movement of 1868 or the intellectual movements of postwar Japan, but for both, the necessity of the contemporary intellectual and historical transformations, and especially for a proper awareness of them, a decidedly historical concept of progress is necessary.

Like all slogans, however, "progress" as a slogan contains myriad uses, but that does not mean it is emptied of all content. Though perhaps at first a slogan may not straightforwardly impose a clear consciousness of the contours and contents of the concept at its base, its freshness alone is enough to make it accepted by people. But as time passes and it is used for absolutely everything, a slogan's original truthfulness is lost. This is the case today with the earlier example of "culture." "Cultural life" and "cultural housing" may be fine, but when it comes to "cultural underwear" and "culture, culture, culture" the word has lost all meaning. Today the concept of "progress" has not been caricatured to that extent, but while the social existence of "progress" is not locked down, there will likely be many who constantly intone "progress" and describe themselves as "progressive." So worldly minds will have to start reflecting on just what "progress" means. Also, in parallel with this constant preaching of "progress," I feel that recent movements in Japan are not, in fact, progressive, but are indeed reactionary—this is just a feeling and not yet true acknowledgment—so today is precisely the time to embark on an interrogation of the concept of progress.

Furthermore, slogans are extremely dangerous. For example, "national unity" [*kyokoku itchi*] is a slogan used by both friend and foe alike. A competition to determine just which "national unity" is the true one has begun. Within such a structure, fascists themselves have begun describing themselves as progressive. A Japan destined to develop the Asian continent in accord with its enterprising national essence would thus likely be called progressive, as would cutting out the bourgeoisie (including landlords) and partisan politicians who injure the beauty of the capitalist system. In this sense, Marxism would clearly not be progressive, and worse, clearly must be reactionary. Such a civilizational perspective in the villages and cities, which holds that both the age of Marxism and liberalism is over, necessarily terminates in this sort of understanding. If it is a simple battle cry, then such a slogan is perfect for friend and foe alike. Progress as an empty signifier is becoming a concept that anybody may use. We are currently facing this danger.

2

Indeed, the concept of progress is not without its own problems as a philosophy of history. As a philosophy of history, progress is assumed to be in the service of some purpose or goal, and it is normally thought of as necessarily moving closer and closer to that goal; but to see progress this way means only that the concept is teleologically posited. Further, if the telos of history is for some reason theoretically elusive or impossible to achieve, then this concept of progress can never become scientific.

Seeing history as the march of progress is an unscientific historical consciousness; it is a prescientific school of history that forces theological assumptions (the actualization of God's plan for the world) or ethical valuations (such as the perfection of the individual or the attainment of the good) into the movement of history. Indeed, in this sense, the concept of progress is ultimately ethical (and thus outside the field of theory); Hegelians' progress (the progress of consciousness) can be thought of as primarily moral, and placing such an ethical value into the historical record clearly and completely loses any objective consciousness. In contrast, for Marxist theory (in this case historical materialism), history is not explained ethically, indeed ethics must be explained historically. There is nothing as scandalous as a prescientific, ethical concept of progress.

It is often mistakenly said by lazy critics of Marxism that Marxist critique cannot theoretically derive personal freedom or ideals—ethics—from its materialism. Yet what do utopians or idealists have that could explain the actual origins of freedom or ideals or ethical value? They merely interpret some of the facts with rarefied conceptual methods using words that match their own personal tastes, merely positing the existence of their assumptions and never once offering proof or explanation for them. I know of no proof or explanation in the philosophy of history beyond the (admittedly first rate) recognition of these sorts of ethical objects. Therefore, it is absolutely disingenuous and designed to fool the layperson that only materialism has the responsibility to prove and justify its ideals. But materialism excels in explaining how particular ethical value relations emerge in a causal fashion from the sociohistorical structures of existence. Like idealism, materialism merely needs the honesty not to make empty promises—such as promising a proof (?) for how freedom is possible. Now, in the manner of such a critic of Marxism, to the extent that it is an ethical valuation, the concept of progress can never be Marxist. For if by chance such a thing existed within Marxism, however incomplete, it would be a Marxism that permitted idealism [*risōshugi*], and thus materialism's worldview would lack any unity—which is another way of saying that for this sort of Marxist critic today, idealism alone may speak of progress. This sort of idealism calls itself either liberalism (Kawai Eijirō) or Japanism (Kanokogi Kazunobu). From their perspectives both liberalism and Japanism, respectively, are "progressive."

To avoid these idealistic difficulties in the concept of progress, today philosophers of history push the concept of "development" (expansion, growth, emergence, evolution). According to Dilthey and others, history has development but does not speak of progress. Here one might think the above difficulties have been avoided. But, in fact, they have merely added another layer of difficulties. This is because the concept of development, just like a spooled thread that is gradually being unspooled, is like progress in that it had its goal right from the start—with development, too, the endpoint is there from the beginning. There can be no "development" of the situation unless one has already started toward the goal. If progress must not be teleological, we should not forget that the organicist concept of development is already teleological. The only difference is whether the telos is internal or external. Even if history is said to be immanent, if it is not teleological, then even an internal telos is external to history.

It is the concept of progress (and thus also development) in Marxism that saves the concepts of progress and development in bourgeois philosophical common sense. Of course, although this word "progress," which is used so casually today, is a mash up of a fragment of the above bourgeois philosophical common sense and a piece of this new Marxist concept, only the latter element of this everyday word is scientific.

Fundamentally, the concepts of progress and development in bourgeois philosophies of history are essentially metaphors. But even so, Marxism is more skillful with this metaphor *as a metaphor*. To wit, progress is that which rolls the wheels of history forward, that is in the direction it had been heading (but by no means in a straight line), and reaction is that which seeks to roll the wheels backward. This is a metaphor familiar to everyone, but let's briefly explain the scientific flavor of this metaphor.

For the concept of progress in bourgeois philosophical common sense, the current situation must be progressing toward a predetermined purpose or goal. Like the pull of two magnets or the way the earth's gravity pulls things toward it, walking toward a goal is an expression that posits some kind of "action at a distance." Although the possibility of action at a distance has been sufficiently and rationally explained for physical objects (field theory), in historical and social theory, action at a distance is nothing more than the ignorance of a historical causal necessity operating in the gap between the current situation and the circumstances of the future goal or end state. In other words, here action at a distance is nothing more than filling in the gaps with idealism. In contrast, in the case of the turning of the wheel of history, one should not consider the gravitational pull of some goal, but only the push and pressures (the masses and the objective circumstances) acting on the wheel while it is touching the ground and in its current track at any given historical moment. A wheel is from the very start turning, and in turning successive parts of the wheel come in contact with the earth. Ideals and goals are not givens, but rather, like the successive parts of the wheel coming into contact with the earth, their possibility and integration into history is only promised through the development of the actual circumstances. The trajectory of history is so drawn: wheels rolling on the ground. In contrast, free-falling objects fly through a void. This metaphor, then, is a good way to compare the materialist and idealist methods of the recognition of history.

This wheel of history theory is also good for the theory of development. In the theory of the spooled thread, the spindle is eternally present until the completion of the development. It is, and forever remains, an absolute origin. In other words, no matter how much history develops, it never escapes the structure of this spool. This sense of development is a total return to the origin, and the secret of this theory lies in the myth of Ariadne's thread. Theseus from the very start intended to return to the origin using the "development" of the thread he received from Ariadne. If we consider the labyrinth of Japan in the state of emergency, "development" would become a "restorationism," and a "development" of the Chinese mainland would be a return to the founding of the Japanese state [肇国]. In contrast, unlike a spooled thread, in their turning, the wheels of history actually do move forward. But after they have passed does nothing remain? The rut remains; history remains. This is not a restorationist "history." It is a progressive and developmental history. It might be said, however, that it is theoretically problematic for progress and development, and with such a broad understanding of change there is nothing that remains constant within them. But it is best to think of the wheel itself as that constant. In fact, is not reality something like this wheel?

If we look at Marxist metaphors of progress (or development)—here see Lenin's "spiral theory"[2]—we would see that Marxists have excellent literary symbols. But, of course, in this case, metaphors are not merely metaphors but metaphors for the easy acceptance of the scientific determinations of this concept. From here it is easy to guess in what sense goals and ideals are established for the Marxist sense of progress and development. Which is, liberated from goals qua "goals" (teleology) or ideals qua "ideals" (idealism, utopianism), progress and development, and goals and ideals, like the wheel of history touching the ground, can be scientifically, materialistically, and actually clarified.

But we can probably say that the vast majority of bourgeois "philosophy" (?) has mostly worked things out, at least this far. Indeed, the Marxist theory of progress is not something from a fantastic other world, yet what bourgeois philosophy could so clearly and precisely explain this understanding of progress? Even the most progressive and developed of the bourgeois philosophies, Nishida philosophy—to the extent that it depends on replacing the goal of being, and the thought of being, the idea of being (à la Hegel) with the goal of nothingness, the thought of nothingness, and the idea of nothingness—cannot explain the actuality of the relations of progress and history. What is actually needed here is not the progressive development of nothingness, but the *actual* progressive development of being. I fear that there will be, as it were, no actual distinction between a progressive nothingness and a reactionary one (a sort of reactionary liberalism?).

3

But even if the turning wheel of history is called progress, such a formal prescription would clearly leave no choice other than metaphysical rules in the case of practical problems. The problem is, just what are the wheels? As the wheels on the vehicle of history is the problem, it matters a great deal whether this car is a bourgeois automobile, a proletarian wagon, or a freight car. That is what all this means.

Today, in a simple sense that has become mostly commonsensical, the concept of progress is generally meant to be that which accompanies the interests of the proletariat. The proletariat has its own international political party and advancing together, within this party, is considered to be progressive. To the extent that they are on this course, even fellow travelers are considered progressive. Of course, this is based on the fundamental theory, widely asserted today, that the proletariat class has been given the singular responsibility for the progressive development of history.

This is fine as far as it goes, but on the other hand, for this concept of progress to be sufficiently accepted as common sense, it must also mean that each individual member of the public must feel that something about him or herself has increased, that there is something "extra" or something "more" [*purasu no mono*]. We must pay special attention, for this requirement must also be satisfied. For a wider adoption of the proletarian concept of progress to become an everyday term adopted by those groups not strictly part of the proletariat (farmers, the middle class, others), it is necessary in the end that they, too, feel some kind of personal "extra." As a common-sense concept, whatever else it may be, "progressivism" is a particular commentary on values and so reduces to an ethical concept—it is an actual psychology. From here various splits and agitations emerge within this concept of progress, so that that public common sense must once again ask, "Just what is progress?"

Here we first encounter the concept of the masses. The relationship between the masses and the proletariat should not be wedded to some mechanistic relation such as: "the proletariat itself is the masses" or "the general public is not quite yet the masses," because the proletariat and the masses must be truly unified in a systematic way. But ordinary mass common sense generally lacks such systematic understanding, and so the masses are simply thought of as the average of some set of the majority. Thus the question naturally arises whether the above proletarian progressiveness is the progressiveness of the masses, as masses who exist here in our everyday world. Even if this question is ultimately unreasonable, the raw fact that this question is asked needs to be taken into account.

MEANING OF "PROGRESSIVE" AND "REACTIONARY"

Recall here that one of the charms of bourgeois sociology is that it generally pays extreme attention to common sense points of view. That is, for bourgeois sociology, society is characterized by common sense—it is extremely phenomenological and characterized by the various matters most close to hand. This is the malignant strength of bourgeois sociology. It is well known in Japan and elsewhere today that sociology is not theoretically an enemy of social science, but surprisingly, within economics, political science, law, and even in social conventional wisdom, there is this persistent and ingrained belief that it is. Indeed, the concept of the masses as social common sense clearly reduces to this sociological perspective, and so this sociological common sense, too, is the concept of the masses. In fact, it is the concept of the masses themselves; it is the masses becoming self-conscious. So, the question is whether proletarian progressiveness results in a mass progressiveness for these masses, in other words, whether the interests and welfare of the masses are *actually* increased and improved in union with the proletarian version of progress.[3] This is why the common sense of the masses has become a question.

Now progressiveness can be thought of generally as the prosperous or improved [*purasu*] relations of these so-called masses or this "society" or this public. For these masses, any characteristics thought of as good will eventually be considered "progressive." Such masses think: since Japan's advance into Manchuria things have got a bit better; if there's nothing to eat at home, why not go to Manchuria, in Manchuria there is work (?). The vast munitions industry prospers with a rise in military tension, and then, at least marginally, jobs and wages will increase, and even the farming villages might be industrialized, and so forth. All this seems to be the acknowledged social awareness based on the so-called common sense of the masses—of course, a huge part of this common sense is constructed by the bourgeoisie, various military men, journalists, social studies teachers, and the like. This means that, put simply, the force that has brought about the above situation is Japanese fascism, and here Japanese fascism can appear progressive, can appear to resolve Japan's difficulties, can appear to create hope for the near future, and develop Japan along these lines.

Unsurprisingly, those who use and encourage this vulgar common sense of the masses are the Japanese ruling classes. According to the common sense of sociology, the distinctions of social classes are no different than the distinctions between a single school class being split into two groups, group A and group B. Any class conflict is purely accidental and not the essence of civil society. Therefore, sociologically, society is a sum total of—not a conflict between—group A and group B; The masses are the average sum total of rulers and ruled. As the masses means the sum of the rulers and the ruled, the sociological understanding of the "masses" organizes the rulers and the ruled as well, but at the same time, the concept itself determines which of them will rule.[4] It is in this way that progressiveness and class conflict become completely unrelated. Progress is national progress (or humanity's progress).

Thus there is no conflict between the ruler and ruled, and the ruler does nothing but rule. What appears on the surface of the phenomenon is of course only the ruler. Now recalling that progress needs some sort of opposing force against which to measure itself, when the masses look for things to oppose in this society, they only see those things given to them by their ruling brethren. The fall of the established parties, the rise of the new bureaucrats, the decline of parliamentary politics, the impasse of liberalism, the denunciation of the senior statesmen, attacks on a government based on [Minobe Tatsukichi's] organ theory, the Control Faction's actions against bourgeois-ification, all this will come to be seen as one big opposition. And thus, all the various forms of fascist movements seen here will overcome the opposition party in the necessary conflict, and thus all will be "progressive." For example—because thanks to the universal manhood suffrage elections done under the auspices of the Japanism of the military and new bureaucrats and the ideology of national unity—a proletarian party was for the first time able to advance, which led not a few proletarian representatives to say that Japanism has a progressive essence, and we should therefore even support a progressive Japanism. The concept of progress based on this pseudoconflict and the previous concept of progress based on national unity have the same essence.

While both tactics may be part of a unified front, inserting oneself into the masses of right-wing labor groups to organize them along progressive lines, and merely partnering with and supporting those right-wing groups, are absolutely two different things. The difference matches the difference between a proletarian organization of the masses and the sociological meaning of the masses. But for the social theorist and social activist, who at first tactically use but then come to eventually have complete faith in the sociological common sense, such differences will come to be seen as nothing but obstacles.

4

The proletarian concept of progressiveness bears some blame for the widespread belief in this rather strange concept of progress. Namely, the good meaning in the common-sense concept of progress was that it thought of progress as linked to the class subjectivity of the proletariat. But to use only that class subjectivity to determine if something is progressive or reactionary, means that it will likely be mixed together with the average social subjectivity called "the masses." And so, at those points where the public common sense is not well organized, that confusion will make its way into the "progressiveness" itself. The determination of such progressiveness naturally must go one step further than this subjective determination to none other than the development of productivity.

It is thus a well-known rule that a form encouraging the development of productivity in society, and especially a form that destroys the obstacles to increased productivity, is progressive, and that which goes against productivity is reactionary. As this understanding that "productivity = progress" is a mechanical rule of economic progress, unlike political or cultural determinations, there are few places for moral common sense to make an appeal. Common sense does little to bring these issues to the fore, and in fact the possessors of this understanding of common sense of progress are true believers.

That said, even this progress is probably politically overdetermined. Even if it encourages forms that develop productive forces, and even if it removes all fetters to productivity, the results and goals of such political action, in truth, are simply the development of the productive forces of society itself. In this line of thinking, productive forces naturally and spontaneously, and even consciously, develop with some sense of goal, so the promotion of the development of these forces, or the resulting behavior or phenomenon, are by definition "progressive."[5]

What catches our attention here is that this sense of progress has at root the prescription of development running through it, but this development is not our above qualitative example of an unspooling a thread; rather it is based on some sort of quantitative increase. So now even all those things possessing qualitative aspects, political, cultural, or ethical progress are all reducible to a corresponding quantitative determination of increased productivity and accumulation. But because an increase in productive forces is nothing but an increase in productivity, here we have a quantitative increase that is directly converted into a qualitative one. It is important to trace the path by which cultural and literary concepts become quantitative determinations (of course first being converted into qualitative ones), for this is the first step toward a scientific concept of progress.

But a mere quantitative determination of the productive forces alone is not a scientific determination of progress. It only becomes scientific as the basic determination, as a precondition for the sufficient self-awareness of the proletarian class's political, cultural, moral, (and literary) concept of progress.

Given this conception of progress, however, it is clear that if we press the issue, we see that such a simple concept contains within it several articulations. That is to say, even if some determination is progressive from a purely productive forces relation, there are countless examples of such determinations being textbook reactionary from a class or political perspective (for example, Japan's imposition of capitalism in Manchuria and China). There are also not a few examples of something seen as progressive from a class or political perspective being a reactionary determination of culture and morals (for example, the formalistic politicism of cultural movements). Take especially the case of something like liberalism. Even though it may have an antifascist political understanding similar to the proletariat, an attempt to establish a liberal party will prove to have a directly reactionary significance as it will actually thwart the development of a proletarian party. In contrast, in its cultural, moral forms (I would call this cultural liberalism), much (not all), of this same (?) liberalism, would consider it sufficiently progressive to stop at cultural and moral interests, never becoming a concrete politics. These facts (facts with actual examples) may only be explained because the concept of progress is not an unchanging single thing, but has multiple, flexible articulations.

If we think about what we have just seen, progress is not unconditionally and absolutely progress, but itself may have living within it the possibility of turning reactionary, which was all based in reality. But if we try to reverse the procedure it becomes a question of whether a so-called reactionary something or other includes a potential moment of progressiveness. But that question is merely Scholasticist speculation. Reaction can only be a spur for true progress; it cannot itself be progressive. History is progress itself. All reaction is nothing but Mephistopheles who desires only evil, and it is too much to expect good from it. The difficulty is that for Mephistopheles and all reaction, the problem is solved not through more reaction but only through actual progress. The very concept of progress itself always demands such optimism. I have to leave to another occasion a discussion of the form of reaction that is not a question of progressive or reactionary (there is no reactionary ideology that does not clothe itself in progressivism), but a form of reaction that claims the concept of progress itself is dubious.[6]

5

So far we have focused on what progress itself is, socially. But now it remains to pose the question in reverse: What is contemporary society's progressiveness? It is said that the current period in Japan is the waning of Marxism and the rise of fascism, and in that sense, Japanese society is in a reactionary period. In a certain sense, that is absolutely correct. Even if it is the case that the current reactionary period has not exterminated progress but only waylaid it, it is impossible to deny that the total characteristics of the current period are reactionary.

But what does it actually mean to say that Marxism has waned? While the original meaning would be that Marxist political parties, labor unions, and their associated cultural and political organizational have been destroyed, in addition to this, or rather more intimately than this, from the perspective of the public's actual feelings, generally, the popularity of Marxist trends has withered. Leftist "thought criminals" no longer appear as heroes on the pages of bourgeois newspapers and have begun being treated as thieves and gangsters (today's heroes are right-wing groups and Japanist gangs[7]). This is because newspapers reflect the day-to-day common sense of society as well as instruct the public in the current common sense, and thanks to this dual role, they have reduced the number of Marxist sympathizers, and even reduced the number of casual observers. Marxism has entered a period of reflection, and this is the meaning of the so-called reactionary period.

This reflection did not take the form of "Is Marxism mistaken?" (of course there were many of the converts to fascism, the *tenkōsha*, who did just this; this issue is outside of Marxism). The reflection was on how to refine Marxist theory through basic education and give it more practical flexibility. The moment of political progress had ebbed, but based on this regression, it is an important point that it strengthened progressiveness as a cultural and moral task.

Indeed, precisely today, Marxist theory is daily becoming common sense, meaning it is becoming a morality and a temperament, and that process is happening even in this reactionary period. In that sense, this is a period where for the first time one could say Marxism is becoming "thought." Now is the time for Marxism and materialism to use this opportunity to infiltrate the morals and attitudes, and eventually the customs, of the masses. The current situation is in fact indispensable to make "progress" an active, lived thought. This is the invisible force for the future. And therefore, today is precisely the moment when Marxist theory should be rigorously studied and developed *as theory*. And indeed, as the reader likely is aware, Japan has thrown itself into the theoretical issues and troubles just as Russia did in the reactionary period after 1905. Now is the age of Marxist literature and philosophy. Of course, no period is exclusively reactionary. Historical progress does not "just happen."

I cannot here write on labor unions and political movements. There is one necessary conclusion to draw on the task of the intelligentsia. The progressiveness of today's cultural and moral forms is nothing less than the progressiveness of the intelligentsia. Progressive activities are waiting on the activities of "intelligence" to a large degree. We have already seen this, but here is the unmistakable general point on the role of the intelligentsia in today's reactionary age. We should not discuss the age of reaction or retreat in vain. It is not only meaningless to observe the turmoil, bewilderment, and despair of the intellectuals; it is also a mistake. Those intellectuals who in this age despair or prevaricate are those who have no social awareness of the particular function of their own intelligence. Which is to say that even if they belong to groups of salarymen or students, they categorically do not belong to the intelligentsia. As long as they hold on to this "intelligence" I do not believe a concept of "progressive intelligentsia" may ever be built. A reactionary age, for better or worse, is an age when the particular progressiveness of intellectuals must be, and can be, mobilized.

Chapter Twenty-two

A RECONSIDERATION OF THE MASSES

It is said that film is a mass art, that samurai and gambler stories are mass literature. But if you look closely, here you can see that there are deep-seated stipulations on the meaning of the modifier "mass" that are not obvious at first glance. Looking closely, we would be forced to notice that there is something here in the concept of the masses—such as simply matching up with the tastes of the majority or appealing to their interests—something that cannot be completely explained by the simple principle of the majority. Actually, the majority of the public is not simply only the majority qua a large number of people. The actual social facts show also that economically, they are, both relatively and absolutely, poor proletarians, and politically they are the powerless—they are the ruled, the governed. And it is no coincidence that in present society, the majority are proletarian and the ruled, but rather, they are, as it were, proletarian and ruled because they are the majority, and they are the majority because they are proletarian and ruled. So here, on the question of the masses, a two-fold, or rather a two-level, concept emerges. On one level, there is the conception of the masses as simply the majority of society, and on the other, there is the conception of the masses as economically proletarian and politically governed. We can distinguish the two levels as: the former is a sociological (definitely not a social-scientific) concept, and the latter is a social-scientific concept.

In general, the mass quality of film and mass literature is of the sociological conception. In contrast, the mass nature of things like proletarian literature or the interests of the masses indicates this social science concept. But we must not forget that this basic distinction between the two concepts of the masses is grounded in various nuances of the concept of the masses. First, there is the commonsensical way of thinking of the masses as the "ignorant masses" [*gushū*]—a "mob" [*mobbu*]. But the great mass within did not come to be imagined as this "mob" as a concrete thing from the very start; in fact, this mob was naturally based in a particular view of human behavior. It began with the particular phenomenon of the undisciplined, unruly, unordered crowd. The word "mob" expresses the fact that the crowd has psychologies and behaviors within it like that of primitive humans: unthinking with an inherent herd-like nature [和雷同性]. From there it was assumed that the great masses of society, should they be assembled into a crowd, would have this mob quality. And so this conception of human behavior induces an assumption of the masses as the ignorant masses. Thus "the ignorant masses" is representative of sociology's conception of the masses.

As just stated, the defining characteristic of the crowd-like masses is ultimately said to be that they are unorganized. Yet clearly this disorganization does not mean that each individual in the crowd acts independently of the others. So, in fact, it is rather their herd-like psychological nature to follow blindly that is the most important characteristic. Thus in other words, "unorganized" here means that each individual has no independence from the others, that is they have no positive individuality, but only a negative individuality. This "unorganized" is the polar opposite of the principle of both a self-centered free individual and the absolute libertarianism of anarchism—a so-called liberalism that seeks maximum freedom. Accordingly, this concept of the ignorant masses is opposed by the concept of a sagely, aristocratic elitism [*kizokushugi*]. There are various forms of [aristocratic] elitism, from oligarchic political elitism to those that come from class objectives and even others that come from elite, aristocratic tastes—the most important of which is the lauding of those with excellent skill and will power: a spiritual elitism. Thus all aristocratic elitisms seek a rational basis in this spiritual elitism.

This aristocratic elitism often appears in numerous economic, political, social, literary, and ethical guises without its explicitly aristocratic garb, but rather as an aristocratic appraisal of the "hoi polloi" [*senmin*]. In the past this was seen in ethics like that of the Stoics, and later in Schopenhauer and Nietzsche's philosophy, the Roman-ha writers, and every sort of egoism and egotism. There are countless cases of literary heroes based on the model of the aristocrat: see Turgenev's Bazarov[1] or Stendahl's Julien Sorel[2] for basically modern examples of this type. But the ultimate source of all these literary, ethical, or spiritual aristocratic elitisms, that is this particular appraisal of the masses as the hoi polloi or the ignorant masses—and eventually all the other economic, political, and cultural conception of the ignorant masses—have their origins in "spirit." For example this weak, limp [ニラ的] form of a so-called brain trust is not in fact merely a brain trust of skills, as other examples would include financier economic elites [*kizoku*], elder statesmen political elites, and socially, imperial subjects holding court ranks. And there also exists the cultural elite: the managing directors of national education. All confront the ignorant masses and the hoi polloi as spiritual elites.

The concept of the chosen people is absolutely not exclusive to folk religion but belongs to nearly every type of faith in the motherland. Whenever love of the motherland becomes patriotic culture (such as the old worldview of China that saw barbarians to the east, west, north, and south, or in the very concepts of "foreign thought" or "foreign civilization"), a chosen elite always appears in times when the motherland has a "mission"—such as, say, to become the leader of world culture or East Asia. But let's leave that aside right now. What is most important here are the concepts of the [chosen] elites (Elite) [選良] and the leader (Duce).[3] "Elites" and "Duce" mean spiritual aristocrats[4] on the one hand, and at the same time, cultural, social, political, and economic aristocrats on the other. Broadly speaking, its political expression is the ultimate principle of fascist political philosophy: the principle (!) of Mussolini the "party leader" or Hitler "the Führer." In general, fascist philosophy likes to turn proper nouns into principles, see Japan-ism. ("Americanism" is more of a nickname given by others.) Further, in this version of fascism, (fascism in all its forms is different), as the ultimate aristocrat, to the extent that the Duce or Führer possesses a specific charismatic and active personality, it does not fully reach complete mysticism or sacredness, and so its authority, too, has not yet reached complete omnipotence or omniscience. (To the extent that the Russian tsar or the pope had a [particular] positive, assertive individual will, they were neither omnipotent nor omniscient.)

The leader is of course the leader of the masses. For the masses are only disciplined and organized by means of this fascist, ultimate sovereign. Thus there is the potential for this leader, who gives order and organization to the masses, to be taken as the masses themselves. In fact, it is only because this potential misrecognition exists that the leader may organize the masses in the first place. Therefore, the medieval masses did not have this sense of organization. Having this sort of grounding in the masses—or seeming to appear as the very organization of the masses—is the unique character of fascism and what distinguishes it from merely powerful authoritarian politics. But there is always a fantasy at work here. The concept of the leader was from the beginning constructed in opposition to the concept of the unorganized masses. These fascist masses do have their own organization within them, yet they are from start to finish considered as the ignorant masses. Which is to say that the masses do not have any organization (because if the masses had their own organization, they would not be the unorganized, ignorant masses). So however much the masses spontaneously engage in organized activity, if that spontaneity itself is due to some external command, then that spontaneity cannot be from within the masses.

Thus, the fascist concept of the masses, that is, the masses in opposition to the "Duce" and the "elites," is today the most active, actual form of the sociological concept of the masses. In fact, what in Germany today is called "the masses" is just whatever 98 percent of the people do.

The key feature of the fascist concept of the masses is that those masses do not recognize their own organizational ability, and in that sense, also then do not recognize their own internal rationality. Blood, belief, intent, different peoples, all of humanity must be found within the masses. Recognition of some sort of rationality in the masses would have to be found in the "Understanding"[5] [*gosei*] of the mass of humanity. Early modern English humanism began from a focus on this human understanding, which later became the philosophical principle of modern liberalism and democracy. Liberty and equality of the French *grand bourgeoisie* is also derived from understanding qua Reason (*rēzon* [*raison*]). It was by means of an assumed, fundamental principle of this understanding that each individual member of the masses could freely calculate, express opinions, and debate, thereby constructing public opinion. In this conception, the masses casts off its unorganized nature and acquires a sort of rationality and organizational capacity.

That said, even in this version, as always, this concept of the masses is supported by the principle of the majority. Through the sense of "one man, one vote," the masses are conceived of as the sum of these votes. Thus, as before, the masses are nothing more than a weakly organized simple majority with only a mechanical rationality. The qualitative results of each instance of limited suffrage (as opposed to universal suffrage) are in fact the result of using the aliquot parts of this mechanistic character. The flaws of the fixed number of parliamentary seats for relatively small electoral precincts, the necessity of proportional representation, and the disconnect between votes received and electoral winners are built on this contradiction. All these instances are the actual form of appearance of the fundamental contradiction found in a (mechanistic) organization of the masses in a capital-dominated society. Thus, this democratic concept of the masses is ultimately the same as the fascist concept in that, to the end, it is based on the principle of large numbers, the majority, and does not escape the sociological conception.

We must not overlook that the democratic concept of the masses must be based on the enlightened nature of each individual's understanding, but as a practical problem, it is not the case that the majority would be necessarily well enlightened, so as before, the qualitative aspect of the masses remains the ignorant masses or mob. Fascism leans into the dregs of the ignorant masses and the mob hitherto dominated by democracy and liberalism, while at the same time mobilizing these same concepts of the masses. In contrast, democracy and liberalism have faith in the gradual reduction of ignorance and the mob aspects of the masses. This is the concept of progress as a liberal term (it means other things in other cases). Nonetheless, everyone must acknowledge the basic truth of this unorganized, ignorant remnant within the fascist and liberal theories of the masses.

We must say that the ignorant manner of this conception of the democratic masses appears in its nature to have a need to be ruled by demagogy [被デマゴギー性]; appears in the inadequacy of enlightened results of each individual of the masses, that is, the immaturity of their understanding; and appears from their holding interests and concerns different from their everyday interests. Their potential for blind action lies in the fact that their concepts are inadequately *actual* and divorced from a material base; "demagogy" is the political leaders' amplification and mobilization of this gap. It is necessary to stress that this demagogic nature is essential for grasping the liberal democratic concept of the masses. But at times, and depending on the person, either sooner or later the actual everyday interests of the masses eventually must be conceptually corrected. This is not, as the liberals occasionally think, due to the progress of the masses' understanding. Quite the opposite, it is that as a result of development of the actual relations, the relation between that development and the interests of the masses has been corrected. The result may frequently be the so-called progress of the masses, but through this conceptual correction demagogy gradually loses its power. Demagogy is already unsuccessful for rulers of the masses. This is because ~~rulers~~ must take responsibility for consciously promulgating demagogy. This is of course understandable, but it is here where demogogy comes to acquire new functions. That is to say, rulers can invert the masses' criticism of demogogy and call that criticism itself demogogic. Thus, cracking down on false rumors becomes the grand policy of the ~~ruling class~~. Further, the masses being seen as unmoved by the ruling class's demagogy can invert to be seen and denounced as the promulgation of demagogy by the masses' themselves.

But these masses that are assumed to be spreading false rumors can no longer be the same ignorant masses of blind action as characterized by their need to be ruled by demagogy. This is because the so-called false rumors were the masses' criticism of the promulgation of demagogy by the ~~ruling class~~. Thus, this criticism was not a false rumor; the real false rumor is the ~~ruling class's~~ new denunciation of the masses criticism as the demagogy of the masses. So, this fact, notwithstanding the abstract remnants of its need to be demagogically ruled is the reason, for the most part, that it is assumed the masses have reasonable [*goseiteki*] political views that lie on the side of democracy and liberalism. At minimum, it means that the masses are able to talk of things close to the truth.

The case of the ~~1939~~ [*sic?*] general election appears to support this view. Despite the cries of a state of emergency, if we leave aside the absolute numbers, proletarian representatives who opposed this socially current ideology of a state of emergency made surprising progress. In contrast, with twelve exceptions, Japanist candidates, all lost. It is thought that this tells the tale of a democratic understanding of the masses. It can be thought that the explanatory power of reason [*gosei*] is growing in the masses. Some say this is the result of political education. Others say it is thanks to new bureaucratic regulation of the elections. Surely this is the case.

A RECONSIDERATION OF THE MASSES

But on the basis of this phenomenon alone, it remains dangerous to buy into this mechanical concept of the masses. First, these masses cannot immediately intuit whether or not some so-called proletarian party is in union with those new bureaucrat or military-tinted ideologies. We cannot forget that today's proletarian party is primed to be social fascist (one kind of national socialism). If the masses are still unaware of this, by the time it is made clear, they may have semi-permanently lost their window of opportunity as far as democratic representation is concerned. In other words, ultimately, we may have to say that at the decisive moment, the masses are captured by fascist demagogy. Thus, as long as the proletarian party is truly and exclusively a proletarian party (we should not forget that there is a proletarian faction that includes even Japanists), the democratic masses will never give assent to the endless advance of the proletarian faction. These masses simply no longer believe in either the past demagogy of the Seiyūkai and Minseitō parties or the too novel demagogy of Japanist parties. The resulting incomplete political vacuum was accidentally filled by this new "proletarian faction" [*musan-ha*], which at present is not demagogic. Accordingly, if a party's ideology is merely somehow "new proletarian," it is always possible for the substitution and adoption of even fascist demogogy.

The above is merely an example from actual circumstances. But I think it alone should prove how fragile and narrow the mechanical organization of the democratic concept of the masses is as its own self-organization. Such is the meaning of the masses in mere parliamentarism—from purely nominal fascist democracy up to actually felt liberal democracy, and eventually social democracy. We can judge from the historical precedents in Italy, Germany, and elsewhere how this legalist parliamentarism gave us legal fascism, and how social democracy was an absolute and necessary element for the establishment of a fascist regime. The actual significance of the inadequacy of the sociological concept of the masses, the masses as founded on a simple principle of the majority, is here laid bare.

So then, we come to the question of the social scientific concept of the masses. This is not a question of the majority. Here the masses are not the majority because they are proletarians and the ruled. Quite the contrary, they are proletarians and the ruled because they are the majority. This quantitative nature of the majority has a qualitative economic, political, social, and cultural content. This qualitiative content is none other than the masses own capacity to organize themselves. Here, for the first time, positivity and spontaneity runs through the masses in every sense, because in this qualitative social scientific concept, the masses, for the first time, may be said to be full-fledged social individuals [*shakaijin*] who can organize themselves. So, in this sense "the masses" means "mass organization." The masses are not the mere uniform mechanical and quantitative majority as in the sociological sense above, and much less an unorganized, chaotic mob; *the masses are organization itself.* Without self-organization there are no masses.

But that said, merely being already organized alone does not make the masses. If that were the case, the masses would be a large number, a mere part or small part. Far from the masses they would end up being a sect or faction. In fact, this concept of the masses as one part often sneaks past the gates of social science. There are concepts of the masses that say only those with extremely high proletarian consciousness are the masses. But it should go without saying that incompletely organized masses are still the masses. In the present situation in Japan, the majority of the masses are unorganized (not only as labor unions but mentally as well). Today, the organization of the masses has not been completed. One portion has been organized, while another, surely larger portion, has not been. But once an organizational policy is eventually put into place, it must be an organization of the politically dominated proletariat, who are, as a matter of course, the majority of all society. Once again, this organization is first possible as an organization when mediated by the majority of society and at at the same time by the dominated proletariat. It is with such an organization that the masses first become the masses.

But it should be noted that though called the masses, the concept has absolutely not lost its determination as a simple majority, meaning that things such as the the "mass readership of mass literature" or the "mass audience of mass films" do not lie outside these masses and this mere sociological concept of their organization. We should therefore not forget that though it is clearly inappropriate to our last social scientific concept, the fascist organization of the masses, or a "fascistic massification" [*taishūka*] is an actual and grave possibility. Even in countries where it did not spring from a mass base, fascist organization of the masses is the rule. And at the same time, mass parliamentary activities, bourgeois democratic activities, remain one of the indispensable regulating principles of the masses today. It is a simple fact that should not be dismissed that the democratic majority (in the sociological sense) in the Diet is directly related to the social scientific concept of the masses.

Even if the already organized portion of the masses is extremely small, when there is a policy of continuing down that line of organization, this numerically small organization is clearly a living mass organization, and a path that leads toward the masses, a mass nature, runs through it. This structure of the masses allows a small number to achieve a mass nature. This is fundamentally different than the role of the minority (the leadership) in fascism. For example, even though Italian fascism was the majority of the regional groups (this was the original meaning in "fasces"), from the very dawn of fascist political rule it adopted every possible means to absolutely prevent the organization of the dominated proletariat—and the news today makes this clear.

The fact that the masses are the majority and at the same time more than the majority would make it seem as if various rules that contradict majority rule can be constructed, so today the concept of the masses is vague and problematic. At times, times necessary from the perspective of ruling class, the masses will be foolish. Other times, including even occasions when the masses rule themselves, the masses will not escape some banal, vulgar average. Despite all that, when the masses do rule themselves, that is when the masses become themselves, "the masses" becomes a new standard of value. Here I have tried to simply give an analytical and conceptual solution, but the paradox of the masses can only truly and actually be solved historically.

Chapter Twenty-three

LIBERALISM, FASCISM, SOCIALISM

In Japan today, social thought is of three types: liberalism, fascism, and socialism. As simple schools of thought these three may be said to be liberalism, Japanism, and materialism. Of course none of these is merely an intellectual phenomenon. They each also have a social existence and a social expression [*ugoki*]. That is, all three types of thought, with each possessing a more or less defined intellectual system, are also produced from some emergent class or social strata that gives rise to them. Each have a social class or a social stratum that is the bearer of their intellectual systems and their social expression. So, each of these types of social thought must be considered from four main points: the intellectual system, the form of its movement [*ugoki*], its social basis, and its subjectivity (the bearers of the thought and its movements).

1

For convenience let us begin by classifying the various sources that motivate liberalism's system of thought. As a system of thought in the strict sense, and especially in Japan, there are very few cases of systematic liberalism; still, there is no thought that does not have at least the possibility of becoming a system.

LIBERALISM, FASCISM, SOCIALISM

Liberalism is motivated by three theoretical sources. Historically, the oldest theoretical motivation is the economic doctrine of laissez-faire. As is widely known, although liberalism shares a basis of support with the concept of the free individual that also lay behind early modern capitalist society, this is not the only feature liberalism shares with capitalism. In this case, "free individual" was an understanding of human freedom centered around being a capitalist: free industry, free trade, and free investment. So, let's borrow general language to describe this and call it "economic liberalism." This economic liberalism was a general feature of the period of ascendant capitalism, and although it lives on as the fundamental spirit of capitalism, under the original conditions of rule by the semifeudal bureaucracy that gave rise to Japanese society, this economic liberalism was never fully ascendant. But this incompleteness is not of course limited to Japan. With entry into the age of monopoly capitalism, the freedom of individual capitalists, even among themselves, became the freedom of only a small number of large, oligarchic capitalists, or rather, the freedom of the individual capitalist was replaced with the freedom of capital itself. Now, in introducing a controlled economy while preserving that spirit of economic freedom, capitalism has itself become a social limit on actual freedom. As everyone knows, this point has become especially notable in Japan today.

This is neither the destruction of capitalism nor its improvement; it is simply the highlighting of what is the essence of capitalism. Regardless, it is a simple fact that in today's capitalism, economic liberalism no longer operates in its original form. In Japan today, the original freedoms of economic liberalism have become all but completely impotent. As the contradiction between the controlled economy and economic liberalism grows ever more noticeable, economic liberalism appears in movements to protect the commercial rights of shopkeepers, in attacks on unions and large department stores, and the like. (Popularly, liberal economic opposition to the controlled economy is linked even with fascist opposition, and thus few would call it liberalism; but this fascist-friendly type of economic liberalism, is it not, in fact, a desperate, strained sort of "liberalism"?) However, because this movement ultimately cannot fight the objective circumstances, it has no future prospects. Outside the unsystematic sentiments of a small number of petit bourgeois and Ministry of Commerce policies, its possesses no form of thought, no system of thought. As thought, economic liberalism is a thing of the past.

The second source of liberalism is "political liberalism." Originally it was the straightforward political implications of economic liberalism, but the conclusion has developed independent of its premise. It is fine to say that political liberalism is largely "democracy" (bourgeois democracy). Generally speaking, if democracy is the political ideal of the age of bourgeois leadership, in times of capitalist decline or when capitalism meets large opposition, liberalism often means a passive political liberalism, a negative freedom. In Japan today, what is thought of as so-called liberalism is thus clearly not "democracy," in general it is nothing more than this passive political liberalism (today an active, positive liberalism would have to recognize present-day socialism as a necessary stage of its own development). Both the original bourgeois and the current negative forms are political liberalisms, but because political liberalism has this passive and active dual nature, it also means that it is inherently problematic to think of liberalism as something necessarily progressive.

Indeed, one of the most striking features of current political liberalism is that it is guided by its negative, passive side. That is, we should take note of the fact that the majority of today's liberals do not themselves belong to the bourgeois (and land owner) political parties who traditionally practiced a positive, aggressive course of liberalism, but are now instead merely relatively independent pundits. This is the case for liberals such as Baba Tsunego, Kiyosawa Kiyoshi, Hasegawa Nyozekan, and even Ozaki Yukio. Thus, one more feature of this political liberalism is that it hardly appears as a system of thought, but only as a liberal attitude or sentiment. A thinker like Nyozekan has a system; it is not a liberal system, but something else (bourgeois materialism?). Nyozekan has been called a liberal (though probably would not be called that now), but that label "liberal" was always merely a function of some sort of liberal feelings his readers got from him.

Kawai Eijirō is probably the most conspicuous liberal here. He is likely the only systematic liberal in Japan today. Kawai's theoretical motivations spring forth from idealism and ethics, and in that respect belong to the third instance of liberalism below, but because of this idealist and ethical base, Kawai's is the rare political liberalism with a system of thought. He does not make use of the above economic liberalism (what he calls first-period liberalism), but rather advocates for the socialistic control of freedom. Here he says that socialism is third-period liberalism. But this "liberalistic socialism" (?) is linked to absolutely no political activity in Japan. In truth liberalistic socialism is likely close to rightwing social democracy (or part of a social mass party), though this university professor's intellectual system has no actual connection to these rightwing movements or subjectivities. In its social existence, Kawai's system hardly differs from the sentimental liberalism mentioned above, though that sentimental liberalism is more extreme than Kawai's in that in being free of partisan politics—as an "enlightened centrism"—sentimental liberalism appears as a *freedom from* all political activity itself.

Yet the greatest strength of sentimental liberalism is that it represents the common sense of a particular social group. In this sense, it has a certain sort of mass quality to it. It is a merely *sentimental* liberalism because it most faithfully reflects this particular mass-like common sense, that is, it corresponds to the political common sense of the middle class with their capacity for free opinion. (It is no accident that the majority of sentimental liberals come from the ranks of newspaper journalists.) Once, back in the Popular Rights and Liberty Movement of the 1870s, journalists had made up a large portion of those who risked their lives fighting the remnants of feudal rule.

Yet in a wider understanding of political common sense, in today's era of universal manhood suffrage, the corresponding common sense of nearly every owner of average political consciousness appears to center on this purely discursive, free-speech liberalism. Yet ironically, this discursive liberalism has no essential connection to the current system of representative democracy ("constitutionalism"). It absolutely is not a political liberalism. In a most vulgar way, this liberalism is thought of simply as a parliamentary system that confronts dictatorship.

But in parallel with the fact that the Japanese parliamentary system has become a fascist body, *while remaining a representative parliamentary system*, the parliamentary system has become completely independent of political liberalism. It is not simply the case that the government, bureaucracy, and military repress the Diet and the bourgeois parties. The important point rather is that the Diet and the bourgeois parties themselves have, *in the name of a representative system*, in fact, become independent of that political form and have become something other than liberalism. The current result is, as it were, a *constitutional fascism*, a type of fascism that has adopted a parliamentary system. It cannot be permitted to think of fascism's political form as dictatorship alone; A fascism that has not taken the political form of dictatorship exists in Britain, the United States, and France.

In spite of all this, in Japan today, the entirety of this constitutional fascism is thought to be "liberal." There is a huge mistake here. One of the main sources of this belief lies in the mistaken public consciousness of the character of liberalism. And that is not all. People are also misled by constitutional fascism's occasional and partial mimicry of liberalism. That is to say, constitutional fascism is a phenomenon that emerges in opposition to the explicit direct action of militaristic Japanese fascism; ~~this is~~ the "liberalism" that is imagined to be lurking behind the liberal ~~mimicry~~ of the senior statesman bloc, or the government's denunciation of [Minobe's] organ theory [of the emperor], or the finance minister's balanced budget, or the fascist bureaucrats of the "control" faction [tōsei-ha]. This liberalism is a liberalism with no substance, it is incidental, a side-effect, an occasional mere shadow of resistance. Of course, in no way can this be taken to be liberalism. In general, today's liberalism differs from the democracy of the era of early capitalism that was an ideology founded on the petite bourgeoisie, or better, founded more or less on the intellectual capacity of the petite bourgeoisie. Today's so-called democracy on the other hand differs from liberalism in that present "democracy" is an explicit ideology of the landowners and the bourgeoisie. Further, based on the particularity of Japanese capitalism and its ~~fundamental condition~~ of the proletarianization of its small-scale farming, by forging links with middle-class farmers, small business owners, and other interests, it becomes a fascist ideology.

The third theoretical motivation for contemporary liberalism is cultural freedom. Let's call it "cultural liberalism." This liberalism locates the final philosophical basis of freedom in the progressive development of culture, the exaltation of humanity, the perfection of personality, and so on. This is a particular ideology of the cultural intelligentsia who have given it an intellectual system, an ideology that represents their interests, and has become in their hands a movement. From the confessional and self-criticism literature of former leftist mea culpas [tenkō bungaku] to literary trends including "pure literature" and popular literature (such as Kikuchi Kan and Kume Masao)—mass literature is different—such literature is undoubtedly a powerful social movement; just look the number of similar journals and magazines. But this literature itself is also the stronghold of today's cultural liberalism. Alongside this literature there is also various forms of bourgeois idealist philosophy (Nishida philosophy, humanism, and so on). It should be noted that Nietzsche, Kierkegaard, and Heidegger are perceived in Japan not as fascist philosophy but as cultural liberal philosophy.

In Japan cultural liberalism may be cultural, but in absolutely no way can it be said to be liberal. That is to say, even beside the fact that there is currently no relationship between cultural liberalism and political liberalism, "cultural freedom" itself has absolutely no relationship to any political goals at all. On this point there is no unity with the progressive liberal literary movement in France. Cultural liberalism in Japan is remarkably literary. Behaviorism has not escaped these limitations and the Liberal Arts Confederation [Gakugei jiyū dōmei] is still asleep.[1]

While of course it is not a question of the above constitutional fascism, all three liberalisms—sentimental liberalism, systematic liberalism, and this cultural liberalism—all emotionally, intellectually, and culturally oppose or feel a gap between themselves and the only scientific socialism: Marxism. Determining the progressive nature of all three liberalisms is one of the practical problems for socialism today, but from the perspective of progress, at the level of principles, cultural liberalism seems the most promising. That is because to the extent that it is not a political liberalism, cultural liberalism has no necessity for a direct contradiction with a politics of scientific (materialist) socialism. The next most promising would be sentimental liberalism. Sentimental liberalism is a political liberalism, but emotions should not be respected as political principles so there's not a huge problem here. Systematic liberalism is the least promising because it shares nearly the same problem, socialism, with scientific socialism, so it would have a direct contradiction with Marxism. The same is also true of Christian socialism and anarchism. However, systematic liberalism, as far as Marxism is concerned, is not a big problem as it is weaker than both Christian socialism and anarchism as a current social movement. Of course, this critique of liberalism should not be considered a socialist criticism of liberalism in general or of the essence of liberalism.

2

As stated, today's so-called democracy, as something with a so-called liberal constitutional and parliamentary essence, is nothing but (constitutional) fascism. This is a fascism of the bourgeois and landlord political parties, but one whose [social] base is not in the bourgeoisie or the landlord classes themselves. Generally, fascism is the necessary social and political system of monopoly and finance capital. Fascism actually represents the interests of the grand bourgeoisie (and thus also the big landlords), and so in that sense it is based on them. But one of fascism's unique characteristics is that its actual constituency and its imagined, ideal constituency are based in different social strata. So as seen in the recent general election, in this type of political-party fascism, the middle class itself imagines that this fascism represents the interests of the average (average political intelligence, too) of the middle class. Yet to the extent that the middle class does not think of its political and economic interests as totally separate, it does not in fact completely trust the political consequences as in its political interest, and thus a certain passive attitude on general elections takes hold through which the middle class becomes unconscious supporters and even fans of these parties and this party fascism.

As is well known, the Seiyūkai is a more of a landlord party and Minseitō more of a capitalist party, but the difference in those actual constituencies also corresponds to a difference in their idealist constituencies. The electoral base of the former is the middle stratum of the agricultural population (the so-called farm villages [nōson]), and the latter, the middle stratum of the commercial and industrial population (the so-called commercial and industrial workers [shōkōgyōsha]). Thus, while there are some differences in the outward appearance of this fascism there are no real, important differences. For example, one side wants the "clarification of the national essence" (perhaps borrowed from other fascists) and an expansionary fiscal policy (which is a fox that has borrowed the power of a tiger); the other side wants the "doctrine of the three Alls": national security [kokubō], economy, and industry. These are the only differences. (This was the situation in February 1936.)[2]

The second fascist strata are the bureaucrats or the "new" bureaucrats. The new bureaucrats have been especially noisy since the Okada administration,[3] but this is just a doubling down of the nature of the Japanese bureaucracy in an emergency, so these new bureaucrats are still bureaucrats in essence and any principled distinction between bureaucrat and new bureaucrat is meaningless. The Japanese bureaucracy (and later military bureaucracy) developed along a path of gradual unification with feudal (and semifeudal) authority and the bourgeoisie. Today's so-called "new bureaucrats" are those semifeudal elements who have retaken the leadership against the pure bourgeoisie.[4] The new bureaucracy is nothing more than the policies of bureaucratic fascism. Formally, party fascism wears the mask of a fascism from below, but as the party itself is of the ruling upper class of society it should in fact be called a fascism from above. In contrast, bureaucratic fascism absolutely must be called fascism from above. Of course, bureaucratic fascism is also a form of constitutional fascism. It is distinguished from and can oppose party fascism, for where party fascism has rendered the constitutional, parliamentary system merely formal and moribund, bureaucratic fascism plans to cut the fat and streamline it all beneath the Cabinet Legislative Bureau. (The differences emerge between the two fascisms in cases such as cabinet elections, regulating elections, and fascify-ing of the judiciary. Against which we get the impotent cry ". . . but liberalism!").

Party fascism, while purporting to represent the interests of the middle classes (which here literally means the interests of the Japanese Empire), is in fact well aware that it actually represents the interests of the party itself, that is it represents the interests of the landlords and the bourgeoisie. But bureaucrats, while they may be an occupational group, are not considered an interest group because they are public servants, and so as the bearers of bureaucratic fascism they are not perceived as having their own interests. (Actual relations between high ranking bureaucrats and the bourgeoisie are conveniently not part of the equation). Thus, there is in bureaucratic fascism a kind of moral confidence and a pretext of a just cause [*taigi meibun*]. But the moral system that justifies this "just cause" is extremely weak. There is no cohesion at all;[5] it is merely an intoning of the thoughts of various individuals like the agrarian fundamentalism (of Home Minister Gotō) or Matsumoto Manabu's "Japanese-ism"[6] [邦人主義]. The party politicians, though they are the representatives of the landlords and the bourgeoisie, are not eloquent or talented ideologues. In fact, even if you look at their slogans, they are largely borrowed ones (see the decidedly nonaltruistic phrases above, like "shining" or "national unity.")

When all this becomes military fascism, the intellectual principles of the just cause are made abundantly clear. Among junior officer elements in the military, the intellectual and national socialist political system of people like Kita Ikki[7] are prevalent, but such an intellectual system is not necessary for thought centered on a just cause. The entirety of "just cause" thought is crystallized in four characters: be loyal to the sovereign and love the nation [忠君愛国]—in short, a loyal patriotism. But military ideology already has a long record of being condensed in this way. Past instances included "Heartland-ism" [nōsonshugi] (an antiurban ideology), national planned economy, and in the extreme, there was even a Herculean-style "the philosophy of battle." But all of these came from the spirit of national security above all else. Now, as may be seen in the army's shouting down of Finance Minister Takahashi in the budget meeting, national security is more important than all else. The spread of the ideology of national security has reached the point to where it emerges in the economic problems of farming villages or the entire controlled economy, both of which earlier had been the responsibility of the cabinet and traditionally not things the military knew much about.

While the bearers of this ideology of military fascism are various military members (mainly active-duty reserve officers), this ideology is different from their corresponding occupational interests and it does not represent these military members' social stratum's true interests. The ideal, conceptual ground of this ideology is largely occupied by the average population of the villages and cities. Reservists, youth groups, students, and others make up a huge part of this population, but it is clear that this ideology of military fascism does not directly represent their interests. The kinds of movements of this ideology is so well known it is not necessary to recount them here.

The groups that seized the opportunity of emergency military actions were the right-wing, reactionary nationalist fascist groups. Immediately after the May 15 Incident[8] there was a rapid increase in the number of such groups. At first this was viewed as an extension of the original reactionary nationalist groups, and accordingly, it was seen as essentially, and as a matter of political program and group members' self-image, based on feudal authority. Yet we must not forget that an extreme number of these groups had a national socialist form with a political program calling for the overthrow of capitalism—though never actually the overthrow of capital-ism, but only the overthrow of capital-ists. Thus, these groups were excellent fascists (see below for the Japanist form of fascism). It is a shared global nature of fascism that at the beginning the slogan "overthrow capitalism" was in service of creating a force to oppose scientific socialism, only later to gradually obfuscate the meaning of the slogan and eventually arrive at a conclusion completely opposite of the overthrow of capitalism. Now, this fascism, while a particular form within Japanese fascism, is relatively close to the Italian and German forms of fascism. Its social cohesion and private militia activities, and unconstitutional direct action all speak to its character. (Among the ~~junior officers~~, too, there are occasionally clear examples of such activities. For example, an extreme opposition to the parliamentary system or the rejection of the chain of command.) Thus, in a way this is a fascism from below. But speaking more strictly theoretically, fascism can never be truly "from below."

It was the right-wing, reactionary, nationalist groups who developed the ideology of Japanese fascism into a first-rate, brilliant (?) fascist ideology. That said, at first, this ideology took each version in turn and did not have a completely systematic truth in any theoretical sense, much less a unified, structured worldview. It was variously split into spiritualism, agrarianism, Japanese nationalism, Asianism, Orientalism, a Doctrine of the Imperial Way—without yet knowing how to consolidate or unify them all. But as the outward forms of these forces slowly boiled down, in parallel with the disciplinary unification of the various fascist groups, it eventually produced a unified Japanese fascist ideology. That is, in passing through the Doctrine of the Imperial Way, it finally reduced down to an "ideology of the clarification of the Japanese national essence"—[*kokutaimeichōshugi*, 国体明徴主義]. With this ideology of the national essence as a polestar, the unification of the fascist groups and the principles of its thought took shape. Yet in looking back on this now, it is clear that "the clarification of the national essence" are mere words with no systematic thought at all, which makes it the perfect partner for militaristic fascist ideology. (Speaking of this point, we should not overlook the unification of right-wing intellectual groups and the parallel birth of rightwing patriotic labor unions. The movements of the Japan Industrial Workers Club and the Trade Union Confederation [*Sōrengō*] are examples.)

The discrepancy between fascism's actual constituency and its ideal constituency means that fascist ideology is especially idealistic and ideological (it may be better to say especially demagogic). But in another sense, fascist ideology lacks other features of an ideology: *As thought*, it cannot have any system of articulation.

(Finally, as touched on before, it is not that popularly, fascism cannot be said to not be a merely controlled economy, but that this is a rather weak feature of fascism's politics, no matter how directly related it may be economically to finance and monopoly capitalism.)

Now, the above has been the various aspects of today's Japanese fascism. But what is the defining fascistic feature of Japanese fascism? (It should no longer be an issue as to whether or not Japan is fascist.) The defining character of Japanese fascism may be summed up as a fascism where the general conditions of fascism could be built upon the basic conditions of the remnants of feudal forces particular to Japan, or again, *where these feudal forces took the form of fascism*. It is possible to indicate the shared characteristics of this Japanese fascism. Of course, there is no room for an analysis of Japanese fascism in general, but such an analysis is precisely the great practical task for socialism from here on. It should be again stated here that this task is directly related to the previously mentioned interrogation of the "progressivity" of liberalism,[9] which is to say that *there is a real relationship between liberalism and fascism*. And turning our attention to this relationship is today the most important task for Japanese social science. The political task, the question of an anti-fascist common or unified front, in labor unions or cultural movements, may be viewed as being gradually solved socially, which we might conceivably see as a form of progress within our so-called reactionary age.

Today is called an age of reaction. Both Marxism and liberalism have waned and Japan is a fascist world, and more, fascism is said to be the only path forward. But this conventional wisdom is completely superficial and vulgar. Socialism will take this opportunity and use it to cultivate the ground for a deeper, more intimate, and more mass-like socialism. Upon such ground, the political path of socialism may be renewed.

AFTERWORD

A *Japanese Ideology* for Our Time

Back in 2015, when I was considering a full translation of *The Japanese Ideology*, a response I heard more than once was, "Is there really anything new to say about fascism?" More than anything I may have said on those occasions, history itself offered its own terrifying rejoinder a year later with the reemergence of the question of fascism in the US election of 2016. Trumpism fit neatly into other contemporary examples of such resurgence: Britain's Brexit, Hungary's Jobbiks, Greece's Golden Dawn, India's Bharatiya Janata, Russian Putinism, Israel's Likud, Brazil's Bolsonarismo, not to mention the increasing use of archaist references by Japan's ruling LDP, and many others. And then, just one year later, actually existing, violent, fascist riots irrupted here in Charlottesville in August 2017, a preview of the sacking of the US Capitol by would-be putschists in January 2021. Suddenly, it seemed fascism was everywhere on the march—I am writing this afterword not twenty yards from the intersection of Fourth and Water Streets, where Heather Heyer was killed by a fascist rioter. The media immediately filled with moments of angsty, liberal handwringing over images of physical violence. This common liberal condemnation reduces fascism to a mere tactic, evacuating it of any ideological content and thereby forestalling any meaningful understanding or critique of fascism in favor of a sentimental liberalism of empty pieties, lamenting and mourning the absence of a "reasonable," "peaceful," yet embarrassingly exposed and impotent "center."[1]

Despite its violence and immediate threat, it would nonetheless be a mistake to focus exclusively on the spectacular aspect of Charlottesville. It was not only embedded in a larger set of Gramsci's "morbid symptoms" that augur a gathering fascism: "trad" wives, incels, superhero films, endless gun blog discussions on "stopping power," Black Rifle coffee sipped out of "Punisher" mugs, all the way to even the "restorationist" doctrine of legal "originalism" that seeks to drag our present back into Jefferson's eighteenth century. But in denouncing only these explicitly fascist social expressions it must be recognized that Charlottesville also took place against a social backdrop that merely reproduces the faux resistance of Tosaka's "sentimental liberalism," a politically impotent "cultural liberalism" that with the rise of monopoly capitalism and imperialism had abandoned politics and economics and confined itself to aesthetic and cultural realms. Both fascism and liberalism had rejected the concreteness of the historical conjuncture and fled to the spiritual (cultural), and thus were, at minimum, open to the cultural essentialism of the eternal and the archaic. In this cultural consciousnesses, the retreat of liberal thought from the economy and society settles into the angst of a liberal identity politics that only allows a purely personal distaste of the more spectacular forms of fascism while leaving the equally ahistorical spiritualisms and archaisms of "normal" capitalist ideology intact.

In the immediate aftermath of Charlottesville's 2017 Unite the Right riot there were countless teach-ins, think-pieces, and op-eds. On those occasions when the form of "historical" critique of Charlottesville did occur, it was to point out that the Robert E. Lee statue at ground zero of the riot was not put up during, or in the immediate aftermath of, the Civil War, but was erected in the 1920s—making things better or worse, no one would say—and thereby reducing historical criticism to nothing more than assigning each event its "proper place" in a linear timeline. Others looked for analogies, aligning 2017 Charlottesville with 1933 Germany or the like. Differently, but with similar results, analogy and allegory also erased history in the name of a static image of an ahistorical and idealist "synchronic displacement."[2] All of these approaches—linear time, allegory, angst—prevent our ability to understand the contemporary historicity of the event that was Charlottesville as all ignore history's temporal unevenness: what Bloch termed "the contemporaneity of the noncontemporaneous" and Tosaka called the "three-dimensional" nature of historical time. Charlottesville, and the question of fascism today, needs to be placed within Tosaka's three-dimensional everydayness, into a present moment "configured by"[3]—and taking its meaning from—its relationship to the myriad other pasts that make up the whole of historical time. In taking temporal unevenness seriously, by historicizing the present while contemporizing the past, the historical question should have been: "What is the ideological content of rallying around a statue of Robert E. Lee while donning historical fascism's swastikas, tiki torches, Norse runes, and Confederate flags—in Charlottesville, Virginia, in August 2017—after the Civil War, Hitler, Jim Crow, the Civil Rights movement, decades of neoliberalism, the 2008 Crash, the 2016 election, and within the contemporary political and economic conjuncture?"

It is not possible to take up each of these present pasts here, but the two biggest differences between fascism of the 1930s and today would surely be the role of the state and the intervening decades of neoliberalism. These two are linked—in more ways than one. They are linked, of course, in the neoliberals' own self-understanding that the problem of fascism is a problem of the state, the famous "state phobia" of the immediate postwar Ordoliberals and Hayek's *Constitution of Liberty*, in which any state regulation or active, political organization of society is a road to serfdom.[4] (In the *Birth of Biopolitics* Foucault criticizes this state fetishization in favor of seeing Nazism as a form of "nonstate governmentality," and the state as limited by the party.)[5] This focus on fascism as first and foremost an institutional apparatus, only seen in a fully formed fascist *state*, while ignoring nonstate, social forms of "fascization" (*fashōka*) has led many, including at times even Corey Robin,[6] to reject the use of the term today. But as seen throughout *The Japanese Ideology*, and indeed in the whole of Tosaka's work, fascism is "from the beginning"[7] a question of not simply of the state, the party, or institutions, but of ideology and thought, fascism as a "political mechanism . . . that takes advantage of the domestic and international anxieties of the petite bourgeoisie—the middle classes in the broad sense" and "creates the fantasy that it shares the middle classes' own interests, yet all the while . . . extending the rule of finance capital."[8] Importantly, it is less the state, or even the nation, but rather the form of accumulation, that produces fascist thought.

AFTERWORD

Our current moment has seen numerous discussions, examinations, and theorizations of fascism. Beyond those that repeat and celebrate a liberal center opposing "extremism" of both left and right, such as Jason Stanley's *How Fascism Works*, there are important interventions into the question of fascism today, notably Ugo Palheta and Enzo Traverso. Traverso has proposed the term "postfascism" to describe Trump, Le Pen, and others, for he notes that there are "new elements," such as Islamophobia or attacks on immigrants over a more active anticommunism, "that do not belong to the [fascist] tradition."[9] This is undoubtedly true, and, crucially, he does believe that the term "fascism" is both "inappropriate and indispensable." But his analysis can at times suffer from a conception of linear time and the internal development of a more classic intellectual history that seeks genealogies, filiations, inheritances, and textual sources, occasionally leading to some less than convincing justifications.[10] Two excellent recent books—from Alberto Toscano, *Late Fascism*, and Harry D. Harootunian, *Archaism & Actuality*—do take on fascism from the question of the historical present as a site of combined and uneven temporalities employed by Benjamin, Bloch, and Tosaka. The critical task becomes how we contend with the presence of these pasts in our present.

Thus today, the concept of fascism must not only be used with respect to the acute global crash of the 1930s, but it must also be taken up as a problem of the social ideology and thought of postwar neoliberalism that was itself born of the historical fascisms. That is, contemporary fascisms must be considered within this historical method of multiple temporalities if we are to arrive at any theoretically and historically grounded understanding of the fascist form of capitalism in both its historical and contemporary expressions.[11] In this sense, fascism, as a concept, is split in two. There is the fascism of the 1930s and the more general understanding of fascism as a form. Which means that on the one hand, there is a broader, more universal sense, and at the same time a fascism in which the concept is more confined and determined by its particular historical circumstances. Following Tosaka's method, the task of a historical critique of fascism, then, is to historically and theoretically "analyze the gap between these two meanings."[12] The historical specificities of both moments—whether considering the reproduction, reemergence, and supersession of fascism today—require that the concept be distinguished from the actually existing historical forms of appearance, but also be able to draw out more general conditions of historical and contemporary fascism that were themselves not wholly determined by their moments. This historical dynamic resonates with Karatani's argument in *History and Repetition* that fascism repeats as form, not content; how the crisis of representation resulting from the failure to answer the national question appears in the state as a morbid symptom of the crisis of accumulation.[13] Whether we adopt Traverso's term "postfascism" or not, paraphrasing Tosaka, what is a required is a concept of fascism that is "at once more general and also more particular."[14]

In the wake of the 2016 US election, countless think-pieces identified the revenge of the forgotten or left behind "white working class" as the key category by which to grasp the meaning of the apparent rupture with the near past.[15] But, like Tosaka's rejection of a the "salaryman" as a class for not proceeding from the material relations of production as the two classes, bourgeois and proletariat, do,[16] "the white working class" is, in Toscano's words, "sociologically spectral." It is not a class—in Tosaka's social-scientific sense—but a "racialized simulacrum of a proletariat"; and thus it is "not a stepping stone toward class politics, but its obstacle, its malevolent and debilitating *ersatz* form."[17] While it is true that, for Tosaka, beneath the level of abstraction of the mode of production, in a historically specific society, the two classes may be further split into social strata, a category that indicates "a particular social status, and thus also names an occupational position in society"—in Tosaka's time, the relevant strata were capitalist and landowner, and proletarians and farmers—the "salaryman" was neither of these. The salaryman was rather a category of superficial "phenomenological sociology" conjured as an imagined sociological object, not from the actuality of the current conjuncture, but a myth produced from superficial sociological discourse, from the readership of journalism, bourgeois sociology, and criticism journals. In our day, the "white working class" exists nowhere more than online and in the media. As such, like the "white working class," in his actuality the salaryman "is simply a salaryman" and was only able to take his place as a representative of contemporary society by being "sutured" to a properly delineated social stratum within class society. In this sense, despite his actual social position, in a pre-Marxist, pre-scientific understanding of ideology, Trump's language and aesthetic, could in fact, appear to be working-class president. It is also here that this imagined white, working pseudoclass can appear to have some social actuality with a mass basis. Yet it will remain a chimera unless sutured to a class or social strata produced by the actually existing material and social relations of production, either becoming the proletariat, or becoming the ideal, but not real, constituency of a fascist demagogy that produces the fantasy that it shares the interests of this "class" all the while "extending the domination of finance capital."[18]

In Tosaka's moment of the 1930s, he identified the ways in which the hermeneutic and philological method of liberalism and Japanism formed the metaphysical ground of "the Japanese Ideology" to become a metaphysics that accompanied, and ideologically veiled, a Japanese imperialism driven by monopoly and finance capital.[19] Tosaka's critique alerts us that we should always be looking for the "fascization" (*fashōka*) of an accumulation regime, a concept that also forms a key part of Ugo Palheta's theory of fascism.[20] Without a robust, theoretical understanding of "fascization" there is danger that fascism can only be defined, and condemned, retroactively, but never in its actual moment of emergence. The question then becomes, why has fascism become an issue now, after decades of neoliberal accumulation? Like Nicos Poulantzas earlier, Ken Kawashima, in a response to Ugo, has pointed out the simple yet deeply obscured answer: we are still in the stage of imperialism, of finance and monopoly capital; and fascism, as a "reaction-formation to capitalist crisis," is "designed to defer the end of the imperialist stage, and thus to defer the end of capitalism itself."[21] We find here, again, a resonance with Tosaka's class theory, that "bourgeois ideology" is not limited to the speaker's class position or sociological status, but indicates *that which is necessary at any given moment* for preserving and extending accumulation. Understanding neoliberalism within this larger framework, like how hermeneutics and philology came together with imperialism to become "the Japanese Ideology" of the 1930s, we must ask how neoliberalism works, both materially and ideologically, to serve, and veil, the preservation and extension of finance capital, and indeed, (late) imperialism, to look for its particular form of fascization.

Gavin Walker has identified the "after-effects" of imperialism following the end of formal colonial empires, the displacement of their political and ideological techniques into the former imperial metropoles, a policed "racialization" he calls "the metapolitics of imperialism."[22] This racial supplement of ostensibly individualist neoliberalism had been there from the start of the neoliberal era, seen in Ronald Reagan's 1980 campaign

AFTERWORD

announcement in Philadelphia, Mississippi, the site of the murder of three civil rights workers in 1964, and in Margaret Thatcher's famous, and awkward, addendum "... and their families" to the more explicitly neoliberal "there is no such thing as society. There are only men and women." As Wendy Brown has shown, it is from within these ellipses that a whole panoply of social issues around gender and race are allowed to emerge, disavowed and implicit, but for all that no less effective.[23] With the cascading crises of the dot-com bubble in 2000, the housing crash of 2008, and the pandemic, what appears to have changed is that this racial subtext has become text. This form of neoliberal racialization is no longer the hard boundaries of imperial citizen and colonial subject, but a "boomerang effect" of an unfettered colonial police applied to the imperial metropole.[24] Crucially, Walker points out that it is not the nation and the old nationalism that fuels the current fascization,[25] but rather the neoliberal deification of market competition, a naturalization and eternalization of a zero-sum game of winners and losers that, when yoked to the afterlives of imperial racial hierarchies rebounding back into the metropole, combine to become a harsh defense of racialized, Nietzschean accumulation.[26] Indeed, just such a Spenglerian defense of eternal "dominance hierarchies" everywhere under siege by debilitating and energy-sapping "woke" society runs through the entirety of Jordan Peterson's Pareto distributions mediated by the archaisms of Jungian archetypes.[27] Of course, we should see here, and in Charlottesville, an example of Tosaka's "primitivization" of thought, complete with its own totemistic and animistic aspects.

Charlottesville, the sacking of the US Capitol, and many other cases are only the latest, spectacular instances of the long American tradition of bands of armed groups operating as a disavowed supplement to the official "police function,"[28] the devolution of the sovereign right to violence to overwhelmingly white armed "gangs"[29] and militias: slave patrols, the Klan, the Pinkertons, the Michigan Militia, the Proud Boys, and so on.[30] As a matter of materialist historical criticism, we must ask, what time does this "class" represent and inhabit? Like the "vague restorationism" of Japan's "long feudal period" in the 1930s, despite the very real political and historical disputes over national history such as the 1619 and 1776 projects, these groups and their corresponding state representatives today are groping for a much more demagogically useful archaic base—an inversion of the contemporaneity of the noncontemporaneous to the mysticism of the "politically more retrograde noncontemporaneous contemporaneity of fascism"[31]—the conversion of historical time into fascist time.

As in Tosaka's day for "salarymen" and "farming villagers," the spectral nature of this "white working class" exposes it as an idealist object of pure ideology mobilized by cultural demagogy: "Despite that fact that [it] is fundamentally an idea which arose from particular, material social conditions, it does not objectively reflect the material foundation that produced it. Thus, as a form of thought . . . [it] has a fundamentally ideological essence."[32] The "thought" that produced this pseudoclass then becomes the seemingly mass-based ideological sign of neoliberalism's hatred of society in favor of pure competition, which has become natural law; this can be seen in economic "research" to prove the market is hard-wired into humanity at the level of biology, in research that maps brain function when thinking about market relations, or that Neanderthals were defeated by Homo sapiens thanks to the market. In this understanding, this spectral class can thus appear as the victim of the old model of the market as a more social and socialized "exchange" with its compromises, flattened, technocratic banalities, and indeed "miscegenation,"[33] and summoned to the raw deathmatch of endless competition in the neoliberal model.[34] As capitalist crisis, especially since the 1970s, has become much more chronic than the acute crash of the 1930s, our "late fascism" of our "late imperialism" is much less a call for national palingenesis, but a more anticipatory, speculative, and permanent "projected sense of loss . . . an act of recuperating something that has not yet been experienced."[35] Together with the obviously restorationist slogan "Make America Great Again," the cry at Charlottesville—"Jews *will not* replace us"—was indeed future oriented: an anticipated, virtual, loss that is nonetheless experienced as already actualized in the present. US media is currently filled with stories of petit bourgeois professionals who are shocked that the structuring practices of capital accumulation have started to come for them. The subjects of these stories almost always reach for a culturalist interpretation, blaming governmental social programs like affirmative action or "open borders," rarely noticing that they have been mere "workers" the whole time.[36]

If, as Tosaka definitively showed, liberalism is hopelessly implicated in fascism's rise, then the solution to a reemergence of fascism cannot be more liberalism. A dropping out of history and politics in favor of "consciousness polishing" when "thought itself has become something to be forged in the dojo just like judo, kendo or Zen." This neoliberal notion of subjectivity as nothing more than personal "investment" in "human capital," though it may imagine itself as a postideological, pragmatic center, "all this idealist rubbish ... does nothing but play a mute Sancho Panza to fascist thought ... [it is] the social ground from which a bona fide fascism emerges."[37] Beyond and behind the more openly fascist archaisms, in our age these individual spiritualisms are everywhere: yoga, mindfulness, "make your bed,"[38] neo-Stoicism, self-help and wellness, Tyler Cowen's trumpeting of Mormonism and other "strict religions" as a cure for poverty,[39] and Silicon Valley's fight against aging and death itself.[40] De te fabula narratur. As currently constituted, identity politics seems inadequate to the challenge. Following Tosaka, to frame the question in philosophical terms, does the current thought that goes by the name "identity politics" have any internal mechanism to deal with "white pride" in any coherent or systematic way?[41] Attempts to do so from within cultural liberalism all too often terminate in repetitions of reified "culture" itself. To proceed along these lines invariably abandons an actually existing global history in favor of interminable, competing philological projects.[42]

What is once again required is Tosaka and the *yuiken's* project, to build an antifascist thought able to critique not just the cultural but the social, political, scientific, and economic expressions of reactionary thought within a consistent, organized system of logic and method. The most promising avenue of recent thought is centered on the development of the theory and practice of the conditions of capitalism itself, its production, and importantly its reproduction, "so-called primitive accumulation," for it is here that the apparent closed-loop of capitalist domination that sidelined much of Western Marxism remains "open" to history, to politics, and to social revolution. In place of the flat spaces of real subsumption, formal subsumption that focuses on the found historical materials marshaled for capitalist accumulation offers ways of contending with the material and historical base that gives rise to the forms of society that produce both liberalism and fascism;[43] the latter can now be thought of as the ideologically veiled, disavowed repetition of the violence of primitive accumulation in our present.[44] It is in the embracing of Tosaka's inescapable, material "now" of everydayness as the historically specific site where primitive accumulation (expropriation) and the daily repetition of the commodification of labor-power (exploitation) are lived. The site of the spectacular Unite the Right riot in Lee Park in Charlottesville was also the site of a previous expropriation of the African American neighborhood of Vinegar Hill. And thus also here where, just as Tosaka said, history *is* theory. The production of an emancipatory politics must start from this base as a way to recapture the political and economic freedoms abandoned by cultural liberalism, to reconnect a cultural freedom to a materialist base. (Black Lives Matter has this potential within it.) At its best, this is what both Marxism and postcolonialism's interrogation of the national question and the refusal to take the nation as a stable unit of analysis offers. Indeed, only by becoming practical materialists (socialists) not reducible to an eternal cultural essence may the liberals' cultural freedoms have any chance of survival.

In short, it should no longer be a question as to whether or not fascism remains an immanent possibility in capitalism—the ghost in the machine, a ghost whose silhouette may always be glimpsed through social, cultural, and above all, historical critique. As we are still within Tosaka's moment and "late imperialism," that method remains Marxist. Far from invoking a fantastic supplement to materialist critique, this fascist specter within capitalism is grounded in theory, theory as the actual, historical development of the laws of motion of capitalist accumulation themselves. It is as simple as dropping the assumption Marx used in *Capital* that all commodities will be paid at their value in order for him to show that the particular form of the exchange of equivalents dialectically inverts to become exploitative in a society characterized by the commodification of labor-power in the production of "absolute surplus value." But the potential, and the material incentive to reduce the value of labor-power below the level necessary for the reproduction of the worker — even down to zero — was and is always there, hiding in the light. The historical/theoretical form, the absolutizing of absolute surplus value, goes by many names: necropolitics,[45] the return of colonialism to the metropole,[46] deformal subsumption.[47] And the name of the ideology that through demagogy enables the disavowed repetition of the violence of primitive accumulation inherent in the production of absolute surplus value in a modern form—is fascism.

NOTES

INTRODUCTION

1. See for example: *On the Scientific Method* (*Kagaku hōhōron*, 1929), *Literature as Thought* (*Shisō toshite no bungaku*, 1936), *Thought and Popular Custom* (*Shisō to fūzoku*, 1937), and *Japan as a Link in a Global Chain* (*Sekai no ikkan toshite no nihon*, 1937).
2. This neo-Kantian undercurrent would find another expression in the postwar period with Hiromatsu Wataru's study of Ernst Mach. See Hiromatsu Wataru, *Hiromatsu Wataru chosaku shū* (Collected works), 16 vols. (Tōkyō: Iwanami shoten, 1996–97).
3. Harry D. Harootunian, *Marx After Marx: History and Time in the Expansion of Capitalism* (New York: Columbia University Press, 2015).
4. Kōzai Yoshishige, *Senjika no yuibutsuronsha tachi* (Tokyo: Aoki shoten, 1982), 41.
5. Kōzai Yoshishige, *Senjika no yuibutsuronsha tachi*, 41.
6. Tosaka Jun, "The Principle of Everydayness and Historical Time," trans. Robert Stolz, in *Tosaka Jun: A Critical Reader*, ed. Ken Kawashima, Schäfer Fabian, and Robert Stolz. Cornell East Asian Series, no. 168 (Ithaca, NY: East Asia Program, Cornell University, 2013), 3–16. See *Tosaka Jun zenshū* (hereafter *TJZ*) 6 vols. (Tokyo: Keisō Shobō, 1966–79), where this untranslated essay is collected in volume 3).
7. Harry D. Harootunian, "Philosophy and Answerability: The Kyoto School and the Epiphanic Moment of World History," in *Confronting Capital and Empire: Rethinking the Kyoto School Philosophy*, ed. Viren Murthy et al. (Leiden: Brill, 2017), 21–57.
8. Harry D. Harootunian, *Overcome by Modernity: History, Culture, and Community in Interwar Japan* (Princeton, NJ: Princeton University Press, 2000), 11.
9. Tosaka Jun, "The Principle of Everydayness and Historical Time," 16.

10. Tosaka Jun, "Film Art and Film: Toward the Function of Abstraction," trans. Gavin Walker, in *Tosaka Jun: A Critical Reader*, 116.
11. Tosaka Jun, "The Principle of Everydayness and Historical Time," 12.
12. Tosaka Jun, "The Principle of Everydayness and Historical Time," 11.
13. See Lenin's "nature is infinite, but it infinitely *exists*." V. I. Lenin, *Materialism and Empirio-criticism* (Beijing: Foreign Languages Press, 1976), 314.
14. Tosaka Jun, "The Principle of Everydayness and Historical Time," 10.
15. Jorge Luis Borges, "Pierre Menard, Author of *Don Quixote*," trans. Anthony Kerrigan, in *Ficciones*, ed. Anthony Kerrigan (New York: Grove, 1962), 45–56.
16. Chapter 4, this translation.
17. Tosaka Jun, *Thought and Popular Custom* (*Shisō to fūzoku*, 1936), in *Tosaka Jun zenshū* (hereafter *TJZ*), 6 vols. (Tokyo: Keisō Shobō, 1966–79), vol. 4:269–469.
18. See chapter 8, this translation.
19. See Massimiliano Tomba, *Marx's Temporalities*, trans. Peter D. Thomas and Sara R. Farris (Chicago: Haymarket Books, 2013).
20. Tosaka Jun, "The Principle of Everydayness and Historical Time," 13.
21. Heidegger's "being-toward-death (*Sein zum Tode*).
22. Tosaka Jun, "The Principle of Everydayness and Historical Time."
23. William Wendell Haver, *The Body of this Death: Historicity and Sociality in the Time of AIDS* (Stanford, CA: Stanford University Press, 1996), 143.
24. Harry D. Harootunian, "The Fantasy of Modern Life," in *Overcome by Modernity: History, Culture, and Community in Interwar Japan*, 3–33.
25. The term *genshikashugi* is literally "primitivizationism" or "originism" but as we will see, it necessarily takes on a historical content from the national past. As such, it is also occasionally translated as "nativizationism." It should be read as a form, however, and different places would have different "nativizationist" content within this form. See for example, Reto Hofmann, *The Fascist Effect: Japan and Italy 1915–1952* Studies of the Weatherhead East Asian Institute, Columbia University. (Ithaca, NY: Cornell University Press, 2020) and further discussion in this introduction.
26. Tosaka consistently insists on a difference between *genjitsu* (reality), accepting things as they are and thus merely interpreting their meaning, which Harootunian associates with the "archaic," and *jissai* (actuality) that involves movement, praxis, and history. See Harry D. Harootunian, *Archaism & Actuality: Japan and the Global Fascist Imaginary* (Durham, NC: Duke University Press, 2023), 101.
27. Kishi Nobusuke (1896–1987), former economic czar of Manchukuo and member of Hideki Tōjō's wartime cabinet. He was indicted as a war criminal during the Allied Occupation, he was released without trial after the United States prioritized anticommunism over war responsibility. Later he became prime minister (from 1957 to 1960) and met with President Eisenhower at the White House for the renewal of the San Francisco Treaty in 1960.
28. Several of the coup's leaders, including Kita, whose writings were merely the inspiration, were executed, and many of the other participants sent to the Chinese front, less than a year before the full-scale invasion of China at the Marco Polo Bridge Incident in July 1937, beginning what is known as the Greater East Asian War from 1937 to 1945.
29. This translation, chapter 23.

INTRODUCTION

30. Kevin Passmore, *Fascism: A Very Short Introduction*, 1st edition (Oxford: Oxford University Press, 2002); 2nd edition (Oxford: Oxford University Press, 2014).
31. See the classic example of Walter Laqueur, *Fascism: Past, Present, and Future* (Oxford: Oxford University Press, 1996) and a recent version, Federico Marcon, "The Quest for Japanese Fascism: A Historiographical Review," *Religion and Thought* 4 (Ca'Foscari Japanese Studies, 2021), 53–86.
32. See, for example, Stanley Payne, *A History of Fascism, 1914–45* (Madison: University of Wisconsin Press, 1995); and George Macklin Wilson, "A New Look at the Problem of 'Japanese Fascism,'" *Comparative Studies in Society and History* 10, no. 4 (1968): 401–412.
33. Harry D. Harootunian, *The Empire's New Clothes: Paradigm Lost, and Regained* (Chicago: Prickly Paradigm Press, 2004).
34. This latter understanding of Japan as not fully modern because of "feudal remnants" was the position of the JCP-aligned "Lecture School" (Kōza-ha) of Japanese Marxism in its immensely important and intense debate on Japanese capitalism with the "Worker-Farmer School" (Rōnō-ha) in the 1920s. Like Uno Kōzō, Tosaka was not a direct participant in this debate, but in chapter 1 of *The Japanese Ideology* he quickly announced his position on the liberal, capitalist nature of modern Japan: "Of course, in neither form nor essence can we say there exists a full and complete bourgeois democracy in Japan. Japan's current democracy has mixed with, compromised with, and been distorted by a host of feudalistic elements such as the bureaucracy, the military, and obedience to authority. Even so, it is important to acknowledge that a distorted democracy is still at its base a kind of democracy. Even if liberal consciousness in Japan today is rather unconvincing, it is still the foundation of our social consciousness."
35. This belief in Japan as unique and sui generis is not limited to the fascism debate but permeates much of the scholarship in general. See, for example, Samuel P. Huntington, *Clash of Civilizations and The Remaking of World Order* (New York: Simon & Schuster, 1996), in which Huntington calls Japan the only nation-state that is also coterminous with a "civilization."
36. Maruyama Masao, *Studies in the Intellectual History of Tokugawa Japan*, trans. Mikiso Hane (Princeton, NJ: Princeton University Press, 1974).
37. For the critique of using militarism to describe Japan see Harootunian, *Overcome by Modernity: History, Culture, and Community in Interwar Japan*, and Tosaka Jun, this translation, chapter 10.
38. Walter Skya, *Japan's Holy War: The Ideology of Radical Shintō Ultranationalism* (Durham, NC: Duke University Press, 2009).
39. Hannah Arendt, following Kaustky on "ultra-imperialism," held that totalitarianism was a policy choice and not produced by political economy and historical circumstances, at which point she must invoke a weak Dostoeyevskian appeal to a Judeo-Christian sense of metaphysical right and wrong in her conclusion—literally a deus ex machina solution to the bind *Origins* has constructed in its previous three sections. But such is the price of her anti-Marxism and the fate of all theories of "totalitarianism." See Slovaj Žižek, *Did Somebody Say Totalitarianism?: Five Interventions on the (Mis)use of a Notion* (London: Verso, 2002).

    This rejection of fascism from nontheoretical, purely subjective, personal feelings not grounded in anything but the personality of the speaker is a move Tosaka saw early and labeled "sentimental liberalism" (*kibunteki jiyūshugi*) some twenty years before *Origins*. See Hannah Arendt, *Origins of Totalitarianism* (New York: Harcourt Brace Jovanovich, 1973).

40. Roger Griffin, ed. *Fascism* (Oxford: Oxford University Press, 1995).
41. Zeev Sternhell, *Neither Right nor Left: Fascist Ideology in France* (Princeton, NJ: Princeton University Press, 1995). Paxton rejects the left-right approach, but then immediately invokes a "center" as way to judge both. See Robert Paxton, *The Anatomy of Fascism* (New York: Vintage, 2005), 12.
42. Chapter 23, this translation.
43. Chapter 20, this translation.
44. See Lukács on the Heideggerian and Nietzschean preparation of the ground for the intelligentsia's later embrace of Hitlerism. Georg Lukács, *The Destruction of Reason*, trans. Peter Palmer (London: Verso, 2021).
45. On the *tenkō* phenomenon, see Max Ward, *Thought Crime: Ideology and State Power in Interwar Japan* (Durham, NC: Duke University Press, 2019), especially chapters 4 and 5.
46. Chapter 23, this translation.
47. See also Tosaka on the propensity for bourgeois philosophy to tend toward religious thought in *Shisō to fūzoku*, chapter 27: "Bourgeois Philosophy and its Nature to Become Religious" in *TJZ* 4:436–443.
48. This observation should be more than enough to remind us that whatever else it may be, fascism is firstly an anticommunism. See chapter 23, this translation: "It is a shared global nature of fascism that at the beginning the slogan 'overthrow capitalism' was in service of creating a force to oppose scientific socialism, only later to gradually obfuscate the meaning of the slogan and eventually arrive at a conclusion completely opposite of the overthrow of capitalism."
49. Laqueur, *Fascism: Past, Present, and Future*, 10 (emphasis added).
50. Gavin Walker, "Revolution and Retrospection," in *The Red Years: Theory, Politics, and Aesthetics in the Japanese '68* (London: Verso, 2020), 5.
51. Chapter 20, this translation.
52. Chapter 8, this translation: "Put another way, it is a primitive religion, and from here emerges a particular totemism. Empirical studies by many sociologists have shown that totemism assumes certain forms of ancestor worship and the existence of prohibited sacred objects [taboos]. Furthermore, it also appears as a kind of animism. The creative powers of the earth, together with the life spirit of plants, can become the objects of worship, as they are when they are united in the animism of agrarian fundamentalism. In this way, familialism can begin in the home and be infinitely expanded out to the nation and finally to all heaven and earth."
53. See Mark Driscoll's discussion in "Apoco-elliptic Thought in Modern Japanese Philosophy," accessed March 6, 2024, https://khora.site/driscoll.html#:~:text=It%20will%20be%20this%20looping,mobilization%20for%20essential%20ethno%2D national.
54. Katsuhiko Endo, "The Multitude and the Holy Family: Empire, Fascism, and the War Machine" in *Tosaka Jun: A Critical Reader*, 274–296.
55. See *"Jiyū no gainen to bunka no jiyū"* in *Gendai yuibutsuron kōwa*, *TJZ* 3:395–400.
56. Tosaka Jun, *"Bunka no kiki to wa, nani ka?"* ("What is a crisis of culture?") in *Sekai no ikkan toshite no nihon* (Japan as a link in a Global Chain, 1937) in *TJZ* 5:62–67.

1. PROBLEMS IN CONTEMPORARY JAPANESE THOUGHT

See also chapter 6 in this translation, where "'Japan' itself is not an object to be explained. Rather it is nothing more than a method or a principle arbitrarily deployed so that all other objects are explained in terms of it."

57. See the notion of criticism as "anti-Japanese" in *"Nachisu geijutsu tōsei ni yosete"* in *Sekai no ikkan toshite no nihon*, TJZ 5:81–84. Thanks to Jonmarc Bennett, Marquette University.
58. See Gavin Walker, *The Sublime Perversion of Capital: Marxist Theory and the Politics of History in Modern Japan* (Durham, NC: Duke University Press, 2016), chap. 2.
59. Ken Kawashima and Gavin Walker, "Uno Kōzō's Theory of Crisis Today" in Uno Kōzō, *Theory of Crisis*, trans. Ken Kawashima. *Historical Materialism* Book Series, vol. 251 (Leiden: Brill, 2022), 177–202.
60. See Naoki Sakai, "Subject and Substratum: On Japanese Imperial Nationalism," *Cultural Studies* 14, no. 3–4 (2000): 462–530.
61. As Uno's postwar writings show, capitalism is necessarily always in crisis, stemming from the "impossibility (*muri*)" of the commodification of labor-power. See Kawashima and Walker, Uno Kōzō's *Theory of Crisis*.
62. "In so far as the effects of ideas infiltrate the material foundations of economic structures and society, Japanism also forces its characteristics on to material social structures. Primarily speaking, however, *Japanism is first and foremost an idea, and despite the fact that it obviously broke out under particular, material conditions of society, it does not objectively reflect these material foundations*. Thus, both as a form of idea and as an unfortunate idea, it carries quite a remarkable ideological disposition from the beginning." Emphasis added. See chapter 10.
63. The scholar of Nazi Germany, Richard Evans, comes close to this understanding, but only at the level of description, not theory, when he argues that the defining characteristic of Nazism was not a set of policies, but a competition between Nazis to anticipate what Hitler wanted, something he called "working toward the Führer." See Richard J. Evans, *The Coming of the Third Reich* (London: Penguin Books, 2005).
64. See chapter 10, this translation, on the difference between the "soldiers" and the socially specific status of "the military."
65. See chapter 6, this translation.
66. *Sekai no ikkan toshite no Nihon*, TJZ 5:1–226.
67. On Italy, see Reto Hofmann, *The Fascist Effect*.
68. One of the more important norms that were altered was when Hideki Tojō become prime minister in 1940 while remaining an active Army general.

1. PROBLEMS IN CONTEMPORARY JAPANESE THOUGHT

1. For reasons that will soon be clear, Tosaka says much the same thing about Japanism in chapter 6.
2. This "liberation from" is closer to the Japanese original where the standard translation of "freedom" is *jiyū* and "liberalism" is *jiyūshugi*.
3. Here and elsewhere Tosaka demonstrates that the idealist base of liberalism tends toward a religious worldview and method. See "Bourgeois Philosophy and Its Nature to Become Religious" (*Burujoa tetsugaku to sono shūkyōkateki honshitsu*) in *Shisō to fūzoku* (1937), chapter 27, TJZ 4:36–43.

1. PROBLEMS IN CONTEMPORARY JAPANESE THOUGHT

4. This is a form of anticlass struggle as a form of class struggle, or "capitalism without capitalism." See Massimiliano Tomba, *Marx's Temporalites*, trans. Peter D. Thomas and Sara R. Farris (Chicago: Haymarket Books, 2013), especially "Political Historiography: Re-Reading the *Eighteenth Brumaire*," 35–59.
5. See for example Tosaka Jun, "On Space" [1931], in *Tosaka Jun: A Critical Reader*, ed. Ken C. Kawashima, Schäfer Fabian, and Robert Stolz. Cornell East Asia Series, no. 168 (Ithaca, NY: East Asia Program, Cornell University, 2013), 17–35, where he states that everyday spatiotemporality can be permanently "open, not closed," but not infinite.
6. J. Victor Koschmann, *Revolution and Subjectivity in Postwar Japan* (Chicago: University of Chicago Press, 1996), 266n59.
7. See especially the work of literary scholar Kobayashi Hideo (1902–1983). For a discussion of Kobayashi in the context of Tosaka's thought, see Harry D. Harootunian, *Archaism & Actuality: Japan and the Global Fascist Imaginary*. Theory in Forms (Durham, NC: Duke University Press, 2023).
8. By contrast, see the ""sense of the actual" in Harry D. Harootunian, *Overcome by Modernity: History, Culture, and Community in Interwar Japan* (Princeton, NJ: Princeton University Press, 2000), 136.
9. See chapter 6, this translation.
10. Part of Tosaka's rejection of the Asiatic Mode of Production in favor of a global understanding of contemporary capitalism and fascism. See, for example, his *Sekai no ikkan toshite no nihon* "Japan as a link in a global chain" (1936), *TJZ* 5.
11. These parenthetical question marks, and occasionally, exclamation marks, are parenthetical in Tosaka's original, and nearly always sarcastically and sardonically express his dismay at the nonsense of the ideas preceding them.
12. This matches his criticism of Heidegger and other phenomenologies as always taking place off stage in "being" or "das Mann," etc. See chapter 2, this translation,
13. Takahashi Satomi, *Zentai no tachiba* (*The standpoint of totality*) (Tokyo: Iwanami shoten, 1932).
14. See chapter 3, this translation, and *Ideorogi gairon* (1932) in *TJZ* 2:95–223.

2. FOUNDATION FOR A CRITIQUE OF JAPANISM

1. Cf. Lenin, who only demonstrated the need of such a science, but it fell to the *yuiken* to actually build one. As Kōzai Yoshishige wrote: "Lenin merely strongly explained the need for this type of progressive natural science, together with philosophical materialists in Marxism to fight reactionary ideology." Kōzai Yoshishige, *Senjika no yuibutsuronsha tachi* (Tōkyō: Aoki shoten, 1982), 41.
2. Cf. Thesis XI from Karl Marx, *Theses on Feuerbach*.
3. Friedrich August Wolf (1759–1824).
4. Tosaka uses kanji, katakana, and romaji scripts throughout this chapter to indicate slightly different historical and conceptual understandings of the word "philology." I have tried to capture some of this, which otherwise would simply be an undifferentiated string of the word in English by adding "Wolfian" to philology or using "philology" in scare quotes when it corresponds to the katakana rendering in Tosaka's original.
5. フィロロギー

3. AN ANALYSIS OF "COMMON SENSE"

6. 文献学
7. Again, this is best understood as either "a philological consciousness" or even "philological epistemology."
8. Johann Salomo Semler (1725–1791).
9. Gerhard Meier (1718–1777).
10. Johann Gustav Droysen (1808–1884).
11. *Issues in the Philosophy of History*, 1892, 1905 2nd edition.
12. Contrast this temporality with the three-dimensionality of historical time in Tosaka Jun, "The Principle of Everydayness and Historical Time [1936]," trans. Robert Stolz, in *Tosaka Jun: A Critical Reader*, ed. Ken C. Kawashima, Schäfer Fabian, and Robert Stolz. Cornell East Asia Series, no. 168 (Ithaca, NY: East Asia Program, Cornell University, 2013), 3–16.
13. See a very similar argument made by Lukàcs on the relation of German intellectuals and Nazism, mediated by Nietzsche, in *The Destruction of Reason* (1962).
14. Emphasis added.
15. Judgment, or the logical activity of connecting concepts with one another.
16. See Marx, *The Eighteenth Brumaire of Louis Bonaparte*, https://www.marxists.org/archive/marx/works/1852/18th-brumaire/; and Massimiliano Tomba, *Marx's Temporalities*, trans. Peter D. Thomas and Sara R. Farris (Chicago: Haymarket Books, 2013), on the difference between the spirit and the ghost of the past.
17. Lucien Lévy-Bruhl (1857–1939), French philosopher and anthropologist. See especially his *Mentalié primitive* (1921) and *L'ame primitive* (1927), which argue for the importance of "collective" and "affective" nature of "primitive" mental processes. Tosaka will invent the neologism "primitivization" (*genshika*) of thought, which under the conditions of capitalist crisis becomes an explicit ideology and the intentional introduction of these elements, or a "primitivizationism" (*genshikashugi*). Further, as seen in chapter 10, when yoked to national history "primitivizationism" often reduces to a "nativizationism" of thought. This ideological aspect of "primitive thought" is not, for Tosaka, a question of the continuity of these primitive processes to the present day, as in Freud's *Totem and Taboo* or, indeed, in Schumpeter's *Capitalism, Socialism, and Democracy* (1942), but rather an explicit and intentional decision to reactivate them in response to the crisis of Japanese and global capitalism.
18. Betty Heimann (1888–1961), German-British Indologist and pioneer of comparative philosophy. See Betty Heimann, "Vergleich der Antithesen europäischen und indischen Denkens," in *Kant-Studien* 31, no. 1–3 (1926): 549–562.
19. See the discussion of historical change within the three-dimensional nature of historical time in Tosaka Jun, "The Principle of Everydayness and Historical Time," trans. Robert Stolz, in *Tosaka Jun: A Critical Reader*, ed. Ken C. Kawashima, Schäfer Fabian, and Robert Stolz. Cornell East Asia Series, no. 168 (Ithaca, NY: East Asia Program, Cornell University, 2013), 14–15.

3. AN ANALYSIS OF "COMMON SENSE"

1. The *tenkō* phenomenon refers to the huge number of Japanese leftists who recanted their views and accommodated themselves to the wartime state. These recantations

3. AN ANALYSIS OF "COMMON SENSE"

sometimes took place after state harassment, arrest, and torture, but even more often were much more voluntary.

2. Tosaka Jun, "The Principle of Everydayness and Historical Time [1936]," trans. Robert Stolz, in *Tosaka Jun: A Critical Reader*, ed. Ken C. Kawashima, Schäfer Fabian, and Robert Stolz. Cornell East Asia Series, no. 168 (Ithaca, NY: East Asia Program, Cornell University, 2013).
3. See Satan's temptation of Christ in the desert, Matthew 4: 1–11.
4. Plato, *Georgias*.
5. In some cases, as here, with "common sense" given in parentheses along with *Gemeinsinn*, Tosaka used the English word as his own gloss of the Japanese term. See later in the chapter with the word "opinion" and "actuality."
6. Cf. V. I. Lenin, *Materialism and Empirio-criticism* (Beijing: Foreign Languages Press, 1976), on the Berkeleyan and similar idealisms defining the truth as the "simultaneous perception of the same."
7. Anthony Ashley Cooper, 3rd Earl of Shaftesbury (1671–1713).
8. Francis Hutcheson (1694–1746).
9. Ralph Cudworth (1617–1688).
10. See, for example, Tosaka Jun, "Laughter, Comedy, and Humor," trans. Christopher Ahn, and Katsuya Hirano, "The Dialectic of Laughter and Tosaka's Critical Theory" in *Tosaka Jun: A Critical Reader*, 50–58 and 176–193, respectively.
11. There exists a separate, materialist proletarian common sense grounded in "everydayness." See Tosaka Jun, *Ideorogi gairon* (1932), *TJK* 2, where this theme is prominent in at least a third of the text.
12. See Tosaka Jun, *Ideorogi gairon*, *TJK* 2 for how this can become eternal norms such as Pareto distributions.
13. Cf. chapter 22, "A Reconsideration of the Masses" on the question of masses and organization.
14. Cf. Fukuzawa Yukichi's "public opinion" as the sum total and average level of a nation's "knowledge and virtue" as a standard of "Civilization" in *An Outline of a Theory of Civilization* (1875).
15. Tosaka Jun, "The Principle of Everydayness and Historical Time [1936]," 3–16.
16. For a discussion of class-riven journalism, see *Ideorogi gairon*, *TJK* 2.

4. ON ENLIGHTENMENT

1. See Gavin Walker, *The Sublime Perversion of Capital: Marxist Theory and the Politics of History in Modern Japan*, Asia-Pacific: Culture, Politics, and Society (Durham, NC: Duke University Press, 2016), for the debate on Japanese capitalism and the contemporary status of feudalism.
2. Emphasis added. See Uno Kōzō's similar use of the reintroduction of feudal affects vs. the persistence of a lingering feudal system. See Ken C. Kawashima and Gavin Walker, "Uno Kōzō's *Theory of Crisis* Today," in Uno Kōzō, *Theory of Crisis*, trans. Ken C. Kawashima (Leiden: Brill, 2021), 177–202.
3. For the Japanese Roman-ha writers of the 1930s see Kevin Michael Doak, *Dreams of Difference: The Japan Romantic School and the Crisis of Modernity* (Berkeley: University of California Press, 1994).

5. A SCIENTIFIC CRITIQUE OF CULTURE

1. See Tosaka Jun, *Sekai no ikkan toshite no Nihon* (Japan as a link in a global chain), 1936 in *TJZ* 5.
2. Vladimir Maksimovich Friche (1870–1929).
3. Victor Francis Calverton (1900–1940).
4. As with *The Communist Manifesto*'s "class struggle" as the motor of history, but also this view also includes the forms of the historical necessities of capital accumulation—necessarily including and built on class struggle.
5. See chapter 10.
6. Abram Deborin (1881–1963).
7. See Gavin Walker, "Filmic Materiality and Historical Materialism: Tosaka Jun and the Prosthetics of Sensation" in *Tosaka Jun: A Critical Reader*, ed. Ken C. Kawashima, Schäfer Fabian, and Robert Stolz. Cornell East Asia Series, no. 168 (Ithaca, NY: East Asia Program, Cornell University, 2013), 218–254, for the difference between Lenin's "reflection" of the economic base in the superstructure and Tosaka's more historically attuned "refraction."
8. See Tosaka Jun, "Laughter, Comedy, and Humor," trans. Christopher Ahn; and Katsuya Hirano, "The Dialectic of Laughter and Tosaka's Critical Theory" in *Tosaka Jun: A Critical Reader*, 50–58 and 176–193.
9. Everydayness structured by the materiality of the capitalist working day.
10. Reto Hoffmann, *The Fascist Effect: Japan and Italy, 1915–1952*, A Study of the Weatherhead East Asian Institute, Columbia University (Ithaca, NY: Cornell University Press, 2020).

6. JAPANIST IDEOLOGY

The title of this chapter in the original appeared in a different Japanese script, one used for loan words and in advertising and emphasis; it read "Nippon Ideorogii," literally "Japan[ese] Ideology," but used a right-wing pronunciation of the word "Japan," written in the katakana script.

1. The Tokugawa discourse sought to purify Japanese of Chinese forms by returning to the divine, spoken language imagined and best captured in the eighth-century imperial genealogies the *Nihon shoki* (Chronicle of Japan, 720) and the *Kojiki* (*Record of Ancient Matters*, 712). See Harry D. Harootunian, *Things Seen and Unseen: Discourse and Ideology in Tokugawa Nativism* (Chicago: Chicago University Press, 1988).
2. September 18, 1931. Japanese military members disguised as "Chinese bandits" blew up a section of the South Manchuria Railway, using this "attack" as a pretense for a military occupation of the region, and one year later, the creation of the Japanese "puppet state" of Manchukuo.
3. January 28, 1932. Another incident orchestrated by the Japanese military and nationalist Buddhists of the Nichiren sect that led to a riot in the Shanghai international settlement.
4. *Yankee Girl* was a 1909 musical comedy with a march by John Philip Sousa, "The Glory of the Yankee Navy."

6. JAPANIST IDEOLOGY

5. Cf. chapter 5: "(this 'Japanese thing' is not something to be concretely explained. Instead, it is thought that 'Japanese things' themselves, now appearing as an abstract principle, become the principle of explanation. Japanese things here are not concrete links in a global chain."
6. An archaic term for "Japanese (language)" that was commonly used in nationalist text and speech in the 1930s.
7. Gondō Seikyō, *Jichi minpan* (Tokyo: Heibonsha, 1927).
8. Dilworth et al. use this phrase to show that Tosaka was amenable to religion and religious organization of society. David Dilworth, Valdo H. Viglielmo, and Augustin J. Zavala, eds., *Sourcebook for Modern Japanese Philosophy: Selected Documents* (Westport, CT: Greenwood Press, 1998). Throughout the translation of this chapter in the *Sourcebook*, the translators consistently translate the Japanese "*shika . . . nai*" (merely, only) as the straight negative "*nai*" (not), and they do so in a way that also consistently makes Tosaka appear to be defending some sort of religious thought.
9. Uda (866–931; r. 887–897).
10. The 1925 Peace Preservation Law established universal male suffrage and criminalized criticism of the emperor and "the system of private property" (capitalism). The penalties were increased to include capital punishment in 1928. For a discussion of this law and its uses see Max Ward, *Thought Crime: Ideology and State Power in Interwar Japan* (Durham, NC: Duke University Press, 2019).
11. On Muneki see John Person, *Arbiters of Patriotism: Right-wing Scholars in Imperial Japan*. A Study of the Weatherhead East Asian Institute, Columbia University (Honolulu: University of Hawai'i Press, 2020).
12. Victor Bulwer-Lytton was the British official in charge of the Lytton Report (1932) to the League of Nations; after investigating and denying the independent status of Manchukuo, he and the Lytton Commission members insisted on Japanese withdrawal from Manchuria.
13. Okawa Shūmei (1886–1957). Japanese nationalist and Pan-Asianist. His focus on the Middle East led to a republishing of his texts after September 11, 2001.
14. May 15, 1932. The May 15 Incident included attacks by young military officers, agrarian fundamentalists (including Tachibana Kōzaburō, cited above), and other radical groups on *zaibatsu* heads, government finance officials, and resulted in the assassination of Prime Minister Inukai Tsuyoshi. This marked the end of party cabinets in Japan until the postwar period and the beginning of "national unity cabinets" that sought to eliminate class struggle in favor of ethnic harmony.
15. Chinese warlord and ally of the Manchukuo government, until his assassination by the Japanese military state. For a discussion of opium and empire see Mark Driscoll, *Absolute Erotic, Absolute Grotesque: The Living, Dead, and Undead in Japanese Imperialism, 1895–1945* (Durham, NC: Duke University Press, 2009).
16. Kita Ikki, *Nihon kaizō hōan taikō*, in *Gendai nihon shisō taikei*, vol. 31 "Chōkokkashugi" (Tokyo: Keiō gijuku keizai gakkai, 1964).
17. The concept of the "Sinosphere," often resolving in a shared Confucian inheritance based in morality and classic texts, now operates as a similar philologistic apology for Chinese political and economic expansion in Asia.
18. 親作と小（子）作. This is also a play on homonyms of *kosaku* (tenant farmer) but with "small" and "child."
19. Othmar Spann (1878–1950). Antisocialist Austrian sociologist and economist.

7. JAPANESE ETHICS AND ANTHROPOLOGY

1. See chapters 5 and 6.
2. This is an alternative reading of the same character, with the same meaning, for "space [*aida*]" shown in earlier in this chapter.
3. "The autumn of life and death" refers to the harvest as the key moment for survival—Three Kingdoms, China.
4. Cf. chapter 12, this translation.
5. Franz Brentano, *Psychology from an Empirical Standpoint*, trans. by A. C. Rancurello, D. B. Terrell, and L. McAlister (London: Routledge, 1973; 2nd ed. with intr. by Peter Simons, 1995).
6. See chapter 2 on all phenomenologies as ahistorical.

8. AN ANALYSIS OF THE RESTORATIONIST PHENOMENON

1. An "undead," intentionally resurrected state of the feudal past—cf. the evolutionary metaphors in *Ideorogi gairon*. Ideology is produced by material conditions but does not directly reflect them, and further seeps back into those conditions.
2. *Genshikashugi* is one of Tosaka's most important neologisms. It literally means "primitivizationism"—an ideology that renders thought primitive and thus is consistently judged negatively. While the broader category of "restorationism" often resolves to the negative and reactionary primitivizationism, there are rare cases, like the Meiji Restoration (1868) and the European Renaissance that can be a progressive restoration. More importantly, as he will show in later chapters of *The Japanese Ideology*, when it is yoked to the national past, primitivizationism is perhaps best translated into English as "nativizationism," becoming not a general primitivization, but a national chauvinistic nativizationism. But it remains a fundamentally and irredeemably reactionary ideological phenomenon and so should not be thought of as a potentially softer "indigenization." In this chapter there are several places where the more general "primitivization" should be used and others where the more explicitly nativist and nationalist "nativizationism" should be used. Later chapters nearly all come closer to the chauvinistic nativization (see especially chapters 10, 21, and 23). But both primitivization and nativization are but slightly nuanced English choices that are translations of the same Japanese word: *genshikashugi*.
3. This is no longer the free-floating, vague liberal sentimentality but a policed content-filled Japanist "sensibility" of national history. See the introduction.
4. See Tosaka's examination of daily customs as expressions of ideology (thought) in such things as clothing in Tosaka Jun, *Shisō to fūzoku* (1937), *TJZ* 2:269–349.
5. This passage comes close a definition of fascism: the disavowed return of the repressed violence of primitive accumulation within the advanced capitalist present during a crisis of capital accumulation (i.e., global 1930s). Modernization here is best understood as "capital accumulation."
6. Marx, in *The Eighteenth Brumaire of Louis Bonaparte* and Walter Benjamin in "Theses on the Philosophy of History" have similar understandings in noting the difference between the *spirit* and the *ghost* of the past—the difference between an inspiration and a haunting. See Massimiliano Tomba, *Marx's Temporalities*, trans. Peter D. Thomas and Sara R. Farris (Chicago: Haymarket Books, 2013).

8. AN ANALYSIS OF THE RESTORATIONIST PHENOMENON

7. See, for example, the Meiji policy of shintō shrine consolidation and nationalization (*jinja gappei*) in the production of "state shintō," and the protests against this policy, perhaps most famously by Minakata Kumagusu (1867–1941).
8. Emphasis added.
9. See the mention earlier in the chapter of *ōsei fukkō*.
10. See Mark Driscoll, *Absolute Erotic: Absolute Grotesque: The Living, Dead, and Undead in Japan's Imperialism, 1895–1945* (Durham, NC: Duke University Press, 2010) for a discussion of the formal, real, and "deformal" forms of capitalist subsumption in the Japanese Empire.

9. THE ESSENCE OF CULTURAL CONTROL

1. See, for example, E. Herbert Norman, *Japan's Emergence as a Modern State: Political and Economic Problems of the Meiji Period* (60th anniversary edition). (Vancouver: UBC Press, 2000).
2. Johann Heinrich Pestalozzi (1746–1827), Swiss pedagogue and educational reformer of some popularity in contemporary Japan, including the agrarian fundamentalist Tachibana Kōzaburō discussed in chapter 6.
3. Cf. Foucault's biopolitics as power saying "yes" to "freedom" and Marx's "Between equal rights, force decides" in chapter 10, Karl Marx, *Capital: A Critique of Political Economy*, vol. 1, trans. Ben Fowkes (New York: Penguin, 1977).
4. Hans Dreisch (1867–1941). Entelechy refers to his term for the vitalist life force.
5. A theory from legal scholar Minobe Tatsukichi (1873–1948), which held that the emperor was a constitutional monarch bounded by law—that the emperor was one "organ" of constitutional rule. Popular during the period of "Taishō Democracy" in the 1910s and 1920s, Minobe was eventually denounced by fascists and the military and expelled from teaching positions and the Diet in 1935.
6. These groups could be described as expressions of the disavowed supplement of state power. See Tosaka Jun, "The Police Function," trans. Ken C. Kasashima, in *Tosaka Jun: A Critical Reader*, ed. Ken C. Kawashima, Schäfer Fabian, and Robert Stolz. Cornell East Asia Series, no. 168 (Ithaca, NY: East Asia Program, Cornell University, 2013), 103–112; and Ken C. Kawashima, "Notes Toward a Critical Analysis of Chronic Recession and Ideology: Tosaka Jun on the Police Function," in *Tosaka Jun: A Critical Reader*, 255–273.
7. I added this "organ theory" for clarity but censored it as all other instances had been before.
8. Emphasis added.
9. See chapter 6 for how Japanese Asianism is the expansion of "Japan" itself to the whole of Asia.

10. THE FATE OF JAPANISM

1. There are countless historical and present examples of this, but the most famous is Nitobe Inazō's *Bushidō: The Soul of Japan* (1899), and more recently, Tom Cruise's film *The Last Samurai* (Warner Bros., 2003).

11. MODERN IDEALISM IN DISGUISE

2. Cf. the Tokugawa-era separation of soldiers and farmers in the early seventeenth century: *heinō bunri*.
3. *Genshikashugi*, introduced in chapter 8 and discussed in the introduction, is one of the most important of Tosaka's neologisms. As described in chapter 8, note 2, it literally means "primitivizationism"—a regressive historical procedure producing an ideology that renders thought primitive and thus is consistently judged negatively. While the broader category of "restorationism" often resolves to the negative and reactionary primitivizationism, there are rare cases, like the Meiji Restoration (1868) and the European Renaissance that can be a progressive restoration (see chapter 8). More importantly, as he will show here and in later chapters of *The Japanese Ideology*, when it infused with historical content, however haphazardly and vague, primitivizationism is perhaps best translated into English as "nativizationism" becoming not a general primitivization, but a national-chauvinist nativizationism. Yet it remains a fundamentally and irredeemably reactionary ideological phenomenon, and so should not be thought of as a potentially softer "indigenization." In this chapter there are several places where the more general "primitivization" should be used and others where the more explicitly nativist and nationalist "nativizationism" should be used. Later chapters nearly all come closer to the chauvinistic nativization (see especially chapters 21 and 23). Both primitivization and nativization are but slightly nuanced English choices that are translations of the same Japanese word: *genshikashugi*.
4. These two words are homonyms: 封建制 (*hōkensei* as feudal system) and 封建性 (*hōkensei* as "feudality"). See Ken C. Kawashima and Gavin Walker, "Uno Kōzo's Theory of Crisis Today," in *Theory of Crisis*, trans. Ken C. Kawashima. Historical Materialism Book Series, vol. 251 (Leiden: Brill, 2022), 177–202.
5. See chapter 3 where Tosaka locates the social place and function of common sense.
6. See Sigfried Kracauer, *The Salaried Masses: Duty and Distraction in Weimar Germany*, trans. Quentin Hoare (London: Verso, 1998).
7. Endo Katsuhiko has followed this reverse course. See Katsuhiko Endo, "The Multitude and the Holy Family: Empire, Fascism, and the War Machine" in *Tosaka Jun: A Critical Reader*, ed. Ken C. Kawashima, Schäfer Fabian, and Robert Stolz. Cornell East Asia Series, no. 168 (Ithaca, NY: East Asia Program, Cornell University, 2013), 274–296.

11. MODERN IDEALISM IN DISGUISE

1. See Kevin Michael Doak, *Dreams of Difference: The Japan Romantic School and the Crisis of Modernity* (Berkeley: University of California Press, 1994).
2. Especially as treated in V. I. Lenin, *Materialism and Empriro-criticism* (Beijing: Foreign Languages Press, 1976).
3. In Tosaka Jun, *Ideorogi gairon* (Tokyo: Risōsha shuppan bu, 1932), also *TJZ* 2:95–222. Tosaka uses the evolutionary metaphor of descent, but later this is further glossed as "historical necessity."
4. See the discussion of historical change in three-dimensional historical time in Tosaka Jun, "The Principle of Everydayness and Historical Time," trans. Robert Stolz, in *Tosaka Jun: A Critical Reader*, ed. Ken C. Kawashima, Schäfer Fabian, and

11. MODERN IDEALISM IN DISGUISE

Robert Stolz. Cornell East Asia Series, no. 168 (Ithaca, NY: East Asia Program, Cornell University, 2013), 14–15.
5. See chapter 2.
6. See the Tosaka's essay "Nichijōsei ni tsuite" on the Manchurian Incident and inability of the Kyoto School and Hegelianism to frame it as a problem of current events, in *TJZ* 4: 136–141.
7. Felix Le Dantec, French biologist (1869–1917).
8. See Martin Heidegger, "Question Concerning Technology," in *Questions Concerning Technology and Other Essays*, trans. William Levitt (New York: Harper Torchbooks, 1977) for the postwar continuation of this method.
9. Tosaka Jun, "The Philosophy of Technology," in *TJZ* 1:229–298.
10. Protagonist of Ivan Turgenev's *Fathers and Sons*.
11. *Ideorogii no ronrigaku* in *TJZ* 2:1–94.

12. "THE LOGIC OF NOTHINGNESS"

1. "Tanabe tetsugaku no seiritsu" in *Gendai tetsugaku kōwa*, *TJZ* 3:177–184.
2. "Kyoto gakuha no tetsugaku" in *Gendai tetsugaku kōwa*, *TJZ* 3:171–176.
3. Aristotle's gloss on Plato's forms; making them something that can be grasped by the human mind.
4. Again, this is a play on words coming from the word "free" (*jiyū*) of liberalism (*jiyūshugi*) in Japanese. The closest meaning in English would perhaps be "all others are *at liberty* to put. . . ."

13. THE SORCERY OF "TOTALITY"

1. See Tosaka Jun, "The Principle of Everydayness and Historical Time," trans. Robert Stolz, in *Tosaka Jun: A Critical Reader*, ed. Ken C. Kawashima, Schäfer Fabian, and Robert Stolz. Cornell East Asia Series, no. 168 (Ithaca, NY: East Asia Program, Cornell University, 2013) for the relation of temporalities and values.
2. Takahashi Satomi, *Zentai no tachiba* (The standpoint of totality) (Iwanami shoten, 1932). In the rest of this chapter Tosaka himself placed the parenthetical page numbers where quoted phrases or passages from this edition of Takahashi's text can be found.
3. Stoic notion of "All in One" or "One in All." This concept has reemerged in recent ecological thought, including the following ecofantasy manga: Eldo Yoshimizu, *Hen Kai Pan* (Titan Comics, 2022).
4. "The concept of pure thinking, and the closely related concepts of *generation* and *origin*, are central to Cohen's project in the *Logic*. All three concepts have to do with the principles that, in Cohen's view, define what an object is for mathematical natural scientific theories. In *Kant's Theory of Experience*, Cohen had been content to identify and exhibit synthetic a priori principles as "present" in experience. But now in the *Logic*, he is concerned with the question of those principles' foundation—that is, with their "origin." His answer to that question is staunchly idealist. Cohen

now argues that pure thinking *generates* those principles from itself. Or in his preferred idiom, pure thinking is "generation." See "Hermann Cohen, section 5, "Pure Thinking, Generation, and Origin," in *Stanford Encyclopedia of Philosophy*, https://plato.stanford.edu/entries/cohen/#ConGenOri (accessed March 17, 2024).
5. Cf. Tosaka's alternative, materialist discussion of historical change as A > B in Tosaka Jun, "The Principle of Everydayness and Historical Time," 14–15: "For example, on one plane, A is [alpha] and, at the same time, is not something else like [beta]. On the other plane, however, A could very well be [beta]. (But if so, it is already not [alpha]). And so in the vertical relationship between these two planes, the law of contradiction is not played out. . . . Rather than displaying A's contradictory nature, this situation demonstrates A's materiality."
6. Here Tosaka is placing together two separate quotes from Takahashi's text.
7. Cf. Lenin's "nature is infinite, but it infinitely *exists*." V. I. Lenin, *Materialism and Empirio-criticism* (Beijing: Foreign Languages Press, 1976), 314.

14. LITERATURE AND PHILOSOPHY IN AN AGE OF REACTION

1. フラーゼ, translated from Ger. *Phrase*.
2. Japan's literary restoration and literaturism is a link in a global chain of the crisis of capitalism. It is the form of appearance in Japan of the global crisis of capitalism.

15. THE ESSENCE OF "LITERARY LIBERALISM"

1. Likely from the German *Charakterkunde* (characterology or personality studies).
2. See chapter 14.

16. THE CONSCIOUSNESS AND CLASS THEORY OF THE INTELLIGENTSIA

1. This reveling in self-debasement, which is itself a form of cultural and intellectual superiority, is part and parcel of the reduction of actually existing liberalism to mere personal sentiment.
2. This translates to a wider ideology of political conversion (apostasy), always from left to right, of the *tenkō* phenomenon.

17. DOUBTS ON THE THEORY OF THE INTELLIGENTSIA

1. Ōmori Yoshitarō (1898–1940). Marxist economist and Japanese translator of Lenin's *Materialism and Empirio-criticism* (1909) in 1927.
2. Gabriel Tarde (1843–1904). French sociologist, criminologist, and social psychologist.
3. See this discussion in chapter 18.

18. THE THEORY OF THE INTELLIGENTSIA AND THE THEORY OF TECHNOLOGY

1. *Gijutsu* translates as both "technology" and "technique" in English.
2. Aikawa Haruki, "*Saikin ni okeru gijutsuronso no yōten*," in *Shakaigaku hyōron* 1, July 1934 (Tokyo: Aoki gakushūdō, 1934).
3. Tosaka Jun, "*Gijutsu no tetsugaku*," *TJZ* 1:229–288.
4. イデー, *idée*,
5. Karl Marx, *Capital: A Critique of Political Economy*, vol. 1, chap. 15, trans. Ben Fowkes (New York: Penguin, 1977), 493n4.
6. Quotes cited above from Marx, *Capital*, but here edited by Aikawa.

19. LIBERAL PHILOSOPHY AND MATERIALISM

1. Aono Suekichi (1890–1961), literary critic and specialist on proletarian literature.
2. Ōmori Gitarō (1898–1940), Japanese translator of Lenin's *Materialism and Empiriocriticism* (1909). Arrested in the antifascist Popular Front Incident (*jinmin sensen jiken*) of 1937.
3. Thomas Hill Green (1836–1882). British idealist. See especially his *Prolegomena to Ethics* (1883).
4. For whatever reason, the words for "organ theory," *kikansetsu*, were not censored in this instance.

20. CONTEMPORARY JAPANESE THOUGHT

1. The two major political parties of Japan through the 1920 and 1930s. See chapter 23 for their respective constituencies and relation to capital accumulation.
2. Sakisaka Itsurō (1897–1985). Japanese Marxist economist and economic historian, and a major *rōnō* (farmer-labor) faction participant in the "debate on Japanese capitalism" (*nihon shihinshugi ronsō*) of the 1920 and 1930s. See Gavin Walker, *The Sublime Perversion of Capitalism*.
3. See chapter 17 on the difference between historical materialism and the salaryman's "pocket-book philosophy of history" (*pokketto shikan*), 157.
4. Miki Kiyoshi (1897–1945). Japanese philosopher, literary critic, and colleague of Tosaka associated with the Kyoto School of Japanese philosophy represented by Nishida Kitarō and Tanabe Hajime.
5. Japanese Marxist involved in the appeal to the emperor (*jikiso*) during the Ashio Copper Mine Incident and later labor organizer of the Ashio miners. He was later found guilty by association and executed in a plot to assassinate the emperor in the Great Treason Incident in 1911.
6. Most likely from the German *Klassenstaat*.
7. This is the main reason Tosaka often rejected the term "reality" (*genjitsu*) in favor of "actuality" (*jissai*) because *genjitsu*, as interpreted by liberal philosophy, "connoted the abstract and immaterial that was prior and superior to the lived reality of

the everyday." See H. D. Harootunian, *Archaism and Actuality: Japan and the Global Fascist Imaginary* (Durham, NC: Duke University Press, 2023), 19.

8. In Buddhist thought, a bodhisattva is one who delays their own post-enlightenment entry into paradise to help others achieve it.
9. Kawakami Hajime (1879–1946). Early Japanese socialist professor at Kyoto University and founder of the journal *Social Problem Studies (Shakai mondai kenkyū)*. He was expelled from his teaching position in 1928. See Gail Lee Bernstein, *Japanese Marxist: A Portrait of Kawakami Hajime, 1879–1946* (Cambridge, MA: Harvard East Asian Monographs 12, 1990).
10. See Marx's 1872 preface to the French edition of *Capital*, vol. 1, translated and included in the standard Penguin edition: "No royal road to science, and only those who do not dread the fatiguing climb of its steep paths have a chance of gaining its luminous summits." Karl Marx, *Capital: A Critique of Political Economy*. vol. 1, trans. Ben Fowkes (New York: Penguin, 1977), 105.

21. THE CURRENT MEANING OF "PROGRESSIVE" AND "REACTIONARY"

1. On customs as "the skin that thought wears," see Tosaka Jun, *Shisō to fūzoku (Thought and popular custom*, 1937) in *TJZ* 4:269–469.
2. V. I. Lenin, *Materialism and Empirio-criticism* (Beijing: Foreign Languages Press, 1976).
3. See first lines of chapter 10 on middle classes losing all confidence in dictatorship of the proletariat.
4. See Katsuhiko Endo, "The Multitude and the Holy Family: Empire, Fascism, and the War Machine," in *Tosaka Jun: A Critical Reader*, ed. Ken C. Kawashima, Schäfer Fabian, and Robert Stolz. Cornell East Asia Series, no. 168 (Ithaca, NY: East Asia Program, Cornell University, 2013), 274–296.
5. See how this existed on the ground in Manchukuo as a necropolitical regime of capital accumulation in Mark Driscoll, *Absolute Erotic, Absolute Grotesque: The Living, Dead, and Undead in Japan's Imperialism, 1895–1945* (Durham, NC: Duke University Press, 2010).
6. In our time, this rejection of the very concept of progress can be seen in those like Jordan Peterson's eternal hierarchies and Pareto distributions, and in Nick Land's manifesto for a "neo-Reactionary movement" based on race and racism. See Nick Land, *The Dark Enlightenment* (Perth: Imperium Press, 2023).
7. See Tosaka Jun, "The Police Function," trans. Ken C. Kawashima, in *Tosaka Jun: A Critical Reader*, 97–102.

22. A RECONSIDERATION OF "THE MASSES"

1. Character in *Fathers and Sons* (1862).
2. The protagonist of *The Red and the Black* (1830).
3. "Elite" and "Duce" appear in roman script in the original.

4. See the discussion of the aristocratic ideal lurking within bourgeois common sense in chapter 3.
5. "Understanding" in roman characters (with capitalized "U") is Tosaka's gloss of *gosei*.

23. LIBERALISM, FASCISM, SOCIALISM

1. The Gakugei jiyū dōmei was a liberal literary organization founded in 1933 to protest against the Nazi concept and control of culture, and as a way to protest the censorship regime in Japan.
2. This refers to the attempted fascist coup d'etat of February 26, 1936, in downtown Tokyo by the "Imperial Way faction" (*kōdō-ha*) of Japanese fascism. It was inspired by the national socialism centered on the concept of "the people's emperor" by Kita Ikki, and it ended in a defeat of the Imperial Way faction at the hands of the "Control faction" (*tōsei-ha*).
3. Keisuke Okada (July 1934–March 1936).
4. See again Uno Kōzō's later discussion of the ideology of "feudality" of "feudal affects" versus the lingering persistence of active resurrection of an entire feudal system. Ken C. Kawashima and Gavin Walker, "Uno Kōzō's *Theory of Crisis* Today," in *Theory of Crisis*, trans. Ken C. Kawashima, Historical Materialism Book Series, vol. 251 (Leiden: Brill, 2022), 177–202.
5. See the discussion of the phantasmagoria of Louis Napoleon in Massimiliano Tomba, *Marx's Temporalities*, trans. Peter D. Thomas and Sara R. Farris (Chicago: Haymarket Books, 2013), 92–158.
6. 「邦人主義」と世界の反響 東京法人社 1936
7. Kita Ikki (1883–1937). Japanese national-socialist. Executed as the spiritual inspiration for, but not a participant in, the attempted fascist coup d'état of February 26, 1936.
8. The May 15 Incident of 1932 (Go ichi go jiken) was an attempted coup planned and carried out by junior naval officers, army cadets, as well as right-wing thinkers including Okawa Shūmei and Tachibana Kōzaburō (examined in chapter 6) in an around Tokyo. Tachibana fled to Manchuria in the wake of the failure. The coup included the assassination of Prime Minister Inukai, grenade attacks on the Mistubishi bank, the head of the Seiyūkai political party, the Keeper of the Privy Seal, and even supposedly included a plan to assassinate Charlie Chaplin, who was touring Japan at the time. The incident marked the end of "party cabinets" in favor of "national unity cabinets" that persisted until the end of the war in 1945. The May 15 Incident was preceded by the similar League of Blood Incident (Ketsumeidan jiken) in March, partly inspired by Gondō Seikyō (who is also examined in chapter 6).
9. See chapter 15.

AFTERWORD

1. See, for example: Ira Bashkow, "Three Lessons I Learned From Charlottesville," sapiens.org, October 13, 2017, accessed March 20, 2024, https://www.sapiens.org

AFTERWORD

/culture/charlottesville-violence-lessons/; Siva Vaidhyanathan, "Why the Nazis Came to Charlottesville," *New York Times*, August 14, 2017, accessed January 18, 2024, https://www.nytimes.com/2017/08/14/opinion/why-the-nazis-came-to-cha rlottesville.html; Mark Edmundson, "Violence in Charlottesville," *American Scholar*, August 28, 2017, accessed March 20, 2024, https://theamericanscholar.org/violence -in-charlottesville/.

2. Harry D. Harootunian, *Archaism & Actuality: Japan and the Global Fascist Imaginary*. Theory in Forms (Durham, NC: Duke University Press, 2023), x.
3. See Tosaka Jun, "The Principle of Everydayness and Historical Time," trans. Robert Stolz, in *Tosaka Jun: A Critical Reader*, ed. Ken C. Kawashima, Schäfer Fabian, and Robert Stolz. Cornell East Asia Series, no. 168 (Ithaca, NY: East Asia Program, Cornell University, 2013), 10.
4. Michel Foucault, *Biopolitics: Lectures at the Collège de France, 1978–79* (Basingstoke: Palgrave Macmillan, 2008), 110, 172.
5. Foucault, *Biopolitics*, 190.
6. Corey Robin's term, "democratic feudalism," captures much of this phenomenon from a standard intellectual genealogy methodology, what Tosaka called an "internal criticism." Yet as it is internal, it remains incomplete. Adding a Marxist framework of historically specific accumulation regimes as an "external criticism" allows the critique to escape mere hermeneutics and thus would satisfy Tosaka's requirements for a full criticism, one that not only gives an *account of* but can at the same time also *account for* the appearance and form of an ideology. See Corey Robin, *The Reactionary Mind* (Oxford: Oxford University Press, 2011) and this translation, chapter 5.
7. See chapter 10, this translation, first paragraph.
8. See chapter 10 this translation. See also, Alberto Toscano, *Late Fascism: Race, Capitalism and the Politics of Crisis* (London: Verso, 2023), xi: "fascism [is] intimately linked to the prerequisites of capitalist domination—which, albeit mutable and sometimes contradictory, have a certain consistency at their core. W. E. B Dubois gave this core a name, still usable today: 'the counter-revolution of property.'"
9. Enzo Traverso, *The New Faces of Fascism: Populism and the Far Right*, trans. David Broder (London: Verso, 2019), 32.
10. "Unlike Mussolini or Hitler, Trump has probably never read Gustave Le Bon's *The Crowd* (1895)—the Bible for charismatic leaders—and his skill as a demagogue instead owes to his familiarity with the codes of television" (Traverso, *The New Faces of Fascism*, 24. See also, Lukàcs on the continuity of Heidegger to Hitler in Georg Lukàcs, *The Destruction of Reason*, trans. Peter Palmer (London: Verso, 2021), which Traverso also notoriously dislikes.
11. Earlier important work on this notion of history and time applicable to this question include Massimiliano Tomba, *Marx's Temporalities*, trans. Peter D. Thomas and Sara R. Farris (Chicago: Haymarket Books, 2013), and Karatani Kōjin, *History and Repetition* (New York: Columbia University Press, 2011).
12. Chapter 4, this translation.
13. Karatani Kōjin, *History and Repetition*, 2–3, 16–18.
14. Chapter 4, this translation.
15. "The white worker class, humiliated over the last thirty years, deceived by endless reformist promises, impoverished by financial aggression, has now elected the Ku

Klux Klan to the White House." Franco "Bifo" Berardi, e-flux conversations, https://conversations.e-flux.com/t/franco-bifo-berardi-on-national-workerism-and-racial-warfare/5272, and also quoted in Toscano, *Late Fascism*, 1. See also, among many others, Arlie Russell Hochschild, *Strangers in Their Own Land: Anger and Mourning on the American Right* (New York: New Press, 2016).
16. See chapter 17, this translation.
17. Toscano, *Late Fascism*, 2.
18. See chapters 10 and 23, this translation.
19. See chapter 10, this translation.
20. Ugo Palheta, "Fascism, Fascisation, Antifascism | Historical Materialism," January 7, 2021. https://www.historicalmaterialism.org/blog/fascism-fascisation-antifascism.
21. Ken C. Kawashima, "Fascism Is a Reaction to Capitalist Crisis in the Stage of Imperialism: | Historical Materialism," March 31, 2021. https://www.historicalmaterialism.org/blog/fascism-reaction-to-capitalist-crisis-stage-imperialism.
22. Gavin Walker, "Fascism and the Metapolitics of Imperialism | Historical Materialism," May 8, 2021. https://www.historicalmaterialism.org/blog/fascism-and-metapolitics-imperialism.
23. Wendy Brown, *Undoing the Demos: Neoliberalism's Stealth Revolution*. Near Futures Series (Brooklyn, NY: Zone Books, 2015).
24. Walker, "Fascism and the Metapolitics of Imperialism | Historical Materialism." This centripetal nature of colonial techniques was of course already prefigured in Aime Césaire's *Discourse on Colonialism* and was key part of the Japanese imperial history when the colonial society built in Manchuria was imported back into metropolitan Japan, most clearly seen in Kishi Nobusuke's move from Manchukuo's economic czar to munitions minister in Tojo's cabinet. See Mark Driscoll, *Absolute Erotic, Absolute Grotesque: The Living, Dead, and Undead in Japan's Imperialism, 1895–1945* (Durham, NC: Duke University Press, 2010).
25. Yet another reason for rejecting the term "ultranationalism" as a substitute for fascism. See the introduction.
26. See also Corey Robin, "Nietzsche's Marginal Children: On Friedrich Hayek," *The Nation*, no. 21 (2013): 27–36, accessed March 20, 2024, https://www.thenation.com/article/archive/nietzsches-marginal-children-friedrich-hayek/tnamp/.
27. Peterson's repressed relation to capitalist accumulation over all else can be seen in the bizarre need to make communists once again the enemy, even in the absence of any real communist movement; enter postmodern, cultural, neo-Marxism (?!).
28. Tosaka Jun, "The Police Function," trans. Ken Kawashima, in *Tosaka Jun: A Critical Reader*. Ed. Ken C. Kawashima, Schäfer Fabian, and Robert Stolz. Cornell East Asia Series, no. 168 (Ithaca, NY: East Asia Program, Cornell University, 2013), 103–112; and Ken Kawashima, "Notes Toward a Critical Analysis of Chronic Recession" in *Tosaka Jun: A Critical Reader*, 97–102 and 255–273.
29. Tosaka "The Police Function"; and Grace Elizabeth Hale and John Grisham, *In the Pines: A Lynching, A Lie, and a Reckoning* (New York: Little, Brown, 2023).
30. Even here, at the level of form, there is a homology with 1930s Japan, which saw the rise of violent patriotic groups and revolts of the "young military officer" ranks.

AFTERWORD

31. Harootunian, *Archaism & Actuality*, 85.
32. Chapter 10, this translation.
33. Walker, "Fascism and the Metapolitics of Imperialism."
34. Foucault, *Biopolitics*.
35. Walker, "Fascism and the Metapolitics of Imperialism."
36. Jodi Kantor and Arya Sundaram, "Workplace Productivity: Are You Being Tracked?," *New York Times*, August 14, 2022, accessed January 17, 2024, https://www.nytimes.com/interactive/2022/08/14/business/worker-productivity-tracking.html?searchResultPosition=18; and Noam Scheiber, "Why Doctors and Pharmacists Are in Revolt," *New York Times*, December 3, 2023, accessed March 20, 2024, https://www.nytimes.com/2023/12/03/business/economy/doctors-pharmacists-labor-unions.html.
37. Chapter 20, this translation.
38. Jordan Peterson, *12 Rules for Life: An Antidote to Chaos* (Toronto: Random House Canada, 2018).
39. Tyler Cowen, "Tyler Cowen on Inequality and What Really Ails America," *The New York Times*, July 30, 2014, accessed March 20, 2024, https://www.nytimes.com/2014/07/31/upshot/tyler-cowen-on-inequality-and-what-really-ails-america.html.
40. See how easily this devolves into contradictory, competing notions of culture: "The burning of non-Aryan books by the Nazis strikes us as barbaric, reminding us of the burying of Confucianists by the first Qin emperor. But to the curators [*shihaisha*] of German Culture, the purification of German Culture, the elevation of German Culture, explicitly requires this "vandalism" (?!). Understand, Hirschfeld's studies of sexuality harm German morality, Marxist texts are immoral, and therefore anti-Cultural [*hibunka*].... Goebbels' ban on Jewish books, too, may look like barbarism. But when seen from Goebbels' perspective [as curator of German morality] it is an urgent and necessary defense of German Culture." Tosaka refers here to the Jewish physician, gay activist, sexologist, and founder of the Institut für Sexualwissenschaft, Magnus Hirschfeld (1868–1935). In May 1933 the Nazis looted the institute and burned its library. See Tosaka, *Sekai no ikkan toshite no Nihon*, in *TJZ* 5:63.
41. See especially Ray Kurzweil on the "singularity" in which matter itself will be converted to computing power allowing humans to become immortal, but also condemning those who do not follow this path to an inferior existence as MOSHs (Mostly Original Substrate Humans). Christian Nagler, "The Singularity, Speculative Subjectivity, and Science Fictional Capital," Historical Materialism Conference: "The Cost of Life" Session 14, SOAS, London, November 12, 2023.
42. Tosaka Jun, "*Ideorogiron no kadai*" in *Ideorogi gairon*, *TJZ* 2:112–131.
43. Harry D. Harootunian, *Marx After Marx: History and Time in the Expansion of Capitalism* (New York: Columbia University Press, 2015).
44. Recent work includes Harootunian, *Marx After Marx*; Gavin Walker, *The Sublime Perversion of Capital: Marxist Theory and the Politics of History in Modern Japan*, Asia-Pacific: Culture, Politics, and Society (Durham, NC: Duke University Press, 2016); Mark Driscoll, *The Whites are Enemies of Heaven: Climate Caucasianism and Asia Ecological Protection* (Durham, NC: Duke University Press, 2020); and Uno

Kōzō *Theory of Crisis*, trans. Ken C. Kawashima, Historical Materialism Book Series, vol. 251 (Leiden: Brill, 2022).
45. Achille Mbembe, *Necropolitics* (Durham, NC: Duke University Press, 2019).
46. Aimé Césaire, *Discourse on Colonialism* (New York: NYU Press, 2000).
47. Driscoll, *Absolute Erotic, Absolute Grotesque*.

BIBLIOGRAPHY

Aikawa Haruki, "Saikin ni okeru gijutsuronso no yōten." In *Shakaigaku hyōron* 1, July 1934. Tokyo: Aoki gakushūdō, 1934.
Arendt, Hannah. *The Origins of Totalitarianism*. New York: Harcourt Brace Jovanovich, 1973.
Bernstein, Gail Lee. *Japanese Marxist: A Portrait of Kawakami Hajime, 1879–1946*. Cambridge, MA: Harvard East Asian Monographs 12, 1990.
Borges, Jorge Luis. "Pierre Menard, Author of *Don Quixote*." Trans. Anthony Kerrigan. In *Ficciones*. Ed. Anthony Kerrigan. New York: Grove, 1962.
Brentano, Franz. *Psychology from an Empirical Standpoint*. Trans. A. C. Rancurello, D. B. Terrell, and L. McAlister. London: Routledge, 1973 [2nd ed. with intro. by Peter Simons].
Brown, Wendy. *Undoing the Demos: Neoliberalism's Stealth Revolution*. Near Futures Series. Brooklyn, NY: Zone Books, 2015.
Césaire, Aimé. *Discourse on Colonialism*. New York: NYU Press, 2000.
Cowen, Tyler. "Tyler Cowen on Inequality and What Really Ails America," *New York Times*, July 30, 2014, accessed March 20, 2024, https://www.nytimes.com/2014/07/31/upshot/tyler-cowen-on-inequality-and-what-really-ails-america.html.
Dilworth, David, Valdo H. Viglielmo, and Augustin J. Zavala, eds. *Sourcebook for Modern Japanese Philosophy: Selected Documents*. Westport, CT: Greenwood Press, 1998.
Doak, Kevin Michael. *Dreams of Difference: The Japan Romantic School and the Crisis of Modernity*. Berkeley: University of California Press, 1994.
Driscoll, Mark. *Absolute Erotic, Absolute Grotesque: The Living, Dead, and Undead in Japan's Imperialism, 1895–1945*. Durham, NC: Duke University Press, 2010.
———. "Apoco-elliptic Thought in Modern Japanese Philosophy," https://khora.site/driscoll.html#:~:text=It%20will%20be%20this%20looping,mobilization%20for%20essential%20ethno%2Dnational.

BIBLIOGRAPHY

——. *The Whites Are Enemies of Heaven: Climate Caucasianism and Asian Ecological Protection*. Durham, NC: Duke University Press, 2020.
Endo, Katsuhiko. "The Multitude and the Holy Family: Empire, Fascism, and the War Machine." In *Tosaka Jun: A Critical Reader*. Ed. Ken C. Kawashima, Fabian Schäfer, and Robert Stolz, 274–296. Cornell East Asia Series, no. 168. Ithaca, NY: East Asia Program, Cornell University, 2013.
Evans, Richard J. *The Coming of the Third Reich*. London: Penguin, 2005.
Foucault, Michel. *The Birth of Biopolitics: Lectures at the Collège de France, 1978–79*. Basingstoke: Palgrave Macmillan, 2008.
Griffin, Roger, ed. *Fascism*. Oxford Readers. Oxford: Oxford University Press, 1995.
Hale, Grace Elizabeth, and John Grisham. *In the Pines: A Lynching, a Lie, a Reckoning*. New York: Little, Brown, 2023.
Harootunian, Harry D. *Archaism and Actuality: Japan and the Global Fascist Imaginary*. Theory in Forms. Durham, NC: Duke University Press, 2023.
——. *The Empire's New Clothes: Paradigm Lost, and Regained*. Chicago: Prickly Paradigm Press, 2004.
——. *Marx After Marx: History and Time in the Expansion of Capitalism*. New York: Columbia University Press, 2015.
——. *Overcome by Modernity: History, Culture, and Community in Interwar Japan*. Princeton, NJ: Princeton University Press, 2000.
——. "Philosophy and Answerability: The Kyoto School and the Epiphanic Moment of World History." In *Confronting Capital and Empire*. Ed. Viren Murthy et al., 21–57. Leiden: Brill, 2019.
——. *Things Seen and Unseen: Discourse and Ideology in Tokugawa Nativism*. Chicago: Chicago University Press, 1988.
Haver, William Wendell. *The Body of This Death: Historicity and Sociality in the Time of AIDs*. Stanford, CA: Stanford University Press, 1996.
Heidegger, Martin. "Question Concerning Technology." in *Questions Concerning Technology and Other Essays*. Trans. William Levitt. New York: Harper Torchbooks, 1977.
Heimann, Betty. "Vergleich der Antithesen europäischen und indischen Denkens," in *Kant-Studien* 31, no. 1–3 (1926): 549–562.
Hiromatsu Wataru. *Hiromatsu Wataru chosakushū* [Collected works]. Tōkyō: Iwanami shoten, 1996–97.
Hochschild, Arlie Russell. *Strangers in Their Own Land: Anger and Mourning on the American Right*. New York: New Press, 2016.
Hofmann, Reto. *The Fascist Effect: Japan and Italy, 1915–1952*. Studies of the Weatherhead East Asian Institute, Columbia University. Ithaca, NY: Cornell University Press, 2020.
Huntington, Samuel P. *Clash of Civilizations and The Remaking of World Order*. New York: Simon & Schuster, 1996.
Katsuya Hirano. "The Dialectic of Laughter and Tosaka's Critical Theory." In *Tosaka Jun: A Critical Reader*. Ed. Ken C. Kawashima, Fabian Schäfer, and Robert Stolz, 176–193. Cornell East Asia Series, no. 168. Ithaca, NY: East Asia Program, Cornell University, 2013.
Kawashima, Ken C. "Fascism Is a Reaction to Capitalist Crisis in the Stage of Imperialism: | Historical Materialism," March 31, 2021. https://www.historicalmaterialism.org/blog/fascism-reaction-to-capitalist-crisis-stage-imperialism.

BIBLIOGRAPHY

Kawashima, Ken C. "Notes Toward a Critical Analysis of Chronic Recession and Ideology: Tosaka Jun on the Police Function." In *Tosaka Jun: A Critical Reader*. Ed. Ken C. Kawashima, Fabian Schäfer, and Robert Stolz, 255–273. Cornell East Asia Series, no. 168. Ithaca, NY: East Asia Program, Cornell University, 2013.

Kawashima, Ken, and Gavin Walker, "Uno Kōzō's *Theory of Crisis* Today." In *Theory of Crisis*. Trans. Ken C. Kawashima, 177–202. Historical Materialism Book Series, vol. 251. Leiden: Brill, 2022.

Kita Ikki. *Nihon kaizō hōan taikō*, in *Gendai nihon shisō taikei*. Vol. 31 "Chōkokkashugi." Tokyo: Keiō gijuku keizai gakkai, 1964.

Koschmann, J. Victor. *Revolution and Subjectivity in Postwar Japan*. Chicago: University of Chicago Press, 1996.

Kōzai Yoshishige. *Senjika no yuibutsuronsha tachi*. Tōkyō: Aoki shoten, 1982.

Kracauer, Siegfried. *The Salaried Masses: Duty and Distraction in Weimar Germany*. Trans, Quentin Hoare. London: Verso, 1998.

Land, Nick. *The Dark Enlightenment*. Perth: Imperium Press, 2023.

Laqueur, Walter. *Fascism: Past, Present, Future*. New York: Oxford University Press, 1996.

Lenin, V. I. *Materialism and Empirio-criticism*. Beijing: Foreign Languages Press, 1976.

Lukács, Georg. *The Destruction of Reason*. Trans. Peter Palmer. London: Verso, 2021.

Marcon, Federico. "The Quest for Japanese Fascism: A Historiographical Review," *Religion and Thought* 4 (Ca'Foscari Japanese Studies, 2021): 53–86.

Maruyama Masao. *Studies in the Intellectual History of Tokugawa Japan*. Trans. Mikiso Hane. Princeton, NJ: Princeton University Press, 1974.

Marx, Karl. *Capital: A Critique of Political Economy*. Vol. 1. Trans. Ben Fowkes. New York: Penguin, 1977.

Mbembe, Achille. *Necropolitics*. Durham, NC: Duke University Press, 2019.

Nagler, Christian. "The Singularity, Speculative Subjectivity, and Science Fictional Capital," Historical Materialism Conference: "The Cost of Life" Session 14, SOAS, London, November 12, 2023.

Norman, E. Herbert. *Japan's Emergence As a Modern State: Political and Economic Problems of the Meiji Period* (60th anniversary edition). Vancouver: UBC Press, 2000.

Palheta, Ugo. "Fascism, Fascisation, Antifascism | Historical Materialism," January 7, 2021. https://www.historicalmaterialism.org/blog/fascism-fascisation-antifascism.

Passmore, Kevin. *Fascism: A Very Short Introduction*. 1st edition, Oxford: Oxford University Press, 2002; 2nd edition, Oxford: Oxford University Press, 2014).

Paxton, Robert O. *The Anatomy of Fascism*. New York: Vintage, 2005.

Payne, Stanley G. *A History of Fascism, 1914–1945*. Madison: University of Wisconsin Press, 1995.

Person, John. *Arbiters of Patriotism: Right-Wing Scholars in Imperial Japan*. A Study of the Weatherhead East Asian Institute, Columbia University. Honolulu: University of Hawai'i Press, 2020.

Peterson, Jordan B. *12 Rules for Life: An Antidote to Chaos*. Toronto: Random House Canada, 2018.

Robin, Corey. "Nietzsche's Marginal Children." *The Nation*, no. 21 (2013): 27–36. Accessed March 20, 2024, https://www.thenation.com/article/archive/nietzsches-marginal-children-friedrich-hayek/tnamp/.

Robin, Corey. *The Reactionary Mind*. Oxford: Oxford University Press, 2011.

Sakai, Naoki. "Subject and Substratum: On Japanese Imperial Nationalism." *Cultural Studies* 14, no. 3–4 (2000): 462–530.
Skya, Walter. *Japan's Holy War: The Ideology of Radical Shintō Ultranationalism*. Durham, NC: Duke University Press, 2009.
Sternhell, Zeev. *Neither Right nor Left: Fascist Ideology in France*. Princeton, NJ: Princeton University Press, 1995.
Takahashi Satomi. *Zentai no tachiba* [*The standpoint of totality*]. Iwanami shoten, 1932.
Tomba, Massimiliano. *Marx's Temporalities*. Trans. Peter D. Thomas and Sara R. Farris. Chicago: Haymarket Books, 2013.
Tosaka Jun. "Film Art and Film: Toward the Function of Abstraction." Trans. Gavin Walker. In *Tosaka Jun: A Critical Reader*. Ed. Ken C. Kawashima, Fabian Schäfer, and Robert Stolz. Cornell East Asia Series, no. 168. Ithaca, NY: East Asia Program, Cornell University, 2013.
———. "Laughter, Comedy, and Humor." Trans. Christopher Ahn. In *Tosaka Jun: A Critical Reader*. Ed. Ken C. Kawashima, Fabian Schäfer, and Robert Stolz, 50–58. Cornell East Asia Series, no. 168. Ithaca, NY: East Asia Program, Cornell University, 2013.
———. "The Police Function." Trans. Ken C. Kasashima. In *Tosaka Jun: A Critical Reader*. Ed. Ken C. Kawashima, Fabian Schäfer, and Robert Stolz, 103–112. Cornell East Asia Series, no. 168. Ithaca, NY: East Asia Program, Cornell University, 2013.
———. "The Principle of Everydayness and Historical Time." Trans. Robert Stolz. In *Tosaka Jun: A Critical Reader*. Ed. Ken C. Kawashima, Fabian Schäfer, and Robert Stolz. Cornell East Asia Series, no. 168. Ithaca, NY: East Asia Program, Cornell University, 2013.
———. *Tosaka Jun: A Critical Reader*. Ed. Ken C. Kawashima, Fabian Schäfer, and Robert Stolz. Cornell East Asia Series, no 168. Ithaca, NY: East Asia Program, Cornell University, 2013.
———. *Tosaka Jun zenshū*. 6 vols. Tokyo: Keisō Shobō, 1966–79.
Toscano, Alberto. *Late Fascism: Race, Capitalism and the Politics of Crisis*. London: Verso, 2023.
Traverso, Enzo. *The New Faces of Fascism: Populism and the Far Right*. Trans. David Broder. London: Verso, 2019.
Uno Kōzō. *Theory of Crisis*. Trans. Ken C. Kawashima. Historical Materialism Book Series, Vol. 251. Leiden: Brill, 2022.
Walker, Gavin. *The Sublime Perversion of Capital: Marxist Theory and the Politics of History in Modern Japan*. Asia-Pacific: Culture, Politics, and Society. Durham, NC: Duke University Press, 2016.
———. "Fascism and the Metapolitics of Imperialism | Historical Materialism," May 8, 2021. https://www.historicalmaterialism.org/blog/fascism-and-metapolitics-imperialism.
———. *The Sublime Perversion of Capital: Marxist Theory and the Politics of History in Modern Japan*. Durham, NC: Duke University Press, 2016.
Walker, Gavin, ed. "Revolution and Retrospection." *The Red Years: Theory, Politics, and Aesthetics in the Japanese '68*. London: Verso, 2020.
Ward, Max M. *Thought Crime: Ideology and State Power in Interwar Japan*. Durham, NC: Duke University Press, 2019.
Wilson, George Macklin. "A New Look at the Problem of 'Japanese Fascism.'" *Comparative Studies in Society and History* 10, no. 4 (1968): 401–412.
Žižek, Slavoj. *Did Somebody Say Totalitarianism?: Five Interventions in the (Mis)use of a Notion*. London: Verso, 2011.

INDEX

Abe Jirō, 260
absolute surplus value, 302
absolutism, 9, 12, 14, 81, 181
abstraction, 182–84, 259
academy, the: and common sense, 53; and literary criticism, 190; and philology, 31–37; and state control of education, 130–32; and Watsuji Tetsurō's ethics, 104–7. *See also* intelligentsia; literature
accumulation. *See under* capitalism
active spirit, 229, 233, 252
actuality (*jissai*), 304n26, 318n7
aestheticism, 191
Age of Enlightenment, 61–76, 260–61. *See also* enlightenment
agrarian fundamentalism, 86, 94–98, 253, 289, 291, 306n52; agrarian villages as a spiritual assemblage, 95–96; and autonomy of village life, 96–97, 102; and feudalism, 139; Gondō Seikyō's "system studies" and, 96–98; and the Japanese family system, 101–2; and Japanism, 14; and mechanization of agriculture, 95; and militaristic consciousness, 139; Tachibana Kōzaburō and, 94–95, 102
agriculture: agriculturalism, 139; and Asiatic Mode of Production, 102; and categories of Japanism, 86; farmers, 212, 286, 288; and Japanese capitalism, 286. *See also* agrarian fundamentalism; village life
Aikawa Haruki, 222–25
Aikawa Takaharu, 99
Anatomy of Fascism (Paxton), xix
ancestor worship, 125, 306n52
angst, xxv, 162, 208–9
animism, xxvi, 125, 306n52
antagonism, production of as means of cultural control, 134–35
anthropology, 15, 200; analysis of Watsuji's *Ethics as Anthropology*, 104–16; and hermeneutics, 29–30; and Marxist philosophy, 30; and philology, 30; Watsuji Tetsurō's use of term, 110, 254
antirationalism, 142
antitechnologism, 86, 141, 142, 155, 156
anxiety, 39, 195, 204, 208–9, 216, 233
Aono Suekichi, 232, 233, 318n1

INDEX

archaic, the, xv; archaic categories transplanted to the present in philological interpretation of classic texts, 13, 33–36; and categories of Japanism, 86; and contemporary problems, 33–35; and critique of philology, 33–36; and formulaic approach, 34–35; and restorationism, xxv, 126; and translation, 36–38
Archaism & Actuality (Harootunian), 296
Arendt, Hannah, xviii, 305n39
Aristotle, 42, 43, 44, 46, 111
Art & Science (journal), x–xi
Artistic Freedom League, 133–34
Artistic Restoration, 192, 198
arts, the, xxvii, 20, 191. *See also* literature; literaturism
Asianism, 14, 88–89, 99–102, 291. *See also* Pan-Asianism
Asian particularism, 79
Asiatic Mode of Production, 102, 308n10
Ast, Friedrich, 24
Aufklärung, 62, 66, 69–70, 73–75, 260, 261
axioms, and common sense, 45–47, 50

Baba Tsunego, 247, 284
Bacon, Francis, 72
"being," xiv; and the dialectic, 174–75; and Heidegger's hermeneutic phenomenology, 112–13; idealism as a philosophy of "being," 148; and materialism, 175; as movement or process, 174–76; and Nishida's philosophy, 167–70; phenomenology and the problem of being, 29; self-interpretation of, 29; and subjectivity and objectivity, 167–68; and Takahashi's philosophy, 181–84; and Tanabe's philosophy, 174; and Watsuji's ethics, 107, 109–10, 112, 115
Benjamin, Walter, ix, xii, 313n6
Bergson, Henri, 91, 150
Bharatiya Janata, 293
Bible, interpretation of, 24, 105
Birth of Biopolitics (Foucault), 295
Black Lives Matter, 302
Bloch, Ernst, ix, 294–96

Boeckh, A., 23, 24
Bopp, Franz, 21
bourgeoisie: and character of democracy in Japan, 286; and common sense, 55, 287; and constitutional fascism, 286; and crisis of capitalism, 155; English bourgeoisie, 48; and enlightenment, 261; and fascism supported by the middle classes, xxviii, 136–37, 288; and fascism viewed as progressive, 287; French bourgeoisie, 47, 276; and liberalism, 233; and Locke's conception of freedom, 72; and materialism, 247; and mechanistic worldview, 192; and Nishida's philosophy, 173; and party fascism, 289; political parties of, xxix, 288; and primitivization, 123. *See also* petite bourgeoisie
bourgeois philosophy: and antiscientism, 154–55; defined/described, xxv, 148; and ethics, 238; and literary liberalism, 236; Nishida's philosophy and, 148, 164, 166–73; and progress and development, 263–65; Takahashi's philosophy and, 184; and technology, 221
Brazil, 293
Brentano, Franz, 27, 114
Brexit, 293
Britain: English bourgeois materialism, 247; English Enlightenment, 62, 66, 71; fascism in, 286, 293; reactionary period of the late 1700s, 47–48
Brown, Wendy, 299
Buddhism, xxv, 9, 13, 30, 36, 87, 111
bungakushugi, xxiv. *See also* literaturism
bunkengakushugi, xxv. *See also* philologism
bureaucracy, xix, xxx, 8, 128–29, 288–89
Burke, Edmund, 47–48, 57
bushidō ("way of the warrior"), xvi, 138, 314n1

Calverton, V. F., 80
capitalism, xiv, xxi; as always in crisis, xxviii, 307n61; antagonism between capitalism and previous feudal system, 122; and antiscientism, 155;

INDEX

and building an antifascist thought, 301–2; and bureaucratic and militaristic conditions in Japan, xix, 128–29; capital accumulation, xxviii, 27, 295, 298, 300, 302, 313n5; capitalists and social strata, 212; character of capitalism in Japan, 283, 286; and classic texts, 253; commodification of labor-power in the production of "absolute surplus value," 302; and controlled economy, 283; crises of the modern era, 299, 300; crisis of the 1930s, xxiv, xxvi–xxviii, 27, 89–90, 148, 155, 317n2; and cultural control, 128–29; democracy of the early capitalist era, 286; as enemy of Japanese liberalism, 237; and fascism, xxviii, 295, 298, 321n8; and feudality, xxvii–xxviii; finance capitalism, xxii, 295, 298; and freedom, 283; and imperialism, xxviii, 136, 298; and individualism, 122; and intelligence, 219; and Kawai Eijirō's liberalism, 237; and liberalism as a historical category, 233; managerial capitalism and the ideology of control, 122; monopoly capitalism, xxvii, 80–81, 122, 283, 298; neoliberalism, 295–96, 298–301; and origins of liberalism, 16, 283 (*see also* economic liberalism); "overthrow capitalism" slogan, 290–91; and political parties, xxix; and primitivizationism and nativizationism, 309n17; and restorationism, 122, 125–26; and retreat of economic liberalism, 283–84; shared capitalist logic of developed nations, 35; and social control, xxix, 80–81, 122; "spirit" of, 78

categories: general theory of, 159; liberalism as a literary category, 161; literary categories, 158–61; literary categories replacing philosophical categories, 194–95, 235; moral categories, 233–35; and Nishida's philosophy, 167; philosophical categories, 159–60; "reality" category, 195; and technology or technique, 220–21, 226; theological categories, 155–56

Catholicism, 9–10, 16, 27, 72
Césaire, Aime, 322n24
characterology, 199
Charlottesville riots of 2017, 293–95, 299–300, 302
China. *See* Manchuria, Japanese conquest of
"chosen" people, 275
Christianity, xviii, xxxi, 9, 78, 155, 305n39. *See also* Catholicism
civilization, 62. *See also* enlightenment
Civilization and Enlightenment (Katō), 259
Civilization and Enlightenment (Miyaki), 259
"Civilization and Enlightenment" slogan, 259–61
civil society: and communalism, xxiv, 108, 110; and control of education, 129–32; and control of speech, 132–33; and cultural control, 128–35; and fascist social expression, 294; and feudalist ideology, 139–40 (*see also* feudalism); ideal of nation of soldiers, 138, 238; and logic of nothingness, 249–50; metaphor of the citizen, state, and society as a family, 123–24; and militaristic consciousness (*see* military); military authorities as a social stratum of society, 137–38; military bureaucrats distinguished from soldiers, 137–38; and Nishida's philosophy, 249–50; and nonstate forms of fascism, 294, 295; and the production of social antagonism, xxix; rural villages (*see* agrarian fundamentalism; village life); social strata and the intelligentsia, 212–15; and Tanabe's philosophy, 249–50; "unity of soldiers and farmers" concept, 140–42; urban vs. rural society, 95–96. *See also* bourgeoisie; class; family system; intelligentsia; masses, the; petite bourgeoisie; proletariat; social control; village life

"clarification of the Imperial Way/ national essence" slogan, xxx, 291

class, xiv; classes giving rise to different types of social thought, 282; and classification of ideologies as fascist, liberal, or Marxist, 242; class struggle and capital accumulation, 311n4; and common sense, 48–49, 58, 60; critique of class theory of the intelligentsia, 203–9, 212–14; distinguished from social stratum, 212; and farmers as citizen-soldiers, 139; fascism supported by the middle classes, xxviii, 28, 136–37, 194, 288, 289, 295, 298; intelligentsia as straddling all social classes, 217; and Marxist view of intelligentsia, 210–13; military authorities as a social stratum of society, 137–38; and samurai heritage, 138, 139; and social antagonism, xxix; and sociology, 267–68; "unity of soldiers and farmers" concept, 140–42; "white working class" as a pseudoclass, 297–98, 300. See also bourgeoisie; middle class; petite bourgeoisie; proletariat

classicism, 75

Clauss, Ludwig Ferdinand, 36

Cohen, Hermann, 111, 179, 316–17n4

colonialism, 92, 298, 299, 302, 322n24. See also imperialism; Manchukuo; Manchuria, Japanese conquest of

common sense, xiii–xvi, 20, 39–60, 310n5; and ancient Greece, 41–42, 55; aristocratic common sense, xxx, 48–49; Aristotle and, 42–44, 46; bourgeois common sense, xxx, xxxi, 49–50, 59; Burke and, 47–48, 57; contradictions of, xxx, xxxi, 41, 50, 53, 58–60; defined/described, xxix–xxx; and demagogy, xxx; and empiricism, 44–47, 48; and enlightenment, 69, 71; and everydayness, 39–40, 57–60; and fascism, xxx; formal content distinguished from content of individual common sense, 51–53; and the human heart, 44–45, 47; inadequacy when classifying ideologies, 244; and inner knowledge, 43–45; intelligentsia and, 40; and intuition, 45–47, 49; Kant and, 49–50; liberal and Protestant common sense in agreement with bourgeois social common sense, 16–17; and the literary world, 40–41; and the masses, xxx, xxxii, 17, 54–57; and materialism, xxxi–xxxii, 60; and the military, 142; as a norm, 53–55, 58; and perception, 42–43; and philosophy, 41–42; and politics, 56; and primitivization, 142; proletarian common sense, xxxi–xxxii, 59, 310n11; and public opinion, 54–57, 59; Reid and, 44–47, 50–51, 54; relation between common sense as content and common sense as a level or standard, xxx, 52–53; shared common sense between individuals in a society, 46; as shared sensation, 43–44; sixth-sense concept of, 42–43; and social class, 48–49, 58–60; and sociology, 267; of soldiers, 51; as a standard and as an ideal, xxx, xxxi, 54–60; and technology, 222; weaknesses in Reid's conception, 47–49

Common Sense School, 44–48, 71

communalism, and Japanese society, xxiv, 108, 110

communism: fascism in opposition to, 306n48; Gondō Seikyō and, 97

Comte, Auguste, 27, 114

Confucianism, 13, 87, 98

consciousness: analysis of the liberal mind, 198–202; and Nishida's philosophy, 168–69; and phenomenology, 27, 113; and the senses, 46; and shared common sense between individuals, 46

constitutional fascism, xx, xxviii–xxxi, 285–89; defined/described, xxviii–xxix

constitutional liberalism, 240

INDEX

Constitution of Liberty (Hayek), 295
constitutive control, xxix, 129–32
A Contribution to the Critique of Political Economy (Marx), 227
control: and capitalism, 128–29; cultural control in Japan, 128–35; Kant and, 130; positive and negative forms of, 129–31; social control (*see* social control)
counter-revolution of property (Du Bois's term), 321n8
Cowen, Tyler, 301
creativity, 52–53
criticism: critique of class theory of the intelligentsia, 203–9, 212–14; difficulties of critiquing unscientific adversaries, 31; and enlightenment, 69; function of, 190; and hermeneutic philosophy, 152–54; and idealism, 147–62; internal and external criticism, 79–84; and the "Japanese spirit," 77–87; literary critics and criticism, 187–95; materialism's method of scientific criticism described, 19–20; and Nishida's philosophy, 163–73; and philology, 30–38; and principle of everydayness, 58; problem of ideological criticism, 79–87; readership of criticism journals, 214; and relation between literature and philosophy, 187–95; and science, 189, 191; and Takahashi Satomi's philosophical method, 176–85; and Watsuji Tetsurō's ethics, 107. *See also other philosophies and topics*
The Critique of Pure Reason (Kant), 67
Cudworth, Ralph, 48
cultural control, 128–35. *See also* social control
cultural freedom, 9–10, 68, 286–87. *See also* cultural liberalism
cultural liberalism, xxi, xxvi, 197, 232–36, 270, 286–87, 301; Aono Suekichi and, 232, 233; and current critiques of fascism, 294; defined/described, 232; and enlightenment, 64–65, 68; examples, 232–33; and individual consciousness, xxi–xxii; liberal philosophy grounded in, 233–36; and Nishida's philosophy, 173; no relation between cultural liberalism and political liberalism, 287; Ōmori Gitarō and, 232; progression from economic liberalism to cultural liberalism, 232; as remaining home of liberalism, 197–98, 233, 235; and socialism, 287. *See also* literaturism
Cultural Unification movement, 17
culture: modern use of term, 260; shifting meanings, 261; and translation issues, 36–37
customs, xiv, xxvii, xxviii, xxix, 96, 97, 119–20, 259–60, 272

Dasein (Heidegger's term), xv, 112
De Anima (Aristotle), 42
Deborin, Abram, xi
Deborinism, 83
deformal subsumption, 302
deism, 72
demagogy, xxix, xxx, 277–79, 298, 300, 302, 321n10
democracy, 7; bourgeois democracy, 197–98; character of democracy in Japan, xxx–xxxi, 8, 285–89; and common sense, 48; constitutional fascism, xx, xxviii–xxxi, 285–89; disconnect from political liberalism in Japan, 285; and the early capitalist era, 286; as ideology of Japanese landowners and bourgeoisie, 286; and liberalism, xx, 8, 252, 285; and literary liberalism, 252; and public opinion, 59; reactions against democratic movements, 89
democratic feudalism (Robin's term), 321n6
Dentsu (communication company), 133
Descartes, René, 45, 74
development, 263–65
The Development of the Monistic View of History (Plekhanov), xi

dialectic, 174–75; and common sense, 50, 53; dialectical inversions and the development of fascism in Japan, xxvi; and enlightenment, 76 (*see also* enlightenment: contradictions of); Hegel and, 50, 182–83; Kant and, 50, 67; and movement and stasis, 180; and Nishida's philosophy, 170–71; and Takahashi's philosophy, 178, 182–84; Tanabe's "absolute dialectic," 174

dialectical materialism, ix, xi, xx, 20, 68, 245–48

dictatorship, 286; as not the only form of fascism, xxviii–xxix, 286

Dilthey, Wilhelm, 26–27, 80, 113, 263

Dilworth, David, 312n8

Dostoevsky, Fyodor, xxv, 148

doxa (ancient Greek concept), 41–42, 55

Driesch, Hans, 130

Droysen, J. G., 26

Du Bois, W. E. B., 321n8

East, the: Eastern elements in Nishida's philosophy, 164–65; and the family system, 101–2; and Japanese fascism, xxx; Ōkawa Shūmei's views of East and West as antagonistic, 99–100; and social antagonism, xxix; as spiritual, 100. *See also* Asianism; Orientalism; Pan-Asianism

Eastern Ethics (Nishi), 32, 104–5, 107

economic freedom, 197

economic liberalism, 64, 72, 197; defined/described, 232; fascist-friendly type of economic liberalism, 283; and Kawai Eijirō's liberalism, 237, 238; and morality, 234–35; as original type of liberalism, 8, 197, 232, 283; political liberalism arising from, 232; retreat of, 283–84

education, state control of, 129–32

elitism, 274–75

emperor: emperor as commander-in-chief of the military, 137; and metaphor of the citizen, state, and society as a family, 124; organ theory of the emperor, 130–32, 241, 268, 286, 314n5

empiricism, 44–49, 66, 72

engineers, xxiv, 217–19

enlightenment, 61–76; active function of, 69; "Civilization and Enlightenment" slogan, 259–61; and common sense, 71; conditions of, 64, 66–68, 72–73; contemporary meaning, 61–64, 68–70, 76; and cultural liberalism, 64–65; English Enlightenment, 62, 66, 71; and fog and darkness of contemporary Japan, 62–63; French Enlightenment, 62, 64–66, 71, 72, 75, 76; Fukazawa Yukichi and, 70; German Enlightenment, 49, 62, 65–66, 72–73, 75, 76, 260; historical Age of Enlightenment, 61–76, 260–61; Japanese Enlightenment, 17, 70; Kant and, 65–68, 72–75; and law of contradiction, 66; and liberalism, 68, 72; Locke and, 64, 72; and mechanism, 74–76; Newton and, 74; and rationalism, 73–74; two senses of word, 61–64, 66–69, 70, 233; Voltaire and, 72, 73; Wolff and, 66, 73–75

entelechy, 130

equality, 48, 57, 199, 200, 232, 276

Essay Concerning Human Understanding (Locke), 72

ethical liberalism, 237–38

ethics: analysis of Watsuji's *Ethics as Anthropology*, 104–16; and anthropology, 30; and history, 262–63; Nish Shin'ichirō's *Eastern Ethics*, 104–5; as the principle of humanity, 107–8; and progress as a philosophy of history, 262–63; superiority of Japanese ethics, 107, 110; Western ethics, 111

Ethics as Anthropology (Watsuji), 15, 30, 31, 104–16

ethics-ism, 115–16, 238–39

ethnicity, xxiv; and enlightenment, 68; ethnic nationalism, xxvi, 125 (*see also* nativizationism); and familialism as representative form of restorationism, 125; the Japanese as the model ethnicity, 111, 254; and the "Japanese reality," 77; "national unity" cabinets and ethnic harmony, 312n14; and state-regulated prostitution, 120

Evans, Richard, 307n63

everydayness, 20; and common sense, xxxi–xxxii, 57–60, 310n11; and current expressions of fascism in the U.S., 295; intelligentsia's view of, 39–40; principle of everydayness, xi–xvi, 40, 57–58; and vulgarism, 39–40

factionalism, 200, 201

facts, and interpretation, 151–54

familialism, 122–27, 140, 306n52

family system in Japan, 101–2; collapse of, 120–23; and individualism, 120–22, 124; metaphor of the citizen, state, and society as a family, 123–24; and prostitution, 119; and restorationism, 119–25; social psychology of, 124; and Tokugawa period, 140; and women, 121, 123

farmers, 212, 286, 288. *See also* agrarian fundamentalism; village life

Farm Village Studies (Tachibana), 102

fascism, ix, xvi–xxxii, 14, 294, 306n39; actual vs. ideal constituency of, xxix, 291; and advancing the interests of finance capitalism, 295, 298, 321n8; alternate labels, xviii–xix; and anticipated losses, 300; and anticommunism, 306n48; and antitechnologism, 86; building an antifascist thought, 301–2; and capitalism, xxviii, 295, 298, 321n8; chosen elites and their leaders, 275–76; and classification of ideologies, 242; and common sense, xxx; and conquest of Manchuria, 267; constitutional fascism, xx, xxviii–xxxi, 285–89; and controlled economy, 291–92; and control of literature, 133; and coup attempts (*see under* Japan); debate over fascism in Japan, xvii–xviii; defined/described, xvii, xix, xxviii, 136, 302, 313n5; defining feature of Japanese fascism, 292; and demagogy, xxix, xxx, 277–79, 298, 300, 302; development in Japan, xxvi–xxxii, 291; dictatorship as not the only possible political form, xxviii–xxix, 286; differences between fascism of the 1930s and today, 295; in Europe, 14, 275, 281 (*see also* Nazism); fascist movements in Japan, 268, 291; fascist movements in the modern world, 293–302; fascization of an accumulation regime, 298–99; and feudalism, xxxi, 292 (*see also* feudalism); and freedom (*see also* economic liberalism); and idealism, 254; and "ideology of the clarification of the Japanese national essence," 291; and imperialism/militarism, 137–39, 298; inadequacy as a system of thought, 291; and Japanese parliamentary system, 285–86; and the "Japanese spirit," 79, 81; Japanism as the Japanese form of, xxvi, 14, 136–43, 231; liberalism's relation to, ix, xix–xxiii, xxvi, xxvii, 17, 283, 292, 300–301 (*see also under* Japanism); liberals' personal opposition to fascism and Japanism, xxi–xxiii, 16, 17, 202, 294, 305–6n39; and literary liberalism, 252; and literaturism, xxv, 194, 252; and the masses, 276, 277, 279–80; materialism as antagonistic to, 231; middle class imagining that fascism represents their interests, xxviii, 288, 289, 295, 298; middle class support for, xxviii, 28, 136–37, 194, 288, 289, 295, 298; military fascism, 267, 289–91; and mimicry of liberalism, 286; and neoliberalism, 295–96, 298–301; and Nishida's philosophy, 165–66; nonstate, social forms of, 294, 295; and organization of the masses under a supreme leader, 276; and philologism, xxv, 253–54;

fascism (*continued*)
  and political parties, 288–89; and progressivism, 261; publications and scholarship on modern expressions of fascism, xvii, xix, 296, 298; and religion, 253–54; self-understanding of fascists, 243, 261; split between fascism of the 1930s and fascism in a broad, universal sense, 296; and totalitarianism, 14; unification of fascist groups, 291; in the U.S., 293–302; viewed as a problem of the state, 295
Fascism: A Very Short Introduction (Passmore), xvii
feudalism, xxvii–xxviii; and agrarian villages, 102, 139–40; antagonism between capitalism and previous feudal system, 122; and Catholic Church, 72; and crisis of the 1930s, xxvii–xxviii; and defining feature of Japanese fascism, 292; as enemy of Japanese liberalism, 237; and enlightenment, 62, 63; and familialism, 140; and fascism, xxxi, 292; feudal elements in Nishida's philosophy, 164–65; historical feudal system distinguished from feudalist ideology in present civil society, 139–40; and the Japanese state, 8, 288–89, 305n34; and liberalism as progressive compared to restorationist thought, 16; liberals' personal opposition to, 202; and militaristic consciousness, 138; and monarchy, 72; and nativizationism, 141; and restorationism, 122, 140; and "unity of soldiers and farmers" concept, 140–41
Feuerbach, Ludwig, 30, 111
Fichte, J. G., xxvii, 67, 167
forces of production, 37, 74, 222, 226, 236
Foucault, Michel, 295
France, 287; fascism in, 286; French bourgeoisie, 47, 276; French bourgeois materialism, 246; French Enlightenment, 62, 64–66, 71, 72, 75, 76; French materialism, 71; French Revolution, 47, 48, 75
Frederick II (Frederick the Great), 62, 65, 69, 75
freedom: and capitalism, 283 (*see also* economic liberalism); cultural freedom, 9–10, 68, 286–87 (*see also* cultural liberalism); and cultural liberalism, xxvi; and development of fascism in Japan, xxvii; economic freedom, 197 (*see also* economic liberalism); and enlightenment, 64–65, 68, 72; "freedom from," xxi, xxii, 9, 12, 285, 307n2; and hermeneutic philosophy's inability to address real-world problems, 162; and idealism, 196, 262–63; and Kawai Eijirō's liberalism, 240; and liberalism, xxvi, 9, 12, 240, 285; and literature, 196; Locke and, 72; and Marxism, 240; and negative control, 131; origin of concept, xxvii, 196–97; and personal "passion," xxv, 162; and philosophy, 196–97; political freedom, 72, 197 (*see also* political liberalism); positive and negative forms of, xxi, 241; and religious consciousness, 9–10; and sentimental liberalism, 285; socialist control of, 284
Friche, V. M., 80
Fujisawa Chikao, 240–41
Fujiwara Mototsune, 96
fukkōshugi, xxv. *See also* restorationism
Fukuda school of thought, 255
Fukuda Tokuzō, 255
Fukumoto Kazuo, x
Fukuzawa Yukichi, 70, 246
Funayama Shin'ichi, 246

Gakugei jiyū dōmei. *See* Liberal Arts Confederation
genjitsu, 99, 151, 195, 304n26, 318n7. *See also* reality
genshikashugi, xv, xxvi, 123, 140, 304n25, 309n17, 313n2, 315n3. *See also* nativizationism; primitivizationism

INDEX

The German Ideology (Marx and Engels), xi, xix, xxvi
Germany, 323n40; German Enlightenment, 62, 65–66, 72–73, 75, 76, 260; German idealism, 28; German Romanticism, 25, 69, 167, 233. *See also* Nazism
Gide, André, 162
gijutsu, 220. *See also* technique
God, 155, 164
Goethe, J. W. von, 74
Gondō Seikyō, 96–98, 320n8
"good wife, wise mother" ideology, 121, 123
Gorai Sosen, 230
grammar, 21, 23, 25
Gramsci, Antonio, ix, 294
Greater Learning for Women (educational text of 1729), 123
Greece, ancient, 31, 41–42, 55, 78, 105
Greece, modern, 293
Green, Thomas Hill, 237–38, 318n3
Griffin, Roger, xviii

Hani Gorō, x, xi
Harootunian, Harry D., xii, 296
Hasegawa Nyōzekan, 233–34, 246–47, 284
Hattori Shisō, x
Hayek, Friedrich, 295
Hegel, G. W. F., xxvii, 27, 50, 57, 67, 74, 167; and the dialectic, 50, 182–83; and ethics, 111, 262; and history, 67–68; and idealism, 149–50; and inference, 244; and logic of existence, 172
Heian period, 140
Heidegger, Martin, xi, xv, xxv, 30, 230; and antiscientism, 154; and cultural liberalism, 287; and hermeneutic phenomenology, 29, 112–14; and philological phenomenology, 27–29; Watsuji Tetsurō and, 110
Heimann, Betty, 36, 309n18
Heisenberg's uncertainty principle, xii
hermeneutic philosophy: and antiscientism, 154–55; critique of, 152–54; and inability to address actual problems, 153–54, 162; and interpretation of facts, 151–54; and *Lebens* philosophy, 153; and literaturism, 162, 252 (*see also* literaturism); metaphysics as, 150–51; and Nishida's philosophy, 252; as the second determination of idealism, 150–51; and theological categories, 155–56
hermeneutics: and ancient Greece, 24; and anthropology, 29–30; application beyond classic texts in the early modern era, 24; and common sense, 60; defined/described, 23; Dilthey and, 26–28; Heidegger and, 29, 112–14; and history, 105–6; and Japanese imperialism, 298; and liberalism, xxiii, 15, 235, 298; and literary liberalism, 235; and logic of nothingness, 250; and philology/philologism, 24–27, 38, 87, 105, 153; and philosophy, 23–25, 28, 30, 106; problems with expansion beyond original use, 106–7; Schleiermacher and, 24–25; and Watsuji Tetsurō's ethics, 105–8, 111–16. *See also* hermeneutic philosophy
Heyer, Heather, 293
Hirano Yoshitarō, 78, 81
Hirschfeld, Magnus, 323n40
history: and categorical logic of nonmodern peoples, 35–36; and critique of philology, 33; and development, 263–65; and development of philology, 25–26; Dilthey and, 26–27, 113; Droysen and, 26–27; and ethics, 262–63; Hegel and, 67–68; and hermeneutics, 105–6; and the "Japanese spirit," 92–93; Kakunoki Inshin and, 93; Kant and, 67; and liberalism, 15; and Marxism, 246, 262–63; and meanings of progress and development, 260–66; Miki Kiyoshi and, 246; and myth, 92–93; and philologism and Japanists' "sense of national history," 14–15; philologism and the literaturist

history (*continued*)
"interpretation" of history, 13; and philology and hermeneutics elevated to philosophical method, 26–29; and principle of everydayness, xi–xvi; relation to philosophy, xi–xiii; and restorationism, xxv–xxvi (*see also* restorationism); and understanding, 25–26; Yasuoka Shōtoku and, 92–93. *See also* philosophy of history

History and Repetition (Karatani), 297

Hitler, Adolf, 89, 275, 307n63

Hobbes, Thomas, 48

Hoffmann, Ernst, 33

How Fascism Works (Stanley), 296

"human": relationality of the human, 108–9; and Watsuji Tetsurō's ethics, 107, 108, 110, 115–16; Western sense of, 110

humanism, 72, 111, 116, 199–200, 233, 235, 287

Humboldt, Wilhelm von, 22, 25

Hume, David, 72

Hungary, 293

Huntington, Samuel P., 305n35

Husserl, E. G. A., 27, 36, 113, 168

Hutcheson, Francis, 44, 46

Ichikawa Kenzō, 121–23

idealism, xv, xxiii–xxiv, 244; absolutism as arising from active, positive idealism in Japan, 14; as antagonistic toward materialism, 244; and antiscientism, 154–55; and common sense, 60; critique of idealism and hermeneutic philosophy, 147–62; current lack of true thinkers, 255; disguised under other names, xxv, 148–62; examples of flaws, 239; and fascism, 254; and feudalism, 140–41; formalism and interpretive philosophy as characteristic of, 12; as a form of thought, 244–45; and freedom, 196, 262–63; German idealism, 28; Hegel and, 149–50; and hermeneutic philosophy, 150–51, 156 (*see also* hermeneutic philosophy); inferiority of idealist philosophies, 249–55; and Japanese spirit, 78; Kawai Eijirō and, 237–39; and liberalism, 8–9, 11, 14, 237–39; and literaturism, 156–62; and Marxism, 237, 239; and metaphysics, 149–50, 156, 250; Nishida and, 172–73; and philology, 38; as philosophy of "being," 148; popular understanding of, 244; and primitivizationism and nativizationism, 141–42; religious idealism, 9; and restorationism, 126, 140–41; Takahashi and, 181, 184; and whole-part relation, 184

identity politics, 294, 301

ideology: and categories of Japanism, 85–86; classification of ideologies as fascist, liberal, or Marxist, 242–44; Japanism as "the Japanese ideology," 136–43; overview of Tosaka's critique, xiii–xxxii; political nature of ideologies, 243; and primitivizationism, 140–41; problem of ideological criticism, 79–87; self-understanding of fascists, liberals, and Marxists, 243. *See also* thought; *specific movements and ideologies*

ideology of literaturism. *See* literaturism

ideology of restoration. *See* restorationism

imperialism, xxii, xxvii, xxx, 322n24; "after-affects" of, 298–99; arising from monopoly and finance capitalism, xxviii, 136, 298; and hermeneutics and philology, 298; imperialistic/militaristic essence of fascism, 137–39, 298; Japanese expansion into Asian continent, xxvii, xxx, 100, 267; and social control, 80–81

Imperial Way, xvi, 102, 291, 320n2

India, 293

individualism, 102; and capitalism, 122; and freedom, xxvii; and the Japanese

INDEX

family system, 120–22, 124; and liberalism, 199–200; and the social contract, 48; and village life, 102; and Watsuji Tetsurō's ethics, 108; and women, 122

individuals: and cultural liberalism, xxi–xxii; individual spiritualisms in the modern U.S., 301; and the masses, 276; and modern concept of "culture," 260; personal opposition to fascism and Japanism, xxi–xxiii, 16, 17, 202, 294, 305–6n39; personal "passion," xxv, 162; physical pragmatism of the individual body, 254; social development of personality, xxvi, 238. *See also* personality; sentimental liberalism

Inquiry into the Human Mind on the Principles of Common Sense (Reid), 46

Institute for Materialism Studies, x

intelligence, 208–9; and capitalism, 219; cult of intelligence, 252; defined/described, 218; and engineers and scientists, 217–19; ideology of the superiority of intelligence, 11–12, 203–4; and intelligentsia, 203–9, 217–18; and the literary arts, 216–17; and material relations of production within society, 217–18; and medieval monasticism, 217; as one of the skills of labor power, 229; and sensation, 218

intelligentsia, 203–19; and anthropology, 30; and anxiety, 39, 204, 208–9, 216; assertiveness and active nature of intellectuals, 215, 217, 219; and class conflict, 208, 210; and common sense, 40–41; critique of class theory of the intelligentsia, 203–9, 212–14; culturalist theory of the intellectual, 215–17; and cultural liberalism, 286–87; dispersed across all social classes, 217; and enlightenment, 63–64; and hermeneutic philosophies, 252–53; impotence/powerlessness of, 204–5, 210–11; and industrial engineers, xxiv, 217–19; and intelligence, 203–9; and leadership, 210–11; and literaturism, 11–12; malignant intellectuals, 205–8; Marxism and, 193, 210–13, 219; and material relations of production within society, 217–19; membership of, 218; negative theory of, 210–12; and Nishida's philosophy, 166; and objectivism, 245; and opposition to the bourgeoisie, 205–6, 216; and opposition to the proletariat, 205–6, 211, 216; and philology, 31–37; positive theory of the active intellectual, 211–12, 215–16; problematization of, 208–19; and progressivism, 272; and religion, 9; and the right to govern society, 204, 216; salaryman ideology theory of the intellectual, 214–15; self-perception of, 205–6; and social strata, 212–14; sociological phenomenology theory of the intellectual, 214–15; and technology, 228–29; translated as the intellectual class, 212; views on everydayness, 39–40

International Culture Promotion Association, 134–35

interpretation: and hermeneutic philosophy, 151–54; and Takahashi's philosophy, 180; and theological categories, 155–56. *See also* hermeneutics

intuition, and common sense, 45–46

Inukai Tsuyoshi, 312n14, 320n8

irony, 40

Ishihara Jun, 254

Ishihara Kanji, xvi

Ishikawa Chiyomatsu, 247

Israel, 293

Itō Shōshin, 91–92

Iwanami Kōza, 36

Jacobins, 47, 48

James, William, 150

Japan: and agriculture (*see* agrarian fundamentalism; agriculture); belief in Japan as unique and sui generis, xviii, 14, 128–30, 305n35; character of capitalism in, 283, 286; character of democracy in (*see* Japanese state); conquest of Manchuria, xxvii, 100, 267, 311n2; and controlled economy, 283; coup attempt of February 26, 1936, x, xvi, 304n28, 320n2; coup attempt of May 15, 1932, 99, 290, 312n14, 320n8; crisis/emergency of Tosaka's era, xxiv, xxvii–xxviii, 89–90, 148, 155, 221, 238, 264, 278, 288; debate over fascism in, xvii–xviii; election of 1939, 278; family system in (*see* family system in Japan); fascism in (*see* fascism; Japanism); feudal elements in, xxvii–xxviii, 62–63 (*see also* feudalism); government of (*see* Japanese state); and ideal of nation of soldiers, 138, 238; and imperialism, 298 (*see also* conquest of Manchuria *under this heading*); Japanese society as being in a reactionary period, 89, 261, 271–72, 292; liberalism as fundamental social consciousness of, 7–8, 16, 305n34; Meiji period (*see* Meiji period); and militaristic consciousness, 137–39, 289–91; and modernity, xvii–xviii; nationalism in, xviii–xix, 89, 90, 97–98, 125, 291 (*see also* Japanism); and national security, xxx, 288, 290; as a nation of "the communion of shrines and grains" (Gondō Seikyō's characterization), 96; political parties (*see* political parties); retreat of Marxist cultural movements in, 156, 211, 233, 271–72; three imperial treasures of, 92–93; three strands of social thought in, 282–92 (*see also* fascism; Japanism; liberalism; materialism; socialism); Tokugawa period, 89, 138, 140. *See also* civil society; Japanese state; military; *and following headings*

Japanese Cultural Institute, 134
Japanese Cultural Spirit Research Institute, 132
The Japanese Ideology (Tosaka), ix; overview of contents, xix–xxxii; relevance for current situation in the U.S. and elsewhere, 293–302
Japanese Literary Institute, 133–34
Japanese spirit, 77–87, 253; and agrarian fundamentalism, 94–98; essence of, 90–94, 98; and fascism, 79, 81, 291; Itō Shōshin and, 91–92; Kakunoki Inshin and, 93; Kihara Masami and, 91–92; Minoda Muneki and, 98–99; and problem of ideological criticism, 79–87; and rejection of the liberal theory of the state, 123; sense of superiority over all others, 98–102; Takasu Hojirō and, 90–91; Yasuoka Shōtoku and, 92–93
Japanese spiritualism, xxvii, 77–87; and agrarian fundamentalism, 94–95; and antitechnologism, 86; expansion of, 101; and familialism as representative form of restorationism, 125; Hiran Yoshitarō and, 78; and Japanism, 14, 98; and militaristic consciousness, xxx
Japanese state: and absolute monarch, 9–10; as authoritative, total state, 241; bureaucrats and "new bureaucrats," 288–89; and constitutional fascism, xx, xxviii–xxxi, 285–89; and constitutional liberalism, 240; and control of education, 129–32; and control of literature, 133–35; and control of public opinion, 133; and control of speech, 132–33; and cultural control, 128–35; and democracy, 8; feudalistic elements, 8, 288–89, 305n34 (*see also* feudalism); and Kawai Eijirō's liberalism, 238; metaphor of the citizen, state, and society as a family, 123–24; and national unity, 268; national unity cabinets, xxx, 30, 312n14, 320n8; and prostitution, 117–21; and sociology,

INDEX

268; and Tanabe Hajime's philosophy, 249–50. *See also* political parties
Japanism: and absolutism, 12, 14; Aikawa Takaharu and, 99; as antagonistic toward liberalism, 8; categories of, 85–86; and common sense, 59 (*see also* common sense); and constitutional fascism (*see* constitutional fascism); defined/described, 14, 307n62; and enlightening the masses, 17; and ethics-ism, 116; and European fascist philosophy, 14; family resemblance to liberalism, 15; and the family system, 101–2; as the Japanese form of fascism, xxvi, 14, 136–43, 231; as "the Japanese ideology," 136–43; and Japanese spirit, 77–87; Japanist ethics, 111, 116 (*see also* Watsuji Tetsurō); liberalism as antagonistic to, 231; liberalism's relation to, xxvi, 12, 15–17; liberals' lack of defenses against, xxii; liberals' personal opposition to, xxii, 16, 17 (*see also* sentimental liberalism); liberal support for the Japanist Enlightenment movements, 17; materialism as antagonistic to, 15, 230–31; Matsunaga Zai and, 99; Matsuoka Yōsuke and, 99; and militaristic consciousness, 137–39; overview of Japanist ideology, 88–103 (*see also* agrarian fundamentalism; Japanese spiritualism; Pan-Asianism); and problem of ideological criticism, 85–87; and the production of social antagonism, xxix; and progressivism, 263; and resolution of real problems replaced by philological interpretation of classic texts, 13; and "sense of national history," 13–15; and the Spirit of the Imperial Way, 142–43; and theory of the state, 241. *See also* agrarian fundamentalism; ethnic nationalism; fascism; Japanese spiritualism; Pan-Asianism; philologism; reactionary thought; restorationism
Jichi minpan (Gondō), 96, 97

jinrin, 107–8
jissai, 304n26, 318n7
journalism, 20, 59, 132, 152–53; and enlightenment, 69; journalists as sentimental liberals, 285; and Nishida's philosophy, 166; and principle of everydayness, 58
Joyce, James, 150

Kakunoki Inshin, 93
Kanokogi Kazunobu, 263
Kant, Immanuel: and common sense, 49–50; control principle, 130; and enlightenment, 65–68, 72–75; and ethics, 111; Newton and, 74
Karatani, Kojin, 297
Katō Hiroyuki, 247
Katō Suekichi, 259
Kawai Eijirō, 237–40, 247, 263, 284–85
Kawakami Hajime, 255, 319n9
Kawashima, Ken, 298
Kawauchi Tadahiko, xi
Keisuke Okada, 288
Kierkegaard, Søren, 287
Kihira Masami, 91–92
Kikuchi Kan, 286
Kimura Taiken, 37
Kimura Takatarō, 31
Kishi Nobusuke, xvi, 304n27, 322n24
Kita Ikki, xvi, 100, 289, 304n28, 320n2, 320n7
Kiyosawa Kiyoshi, 239, 247, 284
knowledge: and ancient Greece, 42; and common sense, 41, 43–45, 51–52, 54, 59; and creativity, 52–53; "ignorant masses" concept, 274–78; intelligentsia's pride in superiority of knowledge, 203–4; knowledge workers, 213–14; and opinion, 51–52
Kobayashi Hideo, 194, 252
Koizumi Shinzō, 239
Kōtoku Shūsui, 247, 318n5
Kōyama Iwao, 163
Kōzai Yoshishige, x, xi, 308n1
Kuchita Yasunobu, 101–2
Kume Masao, 286
Kurzweil, Ray, 323n41

Kuwaki Genyoku, 254
Kyoto School of philosophy, x, xi, 163, 165

Lambert, J. H., 74
Land, Nick, 319n6
language: connection between language and logic, 32–33; and linguistics, 22; translation of archaic texts, 36–38; Watsuji and, 106, 108–10. *See also* philology
Laqueur, Walter, xxiii
Laski, Harold, 72
Late Fascism (Toscano), 296
law of contradiction, 66, 74
law of identity, 66
Lebens philosophy. *See* Life [*Lebens*] philosophy
Lectures on Contemporary Philosophy (Tosaka), 163, 174
Le Dantec, Felix, 154, 316n7
Leibniz, G. W., 73, 74
Lenin, V. I., xi, 83, 148, 223, 265, 308n1
Leonardo da Vinci, 192
Le Pen, Marine, 296
Lévy-Bruhl, Lucien, 35, 309n17
Liberal Arts Confederation (Gakugei jiyū dōmei), 287, 320n1
liberalism, xxi, xxii, 305–6n39; analysis of the liberal mind, 198–202; as antagonistic toward Japanism, 231; as antagonistic toward Marxism, 239, 287; as antagonistic toward materialism, xxii–xxiii, 236; and anthropology, 15; and capitalism, 16, 237 (*see also* economic liberalism); and classification of ideologies, xx–xxi, 242; and common sense, xxx, 16–17; and connection between individuals, 200–201; constitutional liberalism, 240; cultural liberalism (*see* cultural liberalism); defined/described, 12, 196–97, 232, 237–38; and democracy, xx, 8, 197–98; dialectical inversion of, xxvi; economic liberalism (*see* economic liberalism); and enlightenment, 64–65, 68, 72; and equality, 200; ethical liberalism (Green's conception), 237–38; and factionalism, 201; fascism sometimes mimicking liberalism, 286; fascism's relation to, ix, xix–xxiii, xxvi–xxvii, 283, 292, 300–301; as foundation of social consciousness in Japan, 7–8, 16, 305n34; and freedom, xxi, 9, 12, 240, 285; and hermeneutics, xxiii, 15, 298 (*see also* hermeneutic philosophy; hermeneutics); as historical category, 233–34; and history, 15; and humanism, 199–200, 276; and idealism, 8–9, 11, 14, 237–39 (*see also* idealism); and identity politics, 294; and inadequate defenses against Japanism or fascism, 15–17, 293–94, 300–301; and individualism, 199–200; Japanism as antagonistic toward, 8; Kawai Eijirō's liberalism, 237–40, 247, 284–85; liberals' dislike of politics, 201, 202; liberals' personal opposition to fascism and Japanism, xxi–xxiii, 16, 17, 202, 294, 305–6n39; liberals' support for the Japanist Enlightenment movements, 17; as a literary category, 161; literary liberalism (*see* literary liberalism); and literaturism, xxiv, 193–202 (*see also* literaturism); Locke and, 72; and materialism, 16, 231; materialism as defender of, 241; mistaken public consciousness about character of, 286; as a moral category, 233–35; as not a middle ground between left and right, xxi–xxiii, 16; and opportunism, 201; origins of, 8, 197, 232, 283; and partisanship, 201–2; political liberalism (*see* political liberalism); and progress, 277; progression from natural law to utilitarianism to idealism, 237–38; and progressivism, 16, 198, 202, 263; as reactionary, 198, 202, 270; rejection of the liberal theory of the state, 123; and religious consciousness, 9–10, 307n3; resemblance to fascism and Japanism, xx–xxi, 15; retreat from

INDEX

economics and politics, xxiii, 232–33; and sectarianism, 201; self-understanding of liberals, 243; sentimental liberalism, xxi–xxiii, 284–85, 293, 294, 306n39, 317n1; and socialism, 237, 285; sources motivating liberalism's system of thought, 282–87; and stasis, 179; systematic liberalism, 282, 284, 287; and Takahashi's philosophy, 184; two senses of word, 233–34; writers as liberals, 161. *See also* cultural liberalism; economic liberalism; hermeneutics; liberal philosophy; literary liberalism; literaturism; political liberalism; sentimental liberalism

liberal philosophy, 235; and cultural liberalism, 233–36; different meanings of, 232; and hermeneutics, 10–12, 15; and idealism, 8–9, 11; and Japanist philosophy, 12, 15–17, 116; and Kawai Eijirō's liberalism, 237–40; literaturism arising from, 11, 12 (*see also* literaturism); Nishida's philosophy as type of, 236 (*see also* Nishida's philosophy); and opposition to materialism, 16; philologism arising from, 12–13 (*see also* philologism); and religious consciousness, 9–10; and totalitarianism, 15; two forms of, 235–36; and Watsuji Tetsurō's ethics, 116. *See also* literaturism; Nishida's philosophy

Life [*Lebens*] philosophy (Dilthey's conception), xi, 26, 27, 113, 153

Likud, 293

linguistics, 21–22

literary liberalism, 161, 193–202, 235–36, 252; and fascism, 252; and Nishida's philosophy, 236; as the political representation of literaturism, 161; and religious consciousness, 252; separation from political activities of liberalism, 252. *See also* literaturism

literature: assumption that literary arts are the highest standard of human intelligence, 216–17; and common sense, 40–41; and cultural liberalism, 286–87; and freedom, 196; and historical description and philosophy of history, 25–26; idealism and the cult of the literary, 251; liberation from political surveillance, 208; literary critics and criticism, 161, 187–95; literature of despair, 252; materialist literary theorists, 248; and politics, 192, 193; and problem of everydayness, 39; and Romanticism, 69; state control of, 133–35; and *tenkō* phenomenon, 286

literaturism (*bungakushugi*), xxiv, 11–12, 20, 100, 156–62, 186–95, 235–36; active spirit literature, 252; and anthropology and "the study of man," 15; arising from liberalist philosophy, xxiii, 11, 12; and Artistic Restoration, 192, 198; defined/described, xxiv; distinguished from idolatry of art for art's sake and aestheticism, 191; and fascism, xxv, 194, 252; and hermeneutics, 235, 252; and inability to address actual problems, xxv; and intelligentsia and ideology of the superiority of intelligence, 11–12; and interpretation of ancient literary texts, 13; and liberalism, xxiv, 193–202; and life existing for literature rather than literature existing for life, 193; as a link in the global chain of the crisis of capitalism, 317n2; and literary categories, 158–61, 194–95, 235; and literary liberalism, 161; literary representation, 160–61, 195, 251; "literature über alles," 157, 160; literaturization of philosophy, xxiv–xxv, 157–58, 250–51; and material production in society, 217; and philologism, xxv, xxvii, 20–21; and progressivism, 194; relation between literature and philosophy, 187–95, 235, 250–51; and thought, 250–51; and translation issues, xxiv

Locke, John, 44, 64, 72
logic, xiii, xiv; Buddhist logical tradition, 36; categorical logic of nonmodern peoples, 35–36; connection between language and logic, 32–33; and critique of philology, 32–33, 35–38; and familialism, 124; Hoffmann and, 33; liberalism as a logical system built on the idealist interpretation of freedom, 12; Nishida's logic of nothingness, 15, 168–72, 177, 249–50 (*see also* Nishida's philosophy); and partisanship, 201–2; and problem of ideological criticism, 82–83; Takahashi's logic of whole-part relationship, 177–78; and translation, 37–38
Luther, Martin, 24
Lytton, Lord (Victor Bulwer-Lytton), 99, 135, 312n12

managerial capitalism, 122
Manchukuo, x, 89, 92, 311n2, 312n12
Manchuria, Japanese conquest of, xxvii, 100, 267, 311n2
Manchurian Incident, 89, 101, 311n2
Maruyama Masao, xviii
Marx, Karl, 57, 313n6; and agriculture, 94–95; Aikawa Haruki and, 223–25; and ethics, 111; and materialism, 238–39; and problem of ideological criticism, 85; and the "productive organs of man," 224–25; and technology, 223–24, 228
Marxism, x, 7; and anthropology, 30; and building an antifascist thought, 302; and classification of ideologies, 242; and freedom, 240; and idealism, 237, 239; intelligentsia and, 193, 210–13, 219; and Kawai Eijirō's liberalism, 239; liberalism as opposed to, 239, 287; and materialism, 237–39; perspective on Japan as a link in a global capitalist chain, xxxi; perspective on Japan as not fully modern, 305n34; and philosophy of history, 246, 262; and progress, 262–65; and progressivism, 261; retreat of Marxist cultural movements in Japan, 156, 211, 233, 271–72; self-understanding of Marxists, 243; and social strata, 212; and technology, 223–24, as "thought," 272
masses, the, 273–81; and common sense, xxx, xxxii, 17, 54–57 (*see also* common sense); and demagogy, xxx, 277–79 (*see also* demagogy); democratic concept of, 277, 278; and everydayness, 40; and fascism, 276, 277, 279–80; "ignorant masses" concept, 274–78; Japanism and enlightening the masses, 17; as the majority of society, 273, 276–77, 279, 281; and need for rule by a "spiritual elite," xxx, 274–76; organizational capacity of, 276–77, 280; and progressivism, 266–69; proletarian organization of the masses, 268; and public opinion, 54–57, 59; and rationality, 276–77; relation to the proletariat, 266–67, 273–74, 278–81; social science understanding of, 273–74, 279–81; sociological understanding of, 268, 273–81; and spreading false rumors, 278; two-level concept of, 273–74
massification, 56, 59, 69, 76, 280
materialism: as antagonistic toward fascism, 231; as antagonistic toward idealism, 244, 246; as antagonistic toward Japanism, 15, 230–31; as antimetaphysical, 149; bourgeois materialism, 246–47; and common sense, xxxi–xxxii, 60; and criticism, 19–20; current lack of true thinkers, 255; and defense of liberalism, 241; defined/described, 20, 245–46; dialectical materialism, ix, xi, xx, 20, 68, 245–48; distorted understanding of, 245–46; and enlightenment, 66, 72; and ethics, 262–63; examples of

INDEX

materialist thinkers, 247–48; as a form of thought, 244–45; French materialism, 66, 71; Fukuzawa Yukichi and, 246; Hasegawa Nyōzekan and, 246–47; Hegel and, 68; and liberalism, 16, 241; liberalism as antagonistic to, xxii–xxiii, 16, 236; and Marxism, 237–39; Miki Kiyoshi and, 246; and objectivism, 245–46; popular understanding of, 244; and practical approach to "being," 175; and scientific critique of antagonism between the actual world and spirit (culture), 19; and scientific critique of Japanism and liberalism, 17–18; and social antagonism, xxix; superiority of, 17–18, 248–49; Tanabe Hajime and, 246; and technology, 221–22; West as materialistic, 100

Materialism and Empirio-criticism (Lenin), xi, 83, 148

Materialism Studies (journal), ix, x

material relations of production, 115, 217–19, 297

Matsumoto Manabu, 289

Matsunaga Zai, 99

Matsuoka Yōsuke, 99

May 15 Incident (1932), 99, 290, 312n14, 320n8

meaning: and hermeneutic philosophy, 10–11, 152–53; and Takahashi's philosophy, 180; and Watsuji Tetsurō's ethics, 114–15. *See also* hermeneutics

mechanism, 66, 74–76, 228, 231

Meier, Gerhard, 24

Meiji period, 97; and enlightenment, 62, 70; Meiji Constitution, 62; Meiji Revolution (1868), 8; and origins of the Japanese military, 137–38; and restorationism, 126, 313n2; and restoration of imperial rule, 122, 137–38

Mephistopheles, xxx, 40, 58, 271

metaphysics, xxv; and antiscientism, 155; and common sense, 60; and enlightenment, 66; formalism and interpretive philosophy as characteristic of, 12; and German idealism, 28; and hermeneutics, 116, 150–51; and idealism, 149–50, 156, 250; metaphysics of meaning, 28; and Nishida's philosophy, 172–73; and whole-part relation, 184

middle class: and fantasy that fascism shares its interests, xxviii, 288, 289, 295, 298; fascism supported by the middle classes, xxviii, 28, 136–37, 194, 288, 289, 295, 298; and intellectuals as a social stratum of society, 212–13; and military authorities as a social stratum of society, 137–38; and primitivizationism and nativizationism, 142; and sentimental liberalism, 285; spiritualism of the petite bourgeois, 142. *See also* bourgeoisie; petite bourgeoisie

Miki Kiyoshi, x, xi, 112, 246, 251, 252, 318n4

military, 136–43; "common sense" of, 142; emperor as commander-in-chief, 137; and enlightenment, 141–42; and farmers as citizen-soldiers, 139; and fascism, 137–39; and feudalism, 8, 138, 141; and ideal of nation of soldiers, 138, 238; and Manchurian Incident, 311n2; militaristic consciousness in Japan, xxx, 137–39; military authorities as a social stratum of society, 137–38; military bureaucrats distinguished from soldiers, 137–38; military fascism, 289–91; origins of Japanese military, 137–38; and restorationism, 142; and samurai heritage, 138, 139; and Shanghai Incident, 311n3; and the Spirit of the Imperial Way, 142–43; "unity of soldiers and farmers" concept, 140–42; and universal conscription, 138

Minobe Tatsukichi, 268, 286, 314n5

Minseitō (political party), xxix, 288

Miyaki Kaikotsu, 259

INDEX

mode of production, ix, xx, 102, 139, 308n10
A Modern Woman's Reader (Ichikawa), 121–22
monasticism, and intelligence, 217
money, 115
monopoly capitalism, xxvii, xxviii, 80–81, 122, 136, 140, 283
morality, 162, 233–35, 238, 262
moral liberalism, 234–35
Murofuse Kōshin, 255
Mussolini, Benito, 14, 89, 275
mysticism: and crisis of natural science, 192; and enlightenment, 63; and familial nativization, 124–25; and fascism, 14, 275, 300; and German philosophy, 165; and Japanese middle class, 142; and Nishida's philosophy, 15, 165, 169, 171, 249
myth, 92–93

Nagata Hiroshi, x, xi
nationalism, xviii–xix, 89, 90, 97–98, 125, 291; ultranationalism, xviii–xix
National Purification School, 32
national security, xxx, 288, 290
national unity ideology, xxx, 261, 268
"nation of soldiers" concept, 138, 238
nativism, and philology, 87
nativizationism, xxvii; and familialism, 123–26; and feudalist consciousness, 141; and militaristic consciousness, 141–42; and mysticism, 124–25; primitivization understood as, xxvi, 142, 313n2; and restorationism, 123–26; translation issues, 304n25, 313n2
natural law, 237
Nazism, 14, 254, 307n63, 323n40; and authority of the state, 241; Foucault on, 295; and German idealism, 28; and totalitarianism, 15
necropolitics, 302
Neo-Japanism and the Philosophy of History (Kakunoki), 93
neoliberalism, 295–96, 298–301
news media, 58, 133, 152–53, 271

Newton, Isaac, 74
Nietzsche, Friedrich, xxv, 148, 275, 287
ningen, 105, 107, 108, 109. *See also* "human"
Nishida Kitarō, x, 15, 111–12, 148, 163–73, 249. *See also* Nishida's philosophy
Nishida's philosophy, 163–73, 287; and "being," 167–70; as bourgeois philosophy, 164, 166–73; and cultural liberalism, 173; and the dialectic, 170–71; Eastern and feudal elements, 164–65, 249; and fascism, 165–66; and hermeneutics, 252; and idealism and metaphysics, 172–73; and inability to address actual problems, 174; lack of social thought in, 249–50; and literary liberalism, 236; philosophical method based on "nothingness," 15, 165, 168–72, 177, 249–50; and progress, 265; and Romanticism, 167, 172–73; and theology, 250; as type of liberal philosophy, 236
Nishida's philosophy (Kōyama), 163
Nishi Shin'ichirō, 32, 104–5, 107, 253
noesis and *noema*, 168–71
Nogami Toyoichirō, 36
"nothingness": and hermeneutics, 250; and Nishida's philosophy, 165, 168–72, 177, 249–50; and Takahashi's philosophy, 181, 183; and Tanabe's philosophy, 249–50
Nozoe Shigetsugu, 101

objectivism, and materialism, 245–46
Oka Kunio, x, 246
Ōkawa Shūmei, 99–100, 312n13
Ōmori Gitarō, xi, 232, 318n2
Ōmori Yoshitarō, 213, 317n1
On the Establishment of the New Orient (Kuchita), 101–2
ontology, 74, 109, 112
opinion, and common sense, 54–57
opportunism, 201–2
Ordoliberals, 295
organ theory of the emperor, 130–32, 241, 268, 286; described, 314n5

INDEX

Orientalism, 88, 89, 99, 100, 291
Osugi Sakae, 247
Ozaki Yukio, 284

Palheta, Ugo, 296, 298
palingenesis, xxvii, 27, 300
Pan-Asianism, 86, 101–3, 253. *See also* Asianism
pantheism, 164–65
Pan-Turanianism, 101
parliamentarism, 279; and fascism, xxviii–xxix, 285–89
partisanship, xxx, 58, 83, 193, 200–202, 285
"passion," xxv, 162
Passmore, Kevin, xvii
patriarchy, 101, 102. *See also* family system in Japan
Paxton, Robert, xviii–xix, 306n41
Peace Preservation Law, 97, 312n10
perception, 42–43, 49
personality, xxi, xxii, xxvi, 102, 199, 238, 286, 305n39. *See also* individuals; sentimental liberalism
Pestalozzi, J. H., 129, 314n2
Peterson, Jordan, 299, 319n6, 322n27
petite bourgeoisie: and anticipated losses, 300; and class distinguished from social stratum, 212–13; defined/described, 212; and democracy of the early capitalist era, 286; and fantasy that fascism shares its interests, xxviii, 295; and fascism supported by the middle classes, xxviii, 28, 136–37; and intellectuals, 206, 212–13; and liberalism, 198; and literaturism, 194; and Nazism, 28; and primitivization, 142; and salaryman, 213–15; and social strata, 212; spiritualism of, 142. *See also* middle class
phenomenology, 27–29, 74, 112–14
Phenomenology of Spirit (Hegel), 27
philologism, 12; and agrarian fundamentalism, 253; and anthropology, 254; described, 12–13; and fascism, xxv, 253–54; and German philosophy, 15; Heidegger and, 30; and Japanese spirit, 253; and Japanists' "sense of national history," 13–15; and literaturism, xxv, xxvii, 20–21; Nishi Shin'ichirō and, 253; and Pan-Asianism, 253; philology applied to national history, 14–15; philology transformed into philologism once rendered philosophical, 29; and reactionary thought, 13; and real-world problems, 13, 253; and restorationism, xxv, 13–14; Watsuji Tetsurō and, 253–54
philology, 19–38; and ancient Greece, 24; and anthropology, 30; as caricature, 28, 29, 31; and categories of archaism, 87; and classic texts, 22, 31–38; and contemporary problems, 31–38; critique of philological philosophy, 30–38; defined/described, 21–22; development of philological philosophy, 21–30; Dilthey and, 26–28; as distinct from linguistics and the philosophy of language, 22–23; Fujisawa Chikao and, 241; generalization beyond world of language, 22–23, 26, 28–29; Heidegger and, 27–30; and hermeneutics, 27, 38, 87, 105; hermeneutics as philosophical core, 23, 153; and Japanese imperialism, 298; limits of the authority of philology, 38; origins of, 21–22; as philologism once rendered philosophical, 29; and philosophy, 24–25, 28, 30, 38; relation to linguistics, 21–22; Schleiermacher and, 24–25; sole legitimate contribution to contemporary issues, 36; Tosaka's use of different scripts in discussion of, 308n4; and understanding of history, 25–26; Watsuji Tetsurō and, 109–10, 253–54; Wolf and, 21–22
philosophical liberalism, 235. *See also* liberal philosophy

philosophy: and common sense, 41–42, 44–47 (*see also* Common Sense School); focus on "fundamental" problems rather than actual problems, 175; and freedom, 196–97; and hermeneutics, 24–25, 28, 30, 106; literaturification of philosophy, xxiv–xxv, 157–58, 250–51 (*see also* literaturism); materialist philosophers, 248; and philology, 24–25, 28, 30, 38; philology transformed into philologism once rendered philosophical, 29; philosophical categories, 159–60; philosophization of literary criticism, 157–58 (*see also* literaturism); philosophy of possibility, 175–76; relation between literature and philosophy, 187–95, 250–51; relation to history, xi–xiii (*see also* philosophy of history)

Philosophy of Dialectical Materialism (Deborin), xi

philosophy of history: and development, 263–65; Dilthey's *Lebens* philosophy, 26–27, 113; Kakunoki Inshin's neo-Japanist philosophy of history, 93; and Marxism, 246, 262–63; Miki Kiyoshi and Marxism as a philosophy of history, 246; progress as a philosophy of history, 262–65; wheel of history metaphor, 264–65

phraseology, 126

Plekhanov, G. V., xi

political freedom, 72, 197

political liberalism, 64, 72, 236; arising from economic liberalism, 232; defined/described, 232; "fall" of, 232–33; Fujisawa Chikao and, 240–41; and Japanism, 240; Kawai Eijirō and, 237–38, 284–85; liberal theory of the state, 240–41; and morality, 234–35; and organ theory of the emperor, 241; passive and active nature of, 284; and sentimental liberalism, 287. See also systematic liberalism

political parties, xxix, 268, 279; actual vs. ideal constituencies, xxix, 288; bourgeois and landowner parties, xxix, 284, 288; end of "party cabinets" in favor of "national unity cabinets," 30, 312n14, 320n8; and fascism, 288–89; political liberalism, 284–86

politics: and the arts, 192; chosen elites and their leaders, 275–76; and classification of ideologies, 243; and common sense, 56; liberals' dislike of, 201, 202; and literature, 157, 161, 192, 193; and opportunism, 201–2; political concept of the Spirit of the Imperial Way, 142–43

Popular Rights and Liberty Movement, 285

positivism, xii, 19, 27, 114

postfascism, 296, 297

Poulantzas, Nicos, 298

The Practical Philosophy of Primitive Buddhism (Watsuji), 111

primitivizationism (*genshikashugi*), xv, xxvi, xxvii, 299, 309n17; and Charlottesville, 299; defined/described, 313n2, 315n3; and familialism, 123–26; instances described, 142; and restorationism, 140–41; translation issues, xxvi, 304n25, 313n2, 315n3; understood as nativizationism, xxvi, 142, 313n2

principle of actuality, 57–58, 179

principle of everydayness, 40, 57–58

production. *See* forces of production; mode of production; relations of production

"productive organs of man," 224–25

productivity, development of, 269–70

progress: development as alternate term, 263–65; and development of productivity, 269–70; and ethics, 262–63; and liberalism, 277; and Marxism, 262–65; and the masses or the proletariat, 266–69; meanings of progress and progressivism, 260–71; metaphors of, 263–65; and Nishida's philosophy, 265; as a philosophy of

INDEX

history, 262–65; and reactionary thought, 270–71; rejection of, 271, 319n6
progressivism, 30; and development of productivity, 269–70; and enlightenment, 65; and the intelligentsia, 272; and Japanism, 263; and liberalism, 16, 263, 287; and literaturism, 194; and Marxism, 261; and the masses or the proletariat, 266–69; meanings of progress and progressivism, 260–71; nominally progressive things seen as reactionary from a different perspective, 270; self-identification of fascists as progressive, 261. *See also* enlightenment
"progress" slogan, 260–61
proletariat, xiv; and common sense, xxxi–xxxii, 59, 310n11; and dialectical materialism, 246; and the intelligentsia, 205, 211; and progressive development of history, 266–69; regression of power, 208; relation to the masses, 266–67, 273–74, 278–81; and small-scale farming, 286; and social strata, 212; as society's leaders, 204; and "white working class" as a pseudoclass, 297
prostitution, 117–21
Protestantism, 27
Prussia, 62, 69
Psychology from an Empirical Standpoint (Brentano), 27, 114
public opinion, 54–57, 59, 119, 133
Putinism, 293
Pu Yi, 90

racialization, 297, 298, 299
rationalism: antirationalism, 142; and Enlightenment, 66, 67, 68, 73–74, 260; and Reid's conception of common sense, 45–47
reactionary thought, 14, 40; and familialism, 122, 123; Japanese society as being in a reactionary period, 89, 261, 271–72, 292; and liberalism, 198, 202, 270; liberalism as progressive compared to restorationist thought, 16; nominally progressive things seen as reactionary from a different perspective, 270; and philologism/philology, 13, 34–37; and progress, 270–71; and Watsuji Tetsurō's ethics, 104–5. *See also* agrarian fundamentalism; Asianism; Japanese spiritualism; restorationism
realism, 69, 70, 114, 150
reality: actually existing objects, 151; and archaic texts, 13; Fichte and, 167; and hermeneutic philosophy, 11, 25, 152, 162, 250, 252; and idealism, 147; ideology and objective present reality, 83–85; and Japanese agriculture, 95–96, 101; Japanese "reality," 77–78; and literaturism, 159, 162; logic and the relationship between concepts and reality, 32; and logic of nothingness, 250; and metaphorical family of the state and society, 123; and philosophy of totality, 179; "reality" as a philosophical or literary category, 159, 195; reality of Asia, 99–101; and religious freedom, 9; scientific critique of antagonism between actual world and spirit, 19; translation issues, 304n26, 318n7; and wheels of history metaphor, 265
reason. *See* understanding/reason
Reformation, 24
Reid, Thomas, 44–51, 54
relations of production, xiv, xxi, 37, 80–81, 115, 217, 224, 297, 298
religion and religious consciousness: and absolutism, 9–10, 12; ancestor worship, 125, 306n52; animism, xxvi, 125, 306n52; deification of august individuals, 125; deism, 72; and fascism, 253–54; and literary liberalism, 252; and monasticism and intelligence, 217; and nativist familialism, 124–25; Nishida's "logic of nothingness" and, 15; pantheism,

religion and religious consciousness (*continued*)
164–65; and primitivization, 142; religious consciousness arising from liberal philosophy, 9–10, 307n3; and social positivity, 15; theological categories, 155–56; and totemism, xxvi, 125, 306n52. *See also* Buddhism; Catholicism; Christianity; Protestantism; Shintōism
Renaissance, xxvii, 122, 313n2
Rengō (communication company), 133
restorationism (*fukkōshugi*), xxv–xxvi, 117–27; and archaic texts, 126; and capitalism, 122, 125–26; and family system/familialism, 119–27, 140; and feudalism, 122, 140 (*see also* feudalism); liberalism as progressive compared to restorationist thought, 16; and "Make America Great" slogan, 300; and middle-class spiritualism, 142; and militaristic consciousness, 142; and modernization, 125–26; and Nishida's philosophy, 250; and philologism, xxv, 13–14; and phraseology, 126; and primitivizationism and nativizationism, 123–26, 140–41, 313n2; progressive restoration, 313n2, 315n3; and religion, 254; and the Spirit of the Imperial Way, 142–43; and U.S. legal system, 294; "vague restorationism," 140–42, 299. *See also* Artistic Restoration; feudalism
rice, 95, 96
rinri, 105, 106, 107, 108. *See also* ethics
Robin, Corey, 295, 321n6
Romanticism, xiii, 69–70, 75, 233; and Nishida's philosophy, 167, 172–73; two senses of word, 233
Roosevelt, Franklin D., 89
Rousseau, Jean-Jacques, 123
Russia, 293
Russo-Japanese War, 89, 101

Sakamoto Sanzen, 89
Sakisaki Itsurō, 246, 318n2
salaryman, 213–15, 218, 246, 297, 300
samurai class, 138, 139
Satan, 40
Scheler, Max, 230, 231
Schelling, F. W. J., xxvii, 25, 36, 67, 68, 167
Schleiermacher, Friedrich, 24–25
Schmitt, Carl, 241
Schopenhauer, Arthur, 275
science, xxiv, 10, 74; antiscientism in idealist philosophies, 154–55; and criticism, 189, 191; cult of intelligence among scientists, 218–19; materialist natural scientists and mathematicians, 248
Scottish School of Common Sense, 44, 48, 72
sectarianism, 201
Seiyūkai (political party), xxix, 288
The Self-Conscious Determination of Nothingness (Nishida), 163, 169–72
self-consciousness, and Nishida's philosophy, 168–70
Semler, Johann Salomo, 24
sensation, 43, 218
sensory organs, 42–43, 44
sentimental liberalism, xxi–xxiii, 284–85, 293, 294, 306n39, 317n1
Shaftesbury, Lord, 44, 46
Shanghai Incident, 89, 311n3
Shestov, Lev, xxv, 148, 195, 251, 252
Shintōism, xviii, 125
Shisō (journal), 77, 78, 79
Simmel, G., 26
Sino-Japanese War, 89, 101
skepticism, 44
slogans: "Civilization and Enlightenment" slogan, 259–61; "clarification of the Imperial Way"/"clarification of the Japanese national essence" slogan, xxx, 291; dangers of, 261; "Make America Great" slogan, 300; "national unity" slogan, 261, 289; "overthrow capitalism" slogan, 290–91; "progress" slogan, 260–61
social class. *See* class
social contract, 48, 123

INDEX

social control: and capitalism, xxix, 80–81, 128–29; "constitutive control," xxix, 129–32; managerial capitalism and the ideology of control, 122; and the production of social antagonism, xxix. *See also* cultural control

socialism, xx, 292; fascism as antagonistic to, 306n48; Gondō Seikyō and, 97; intelligentsia and, 219; and Kawai Eijirō's liberalism, 237, 285; Kuchita Yasunobu and, 102; liberalism as antagonistic to, 287; Marx and, 238–39; and "overthrow capitalism" slogan, 290; and social antagonism, xxix

social science: and antagonism between materialism and idealism, xxi; and definition of fascism, xix; materialist social scientists, 248; and problem of ideological criticism, 80–87

social strata, 212–15, 282, 297–98

sociology, xx; and class and social strata, 212–13; and classification of ideologies, 243–44; and common sense, 267; and idealism and the cult of intelligence, 251–52; and the Japanese state, 268; and the masses, 268; and problem of ideological criticism, 80–87; and social class, 267–68, 297; sociological phenomenology theory of the intellectual, 214–15

Sōda Kiichirō, 255

Sōda school of thought, 255

sono mama, xx, xxii, xxxi

sonzai, 105, 107, 109–10, 112. *See also* "being"

Spann, Othmar, 102, 312n19

speech, control of, 132–33

Spirit of the Imperial Way, 142–43

spiritualism, 77–87; and Asianism, 100–101; and development of fascism in Japan, xxvii; the East as spiritual in contrast to the materialistic West, 100; individual spiritualisms in the modern U.S., 301; and restorationism and middle-class spiritualism, 142. *See also* Japanese spirit; Japanese spiritualism

The Standpoint of Totality (Takahashi), 15, 176–85

Stanley, Jason, 296

stasis, and Takahashi's philosophy, 179–80

state, the: and constitutional fascism, xx, xxviii–xxxi, 285–89; and constitutional liberalism, 240; fascism viewed as a problem of the state, 295; idea of the total state, 240–41; and Nazism, 241. *See also* Japanese state

Stendhal, 275

Sternhell, Zeev, xviii–xix

Stoics, 275

Studies of the Agrarian Village (Tachibana), 94–95

subjectivity and objectivity, and Nishida's philosophy, 167–69

Sugimori Kōjirō, 255

suicide, 152

systematic liberalism, 282, 284, 287

systems and systemism, 180–82

Tachibana Kōzaburō, 94–96, 102, 320n8

Taine, Hyppolite, 218

Takahashi Satomi, 15, 175–85. *See also* Takahashi's philosophy

Takahashi's philosophy, 176–85; and absolutism, 181; and abstraction, 182–84; and "being," 181–84; Cohen and, 179; and the dialectic, 178, 182–84; and distinction between method and system, 180; and idealism, 181, 184; and inability to address actual problems, 180, 181; and liberalism, 185; and nothingness, 181, 183; and stasis and movement, 179–80, 183; and systemism, 180–82; and "totality," 176–85; and whole-part relation, 177–79, 184

Takami Kakushō, 30

Takasu Hojirō, 90–91

Tanabe Hajime, x, 163, 167, 172; and logic of nothingness, 249–50; and materialism, 246; philosophy of, 174

Tarde, Gabriel, 214, 317n2
technical standard, 226–28
technique, 220, 227–29; Aiwaka Haruki's definition, 222–25; distinction between technology and technical skills, techniques, and methods, 221; Marx and, 227; social category of, 220–21
technology: Aikawa Haruki and, 222–25; and antiscientism of idealist philosophies, 155; antitechnologism, 86, 141, 142, 155, 156; and bourgeois philosophy, 221; and cultural theory, 228; definitions, 221–25; distinction between technology and technical skills, techniques, and methods, 221; intelligentsia and, 228–29; Marx and, 223–24, 228; materialism's theory of, 221–22; mechanization of agriculture, 95; and the "organization of the means of labor," 223–27; "Philosophy of Technology" (Tosaka), 222; science of technology, 227; technical standard, 226–28
teleology, and progress/development, 263–65
tenkō phenomenon, xxi, xxvii, 40, 79, 116, 133, 208, 211, 220–29, 235, 252, 286, 309–10n1, 317n2
texts: and capitalism, 253; classic literary texts and Japanists' sense of national history, 13; and early hermeneutics, 24; and Humboldt's comparative linguistic research, 22; and interpretation and tools of understanding, 23; and philology, 22, 31–37, 253; resolution of real problems replaced by philological interpretation of classic texts, 13, 31–37, 253; and restorationism, 126; textual interpretation and Watsuji Tetsurōs ethics, 105; and translation, 36–38. *See also* archaic, the; philologism
Thatcher, Margaret, 299
theology, 148; and literaturism, 191, 192; and Nishida's philosophy, 164–65,
250; and Tanabe's philosophy, 250; theological categories, 155–56
thought, xiii–xiv, xxiii, 7, 242–55, 259–60; characteristics of a proper thinker, 244–45, 255; Cohen and the concept of pure thinking, 316–17n4; defined/described, 244–45; discrepancy between a thinker's subjective experience and thought's objective meaning, 243; division into fascist, liberal, and Marxist thought, 242; division into idealism or materialism, 244; division into right-wing, centrist, and left-wing thought, 242–44; examples of materialist thinkers, 247–48; and idealism, 246, 249–55; and inferiority of idealist philosophies, 249–55; and literature, 250–51; and Marxism, 272; and materialism, 245–48; and Nishida's philosophy, 249–50; and political nature of ideologies, 243; primitivization/nativization of thought (*see* nativizationism; primitivizationism); prominent people who are not thinkers, 255; and superiority of materialism, 248–49; thinkers requiring a larger trend or school, 254–55; thought requiring a worldview and a logic, 244–45; thought requiring deployment toward actual social problems, xiii, 7, 244, 250. *See also* ideology; philosophy; reactionary thought
Tōjō Hideki, xvi
Tokugawa period, 89, 138, 140
Tokutomi Sōhō, 255
Toland, John, 72
Tomomatsu Entai, 245
Tosaka Jun: career, ix–x; imprisonment and death, x–xi; Miki Kiyoshi and, 246; overview of ideas, xi–xvi
Toscano, Alberto, 296, 297, 321n8
totalitarianism, xviii, xxix, 14, 15, 305n39

INDEX

totality, and Takahashi Satomi's philosophical method, 176–85
totemism, xxvi, 125, 306n52
translation, and archaic texts and the critique of philology, 36–38
Traverso, Enzo, 296, 297
Trump, Donald, 321n10
Trumpism, 293, 296
"truth of the streets," xii, xv, xxxi
Tsuchida Kyōson, 255
Turgenev, Ivan, 275

Uda, Emperor, 96
Ueda Jūzō, 172
Ui Hakuju, 111
ultranationalism, xviii–xix
Ulysses (Joyce), 150
Under the Banner of New Science (journal), xi
understanding/reason, 49–50, 67–68; and common sense, 45–46; and enlightenment, 64–65, 72, 73; and philology, 25–26; and political freedom, 72. *See also* common sense; knowledge
unemployment, 121
United States: Black Lives Matter, 302; Charlottesville riots of 2017, 293–95, 299–300, 302; election of 2016, 293, 297; examples of fascist social expression, 294; fascism in, 286, 293–302; and identity politics, 294, 301; individual spiritualisms in, 301; sacking of U.S. Capitol, 293, 299; and Trumpism, 293, 296; violent groups in, 299; "white working class" as a pseudoclass, 297–98, 300
"unity of soldiers and farmers" concept, 140–42
Uno Kōzō, xxvii, 305n34, 307n61
utilitarianism, 237

village life: and autonomy, 96–97, 102; and feudalism, 102; Kuchita Yasunobu and, 101–2; and militaristic consciousness, 139, 141–42; Tachibana Kōzaburō and, 94–95

Voltaire, 72, 73, 74
vulgarism, 39–40

Wach, Joachim, 24
Walker, Gavin, 298
Watsuji Tetsurō, xviii, 15, 30, 31, 37, 98; *Ethics as Anthropology*, 15, 30, 31, 104–16; and hermeneutics, 108, 111–16; and Japanese ethics as supreme model, 107, 110; and the Japanese spirit, 101; and language, 106, 108–10; and philology, 109–10, 253–54; *The Practical Philosophy of Primitive Buddhism*, 111; and use of term "anthropology," 110, 254
Weber, Max, 78
West, the: and the "human," 110; Ōkawa Shūmei's views of East and West as antagonistic, 99–100; and social antagonism, xxix; West as materialistic, 100; Western ethics, 111
"white working class," 297–98, 300
"woke" society, 299
Wolf, Friedrich August, 21–22, 24
Wolff, Christian, 66, 73–75
women: and employment/unemployment, 121; and the family system, 121, 123; "good wife, wise mother" ideology, 121, 123; and individualism, 122; and prostitution, 117–21
workers, xiv, xv; and "absolute surplus value," 302; anti-prostitution movement, 117–21; commodification of labor power, 302, 307n61; knowledge workers, 213–14; labor issues and interpretation of Buddhist texts, 13; unemployment, 121; "white working class" as a pseudoclass, 297–98, 300. *See also* proletariat
"world," Japanese word for, 109
worldview, xiii; bourgeois and proletarian worldviews, xiv; and concept of the "chosen" people, 275; and democracy, 197; and empiricism and the English Enlightenment, 66; and everydayness, 58; idealist

worldview (*continued*)
   worldview of liberalism, xiv; and Japanese fascism, 291; and literature or literary criticism, 158, 160, 189, 190; and materialism, 248, 263; and philology and hermeneutics, 25, 28; and philosophy, 187; religious worldview, 10, 307n3; and science, 192; and technology, 221, 228; and thought as the unification of worldview and intellectual method, 244–45; worldview, being, and logic, xv

World War I, 89, 99

Yasuoka Shōtoku, 92–93
Yoshino Sakuzō, 7
yuiken project, x, xi, xxiv, 301, 308n1

GPSR Authorized Representative: Easy Access System Europe, Mustamäe tee
50, 10621 Tallinn, Estonia, gpsr.requests@easproject.com

www.ingramcontent.com/pod-product-compliance
Lightning Source LLC
Chambersburg PA
CBHW031230290426
44109CB00012B/227